'Beginning in the early years of the 21st century people have been increasingly enervated by environmental concerns and Green Criminology has emerged as one of the most pressing issue areas for academics. This collection presents a marvelous compilation of essays by some of Criminology's most interesting scholars in a piercing examination of these vital and disquieting topics. The volume offers a critical perspective on the global opportunity structure of capitalist consumption and production showing that the institutions intended for the manufacture and fulfillment of human desire have been built on criminal environmental degradation.'

James Sheptycki, *McLaughlin College, York University, Toronto, Canada*

'Environmental crime, unsurprisingly, often tends to be concerned with financial gain. This collection – edited by leading international scholars – offers an insightful, thought-provoking examination of the 'finances' of environmental crime, with perspectives from different disciplines and jurisdictions. I highly recommend it.'

Colin King, *University of Sussex, UK*

'This collection reinvigorates the critical nature of green criminology, returning the field to its origins by questioning the processes of capitalism that have so irreversibly touched global ecology. This is essential reading for those concerned about the future of the planet and the profit motives that threaten it. An outstanding achievement!'

Bill McClanahan, *Eastern Kentucky University, USA*

'This is a fascinating analysis of environmental crime, seen through the lens of finance. It brings together research on seemingly diverse topics including the waste trade, the illegal wildlife trade and carbon trading, but demonstrates how they harm the environment, and crucially, how they reproduce and deepen social and economic inequalities.'

Rosaleen Duffy, *University of Sheffield, UK*

'This book shows that the interplay of actors both from the under- and upper-world are crucial to the resilience and reproduction of environmental crimes. In the age of climate change denialism and unprecedented environmental destruction, the collusion of corporations, industrial lobbies, politicians and criminals in the perpetration of such crimes should be of particular concern to readers. Some of the world's top researchers in the field of green criminology and related disciplines offer novel perspectives on the interplay between legal and illegal markets, systemic drivers of environmental crimes and how to best address them. A must read to anyone who cares about our environmental futures.'

Annette Hübschle, *University of Cape Town, South Africa*

Green Crimes and Dirty Money

Environmental crimes are primarily driven by financial motives. The combined financial value of illicit trade in protected wildlife, illegal logging and waste trafficking is estimated to come directly after counterfeiting, the narcotic drugs trade and illegal gambling. Logically, the proceeds of these crimes must also be laundered. Goods, however, are not the only money maker for environmental criminals. Corporations may also try to 'save' costs by not complying with environmental regulations and thus commit crimes of omission rather than commission. From an enforcement and compliance perspective focusing on the proceeds of crime may therefore be an effective strategy.

This book brings together different perspectives on the financial aspects of environmental crime and harm from a green criminological viewpoint. It addresses the role of economic systems, the value of environmental performance for corporations, money laundering in the context of environmental crime, financial investigation and questions of regulation and penalties.

Discussing these topics from the view of green criminology, sociology and governance, this book will be of great interest to all those concerned about the financial dimensions of crime and the environment.

Toine Spapens is Full Professor of Criminology at Tilburg University, the Netherlands.

Rob White is Professor of Criminology at the University of Tasmania, Australia.

Daan van Uhm is Assistant Professor of Criminology at the Willem Pompe Institute for Criminal Law and Criminology, University of Utrecht, the Netherlands.

Wim Huisman is Professor of Criminology and Chair of the Department Criminology at VU University Amsterdam, the Netherlands.

Green Criminology

Now two decades old, green criminology – the study of environmental harm, crime, law, regulation, victimization, and justice – has increasing relevance to contemporary problems at local, national, and international levels. This series comes at a time when societies and governments worldwide seek new ways to alleviate and deal with the consequences of various environmental harms as they relate to humans, non-human animals, plant species, and the ecosystem and its components. Green criminology offers a unique theoretical perspective on how human behavior causes and exacerbates environmental conditions that threaten the planet's viability. Volumes in the series consider such topics and controversies as corporate environmental crime, the complicity of international financial institutions, state-sponsored environmental destruction, and the role of non-governmental organizations in addressing environmental harms. Titles also examine the intersections between green criminology and other branches of criminology and other areas of law, such as human rights and national security. The series is international in scope, investigating environmental crime in specific countries as well as comparatively and globally. In sum, by bringing together a diverse body of research on all aspects of this subject, the series makes a significant contribution to our understanding of the dynamics between the natural world and the quite imperfect human world, and sets the stage for the future study in this growing area of concern.

Series Editors:

Michael J. Lynch, *University of South Florida, USA*
Paul B. Stretesky, *University of Northumbria, UK*

Other titles in this series:

Environmental Crime in Transnational Context
Global Issues in Green Enforcement and Criminology
Edited by Toine Spapens, Rob White and Wim Huisman

Greening Criminology in the 21st Century
Contemporary Debates and Future Directions in the Study
of Environmental Harm
*Edited by Matthew Hall, Tanya Wyatt, Nigel South, Angus Nurse,
Gary Potter and Jennifer Maher*

For more information about this series, please visit:
www.routledge.com/Green-Criminology/book-series/GREENCRIM

Green Crimes and Dirty Money

Edited by
Toine Spapens, Rob White,
Daan van Uhm and
Wim Huisman

LONDON AND NEW YORK

First published 2018 by Routledge

2 Park Square, Milton Park, Abingdon, Oxfordshire OX14 4RN
52 Vanderbilt Avenue, New York, NY 10017

Routledge is an imprint of the Taylor & Francis Group, an informa business

First issued in paperback 2020

Copyright © 2018 selection and editorial matter, Toine Spapens, Rob White, Daan van Uhm and Wim Huisman; individual chapters, the contributors.

The right of Toine Spapens, Rob White, Daan van Uhm and Wim Huisman to be identified as the authors of the editorial material, and of the authors for their individual chapters, has been asserted in accordance with sections 77 and 78 of the Copyright, Designs and Patents Act 1988.

All rights reserved. No part of this book may be reprinted or reproduced or utilised in any form or by any electronic, mechanical, or other means, now known or hereafter invented, including photocopying and recording, or in any information storage or retrieval system, without permission in writing from the publishers.

Notice:
Product or corporate names may be trademarks or registered trademarks, and are used only for identification and explanation without intent to infringe.

British Library Cataloguing-in-Publication Data
A catalogue record for this book is available from the British Library

Library of Congress Cataloging-in-Publication Data
Names: Spapens, A. C., editor. | White, R. D. (Robert Douglas), 1956– editor. | Uhm, Daan van, editor.
Title: Green crimes and dirty money / [edited by] Toine Spapens, Rob White, Daan van Uhm.
Description: 1 Edition. | New York : Routledge, 2018. | Series: Green criminology | Includes bibliographical references and index.
Identifiers: LCCN 2018000369 | ISBN 9780815372219 (hardback)
Subjects: LCSH: Offenses against the environment. | Offenses against the Environment—Law and legislation. | Pollution—Law and legislation. | Environmental law, International.
Classification: LCC HV6401 .G754 2018 | DDC 364.1/45—dc23
LC record available at https://lccn.loc.gov/2018000369

ISBN: 978-0-8153-7221-9 (hbk)
ISBN: 978-0-367-89905-9 (pbk)

Typeset in Galliard
by Florence Production Ltd, Stoodleigh, Devon, UK

Contents

List of figures   xi
List of tables   xii
Notes on contributors   xiii
Preface and acknowledgements   xvii

Introduction   1
TOINE SPAPENS, ROB WHITE, DAAN VAN UHM AND
WIM HUISMAN

PART I
Systemic drivers of green crimes   7

1 Destruction and the philosophy of desire   9
   VINCENZO RUGGIERO

2 Environment, conflict and profit: Harmful resource
   exploitation and questionable revenue generation   19
   AVI BRISMAN AND NIGEL SOUTH

3 Eco-mafia and environmental crime in Italy. Evidence from
   the organised trafficking of waste   42
   ANNA RITA GERMANI, ANTONIO PERGOLIZZI AND
   FILIPPO REGANATI

4 Supply and demand: Regulation and the trade in illegal wildlife 72
   AMY COUPER AND REECE WALTERS

PART II
Corporations, environmental violations and the money   89

5 The 'Dieselgate' scandal: A criminological perspective   91
   TOINE SPAPENS

6   Environmental responsibility and firm value   113
     NADJA GUENSTER AND JAKOB KOEGST

7   Too big to deter, too small to change? Profitability and
     environmental compliance in the waste and chemical
     industry in the Netherlands   129
     KARIN VAN WINGERDE AND MARIEKE KLUIN

8   Waste crime from three criminological perspectives:
     Implications for crime control and harm prevention   148
     LIESELOT BISSCHOP AND WIM HUISMAN

PART III
Financial regulation and enforcement   177

9   Green with envy: Environmental crimes and black money   179
     MICHAEL LEVI

10 Wildlife and laundering: Interaction between the under
     and upper world   197
     DAAN VAN UHM

11 The limits of ecological modernisation to effectively
     manage greenhouse gas emissions: A case study of
     carbon market crime   215
     RUTH MCKIE

12 Financial investigation in environmental crime cases
     in the Netherlands   233
     RUBIE IIBWE AIID IIAIIIIA VAII EAIIDIII

13 Sentencing environmental offenders: It is not just
     about the money   250
     ROB WHITE

     Index   267

Figures

3.1 Urban household waste sector: actors and vulnerabilities   45
3.2 Special waste sector: actors and vulnerabilities   48
3.3 The total number of reported cases of organised illegal
     trafficking of waste by year   52
3.4 The total number of reported cases of organised illegal
     trafficking of waste by region (2002–2013)   52
3.5 The total number of offenders charged and arrested   54
3.6 Percentage of cases in organised illegal trafficking of waste
     that have an identified mafia connection, 2002–2013   54
10.1 Categories of perpetrators   200
10.2 Wildlife laundering   202
10.3 Caviar laundering   205
10.4 Money laundering from the sale of drugs   207

Tables

3.1 The number of regions involved in the investigations
(2002–2013)   53
3.2 Basic descriptive statistics   58
3.3 The determinants of organised trafficking of waste in Italy   60
3.4 The determinants of organised trafficking of waste in the
North-Centre of Italy   64
3.5 The determinants of organised trafficking of waste in the
South of Italy   66
6.1 Overview profitability studies   119
7.1 Overview of the data: characteristics of ten firms   136
7.2 Average net turnover in euros (x 1.000)   136
7.3 Average net profit in euros (x 1,000)   137
13.1 Types of penalties imposed by the NSWLEC 2002–2013   262

Contributors

Lieselot Bisschop is Assistant Professor at the Erasmus University Rotterdam (the Netherlands). Her areas of interest and expertise include environmental crime, social harm, organisational crime, environmental governance, and environmental justice. Ongoing research focuses on state-corporate crime, coastal land loss, e-waste, shipbreaking, oil and gas industry, and green energy. Lieselot is also an assistant editor for the *European Journal of Policing Studies*.

Avi Brisman Avi Brisman (MFA, JD, PhD) is Associate Professor in the School of Justice Studies at Eastern Kentucky University (Richmond, KY, USA), an Adjunct Associate Professor in the School of Justice at Queensland University of Technology (Brisbane, Queensland, Australia), and a Conjoint Associate Professor at Newcastle Law School at the University of Newcastle (Newcastle, New South Wales, Australia). His research interests include the anthropology of law, critical criminology, cultural criminology, and green criminology. Within the area of green criminology, he has written extensively on environmental rights, linkages between armed conflict and environmental degradation, representations of environmental crime and harm in film and literature, and individual and collective resistance to environmental crime and harm.

Amy Couper is Associate Lecturer in the School of Justice at Queensland University of Technology. She is completing a PhD in Wildlife Law and Green Criminology, notably examining Australia's policies for culling and controlling sharks.

Anna Rita Germani is an economist with research interests on environmental law and economics issues, such as public enforcement of environmental laws and judicial and prosecutorial discretion in prosecuting environmental crimes, and on environmental justice studies. She teaches Economics, International Economics, and Economics of Public Procurement at the University of Rome 'La Sapienza' and has published referred empirical articles on environmental enforcement, on environmental justice discrimination, on illegal trafficking of waste and, most recently, she is working on environmental crime and victims issues.

Nadja Guenster is Professor of International Financial Management at the Muenster School of Business and Economics, University of Muenster, Germany. Nadja's research focuses on the intersection of corporate social responsibility and finance. Previously, Nadja was visiting faculty at the Haas School of Business, UC Berkeley and Assistant Professor of Finance at Maastricht University.

Wim Huisman is Professor of Criminology and the head of the School of Criminology of the Vrije Universiteit (VU) in Amsterdam, the Netherlands. His research areas include white-collar crime, corporate crime, environmental crime, and organised crime. Recent projects focus on criminal careers of white-collar offenders, corporate complicity to gross human rights violations, causes of corruption, corporate environmental crime, and the prevention of food fraud.

Marieke Kluin is Assistant Professor of Criminology at the Institute of Criminal Law and Criminology, Leiden University, the Netherlands. She received her PhD from the Delft University of Technology in 2014. Her research interests include the regulation and enforcement of corporations, corporate crime, environmental crime, and state-corporate crime. Her research focuses currently on longitudinal white-collar crime and takes a life-course approach to corporate crime.

Jakob Koegst is a PhD student at the chair of International Financial Management at the Muenster School of Business and Economics, University of Muenster, Germany. He obtained his bachelor's and master's degree in Business Administration at the Free University of Berlin. Jakob's research focuses on the intersection of sustainability and finance.

Michael Levi has been Professor of Criminology at Cardiff University School of Social Sciences since 1991. Since 1972 he has been conducting international research on fields including the organisation and control of white-collar and organised crime, corruption and money laundering/financing of terrorism. In 2013 he was given the Distinguished Scholar Award by the International Association for the Study of Organised Crime, and in 2014 he was awarded the Sellin-Glueck prize for international and comparative criminology by the American Society of Criminology.

Ruth McKie is Lecturer in Criminology at De Montfort University, United Kingdom. Her areas of research interest include climate change, social movements, green criminology and environmental crime, transnational and international crime.

Rudie Neve is a Sociologist and Senior Researcher at the Analysis & Research Department of the National Police of the Netherlands. He published reports on organised crime, terrorism and environmental crime. Before joining the police in 2007, he started his criminological research at Maastricht

University, where he studied drug scenes and later worked at the Research Centre of the Ministry of Security and Justice (WODC), where he worked on projects concerning synthetic drug production, cybercrime, and terrorism.

Antonio Pergolizzi is Adjunct Professor of Waste Management at the University of Camerino and environmental consultant for public and private organisations. Since 2006, he has written the 'Ecomafia report' published yearly by the Italian NGO Legambiente. He published the book '*Toxic Italy*' that won the 2012 literary prize 'AcquiAmbiente' and several academic articles. He has participated as an expert in European Union projects on environmental crimes such as EFFACE and LIFE SMART Waste. As a scientific environmental journalist, he regularly writes in magazines and newspapers and has a blog on the website of the Italian newspaper 'La Stampa' on ecomafia issues.

Filippo Reganati is Professor of Economics at the Department of Law, Philosophy and Economic Studies of the 'Sapienza', University of Rome. His research has focused on foreign direct investment and multinational enterprises; international trade in imperfect competitive markets; applied industrial organisation. Currently he is working on the economics of crime with particular reference to environmental crime, money laundering and corruption.

Vincenzo Ruggiero is Professor of Sociology at Middlesex University in London. He has conducted research of behalf of many national and international agencies, including the European Commission and the United Nations. His most recent monographs are: *The Crimes of the Economy* (2013), *Power and Crime* (2015), and *Dirty Money* (2017).

Nigel South is Professor of Sociology and Director of the Centre for Criminology, University of Essex, UK, and a visiting Adjunct Professor at the Crime and Justice Research Centre, Queensland University of Technology. Recent books include H. Mol, D. Rodríguez Goyes, A. Brisman and N. South (2017) (eds) *Environmental Crime in Latin America: The theft of nature and the poisoning of the land*, London: Palgrave; A. Brisman, B. McClanahan, N. South and R. Walters (2018) *Water, Crime and Security in the Twenty-First Century: Too dirty, too little, too much*, London: Palgrave.

Toine Spapens is full Professor of Criminology at Tilburg University, the Netherlands. He specialises in research on organised crime, environmental crime, and cross-border enforcement cooperation. His empirical studies include the trafficking in illicit firearms, large-scale cannabis cultivation, environmental crime, illegal gambling, and match-fixing. His theoretical work focuses on organised crime networks, the regulation of (former) illegal markets and multi-agency approaches to serious and organised crime problems.

Daan van Uhm is Assistant Professor in Criminology at the Willem Pompe Institute for Criminal Law and Criminology of the Utrecht University. He has conducted research in the area of flora- and fauna crimes and the illegal trade in wildlife with a focus on the EU.

Reece Walters is Professor of Criminology in the Centre for Crime and Justice Research and Assistant Dean Research in the Faculty of Law at Queensland University of Technology, Brisbane, Australia. He has published widely on crimes of the powerful and crimes against the environment. His current research focuses on crimes against the essentials of life, namely food, air, and water. He is the author of *Eco Crime and Genetically Modified Food* (2011) and is Editor of Palgrave Macmillan's series on Critical Criminological Perspectives.

Rob White is Professor of Criminology at the University of Tasmania, Sandy Bay, Australia. He has written widely in the areas of criminology and youth studies, and has a particular interest in issues related to environmental harm, ecological justice, and green criminology. His recent books include *Transnational Environmental Crime: Toward an Eco-global Criminology* (2011), *Climate Change from a Criminological Perspective* (2012) and *Environmental Harm: An Eco-justice Perspective* (2013), and he is also the author of *Crimes Against Nature* (2008).

Karin van Wingerde is Assistant Professor of Criminology at Erasmus School of Law, Erasmus University Rotterdam, the Netherlands. Her research interests include the regulation and enforcement of business behaviour, and corporate, financial, and environmental crimes. In particular, she is interested in the relationship between various legal and extra-legal mechanisms of social control and the behaviour of business firms.

Nanina van Zanden is a Criminologist and Project Leader at the Dutch National Police. She worked on projects in the field of environmental crime and is currently focusing on crime related to the dark web.

Preface and acknowledgements

There is increasing evidence that green crimes are globally one of the most profitable illegal activities in financial terms. At the same time these crimes are also extremely damaging to both humans and non-human species as well as ecosystems. Few benefit financially whereas many suffer the costs: the money is 'dirty' in many respects.

This book addresses financial aspects of green crimes from a broad perspective. Authors from different disciplines focus on economic systems, politics and the struggle for resources; links between environmental compliance and the financial performance of corporations, and on how regulators and enforcement agencies use financial incentives, legislation and financial investigation methods to prevent and tackle green crimes and harms.

As editors, we wish to thank Tilburg University, the University of Tasmania and VU University for their financial support, which made this book possible. We would also like to thank Routledge and the editors of the Green Criminology Series, Michael J. Lynch and Paul B. Stretesky, for enthusiastically agreeing to publish this volume in the series.

Toine Spapens
Rob White
Daan van Uhm
Wim Huisman
Tilburg, Hobart, Utrecht, Amsterdam,
October 2017

Introduction

*Toine Spapens, Rob White, Daan van Uhm
and Wim Huisman*

Green crimes and environmental harm encompass a broad range of acts, and they almost always involve a financial component. Individuals, crime groups and corporations aim at making money or saving money, and in the process, they may cause severe damage to humans, flora and fauna and ecosystems either directly or indirectly. Governments may allow or even promote environmental harm in favour of economic goals.

Already, for a number of years, the main environmental crime markets have been considered the third (sometimes fourth) biggest 'dirty money' makers. Only the revenues of drug trafficking, counterfeiting and human trafficking – and sometimes illegal gambling – are estimated to be higher. Recently, a UNEP/ Interpol study concluded that the annual proceeds of the five most important types of environmental crime are between 91 and 259 billion dollars. Illegal logging is estimated to amount to 51–152 billion; illegal and unregulated fishing at 11–24 billion; illegal extraction and trade in minerals/mining at 12–48 billion; illegal trade and dumping of hazardous waste at 10–12 billion and illegal trade and poaching of plants and other wildlife at 7–23 billion (Nelleman *et al.* 2016).

Of course, one may challenge such estimates for being highly speculative, caused by a lack of reliable data. Many of these crimes are not reported to the police and are detected only after inspection or investigation, unless of course disaster strikes. Such uncertainties are expressed in the wide margins of the estimated total size of the environmental crime market as well as specific markets. Environmental crimes often require complex chains of logistics and it is difficult to assess how much money the different actors make. In addition, a specific problem in calculating the 'value' of environmental crime is that it often concerns crimes of omission (Huisman and van Erp 2013). In other words, perpetrators save money rather than earn it, for instance corporations disposing waste illegally instead of having it processed in the legally prescribed – and more costly – manner. This makes it difficult to calculate how much profit is actually generated.

As noted above, a wide variety of perpetrators commit green crimes. These include individuals, some of whom commit these as a means to gain survival necessities such as food and income; organised groups, for whom environmental crimes can be as profitable as for instance drug trafficking; insurgent or terrorist groups, who do so in order to gain funding for armament and ammunition;

corporations, which benefit by calculating the costs of complying or not complying with environmental regulations; and states, which may facilitate the breaking of environmental regulations or fail to regulate specific harmful activities in favour of specific economic and political interests.

Just as with other crimes that are committed for financial gain, many make little money but few very much (van Duyne and Miranda 1999). For example, a man who killed over 70 elephants claimed he received 58 dollars per kilogram of tusks (Messenger 2014). In 2014, the street value of ivory in Beijing was estimated at 2.205 dollars per kilogram (Lawson and Vines 2014). Another example is the fact that worldwide more than a million miners scratch out an illegal living digging for gold in at least 850 hot spots, whereas corrupt authorities gain the most of these activities, by taking a percentage in exchange for not enforcing the law (Paddock 2016).

However, the 'top-earners' in the business of environmental crime are probably legitimate corporations. For example, a Dutch study of the mixing of chemical waste with heavy fuel oil used as a propellant in sea going ships calculated the estimated illegal gain of this activity at 200–500 dollars per ton for the producers, which are oil companies based in the port of Rotterdam (Spapens *et al.* 2013). Total profits are huge because annually over 20,000 ships refuel in Rotterdam and in 2007 13.4 million tons of fuel oil were sold. In 2011, the Dutch police found during a three-week inspection of tankers shipping fuel oil from Rotterdam to the nearby port of Antwerp, that a majority required further investigation for carrying 'dirty oil' or because of other irregularities (van Erp *et al.* 2016). If this was indeed be an indication of a widespread problem, this single case could add several billion dollars to the estimated global value of the illicit waste market.

In particular, corporate environmental crime is sometimes seen as systemic, as an inherent feature of the capitalist economic system, and promoted by a political system that supports economic rather than environmental interests (White, 2013). For example, the 'treadmill of production' theory assumes that capitalism is an ecologically destructive means of production, and that the processes of producing and consuming goods generate ecological disorganisation (Stretesky *et al.* 2013). Enforcement is often problematic because relationships between the managers of important companies and politicians are usually cordial, resulting in perpetrators not being punished, but gently nudged to comply with environmental regulations, at least for a number of years and as long as there is no public outcry or visible disaster (Spapens 2012). Key appointments in the Trump administration, including a known climate change denier and climate science contrarian as head of the US Environmental Protection Agency, reinforce this point about economic and political elites being intertwined and sharing similar interests. The Volkswagen diesel emission scandal further illustrates this point, as the revolving doors between top governmental offices and corporate boardrooms have facilitated the lax regulation and enforcement of diesel emission standards in Germany and the EU (Spapens, in this volume).

Whereas committing green crimes may be highly profitable for the select few, many ordinary people suffer the costs, although it may be impossible to calculate these in terms of money and the impact goes well beyond the financial. Overall costs can be seen in terms of damage to the health and wellbeing of humans and non-human species as well as ecological destruction, for instance the contribution of pollution to global warming. Diverse indirect costs also contribute to the problem. For instance, insurgent groups such as Al Shabaab make 38–56 million dollars annually on the illicit charcoal trade, which they use to buy arms that in turn cause death and destruction (Nelleman *et al.* 2016). Environmental crimes may also rob governments of taxes that could have been used for the public good.

Apart from gains and costs, we can look at the topic of environmental crime and money from the perspective of financial incentives to promote the reduction of environmental harm, as well as applying financial instruments in order to regulate and enforce rules designed to minimise harm and protect the environment. Taxation is of course a traditional instrument at the disposal of governments to influence customers' behaviour, but more unorthodox measures may also be possible. An example here is initiatives to provide wildlife poachers with alternative sources of income, such as tourism or even by employing them as game wardens. The EU emissions trading system aimed at reducing greenhouse gas emissions, is likewise a good example of using the market mechanism to achieve environmental goals. The fact that so much dirty money is made from environmental crime, also brings the problem of money laundering. To be able to spend and invest the proceeds of waste trafficking or poaching on legitimate markets, offenders need to give those proceeds a seemingly legitimate origin. Large-scale investment of dirty money disrupts legitimate markets (Reuter and Truman 2004). Just like money made in other illicit markets. However, compared to other forms of money laundering, not much is known about the specifics of laundering the proceeds of the various forms of environmental crime by the various types of perpetrators discussed above (Rose 2014; Das and Young 2017).

Finally, because environmental crime is almost always aimed at financial gain, the issue of how police, regulators and courts respond to such crimes always has an economic dimension. For instance, stripping perpetrators of illegally obtained assets may be very effective, particularly because the courts usually do not impose lengthy prison terms on environmental criminals. Confiscating assets, however, requires complex financial investigations, particularly when legitimate corporations are involved in the crimes, and subsequently combine expertise with investigative authorities, which is not always available. On the other hand, fines by themselves may prove largely ineffectual as a criminal justice response and this, too, requires greater scrutiny.

The contributors to this volume address many of the issues raised above. Part I 'Systemic drivers of green crimes' focuses on the question of how economic systems, the struggle for resources and political-economic relations may promote environmental harm. In Chapter 1 Vincenzo Ruggiero looks at green criminology from the viewpoint of neoliberal economics and what can be called the philosophy of desire. After examining institutional responses to environmental damage, he argues that even attempts to reduce emissions and the problematic 'carbon trade' result in further damage and novel forms of financial crime. In Chapter 2, Avi Brisman and Nigel South examine the link between conflict and environmental harm. Their chapter builds on a four-pronged typology of conflict-environmental relationships: (1) conflict over natural resources possession; (2) conflict over declining resources; (3) conflict that destroys environments; and (4) conflict over natural resource extraction processes (Brisman *et al.* 2015).

In Chapter 3, Anna Rita Germani, Antonio Pergolizzi and Filippo Reganati conclude that environmental crimes in the Italian waste market are the outcome of a lack of economic resources devoted to crime prevention and enforcement, the strong interaction and collusion between political parties and industrial lobbies, and the lack of a culture of legality. In Italy, this system allows for the creation of high margins of private profits, hampering both the market and economic policy makers in their efforts to allocate or re-allocate resources.

In Chapter 4, Amy Couper and Reece Walters look at illegal wildlife trade through a green criminological lens and draw on both the treadmill of production theory and the Anthropogenic Allee Effect. In doing so, they critically examine the regulatory policies and practices of the Australian Government, a reported world leader in the fight against illegal wildlife trade, through a detailed examination of reported court cases.

Part II 'Corporations, environmental violations and the money' examines the links between environmental compliance and company's performance. In Chapter 5, Toine Spapens analyses the Volkswagen 'dieselgate' scandal. In September 2015 it transpired that the company had installed illegal software in its cars that reduced emissions during laboratory tests. As a result, Volkswagen was confronted with huge financial penalties and damage compensation claims. The chapter looks at the question of why Volkswagen may have installed the software from a criminological perspective, one that focuses on CEOs' personalities, company characteristics and state-corporate crime.

In Chapter 6 Nadja Guenster and Jakob Koegst study the link between environmental performance and firm value. Although numerous empirical studies have shown that higher environmental standards are associated with a higher firm valuation, little is known about the direction of the effect. Does better environmental performance lead to a higher valuation or vice versa? The authors examine the effect of environmental performance on the main drivers of firm value. Their findings confirm a positive link between profitability and environmental performance. Similar to consumers, investors and creditors prefer firms with less environmental problems and provide capital at a lower cost.

Karin van Wingerde and Marieke Kluin examine a similar question in Chapter 7, looking in depth at how very large and profitable firms deal with environmental compliance. They use data on ten firms in the Dutch waste industry and chemical industry. Comparing financial revenues with information on environmental violations the authors characterise the corporations based on a typology developed by Gunningham *et al.* (2003), dividing companies into the categories 'environmental laggards; reluctant compliers; committed compliers; environmental strategists and true believers'.

Chapter 8, written by Lieselot Bisschop and Wim Huisman, adds the activities of criminal organisations in the waste market to the perspective, noting that criminogenic opportunities offered by waste are utilised by legitimate corporations as well as criminal organisations. The authors discuss different criminological approaches to the waste-crime nexus and their respective etiological explanations, as well as views on financial incentives for crime control and harm prevention. They analyse what consequences the theories have for controlling and preventing waste crime and whether the contemporary regulation and enforcement answers to these requirements.

Part III, 'Financial regulation and enforcement', addresses how regulators and enforcement agencies may use financial incentives, regulations and investigation to prevent and tackle environmental crime. In Chapter 9, Mike Levi explores to what extent global initiatives to combat money laundering encompass environmental crimes, focusing specifically on the proceeds of illegal logging and cooperation between the Global North and Global South.

In Chapter 10, Daan van Uhm examines the 'laundering' of protected animals caught illegally in the wild, which also is a method to launder the proceeds of this type of environmental crime. The Convention on the International Trade in Endangered Species of Wild Fauna and Flora (CITES) aims at regulating rather than prohibiting wildlife trade. Although commercial trade in species listed in Appendix 1 – the most endangered flora and fauna – is prohibited, captive bred animals are exempted. This creates a massive loophole, not in the least because it is impossible to distinguish between animals caught in the wild and those bred in captivity. This chapter describes the process of wildlife laundering through breeding farms, legitimate wildlife traders and sanctuaries, based on seizures in the EU and the results of fieldwork in China, Russia and Morocco.

In Chapter 11, Ruth McKie critically reflects on the EU emissions trading system from the perspective of ecological modernisation; one theory in which we can explore human's responses to environmental challenges. She examines three contours of carbon market crime, to answer the question whether ecologically modernised policy can generate action that will mitigate anthropogenic harm caused by human's polluting activities.

The final two chapters address green crimes from the perspective of law enforcement, courts and sanctions. In Chapter 12, Rudi Neve and Nanina van Zanden describe the efforts of the Dutch police to confiscate perpetrators' illegal assets acquired through environmental crimes. Although a financial approach has been quite common in organised crime cases, applying financial investigation methods to environmental crimes has been taken up relatively recently. Because in the Netherlands this type of crime is mostly corporate crime, financial investigation requires advanced financial and administrative expertise, as illegal and legitimate activities are often (but not always) intertwined.

In Chapter 13, Rob White presents a case study of the New South Wales Land and Environment Court, which is the oldest specialist court of its kind in Australia. The court has the options to impose a wide range of penalties, such as fines, imprisonment and remediation. This allows it to deal with environmental crime in ways that involve not only monetary penalties but, also, action requirements that are designed to repair the environmental harm. The emphasis is on measures that are both punitive and reparative, thus serving the purposes of deterrence while ensuring good environmental outcomes.

References

Brisman, A., South, N. and White, R. 2015. 'Toward a criminology of environment-conflict relationships', in *Environmental Crime and Social Conflict: Contemporary and Emerging Issues* edited by A. Brisman, N. South and R. White. Farnham: Ashgate, 1–38.

Das, O. and Young, M.A. 2017. *Environmental Crime and Money Laundering: Tracing the Proceeds of Crime from Illegal Wildlife Trades.* London and New York: Routledge.

Duyne, van, P.C and Miranda, de, H. 1999. 'The emperor's clothes of disclosure: hot money and suspect disclosures', *Crime, Law and Social Change* 31(3), 245–271.

Erp, van, J., Spapens, T. and Wingerde, van, C. 2016. 'Legal and extralegal enforcement of pollution by sea-going vessels', in *Hazardous Waste and Pollution: Detecting and Preventing Green Crimes* edited by T. Wyatt. New York: Springer International Publishing, 63–176.

Gunningham, N., Kagan, R. and Thornton, D. 2003. *Shades of Green: Business, Regulation, and Environment.* Stanford: Stanford University Press.

Huisman, W. and Erp, van J. 2013. 'Opportunities for environmental crime. A test of situational crime prevention theory', *British Journal of Criminology* 53(6), 1178–1200.

Lawson K. and Vines, A. 2014. *Global Impacts of the Illegal Wildlife Trade: The Costs of Crime, Insecurity and Institutional Erosion.* London: Chatham House.

Messenger, S. 2014. 'Exclusive interview with an elephant poacher', *The Dodo*, 15 January www.thedodo.com/interview-with-an-elephant-poa-390317914.html.

Nellemann, C., Henriksen, R., Kreilhuber, A., Stewart, D., Kotsovou, M., Raxter, P., Mrema, E., and Barrat, S. 2016. *The Rise of Environmental Crime – A Growing Threat to Natural Resources Peace, Development and Security.* Nairobi: UNEP.

Paddock, R. 2016. 'The toxic toll of Indonesia's gold mines', *National Geographic*, 24 May.

Rose, G. (ed.) 2014. *Following the Proceeds of Environmental Crime: Fish, Forests and Filthy Lucre.* London and New York: Routledge.

Spapens, T. 2012. *De Complexiteit van Milieucriminaliteit.* Den Haag: Boom Lemma uitgevers.

Spapens, T., Bruinsma, M., Hout, van, L. and Jong, de, J. 2013. *Vuile Olie. Onrechtmatig Verwerken en Mengen van Olieproducten als Vormen van Milieucriminaliteit.* Den Haag: Boom Lemma uitgevers.

Stretesky, P., Long, M. and Lynch, M. 2013. *The Treadmill of Crime: Political Economy and Green Criminology.* London and New York: Routledge.

White, R. 2013 'Eco-global criminology and the political economy of environmental harm', in *Routledge International Handbook of Green Criminology*, edited by N. South and A. Brisman. London: Routledge, 243–260.

Part I
Systemic drivers of green crimes

1 Destruction and the philosophy of desire

Vincenzo Ruggiero

Looking at green criminology from the perspective of neoliberal economics can add some elements to this growing area of enquiry (for a definition of neoliberalism, see Harvey 2005). Complementing economic reasoning with references to what I describe as the philosophy of desire can compound arguments against environmental destruction. This chapter attempts both enterprises.

The abysmal science

We spend money we don't have, on things we don't need, to make impressions that don't last, on people who don't care. Because we do not pursue what is necessary, but what is superfluous, neoliberal economic thought needs to turn the superfluous into a natural product of human activity or even into an element of human organic reproduction. Hence its need to imitate the natural sciences. Biologists, physicists, mathematicians and other scientists have been called upon to make economic theories more 'realistic and effective', namely to inoculate doses of dogma into them. The major opus of economics produced in the twentieth century, the *General Theory* of Keynes (1973 [1936]), out of a total 400 pages included, mainly in the appendix, three or four simple equations. In 1950 only in 2–3 per cent of the articles published by the influential *American Economic Review* contained mathematic formulas, which normally were not at all sophisticated. In 1980 the papers with mathematical calculations were 44 per cent and formulas had become much more complex. Currently the percentage is close to 90 per cent. The only 'real' science within the human sciences, this increasingly esoteric discipline, in its neoliberal version, dominates in university courses, in the specialist literature, and in most schools of management and business. It is the core religion of business administrators, large enterprises, financial institutions, ministries of the economy, central banks, international organisations, the World Bank, the World Monetary Fund and the European Commission.

> The economy is seen as a physical system, implying flows of goods, information and energy, so that it might be useful to model the economy as a system, like physics does. However, while economic theory uses the concept of equilibrium, the same concept used by physics cannot be applied

to the economy, because this is an open system and equilibrium refers to closed systems.

(Gallino 2011, p. 92)

Neo-liberalism does not observe and describe the economic reality; it creates this reality (Ruggiero 2013). It also contradicts one of the very axioms of free markets, namely that the full costs of a transaction must be borne by the involved parties. Many economic activities and transactions, however, exact a significant price on humans and ecosystems, although economists label such price with the reassuring euphemism 'externalities'. In brief, neo-liberalism regards environmental harm as an accidental, unintentional, externality.

Applying the *meum-tuum* distinction suggested by Hayek (1973), we can formulate the following question: Is the environment a public good? The answer is 'Yes', if we, in abstract terms, assimilate it to other non-rival, non-excludable goods, in the sense that one person's enjoyment of the environment does not exclude its enjoyment by others, and in the sense that the good environment is provided to one and all at the same time. However, the answer is 'No' if we believe that goods and resources belong to those who turn them into wealth. Neoliberalism embraces the latter assumption, thus reiterating early liberalist notions according to which the earth has to be turned into property through manipulation, improvement and work. By leaving fruits to rot and venison to putrefy, and for that matter by leaving the earth untouched, we offend the common law of nature (Ruggiero 2013). With neoliberalism, the entire world is given to those who are more capable of exploiting it, and the environment, therefore, is both *meum* and *tuum*, provided we both know how to extract value out of it. The boundaries, in this case, are not determined by the identification of objects upon which the different individuals exercise control, but merely by their capacity and ingenuity, which constitute the only limit to initiative and development. The ultimate resource, in brief, is the human mind, and throughout history human genius always wins out against natural resource restraints.

The harm caused by economic initiative, therefore, amounts to 'externality'. This includes climate change, disposal of toxic waste, de-forestation, pollution of sea, air and land, gigantic disparities in income, transference of toxicity to poor regions and countries, impoverishment of vulnerable populations and destruction of communities (White 2010; South and Brisman 2013). These 'ecocidal' tendencies (South 2010) implicit in unfettered development are masked in a process whereby the specific victims of development itself disappear. Ideological strategies preside over this disappearance, among which a hierarchical positioning of populations and individuals is of crucial importance. Ontological priorities are established so that some lives are deemed less valuable than others: in fact, some lives are never lived nor lost in the full sense. There are lives worth living and lives worth destroying, the former being valuable and grievable, the latter devalued and ungrievable (Butler 2009). Utilitarian reasoning does not object to such distinction, as the suffering of some does not diminish the total happiness generated by the economy. This distinction, in other words, implies the neglect of individual wellbeing and happiness, while the ranking of social goodness and the selection of what is to be chosen are done simply on the basis of the sum total of individual welfares (Sen 2009).

> The utilitarian calculus based on happiness or desire-fulfillment can be deeply unfair to those who are persistently deprived since our mental make-up and desires tend to adjust to circumstances, particularly to make life bearable in adverse situations. It is through 'coming to terms' with one's hopeless predicament that life is made somewhat bearable by the traditional underdogs, such as oppressed minorities in intolerant communities, sweated workers in exploitative industrial arrangements, precarious share-croppers living in a world of uncertainty, or subdued housewives in deeply sexist cultures.
>
> (ibid., p. 282)

This 'coming to terms' includes the acceptance of differentiated distribution of vulnerability and precariousness that neoliberal economy promotes.

Habit and domination

Social scientists who intend to critique the economic logic do not have to go far, in that a return to classical texts may provide enough food for thought. Max Weber argues that markets are antithetic to all other communities, because the latter, not the former, presuppose 'brotherhood' among people. But let us expand on Weber's thought.

In trade, the guarantee of legality on the part of two individuals involved is based on the presupposition, often shared by both, that each of them will have an interest in continuing the exchange in the future, and that therefore will respect the pacts and the promise given. But because trade is a form of socialisation with strangers, therefore with enemies, at the origin, the supervision of legality was entrusted to the religious authority, under the tutelage of the temple, which with time became the state. Supervising over legality, however, does not guarantee the rationality of economic initiative, which by pursuing maximum profitability is constantly urged to cross the boundaries of legality itself. There is, therefore, an element of substantive irrationality in the economic order, determined by attempts to make short-term speculative profit, described by Weber as 'pure gambling interest', which 'is one of the sources of the phenomena known as the 'crises' of the modern market economy' (Weber 1978, p. 40).

Weber adds that humans are creatures of habit, but they are also strongly motivated by their material and ideal interests to circumvent conventional and legal rules, and 'in all societies the economically powerful tend to have a strong influence on the enactment and interpretation of the law' (Roth 1978, p. lxix). For this reason, Weber's work on economic issues is in a sense a sociology of domination, in which the gradual usurpation of collective power results in legitimate institutional force.

Following a Weberian classification, power implies the use or threat of coercive force on those who are given orders, whereas domination is to be understood as legitimised, internalised propensity to obey orders (Ruggiero 2015). This also applies to the economic sphere.

Legitimacy, however, though internalised, needs constant justification on the part of those who have authority, wealth and honour to give reason for their good fortune. Economic thought offers such constant justification.

Ultimately, what prevails in Weber's examination of economic activity is a sense that such activity follows a goal-oriented rationality, which is mainly 'traditional' in its orientation. 'Even in cases where there is a high degree of rationalization of action, the element of traditional orientation remains considerable' (Weber 1978, p. 69). It is against this tradition that the next section of this chapter will now turn.

Poverty as the trigger of development

Practitioners of economics are not allowed friendliness, they are required to describe human motivations as pure and simple, and keep their economic models devoid of such things as goodwill and moral sentiments. It is extraordinary that economic thought has evolved in this way, describing human goals in such spectacularly narrow terms, also because 'economics is largely an offshoot of ethics' (Sen 1987, pp. 1–2). Individuals may well understand and wish to maximise their interest, but practical morality should perhaps lead them to the recognition that theirs and other people's interests are interdependent.

> The recognition of interdependence may suggest following certain rules of behaviour, which are not necessarily of intrinsic value, but which are of great instrumental importance in the enhancement of the respective goals of the members of a group.
>
> (ibid., p. 85)

Many economic schools of thought fail to recognise this interdependence, although they attempt to persuade us (along with Adam Smith) that the interests of the butchers are linked with those of their customers. We have to infer that the values of economics are found in economics itself and accept, for example, a notion of justice as inequality, because inequality supposedly encourages the disadvantaged to follow in the footsteps of their role models, namely the privileged. The reality is that the example set by the privileged does not indicate how to create wealth, but how to take it from others. If not acquisitive crime, this gives rise to instability, and the latter to social harm, and the irony is 'that while inequality gives rise to instability, the instability itself gives rise to more inequality' (Stiglitz 2012, p. 91).

It is inequality itself, its explanation and rationalisation, which have mobilised the most ingenious talents in the economics profession.

In nearly all economic history most people have been poor and a comparative few have been very rich. Accordingly, there has been a compelling need to explain why this is so – and, alas, on frequent occasion, to tell why it should be so.

(Galbraith 1987, pp. 2–3)

Poverty as the result of divine displeasure was turned by economists into inequality as the trigger of development and happiness, and while political economy merged with theology, existing social relations were sanctified. As Thomas More (1997, p. 127) argued centuries ago, one can perceive a 'conspiracy' on the part of the wealthy, who through devices and 'all means and crafts', try to 'keep safely without fear of losing what they have unjustly gathered together'. These devices are then turned into laws, whereby the only legitimate thing the non-wealthy can do is endeavour to imitate the wealthy.

That such an endeavour is implausible is proven by another core notion we find in economic thought, where freedom and equality are deemed irreconcilable. Economics posits that distribution of resources is spontaneous, neutral and market-driven. Following the examples of the privileged, therefore, will only generate acquiescence for a system allowing the privileges openly displayed to remain accessible to a few. If left alone, markets will produce, so we are told, the most efficient and just outcome. This self-serving notion, in fact, justifies a mere upward redistribution of income, and making rich people richer does not make everyone else richer. In brief, wealth trickles up. Moreover, the very 'trickle-down' metaphor does not refer to a gushing waterfall or a potent flow, but to a mere leaking tap.

Economic thought is, indeed, framed in metaphorical terms; nevertheless it constrains our lives, and by virtue of what it hides, can lead to the acceptance of human and environmental degradation. I call this degradation and the social harms thus produced 'the crimes of the economy', which affect workers, consumers, creditors, investors and taxpayers, and of course the environment. Such victims undergo a process of disappearance set off by specific ideological strategies. There are numerous ways of rationalising the crimes of the economy, the first being the mobilisation of the variable externalities, as already remarked. These crimes are often downplayed to the rank of unwanted effect of industrial production or commercial transaction. This is to say, whoever suffers the consequences of an economic operation in which he/she does not take part is the victim of unintentional actions: he or she is an 'externality'.

Enough is enough

Economic history is not a noble history: habit and tradition, as indicated by Weber, urge human action into limitless development and growth, irrespective of consequences. Some economic conducts seem hardly susceptible to the control and discipline of legal norms. If we adhere to Weber's point of view in a more comprehensive way, we have to conclude that development itself, and the growing complexity of markets, make legal coercion increasingly difficult to apply to the economic sphere. As a logical consequence, we may advocate a halt to economic development as the only way of reducing and preventing the crimes of the economy. Arguments against insatiability might be put forward as a challenge against the current obsession with growth: 'enough is enough'. 'To say that my aim in life is to make more and more money is like saying that my aim in eating is to get fatter and fatter' (Skidelsky and Skidelsky 2012, p. 5).

The prosperity of a country cannot be narrowly measured through the amount of money available for a given number of individuals, but also and primarily depends on how resources are distributed, how people live, their degree of participation in the civic and political arena, their capacity to function, make choices and control their outcomes.

Against insatiability, the notion of 'de-growth' can be mobilised, as infinite growth is not only a metaphor for unpleasant and unhealthy obesity, but also because it is criminogenic: it depicts greed and acquisitiveness in a positive light, making them core values of individual and collective behaviour (Latouche 2008, 2010). Simultaneously, growth as we have experienced it over the decades exacerbates the polarisation of wealth, therefore increasing relative deprivation, one of the central variables in the analysis of crime. Ultimately, as a manifestation of insatiability, growth is a form of pathology, such as the uncontrollable, neurotic desire to collect things or to swallow enormous quantities of food. Economists cannot keep preaching that such manifestations of neurosis signal healthy collective conditions.

Challenging growth implies a distinction between needs and wants, the former being characterised by an absolute and the latter by a relative nature. We feel the importance of the former whatever the condition of our fellow human beings may be, while we pursue the latter in order to feel superior to our fellows (Keynes 1972 [1931]). Wants are infinite and are lured towards both 'bandwagon goods', which are desired because others possess them, and 'snob goods', which are desired because others do not possess them (Veblen 1924). The latter are mere advertisements of wealth, status consumptions, which legitimise permanent growth and constant deviations from the rules officially governing it. Growth satisfies both types of wants while creating new ones, it is like a Faustian Man, ambitious, omnivorous, perpetually driven beyond the limits, the infinite, in a vortex that brings 'goods' and 'bads', namely what I term the crimes of the economy.

Desire of nothing

In the second and final part of this chapter I would like to connect these ideas we find in the economic sphere to more general concepts that I group under the definition 'the philosophy of desire'. Here, we shall see how green criminology has to struggle not only against the logic of markets, but also against a powerful set of notions that belong to our own Western philosophical tradition.

The concept of being is often likened to an idea of 'lacking', referred to a deficit, something we will never attain. To be means to feel a possibility, to reach something that is not there yet, that has not yet become, or will never become real. This notion of being contains ideas revolving around the human uncertainty about the future. Lacan (2014) offers a powerful analysis of this uncertainty, when he describes the subject as 'nobody', being fragmented and decomposed. Thus, human subjects are characterised by a 'void', that they attempt to fill with dynamic responses in the form of desires, although desires often fail to address precise objects. Humans are not satisfied by the attainment of a thing, an object, a value item and so on. Therefore, desires never nullify or fill a void: once humans identify an object of desire, and even when they gain possession of that object, their desires grow, move on, turning into desire of nothing. In sum, lack and want are inherent in the human condition. The infinite pursuit of nothing, in its turn, makes the identification of reference points necessary: we need stability and only idols can provide it to us (Ruggiero 2017). Economic growth is one such idol.

On the other hand, humans are aware that they are finite and mortal: we are lucid about this, and as a consequence, we have a special relationship with temporality. This is why we tend to measure, calculate, as a way of assessing what we have done in the past and what we plan to do in the future. Calculate, plan, build, construct, produce, but also optimise: all of these are carried out with the urgency dictated by our awareness of time and mortality.

To reiterate, one of the possibilities for humans is to identify idols, phantom entities as a point of reference, as carriers of stability in a condition otherwise characterised by constant anxiety. But how can this be done, if desire is infinite? Instead of trying to possess things, humans may choose to be possessed by them: they become, in this way, prisoners of the things they want, so that anxiety and uncertainty may cease. We then become totally alienated: we dissolve ourselves in the objects we desire, we become objects and things ourselves. Humans, ultimately, can choose to assert themselves as slaves rather than as subjects.

The idolatry of infinite development causes destruction while encouraging consumption, which has nothing to do with need or even less with desire. Markets, in fact, possess a specific capacity, that of attributing human anxiety to the lack of something they can provide. You are anxious because you need this, and here it is, I can give it to you. This is the answer to your restlessness. Commodities, in this sense, have a metaphysical subtlety and a theological character, they are independent entities, acquiring their own life. Of course, we find these suggestions in Marx, although in classical literature we may find even more powerful renditions of them.

When Balzac's Père Goriot is dying, his daughter attends a sumptuous ball, which she prioritises over tending her father on his deathbed. The ball is a display of wealth, luxury and status, and the things in view seem to take on their own independent life (Balzac 1966). The lamps light out the Hotel de Beauseant, a gendarme in all the glory of his uniform stands on either side of the resplendent gateway, while the great world flocks in. The attire of the most beautiful women in Paris is dazzling, while the most distinguished men proudly deploy their decorations, stars and ribbons, as if showing less their military honour than their bank account. The music of the orchestra vibrates and the waves of notes confer more splendour to the golden ceiling of the palace. It is a society adorning itself with things that speak, move and dance by themselves. In that ball we can see not only a ghostly dance that repels the 'spectre haunting Europe', but also an assemblage of commodities endowed with invincible force and frightening power. Lamps and golden ceilings are not just things, and their properties do not merely respond to human needs. They are on a stage as commodities, symbolic entities acting and interacting among one another, presenting themselves as marked by their specific market value (Ruggiero 2015). The ball is a coup de théâtre, in which the ordinary is transfigured and metamorphosed into a supernatural thing. Commodities assume ghostly silhouettes, invade the stage with their spectral moves, come alive and address other commodities, their ghostly fellows (Derrida 2006). In brief, Balzac's characters prefigure the insatiability of consumerism (Eagleton 2009).

Conclusion

Neoliberalism posits this type of insatiability. It attempts to transform subjects as we know them in specific social contexts into universal beings, unchanged by circumstances and unchangeable by political events. These universal beings are required to produce not something they need to use, but something they need to destroy, as enjoyment of a commodity is less important than its death. As Baudrillard (2005) put it, production survives and continues only because of this massacre: things have to become obsolete, their use-value has to diminish, otherwise the process as a whole comes to a halt. Green criminology cannot avoid addressing these destructive effects of production and economic growth.

Destruction is fed by a mimetic mechanism, as we have seen: we want what other people have, but then we also want what other people do not have. And this mimetic behaviour is justified by neoliberalism, which also preaches increasing social inequality, as the deprived can look to the advantaged and find their role model in them. The advantaged, in this way, become ideals or indeed idols to which all are expected to conform their conduct and activity.

This mechanism was clear in the mind of Saint Thomas, who argued that we are sad when faced with the wellbeing of others because we regard it as the cause of our own humiliation. Sadness, impotence and failure: these are all associated with dissatisfaction, and as a consequence they are experienced as reasons for compensation if not revenge. Inequality and consumerism foster envy. The subject does not consume, he/she is consumed.

To conclude, green criminology may find inspiration and novel impetus from the radical critique of economic thought and a dissection of the philosophy of desire. These are epitomised by the motto 'the car is war', with which Walter Benjamin (2011, p. 167) meant that our societies develop technical means without being able to control them morally. The destructive impetus of neoliberal doctrines reveals the ruinous 'discrepancy between the enormous efforts of technology and its miserable moral illumination' (ibid.). This moral void echoes the legendary figure of Mephistopheles, who pursues evil while producing good, who follows his vices claiming that they will turn into public virtues, who is guided by egoistic desires but claims to cause collective benefit. In his radical critique of 'development', Benjamin (ibid., p. 309) looks at a painting by Klee called 'Angelus Novus', in which an angel walks away from something she stares at. Her eyes are wide open, her mouth is gaping, her wings are spread out. The angel of history must possess similar traits: where we see a chain of events she sees total catastrophe, an accumulation of debris upon debris. The angel would like to fly into the past, attempt to awaken the dead and mend the damage caused. But from heaven a storm blows that pushes her towards the future, while the heap of ruins grows in front of her. 'What we call progress is this storm'.

References

Balzac, de H. 1966. *Le Père Goriot.* Paris: Garnier-Flammarion.
Baudrillard, J. 2005. *The System of Objects.* London: Verso.
Benjamin, W. 2011. *Scritti politici.* Rome: Editori Internazionali Riuniti.
Butler, J. 2009. *Frames of War: When is Life Grievable.* London: Verso.
Derrida, J. 2006. *Spectres of Marx.* London: Routledge.
Eagleton, T. 2009. *Trouble with Strangers. A Study of Ethics.* Oxford: Wiley-Blackwell.
Galbraith, J.K. 1987. *A History of Economics: The Past as the Present.* London: Penguin.
Gallino, L. 2011. *Finanzcapitalismo: La civiltà del denaro in crisi.* Turin: Einaudi.
Harvey, D. 2005. *A Brief History of Neoliberalism.* Oxford: Oxford University Press.
Hayek, F.A. 1973. *Law, Legislation and Liberty.* London: Routledge & Kegan Paul.
Keynes, J.M. 1972 [1931]. *Essays in Persuasion.* London: Macmillan.
Keynes, J.M. 1973 [1936]. *The General Theory of Employment Interest and Money.* London: Macmillan.
Lacan, J. 2014. *Anxiety.* Cambridge: Polity Press.
Latouche, S. 2008. *Breve trattato sulla decrescita serena.* Turin: Bollati Boringhieri.
Latouche, S. 2010. *L'invenzione dell'economia.* Turin: Bollati Boringhieri.
More, T. 1997. *Utopia.* London: Wordsworth.
Roth, G. 1978. 'Introduction', in *M. Weber, Economy and Society: An Outline of Interpretive Sociology* edited by G. Roth and C. Wittich. Berkeley: University of California Press.
Ruggiero, V. 2013. *The Crimes of the Economy.* London and New York: Routledge.
Ruggiero, V. 2015. *Power and Crime.* London and New York: Routledge.
Ruggiero, V. 2017. *Dirty Money: On Financial Delinquency.* Oxford: Oxford University Press.
Sen, A. 1987. *On Ethics and Economics.* Oxford: Basil Blackwell.
Sen, A. 2009. *The Idea of Justice.* London: Allen Lane.
Skidelsky, R. and Skidelsky, E. 2012. *How Much is Enough? The Love for Money and the Case for the Good Life.* London: Allen Lane.
South, N. 2010. 'The ecocidal tendencies of late modernity: Transnational crime, social exclusion, victims and rights', in *Global Environmental Harm*, edited by R. White. Cullompton: Willan Publishing, 228–247.
South, N. and Brisman, V. (eds.) 2013. *International Handbook of Green Criminology.* London: Routledge.

Stiglitz, J. 2012. *The Price of Inequality.* London: Allen Lane.

Veblen, T. 1924. *The Theory of the Leisure Class: An Economic Study of Institutions.* London: Allen & Unwin.

Weber, M. 1978. *Economy and Society: An Outline of Interpretive Sociology.* Berkeley: University of California Press.

White, R. (ed.) 2010. *Global Environmental Harm.* Cullompton: Willan Publishing.

2 Environment, conflict and profit

Harmful resource exploitation and questionable revenue generation

Avi Brisman and Nigel South

Introduction

In 'Toward a Criminology of Environment-Conflict Relationships', Brisman, South and White (2015) set forth a four-pronged typology of conflict-environmental relationships: (1) conflict over natural resources possession; (2) conflict over declining resources; (3) conflict that destroys environments; and (4) conflict over natural resource extraction processes. Conceptualising 'conflict' as 'violence or the threat of violence stemming from incompatibilities in stakeholders' interests, priorities, values or understandings' (Brisman *et al.* 2015, p. 1, emphasis in original)),[1] we set out to provide examples of conflicts that bring about negative/damaging environmental consequences.

In so doing, we (a) acknowledged that other typologies exist (see Brisman *et al.* 2015, pp. 2–3); (b) recognised that some conflicts and environmental harms can "fit" into more than one category; and (c) emphasised that linkages between conflict and the environment are varied and not all negative – – that some factors, such as contested resource wealth, that in some circumstances may precipitate or support or subsidise conflict, may, in other circumstances, provide a route out of, or insulation from, conflict (see Amster 2015, pp. 8–9, 15–16, 69, 130, 144, 157, 160, 163, 165, 170 for examples and a discussion). We noted that post-conflict countries 'increasingly attract investors' and often 'face a . . .

---

1 We focused on conflict(s) between humans rather than on conflict between humans and non-human animals – or 'human-wildlife conflict', as it is often known, and that refers to 'the competition between humans and wildlife in relation to habitat, livelihood aspects (e.g., crops and livestock) and physical safety' (Bond 2015, p. 312). Given the threatened or endangered status of some of these non-human animals (see, e.g., Bond 2015; Gore *et al.* 2006, 2007, 2008; Kahler and Gore 2015; Moen 2015; Romans 2014; Teasdale 2017; cf. Howard 2016), human-non-human animal conflict could fall into either the first or second category of our typology. We leave such a discussion for another day.

rush on their lands, forests, and mineral resources' (Hennings 2016, p. 34). Such developments may, on the surface, appear promising in terms of 'reconstruction and economic prosperity', but 'they may also entail risks for reconciliation and processes and long-term peace prospects due to changing formal and informal land ownership and the often unjust distribution of negative externalities and benefits' (Hennings 2016, p. 34). As such, we urged exercising caution in assuming that the presence of desirable natural resources would necessarily result in economic recovery and successful reconciliation in post-conflict areas. Rather, we stressed that access to land and valuable natural resources, if well managed, have the potential to promote and consolidate peace, and to secure sustainable growth, raise living standards and increase economic equality. We also under-scored the need to update and expand typologies in order to keep them current and fresh, and to reorient them to help analyse more specific or underlying issues and phenomena. This is the goal of the present chapter. More specifically, we seek to complement, illustrate and develop aspects of this typology in two ways.

First, this chapter notes that a wide variety of 'high value' natural resources can be subject to legal and illegal transactions. These have influential effects on the relationship or balance between social stability and unrest, violence and security, environmental degradation and violations of human rights. In so doing, this chapter examines ways in which various enterprises that are engaged in extracting, monopolising and trading resources, have been identified and linked to the funding of conflict. Second, this chapter considers how violence, conflict and war-making have consequences for environmental systems and dependents. Although these scenarios have been analysed in relation to security, politics and resource competition, they have yet to be explored through a criminological lens focused on the role of money and profit. Before beginning this exploration, however, we provide an overview of our quadripartite typology.

An overview of a four-part typology of environment-conflict relationships

Conflict over natural resources possession

This type of conflict is concerned with issues of access to, control over and use of natural resources, including the abundance of natural resources and greed-motivated violence. While there is nothing new about territorial disputes (see Hennings 2016), the desire to acquire or otherwise obtain control over the land of others may be based on ambitions to extend power, to improve or ensure security, to punish or to repatriate (see generally Amster 2015, pp. 63, 115, 129, 144). Almost always, there is a consideration regarding the resources that such land – or waterbodies – can yield. As Amster (2015, pp. 2–3) describes,

> When the United States invaded Afghanistan, it was billed as a war on Al Qaeda and those who would harbor them, including the Taliban (who were actually then-recent US allies). It was also asserted, in something of a

side note, that the effort was intended to liberate Afghan women from oppression and mistreatment. Less well known, although not entirely absent from the dialogue for more careful readers of the news, were issues of resource control including oil and gas transport from the Caspian Basin and the presence (established by the Soviets decades earlier) of potentially trillions of dollars in rare-earth minerals essential to the workings of the digital age.

(Risen 2010)[2]

Other relatively recent examples would include tensions between China and Japan regarding the delimitation of their Exclusive Economic Zones (EEZ) and the sovereignty of the Diaoyu/Senkaku Islands. As Branigan and colleagues (2015, p. 17) report,

> China claims almost all of the South China Sea in a complex dispute which also involves the Philippines, Vietnam, Malaysia, Brunei and Taiwan. Tensions have risen in recent years, due partly to growing interest in the area's energy reserves and partly to broader anxieties about China's rise and increasing assertiveness. The sea also boasts valuable fisheries and is a crucial shipping route.

The role of natural resources (specifically, minerals and forests) has been clear in the recent history of violent conflict in the Democratic Republic of Congo (DRC). Indeed, in the DRC and elsewhere, the damaging and divisive exploitation and trade in diamonds, minerals (such as gold, tantalum, tin and tungsten), timber and wildlife have generated funds – and here we see the link to money, the theme of this edited volume – that have, according to some, spurred, supported and perpetuated internal conflicts, corruption and the externalising of economic surplus (see, e.g., Brisman and South 2013; Cao and Wyatt 2016; Global Witness 2015; Milburn 2015; see also Kristof 2010; see

---

2 In a recent article in *The New York Times*, Landler and Risen (2017, p. A1) report: 'President Trump, searching for a reason to keep the United States in Afghanistan after 16 years of war, has latched on to a prospect that tantalized previous administrations: Afghanistan's vast mineral wealth, which his advisers and Afghan officials have told him could be profitably extracted by Western companies'. While Mr Trump has been sceptical of sending more troops to Afghanistan, he has also discussed mining as an economic opportunity with Afghan president, Ashraf Ghani, and has suggested that Afghanistan's mineral deposits could be a justification for the United States to stay engaged with the country. Landler and Risen (2017, p. A1) report that '[i]n 2010, American officials estimated that Afghanistan had untapped mineral deposits worth nearly $1 trillion' – an estimate, they note, 'that was widely disputed at the time and [that] has certainly fallen since, given the eroding price of commodities'. Landler and Risen (2017, p. A1) state that 'the $1 trillion figure is circulating again inside the White House', but cite former officials who 'warn that the Trump administration is fooling itself if it believes that extracting minerals is a panacea for Afghanistan's myriad ills'.

generally Associated Press 2015; Gettleman 2016; for discussions of the 'blood ivory' trade and the link between elephant poaching and terrorist attacks, see White 2014, and of the global 'blood oil' economy, see South 2016; for challenges to assertions regarding the relationship between natural resources/ mineral abundance and armed conflict, see, e.g., Duffy 2016, Duffy *et al.* 2015; Vogel and Raeymakers 2016).[3]

Global Witness (2014, p. 3) reports that '[a]s global demand for natural resources intensifies, more and more ordinary people are having to defend their rights to land and the environment from corporate or state abuse'. Indeed, as Cao and Wyatt (2016, p. 423) point out, '[i]t is not rare to see cases of timber trafficking that involve murder, violence, threats and atrocities against indigenous forest-living people, journalists and local environmental activists (Boekhout van Solinge 2010; EIA 2012; Interpol and World Bank 2009; Nellemann 2012)'. Global Witness (2014, p. 3) notes that '[m]any of the killings stem from conflicts over the ownership and use of land, particularly in the face of expanded mining and logging activities' – and here, again, we see a link between money, environmental harm and conflict. According to Global Witness, Brazil, Honduras, the Philippines and Peru are the top four deadliest countries for environmental or land defenders.[4] In Peru, the focus of its report, at least 57 environmental activists were killed between 2002 and 2014. Given the low levels of reporting of killings and a lack of official data collection, the actual number is likely higher, leading Global Witness (2014, p. 13) to conclude that '[t]he historic trajectory of killings is clearly rising', which we could take as a tragic indicator of the financial value of what is being 'protected' from the attention of activists and protestors. Ironically, violence related to land disputes can also arise as a result of what may be seen by some as, or intended to be, environmentally positive developments. Lakhani (2014), for example, notes how the Western 'drive to reduce its carbon footprint cheaply is fuelling a dirty war in Honduras, where US-backed security forces are implicated in the murder, disappearance and intimidation of peasant farmers involved in land disputes with local palm oil magnates'.

Finally, we would note that while climate change is usually associated with concerns over declining resources (our second category), melting sea ice in the Arctic has opened up areas that were previously impassable and/or impenetrable (see, e.g., Brisman 2013; Waldman 2016) and which are expected to yield new sources of natural wealth. As Waldman (2016) explains, '[l]ess ice means more access to untapped gas and oil reserves as well as new fishing stocks and strategic military potential'. With a rich array of resources that are now available as a result of climate change, cooperation among the eight nations that have a claim to

---

3 Hennings (2016, p. 36), drawing on Unruh and Williams (2013), makes the important point that 'contested access and control over land and natural resources not only encourages (armed) conflicts but that the (re-)distribution of land remains a key risk factor during conflict transformation'.

4 For a recent report on the killing of wildlife conservationists who attempted to stop poaching and the illegal ivory trade in Africa, see Hauser (2017).

Arctic territory (Canada, Denmark, Finland, Iceland, Norway, Russia, Sweden and the United States) will be paramount not only to avoid tensions and conflict over resource claims, but also to mitigate against new environmental catastrophes, for example, if newly discovered oil spills into an area where little clean-up infrastructure exists.

Conflict over declining resources

This type of conflict is concerned with issues of scarcity and the consequences of the broad degradation of environments related to conflicts and compromises over the use of resources. As Homer-Dixon (1999, p. 48) explains, scarcity can undermine human wellbeing in three interrelated ways – 'through a drop in the supply of a key resource, through an increase in demand, and through a change in the relative access of different groups to the resource' – which he refers to as supply-induced, demand-induced and structural scarcities. According to Homer-Dixon (1999, p. 48),

> [s]upply-induced scarcity gets worse when the resource pie shrinks because it has been depleted in quantity or degraded in quality. Demand-induced scarcity rises when, for example, a growing population divides a static resource pie into smaller slices for each individual. Structural scarcity is aggravated when some groups get disproportionately large slices of the pie while other groups get slices that are too small.

All three types of scarcities are likely to be more pronounced in the coming years. As Hamilton and colleagues (2015:4–5) contend,

> living in the Anthropocene means living in an atmosphere altered by the 575 billion tonnes of carbon emitted as carbon dioxide by human activities since 1870 (Le Quéré *et al.* 2014). It means inhabiting an impoverished and arti-ficialised biosphere in a hotter world increasingly characterised by catastrophic events and new risks, including the possibility of an ice-free planet. It means rising and more acidic seas, an unruly climate and its cortege of new and unequal sufferings. It's a world where the geographical distribution of population on the planet would come under great stress. And it is probably a more violent world, in which geopolitics becomes increasingly confrontational (Dyer 2008).

While Hamilton and colleagues are prognosticating, there is evidence to suggest that their predictions have already been realised. To take one example, studies suggest that drought – referred to by some commentators as a 'creeping disaster' (see Prud'homme, 2011, p. SR3) – fuelled social unrest in Syria to the point of open uprising in 2011 and a subsequent and ongoing civil war with international involvement and global repercussions (see Brisman *et al.* 2018). According to a report from Fischetti (2015),

Drying and drought in Syria from 2006 to 2011 – the worst on record there – destroyed agriculture, causing many farm families to migrate to cities. The influx added to social stresses already created by refugees pouring in from the war in Iraq. . . . The drought also pushed up food prices, aggravating poverty.

While no one has indicated that the drought in Syria caused the current civil war, experts contend that it exacerbated existing stressors to the point of conflict. In order to connect the dots, it is worthwhile taking a few moments to sketch out Syria's geopolitical and hydropolitical history.

Under President Hafez al-Assad (1971–2000), the Syrian government initiated a number of policies to increase agricultural production (e.g. land redistribution, irrigation projects) in order to win the support of rural constituents. These projects exploited Syria's limited land and water resources at a time when the country was already experiencing growing water scarcity and frequent droughts. As Kelley and colleagues explain (2015, p. 3241), one of the significant consequences of these unsustainable policies was the decline of groundwater. (One-third of cultivated land in Syria relies on irrigation and groundwater; the rest is rain fed.) This reduced supply of groundwater markedly increased Syria's vulnerability to drought, and while the government attempted to reduce the rate of groundwater depletion through legislation requiring licences to dig wells, the law was not enforced. When a severe drought began in late 2006/early 2007, as Kelley and colleagues (2015, p. 3241) describe, the agricultural system in the north-eastern region of the country – responsible for more than two-thirds of the country's crop yields – collapsed, forcing Syria to import large quantities of wheat for the first time since the mid-1990s. By this time, Bashar al-Asad had succeeded his father and, in an effort to liberalise the economy, cut the fuel and food subsidies that had become vital to many Syrians. At this point, unjust finance policy meets environmental conditions, with both contributing to the creation of poverty.

Because the rural regions in Syria were so reliant on year-to-year agricultural production and with the further instabilities caused by Bashar al-Asad's cuts, many rural farming families migrated to the country's urban areas – specifically, the peripheries of the cities, which were already struggling from an influx of over one million Iraqi refugees. Kelley and colleagues (2015, p. 3242) state that '[b]y 2010, internally displaced persons (IDPs) and Iraqi refugees made up roughly 20% of Syria's urban population. The total urban population of Syria in 2002 was 8.9 million but, by the end of 2010, had grown to 13.8 million, a more than 50% increase in only 8 years, [and] a far greater rate than for the Syrian population as a whole'. Unsurprisingly, this population surge placed additional strain on the resources of Syria's urban areas; crime, illegal settlements, overcrowding and unemployment grew. The government under Assad, however, offered little in the way of response, helping to sow – if not fertilise – the seeds of discontent and unrest. Thus, as Kelley and colleagues (2015, p. 3242) observe, 'the migration in response to the severe and prolonged drought exacerbated a number of the factors', such as unemployment, corruption and rampant inequality, which are often cited as contributing to the unrest. Importantly for our purposes here, it is noteworthy that these 'factors' are a reflection of who was, and who was not, receiving money.[5]

While Kelley and colleagues (2015, p. 3242) are reluctant to designate drought as 'a primary or substantial factor', they stress that it can 'lead to devastating consequences when coupled with pre-existing acute vulnerability, caused by poor policies and unsustainable land use practices in Syria's case and perpetuated by the slow and ineffective response of the Assad regime'. Kelley and colleagues (2015, p. 3245) conclude by admitting that while they have

> pointed to a connected path running from human interference with climate to severe drought to agricultural collapse and mass migration [. . .] An abundance of history books [. . .] tell us that civil unrest can never be said to have a simple or unique cause. The Syrian conflict, now civil war, is no exception.

They conclude, however, that

> [t]his recent drought was likely made worse by human-induced climate change, and such persistent, deep droughts are projected to become more commonplace in a warming world.

Indeed, if expectations hold true, warmer temperatures due to climate change will stress water resources and agriculture across the Middle East in two ways: higher temperatures will increase evaporation from soils that are already parched and weaker winds will bring less rain from the Mediterranean Sea during the wet season of November to April. This, in turn, could raise food prices, which could fuel (further) conflict (see Kelley *et al.* 2015; see also Fischetti 2015).

In our initial formulation of a four-pronged typology of conflict-environmental relationships, we noted that conflict over declining resources could also entail tensions over the hunting and fishing of non-human animals – species that are endangered or in decline but who represent or reflect human spirituality, culture and tradition (see, e.g., Waldholz 2015). Such tensions and competing visions over the endangered status, welfare and right-to-life of nonhuman animals, on the one hand, and endangered human cultures, traditions and ways of life, on the other, will continue to be sources of controversy and contestation.

---

5 Dawson (2016, pp. 95–96) asserts that 'climate change-catalyzed conflicts such as the war in Syria devastate entire societies, generating millions of refugees', and adds that many of these refugees 'have been left in limbo by the refusal of European nations to offer safe harbor'. At the same time, Duffy and colleagues (2016, p. 17) point out that 'conflicts can produce large-scale population displacements and refugee camps; refugees and internally displaced people can turn to illegal wildlife hunting to feed themselves or to earn cash income'.

Conflict that destroys environments

This type of conflict is concerned with instances where: (a) environmental destruction and degradation are a result of war and other social conflict, including the 'waste of war' (O'Sullivan and Walters 2016, pp. 85, 89); (b) where environmental destruction is used as a tactic or technique of war (or where the forces of nature are utilised as weapons), and (c) where military activities and exercises in preparation for armed conflict have adversely affected the environment.

With respect to the first subcategory – environmental destruction and degradation stemming from conflict and war – we might point to the Reagan Administration's 'War on Drugs' in the 1980s, whereby crop eradication interventions attempted to address the 'supply side' of the drug trade through the liberal use of toxic chemicals on cocaine and marijuana crops. Such indiscriminate aerial sprays, however, were widely disseminated over large areas, contaminating food, poisoning waterways and causing human health and environmental problems. While some might argue that the 'War on Drugs' should be conceptualised as a US domestic and foreign campaign of enforcement against the illegal international drug trade, rather than a conflict between two or more nation-states, the consequences of this campaign have been no less devastating for individuals and societies – and environments – around the world, amounting in some cases to what del Olmo (1987) called 'eco-bio-genocide'.

Amster (2015, p. 3) points out that '[t]he recognition of the environment itself as a casualty of war is a relatively recent phenomenon, although in practice war has been environmentally unfriendly throughout recorded history'. Thus, examples of more 'traditional' wars causing environmental destruction would be the First Gulf War, where the Iraq occupation ignited Kuwaiti oil wells, sabotaged petroleum and natural gas facilities and discharged stored petroleum onto land and into the Persian Gulf (see Amster 2015, pp. 17, 133). The 2006 'Summer War' between Israel and Lebanon would serve as another example wherein Lebanese drinking water systems and reserves were destroyed during the fighting between the neighbouring Middle Eastern countries. For O'Sullivan and Walters (2016, p. 80), '[a]cts of war cause environmental harm and ecological degradation' in that '[f]orests, wetlands and agricultural lands can be destroyed by bombs and chemical weapons or when they are "cleared away" to achieve a military goal'. The instances of harm 'incidental to the conduct of war' or 'environmental harm as "collateral damage"' are distinguishable from the deleterious '"leftovers" of war' (O'Sullivan and Walters 2016, pp. 79, 80). But war detritus can still be dangerous to all life, as for example with unexploded mines or bombs, or used or unused depleted uranium shells (O'Sullivan and Walters 2016; White 2008).[6] As O'Sullivan and Walters (2016, pp. 88–89) explain,

---

6 Although Amster distinguishes between environmental degradation as an 'ancillary casualty of war' and as an 'intentional tactic of war', he admits that '[i]n both instances, collateral or intentional, the outcome is equivalent for people living in war-torn areas as the basic elements necessary for their survival are impinged' (2016, p. 69).

the machinery and infrastructure of war, by its very contemporary and mobile nature, is an environmental hazard. Militaries are machines of mass production. Each soldier's food often comes in disposable containers with disposable forks and knives. Each soldier's uniform often comes in plastic wrappings. Soldiers fire weapons during firefights leaving mass amounts of shell casings on the ground. This means that a military can produce a huge volume of refuse as they move through a country fighting the enemy. In war, this waste is not always disposed of correctly.

O'Sullivan and Walters (2016, pp. 81, 82), echoing Amster (2015, pp. 3, 17), assert that '[t]he water, soil and air are . . . common victims in war' (although they acknowledge that the environment 'is generally not recognised academically or legally as a victim'). What is particularly noteworthy about the serious environmental harm and ecological degradation caused by war – is that '[p]eople's livelihoods are also affected as they may not be able to cultivate their land due to environmental degradation . . . or people may not be able to avail of their state's natural resources'. This can, in turn, contribute to poverty and insecurity and destabilise post-conflict peace building.

With respect to the second subcategory – where environmental destruction is used as a tactic or technique of war (or where the forces of nature are utilised as weapons) – we might try to differentiate between instances where the environment, itself, is a target (such as the use of pesticides in Vietnam or the deliberate contamination of agricultural water supplies or the destruction of farmland – a strategy pursued by the United States during the Korean War (see Dawson 2016, pp. 15, 59–60; O'Sullivan and Walters 2016, pp. 81, 82; see generally Amster 2015, pp. 16–17, 69, 116)), and cases where the environment is employed as a conduit for or instrument of violence and destruction, such as releasing chemical or biological weapons into the atmosphere. Note, however, that the distinction is far from clear. An attack on an oil facility or tanker or natural gas plant could be intended as a means of generating a giant bomb or (given our fossil fuel reliance) as a means of creating an extreme economic crisis (see generally Wittenberg 2015b). For Dawson (2016, pp. 59–60), environmental destruction as a tactic of war and environmental destruction as a technique of war can, at times, be subsumed under the term 'ecological warfare': 'In some cases, ecocide is a conscious strategy of imperialism, generating what might be termed ecological warfare. For example, the destruction of the great herds of bison that roamed the Great Plains of North America was a calculated military strategy designed to deprive Native Americans of the environmental resources on which they depended'.[7]

If conflict can destroy environments – and if environments can serve as targets or as conduits for or instruments of violence and destruction – it should come

---

7 For a discussion of how an international law against ecocide would apply, see Higgins *et al.* (2013).

as no surprise, then, that military activities and exercises in preparation for armed conflict have adversely affected the environment. These are, in other words, adverse environmental impacts of running the war machine itself. Examples include the methods employed to produce nuclear weapons (including the transportation and storage of radioactive and hazardous waste), which have resulted in tremendous contamination of the environment, as well as the 'equipment and technologies that can be difficult to dispose of once they are no longer functional' (O'Sullivan and Walters 2016, p. 89). The US military's heavy reliance on energy-inefficient equipment and vehicles also contributes substantial greenhouse gas emissions (see, e.g., Amster 2015, pp. 38, 114, 133; White 2014, p. 846).[8] While consumption of fossil fuels obviously occurs during armed conflict – O'Sullivan and Walters (2016, p. 81) note that 'the US military in Iraq devoured around 1.2 million barrels of fuel per month in order to run its fleet of helicopters, planes and ground vehicles (Associated Press 2008)' – making it a war for oil that has used a lot of oil! – militaries are hardly ecologically friendly during peacetime (see Mathiesen 2014). Indeed, the US Department of Defense is the world's largest consumer of energy (Dawson 2016, p. 60; Watson 2016).[9] In addition, US military training exercises have sparked fires and destroyed countless flora and fauna on land and at sea, while the US Navy's use of sonar has caused harm to unknown numbers of whales and other marine mammals (see, e.g., Mayton 2015; Palmer 2015a, 2015b) and the British Royal Navy's detonation of underwater bombs have caused mass stranding of long-finned pilot whales (see Edwards 2015).[10] The impact of military activities on nonhuman animals is particularly troubling for scholars such as Beirne (2014, pp. 58–59), who asserts:

> Militarism . . . intersects with pollution as a site of theriocide [animal killing]. One of militarism's major effects is environmental degradation, including space junk, contaminated military bases, the dumping of jet and other fuels,

---

8 Amster (2015, p. 114) adds that warfare's 'enormous cost. . .takes resources away from mitigating climate change'.

9 Note that while the US Navy uses more than a third of the energy consumed by the US Department of Defense, in January 2016, it launched its first carrier strike group powered partly by biofuel and its 'Great Green Fleet' initiative aims to draw 50 per cent of its power from alternative energy in four years (Watson 2016). It also bears mention that the United States shoulders much of the responsibility for ensuring the flow of oil in the Middle East and for protecting global oil shipping lanes. For example, the US Navy protects the Strait of Hormuz, through which roughly one-fifth of the world's petroleum passes (Plumer 2014). Thus, not only is the US military 'the single most polluting organization on the planet', to quote Dawson (2016: 60), but it also serves to protect and ensure continued polluting by others.

10 Debates over whether wildlife protections in the United States under the Endangered Species Act (ESA) present a threat to military readiness have a long history – most recently with sage grouse (Taylor 2015). While past ESA listing decisions have encroached on military exercises, such as in the case with the red-cockaded woodpecker

overboard ship discharges, and the use of bombs and toxic weapons such as Agent Orange. All these activities kill animals either directly or indirectly by degrading or destroying their habitat. . . . Military experiments and military training exercises are conducted with the use of birds, cats, dogs, dolphins, ferrets, fish, goats, mice, pigs, rabbits, rats, and sheep and – until quite recently – with primates, including 4,000 monkeys at the Oregon National Primate Research Center.

While the US military has often considered nonhuman animal life as acceptable collateral damage in its training exercises (just as it has during war, as noted above), it bears mention that the US military does, at times, engage in some environmentally-friendly behaviours and practices. For example, in the past, lead from ammunition has poisoned some 75 species of birds – especially waterfowl and scavengers, such as condors, eagles, and ravens (*New York Times* 2010). Lead exposure to scavenging animals also presents a human health risk to humans who eat hunters' kills (Barringer 2010b). In August 2010, the US Environmental Protection Agency rejected a request (from the American Bird Conservancy and the Center for Biological Diversity) that it ban lead bullets, on the grounds that it does not have the legal authority to do so (Barringer 2010a). According to the EPA, the Toxic Substances Control Act exempts ammunition from its controls (Barringer 2010a). The American military has now begun to embrace 'green bullets' (Barringer (2010b) – as part of what might seem like an effort to cause less damage to birds and other animals poisoned by discharged ammunition. But the US Army's 'eco-friendly quest' has not, however, been undertaken with only the environment in mind. The goal has been to produce a 'more effective' bullet – one with the ability to pierce protective shields and cause more bodily harm than lead bullets (Wittenberg 2015a).[11]

In the coming years, we envision heightened concern on the part of the military towards environmental issues. For example, in October 2016, reports

and the desert tortoise, the ESA allows the Secretary of Defence to obtain an exemption from restrictions to protect national security. Endangered Species Act of 1973, Pub. L. No. 93–205, 87 Stat. 884 (1973) (codified as amended at 16 U.S.C. §§ 1531–44 (2006)). The relevant portion of the statute, Section 1536(j) [ESA §7(j)], provides: 'Notwithstanding any other provision of this chapter, the [Endangered Species] Committee [which reviews applications submitted to it pursuant to ESA §7(e)(1)] shall grant an exemption for any agency action if the Secretary of Defense finds that such exemption is necessary for reasons of national security'. For an in-depth discussion of the Secretary of Defence's exemption for the purpose of national security, see Wells (2006). For an overview of how the US Department of Homeland Security has exempted itself from the Endangered Species Act and other environmental laws and regulations, such as the Clean Air Act and the Clean Water Act, see Amster (2015:168).

11 For a discussion of how unmanned aircraft systems (UAS) or 'drones' – well known for their military functions – might be used in environmental monitoring and enforcement (such as for detecting oil leakage from pipelines and storage tanks and air and water quality compliance), see Satterlee (2016).

indicated that the US Air Force's radar installation project, Space Fence, designed to track fragments of space junk to improve the safety of astronauts and satellites, was becoming increasingly vulnerable to rising sea levels, due to its location – an atoll in the Marshall Islands (see, e.g., Associated Press 2016a; Perry 2016). Similarly, studies have found that coastal naval bases, including Naval Station Norfolk, the world's largest naval base, are profoundly threatened by rising seas. As Gillis (2016) explains, '[n]aval bases . . . can hardly be moved away from the ocean, yet much of their land is at risk of disappearing within this century'. But here, as above, the US military's awareness and interest in environmental degradation and climate change has developed not out of a new appreciation for nonhuman animals and Earth's ecosystems, but from fears, to quote Gillis, that 'national security is on the line' and there will be a significant financial cost to losing strategically-valuable land to the sea. So, too, with conservation, where the framing of 'poachers-as-terrorists' has gained traction because it fits with pre-existing concerns about global security and allows the 'greater use of force . . . for any perceived or actual threat to certain iconic species (notably elephants)' (Duffy 2016, p. 239) – a point to which we return in the next part.

Conflict over natural resource extraction processes

This type of conflict is concerned with issues pertaining to group conflicts over methods and techniques of, and the necessity for, certain types of resource extraction (including not just the 'raw resource', but also the infrastructure, such as transmission and transportation routes and pipelines). For example, the chapter by Paulson, Zagorski and Ferguson (2015) in our Environmental Crime and Social Conflict volume examined the 2010 Deepwater Horizon oil spill in the Gulf of Mexico – an incident that illuminates the fundamentally economic conflict over natural resource extraction processes, including who benefits, who does not, and, most significantly, who is considered a legitimate actor in relation to such processes. Similarly, Carrington, Hogg and McIntosh (2015) describe the harmful effects of mining on local communities and the environment – and the ways in which the global expansion of mining has contributed to localised patterns of violence, conflict, work and community life in mining towns in Australia, again, all driven by economic imperatives and a boom in extraction industries.

One defining feature of the conflict over natural resource extraction processes is that it is often not just the fact of extraction of declining resources or the means by which the extraction is occurring (or proposed to take place) that bring about disagreement, struggle and strife, but the theft of land that often accompanies mining and other extractive processes (Rodríguez Goyes *et al.* 2017; see also Wyatt and Brisman 2016; see generally Damonte 2016; de Vos 2016; Hennings 2016). For example, an editorial published by *The New York Times* in January 2015 described the violence perpetrated by Myanmar's police against the Burmese people, who were protesting the theft of their land and their evictions in order to make room for the Letpadaung copper mine.[12] Likewise, in Peru, Global Witness (2014, pp. 3, 10), reports that:

> Many of the killings of environmental and land defenders . . . are attributed to conflicts between local communities and extractive projects, with opposition to mining the principal locus for violence against activists [. . .] The mining sector in Peru, like the forest sector, is beleaguered by poor governance. Peru is currently the world's third-biggest producer of copper and 6th largest producer of gold, with mining accounting for 15 percent of GDP overall and 5.4 percent of Peru's total greenhouse gas emissions. The vast majority of mineral deposits are located near indigenous community lands resulting in extensive conflicts over land and the environmental impacts of mining projects [. . .] [T]he gold mining industry, which is prominent in the Amazon region, is leading to dramatic increases in deforestation and mercury poisoning, affecting the health and livelihoods of local indigenous communities.

Global Witness' research found that 80 per cent of all killings of environmental and land activists in Peru between 2002 and 2013 stemmed from local opposition to extractive projects.

Whether the extraction process involves the theft of lands, pollution of waters or illegal and over-fishing, resistance is a common response (see Hennings 2016, p. 35 for a discussion). For example, the Sea Shepherd Conservation Society (SSCS) has gained an international reputation for obstructing whale-fishing vessels (see, e.g., Jacobs 2015), as well as impeding vessels engaged in illegal fishing (see, e.g., Pala 2015). According to a report by Lampen (2016), on 15 April 2016, the SSCS used a night-vision drone to capture footage of totoaba poachers operating under the cover of darkness in the Gulf of California; it then sent the coordinates of the bandits to the Mexican Navy.[13] (The Mexican government has given the SSCS permission to police gillnets in the Gulf of California.) Here, the conflict is not one involving groups that both want the same resource (as with water or food, described above in Category #1), but between one group that wishes to obtain the declining resource (the poachers) and another that wishes to preserve it (SSCS). Similarly, sHellNo! Action Council has engaged in a wide range of efforts (including kayak blockades) to try to prevent Royal Dutch Shell from drilling in the Arctic (Lewis 2015). Here, too, the conflict does not entail groups fighting to obtain and consume the same resource, but is between one group that seeks the declining resource (oil) and

---

12 Other plunder in Burma (Myanmar) has included illegal logging (and timber sales to China) and animal trafficking due to high demand in China for tiger and leopard parts, bear bile and pangolins (*New York Times* 2015).
13 For a discussion of other instances in which Greenpeace has used drones as part of its 'arsenal of activism', see Satterlee (2016, p. 11081).

another that wishes to leave it in the ground (in order to avoid disastrous drilling accidents in the unpredictable weather of the Arctic region, as well as to avoid the negative impacts of climate change).

'Keep it in the ground!' became a familiar refrain and chant in 2016, as highlighted by the protests by Native Americans and non-Native Americans fighting to prevent construction of a portion of the Dakota Access Pipeline (also known as the Bakken pipeline) near the Standing Rock Sioux Reservation in North Dakota (Healy 2016b; Samson 2016). The pipeline threatens water supplies for the Standing Rock Sioux, as well as for millions downstream, and its route would destroy tribal burial grounds and sacred cultural lands (Aisch and Lai 2016; Healy 2016a; see also Associated Press 2016b, 2016c; Healy 2016b; www.waterprotectors.com; see generally Associated Press 2016b). At the time of this writing (December 2016), the future of the pipeline – and the resistance to it – hangs in the balance. What is clear, however, is that natural resource extraction processes – especially those that threaten water supplies and culturally significant places and spaces – will continue to incite opposition in years to come (see generally Pearson 2015). In cases such as this, financial goals are very clearly prioritised over cultural, religious and historical claims (for a rare exception, see *New York Times* 2016).

In our original typology we did not place any particular emphasis on money or finance as part of the environment-conflict nexus, in part because it is so self-evident that much environmental harm and a great deal of conflict are the result of the pursuit of advantage, including political and financial gains. If we adopt a more explicit focus on the impact or influence that money might have on our understanding of the relationships between environment and conflict, then we can see in even sharper relief the tragic and dismaying truth that a key source of so much violence, conflict and war affecting environments, humans and other species, is the pursuit of profit. The next section illustrates this point further.

Environmental harm and illegal and questionable financial behaviours

For present purposes, we can take two starting points. First, various enterprises have been identified as engaged in extracting, monopolising and trading in resources in ways that have been linked to the funding of conflict; and, second, conflict and war-making are pursued with the intention of making profits for some, while others die and suffer injury, and environmental systems and their dependents are impoverished.

A wide variety of 'high value' natural resources can be subject to legal and illegal transactions whether in cases such as mining, logging, oil or even fishing of the endangered totoaba fish and vaquita porpoise (Hance 2016). The profitability of such activity can support or encourage commercial, political and religious activities, which, in turn, can have influential effects on the prospects for social stability and security versus unrest and violence, with the consequences of the latter including environmental degradation and violations of human rights.

The currency involved will often be environmental wealth, wildlife and the fruits of nature and riches of the earth. Such transactions can generate profits that 'directly finance' various groups engaging in conflict, such as 'tribes, ideologically driven organisations, nations' that will use 'crime and violence to advance their interests' (Douglas and Alie 2014, p. 271).

In more detail, a useful review by Bergenas and Knight (2015, p. 119) provides examples different from those offered in the previous section and different from each other. The important connection here is that although some conflicts are driven by the objective of achieving control over valuable resources, and others are simply supported by the environmental assets available, it is the wealth that nature provides that is noteworthy. For instance, Bergenas and Knight describe 'terrorist groups and transnational organized criminals around the world' that 'prey on Mother Earth to finance their destructive activities'. In 2014, they note, 'the United Nations reported that the Islamic State's largest revenue stream comes from the terrorist organization illegally trading oil', apparently 'collecting as much as a million dollars a day' (ibid., p. 123). Without this flow of oil revenue, the conflict might not continue/have continued. In other words, the point here is not whether oil extraction is more harmful to the environment in one context than another but the fact that an environmentally harmful activity is helping to perpetuate a conflict.

In East Africa, al-Shabaab (an organisation that has been linked to al-Qaeda) is said to generate millions of dollars per year from involvement in the illicit charcoal trade. In the past, in Colombia, the Revolutionary Armed Forces of Colombia (FARC) was known to control the country's only tungsten mine, which according to Bergenas and Knight (ibid., p. 122), would have made it a 'key supplier for a number of multinational companies'. In Southeast Asia, as is more widely known, 'transnational organized criminals' have profited from the 'lucrative illegal ivory market', which has helped maintain demand thereby being directly linked to 'the slaughter of increasingly endangered elephants and rhinos' (ibid., pp. 124–125). In the Democratic Republic of Congo (DRC), noted above, militias 'earned an estimated US$1 billion from illegal mining in 2013', making this the primary source of terrorism financing in the region and in Afghanistan, 'the Taliban earns a minimum of US$17 million per year from its own illegal mining, primarily of lapis lazuli and ruby' (ibid., p. 123). There are also suggestions of direct links between wildlife trafficking and terrorism in the cases of Sudanese groups, militias in the DRC and the Central African Republic and the Lord's Resistance Army. According to estimates from the United Nations Environment Programme, 'the annual income to militias in all of Sub-Saharan Africa' – just derived from the ivory trade – is 'approximately US $4 – 12 million' (ibid., pp. 120–121). Bergenas and Knight (2015, p. 119) conclude that 'environmental crime is a geostrategic issue with serious implications for national and international security'.

There are, of course, challenges to this kind of analysis. Duffy (2016, p. 242), for example, questions the 'link between natural resources as a financial underpin for conflicts (Berdal and Malone 2000; Le Billon 2008, 2012; UN 2013)', claiming that the evidence suggesting that ivory is funding Al Shabaab operations is lacking: 'The idea that ivory poaching funds terrorism . . . circulates in high political circles, but it does so on a paucity of clear evidence and using simplifications of a complex political economy of poaching' (Duffy *et al.* 2015, p. 246). Rather, she argues that 'the discursive link between poaching and terrorism is used to further the interests of the US-led War on Terror and has meant that conservation has been integrated into much wider sets of policy debates and initiatives linked to global security' (Duffy 2016, p. 242).

There are thus some grounds for caution when drawing linkages between environmental crime/harm, conflict and security (McClanahan and Brisman 2015), insofar as this easily leads to calls for pacification and measures involving the amplification of 'war' rhetoric and the use of force, as in the declaration of a 'war on poachers' employing mercenaries and security forces, and the militarisation and 'weaponising' of conservation (McClanahan and Wall 2016; Wall and McClanahan 2015; see also Smith and Humphreys 2015). Wall and McClanahan (2015, p. 224) are particularly critical of the 'coupling of security logics and conservation logics through the practice of the hunt for human prey [poachers]'. Similarly, Duffy (2016, p. 238) points out the problematic dynamic of what she calls the 'war by conservation', which she describes as 'an "offensive position" in certain locations whereby conservation is the intervening aggressor, not simply the defender of wildlife' (emphasis added). As she explains,

> this new phase of war by conservation differs because it combines anxieties about global security, with environmental concerns and counter-insurgency (COIN) techniques. One of its main driving objectives is security and stabilization of areas that are of geostrategic interest to the US-led War on Terror. Furthermore, this new phase can be characterized as war by conservation because conservation agencies themselves are becoming . . . engaged in use of force against people they identify as poachers and as members of terrorist networks (emphasis in original).

This increasing tendency to discursively frame poaching in reference to terrorism, while troubling for a number of reasons, is especially so given that the narrative of what Duffy calls 'poachers-as-terrorists', noted above, 'renders the complexity of poaching invisible; further it has the effect of displacing alternative, longer standing approaches to poaching which seek to understand the very different reasons why different people engage in illegal hunting in a range of locations' (2016, p. 238). These different reasons will reflect and involve various cultural histories, motives and opportunities, but some form of financial element will be common, whether in the form of contributions to subsistence and trade, or as the expensive costs of luxury hunting 'safaris' marketed to the rich.

These scenarios have been analysed in various ways related to security, politics and resource competition but their relevance to this chapter is that it is also criminologically interesting to note the central importance of money and profit.

There are significant economic and structural costs to the nations and regions affected by environmentally related conflict. As Douglas and Alie show (2014, p. 275):

> The violence (or threat of violence) surrounding poaching and the 'wildlife wars' also undermine other legitimate economic activities by contributing to a perception of regional insecurity. [. . .] The crime and violence associated with the illegal wildlife trade can, therefore, undermine governments, economic development and stability broadly (emphasis added).

It is also the case that various 'legitimate economic activities' and examples of 'economic development' can play their own influential roles in creating the conditions for environmentally-related conflict. For example, speculation, fraud and corruption generate illicit profits that may be invested in arms and militia, conflicts and coups, mobilised to secure the environmental wealth of a particular territory (see generally Hennings 2016). In various parts of the world now, and increasingly in the future, demand for meat and for bio-fuels will increase pressure on land availability, leading to contestation over land ownership and conflict over traditional versus genetic modification farming methods (Rodríguez Goyes and South 2016). Corruption can undermine conservation programmes as a result of laws that are unequally enforced; this failure of both procedural and substantive justice can lead to disillusionment, social tension and conflict (Gore *et al.* 2013).

The finance and accounting industries in themselves are contributors to the toll on societies and environments exacted by profiteering and conflicts. Illegal logging, mining, fishing and so forth produce funds that require the services and facilities of accountants and banks. Further, capital-intensive extraction often requires considerable loans and investments by the financial industry.

These 'reputable' professionals and institutions create the mechanisms for tax fraud and money laundering that increase profits and deprive producer nations of income (Nelleman *et al.* 2016). As part of global chains of commodities and consumption, illegally produced environmental goods, or abducted/captured/hunted/poached wildlife, are merged into legal trade flows and markets producing the profits and motives to continue to formally and informally support and enable these activities. Across the planet, harmful forms of resource extraction and questionable methods of revenue generation seem to be expanding unchecked with little regard for medium-to-long-term consequences.

Conclusion

Bergenas and Knight (2015, p. 120) suggest that:

> Environmental crime has all of the characteristics of a twenty-first century problem. It is a hybrid challenge that cuts across the defense, security, development, and conservation worlds. It has a global reach and is transnational in nature.

Furthermore, environmental crime, like war, is often highly profitable – or, to put it another way, it is often less expensive and more expedient to engage in environmental crime and harm (e.g., flouting pollution laws) than to undertake (potentially costly) practices that abide by the law and respect the Earth's limits (see generally Vogel and Raeymaekers 2016, p. 1104). Around the world, regressive laws have extended land use rights, and supported and legitimised expectations of high profits for investors involved in the expansion of large-scale agriculture, mining, logging and infrastructure projects. These same laws have also facilitated the movement of extractive activities into encroachment upon indigenous territories (Global Witness 2014, pp. 6, 7). As one counter-response, recognising indigenous land claims may assist with the protection of the lives and cultures of indigenous peoples and their environment – and, indeed, the planet as a whole (because the destruction of tropical forests around the world is one of the largest sources of emissions contributing to climate change) (Global Witness 2014, p. 3). Thus, for example, if the problem of illegal logging is linked to insecure land tenure and has given rise to increased violence against indigenous communities – as Global Witness (2014, p. 5) claims – then the 'solution' would seem to be to secure land tenure for indigenous communities as a means of reducing deforestation.[14] Clarifying who owns what and where may help break the money-environmental harm-conflict chain (see de Vos 2016, pp. 13, 15, 28 for a discussion), although, of course, this may not be applicable in all situations. The presence of democratic governance and institutions can (although, admittedly, does not always) disrupt or prevent the processes of 'resource capture' and 'ecological marginalization' (see Amster 2015, p. 30 (discussing Homer-Dixon 1999)), but further work is needed.

We suggest that typologies such as ours can help to conceptualise and grasp the scale of the challenges faced – and the amount of financial interest at stake. Thus we should continue to expand and refine our typology – looking at both present and past examples – not just as an academic exercise, but as a means of illuminating nuance and difference in order to help identify better ways to protect and respond.

References

Aisch, G., and Lai, R. 2016. 'The conflicts along 1,172 miles of the Dakota access pipeline', *The New York Times*, 25 November.
Amster, R. 2015. *Peace Ecology*. Boulder and London: Paradigm Publishers.
Associated Press. 2008. 'Facts on military fuel consumption', 2 April.
Associated Press. 2015. 'Armed poachers slaughtering hundreds of elephants in Congo', 8 November.

14 According to Global Witness (2014, p. 6), '[a]cross Latin America, secure land tenure for indigenous communities has proven to be one of the most effective ways to reduce deforestation' (footnote omitted).

Associated Press. 2016a. 'Rising seas could threaten $1 billion Air Force radar site', 18 October.

Associated Press. 2016b. 'The latest: Dakota access protestors beginning to leave', 9 December.

Associated Press. 2016c. 'Law officers ask Obama for help policing pipeline protests', 12 December.

Barringer, F. 2010a. 'National briefing: Washington: E.P.A. turns down request to ban lead bullets', *The New York Times*, 31 August.

Barringer, F. 2010b. 'Groups seek ban on lead in sporting ammunition', *The New York Times*, 3 August.

Berdal, M. and Malone, D.M. (eds.) 2000. *Greed and Grievance: Economic Agendas in Civil Wars*. Boulder, CO: Lynne Rienner.

Bergenas, J., and Knight, A. 2015. 'Green terror: environmental crime and illicit financing', *SAIS Review of International Affairs* 35(1), 119–131.

Beirne, P. 2014. 'Theriocide: naming animal killing', *International Journal for Crime, Justice and Social Democracy* 3(2), 49–66.

Boekhout van Solinge, T. 2010. 'Equatorial deforestation as harmful practice and criminological issue', in *Global Environmental Harm*, edited by R. White. Cullompton: Willan Publishing, 20-36.

Bond, J. 2015. 'Making sense of human-elephant conflict in Laikipia County, Kenya', *Society and Natural Resources* 28(3), 312–327.

Branigan, T. 2015. 'Satellite images boost concern over Chinese airstrip in disputed waters', *The Guardian*, 18 April.

Brisman, A. 2013. 'Not a bedtime story: climate change, neoliberalism, and the future of the Arctic', *Michigan State International Law Review* 22(1), 241–289.

Brisman, A. and South, N. 2013. 'Resource wealth, power, crime, and conflict', in Emerging Issues in *Green Criminology: Exploring Power, Justice and Harm*, edited by R. Walters, D. Westerhuis and T. Wyatt. Basingstoke: Palgrave Macmillan, 57–71.

Brisman, A., South, N. and White, R. 2015. 'Toward a criminology of environment-conflict relationships'. In *Environmental Crime and Social Conflict: Contemporary and Emerging Issues*, edited by A. Brisman, N. South and R. White. Farnham: Ashgate, 1–38.

Brisman, A., McClanahan, B., South, N. and Walters, R. 2017. *Water, Crime and Security in the Twenty-First Century: Too Dirty, Too Little, Too Much*. London: Palgrave Macmillan.

Cao, A. and Wyatt, T. 2016. 'The conceptual compatibility between green criminology and human security: a proposed interdisciplinary framework for examinations into green victimisation', *Critical Criminology* 24(3), 413–430.

Carrington, K., Hogg. R., and McIntosh, A. 2015. 'The hidden injuries of mining: frontier cultural conflict', in *Environmental Crime and Social Conflict. Contemporary and Emerging Issues*, edited by A. Brisman, N. South and R. White. Farnham: Ashgate, 241–264.

Damonte, G.H. 2016. 'The "blind" state: government quest for formalization and conflict with small-scale miners in the Peruvian Amazon', *Antipode* 48(4), 956–976

Dawson, A. 2016. *Extinction: A Radical History*. OR Books: New York and London.

de Vos, R.E. 2016. 'Multi-functional lands facing oil palm monocultures: A case study of a land conflict in West Kalimantan, Indonesia', *ASEAS – Austrian Journal of South-East Asian Studies* 9(1), 11–32.

Duffy, R. 2016. 'War, by conservation', *Geoforum* 69, 238–248.

Duffy, R. and Humphreys, J. 2014. Mapping Donors: Key Areas for Tackling Illegal Wildlife Trade (Africa and Asia). Evidence on Demand Report HD151.

Duffy, R., St. John, F., Büscher, B. and Brockington, D. 2015. 'The militarization of anti-poaching: undermining long term goals?', *Environmental Conservation* 42(4), 345–348.

Duffy, R., St. John, F., Büscher, B. and Brockington, D. 2016. 'Toward a new understanding of the links between poverty and illegal wildlife hunting', *Conservation Biology* 30(1), 14–22.

Dyer, G. 2008. *Climate Wars*. Oxford: Oneworld Publications.

Edwards, R. 2015. 'Royal Navy bomb explosions caused mass whale deaths, report concludes', *The Guardian*, 24 June.

EIA. 2012. *Appetite for Destruction: China's Trade in Illegal Timber*. London: Environmental Investigation Agency.

Fischetti, M. 2015. 'Climate change hastened Syria's Civil War', *Scientific American*, 2 March.

Gettleman, J. 2016. 'Where wars are small and chaos is endless', *The New York Times*, 1 May.

Gillis, J. 2016. 'Global warming's mark: coastal inundation', *The New York Times*, 4 September.

Global Witness. 2014. *Peru's Deadly Environment: The Rise in Killings of Environmental and Land Defenders*. London: Global Witness.

Global Witness. 2015. *Blood Timber: How Europe Played a Significant Role in Funding War in the Central African Republic*. London: Global Witness.

Gore, M.L., Knuth, B.A., Curtis, P.D., and Shanahan, J.E. 2006. 'Stakeholder perceptions of risk associated with human-black bear conflicts in New York's Adirondack Park campgrounds: Implications for theory and practice', *Wildlife Society Bulletin* 34(1), 36–43.

Gore, M.L., Knuth, B.A., Curtis, P.D., and Shanahan, J.E. 2007. 'Factors influencing risk perception associated with human-black bear conflict', *Human Dimensions of Wildlife* 12(2), 133–136.

Gore, M.L., Knuth, B.A., Scherer, C.W., and Curtis, P.D. 2008. 'Evaluating a conservation investment designed to reduce human-wildlife conflict', *Conservation Letters* 1(3), 136–145.

Gore, M., Ratsimbazafy, J. and Lute, M. 2013. 'Rethinking corruption in conservation crime', *Conservation Letters* 6(6), 430–438.

Hamilton, C., Bonneuil, C. and Gemmene, F. 2015. 'Thinking the anthropocene', in *The Anthropocene and the Global Environmental Crisis: Rethinking Modernity in a New Epoch*, edited by C. Hamilton, C. Bonneuil and F. Gemmene. London and New York: Routledge, 1–13.

Hance, J. 2016. 'China's craze for "aquatic cocaine" is pushing two species into oblivion', *The Guardian*, 11 January.

Hauser, C. 2017. 'A Crusader for elephants is shot dead in Tanzania', *The New York Times*, 19 August.

Healy, J. 2016a. 'Tension rising over pipeline, tribes dig in: "we're staying" ', *The New York Times*, 11 October.

Healy, J. 2016b. 'On frozen Dakota prairie, readying for one final stand', *The New York Times*, 4 December.

Hennings, A. 2016. 'Assembling resistant against large-scale land deals: Challenges for conflict transformation in Bougainville, Papua New Guinea', *ASEAS – Austrian Journal of South-East Asian Studies* 9(1), 33–52.

Higgins, P., Short, D. and South, N. 2013. 'Protecting the planet: a proposal for a law of Ecocide', *Crime, Law and Social Change* 59(3), 251–266.

Homer-Dixon, T.F. 1999. *Environment, Scarcity, and Violence*. Princeton, NJ: Princeton University Press.

Howard, B.C. 2016. 'Man who punched kangaroo to save his dog risked his life', *National Geographic*, 5 December.

Interpol and World Bank. 2009. 'Chainsaw project: An Interpol perspective on law enforcement in illegal logging'. *Rural Development and Natural rResources*. World Bank & Interpol.

Jacobs, J.P. 2015. 'Supreme Court won't review Sea Shepherd piracy case', *Greenwire*, 8 June.

Kahler, J.S. and Gore, M.L. 2015. 'Local perceptions of risk associated with poaching of wildlife implicated in human-wildlife conflicts in Namibia', *Biological Conservation* 189, 49–58.

Kelley, C.P., Mohtadi, S., Cane, M., Seager, R. and Kushnir, Y. 2015. 'Climate change in the Fertile Crescent and implications of the recent Syrian drought', *Proceedings of the National Academy of Sciences* 112(11), 3241–3246.

Kristof, N.D. 2010. 'Death by gadget', *The New York Times*, 27 June.

Lakhani, N. 2014. 'Honduras and the dirty war fuelled by the west's drive for clean energy', *The Guardian*, 7 July.

Landler, M. and Risen, J. 2017. 'Mineral wealth In Afghanistan tempts Trump', *The New York Times*, 26 July.

Le Billon, P. 2008. 'Diamond wars? Conflict diamonds and geographies of resource wars', *Annals of the Association of American Geographers* 98, 345–372.

Le Billon, P. 2012. *Wars of Plunder: Conflicts, Profits and the Politics of Resources*. London and New York: Hurst and Columbia University Press.

Le Quéré, C. *et al.* 2014. *Global Carbon Budget 2013*. Earth System Science Data 6, 235–263.

Lewis, R. 2015. 'Seattle "kayaktivists" form blockade as Shell rig heads to Alaskan waters', *Al Jazeera America*, 15 June.

Lampen, C. 2016. 'Sea Shepherd conservation society uses drone to take out poachers', *Mic/Yahoo!News*, 24 April.

Mathiesen, K. 2014. 'What's the environmental impact of modern war?', *The Guardian*, 6 November.

Mayton, J. 2015. '"A deaf whale is a dead whale": US navy sonars could be cause of strandings', *The Guardian*, 14 June.

McClanahan, B. and Brisman, A. 2015. 'Climate change and peacemaking criminology: ecophilosophy, peace and security in the "War on Climate Change"', *Critical Criminology* 23(4), 417–431.

McClanahan, B. and Wall, T. 2016. '"Do some anti-poaching, kill some bad guys, and do some good": Manhunting, accumulation, and pacification in African conservation', in *The Geography of Environmental Crime*, edited by G. Potter, A. Nurse and M. Hall. London: Palgrave Macmillan, 121–148.

Milburn, R. 2015. 'Gorillas and Guerrillas: environment and conflict in the Democratic Republic of Congo', in *Environmental Crime and Social Conflict*, edited by A. Brisman, N. South and R. White. Farnham: Ashgate.

Moen, B. 2015. 'Grizzly bear-human conflicts rise in Wyoming in 2014'. Associated Press, 22 January.

Nellemann, C. 2012. Green carbon, black trade: Illegal logging, tax fraud and laundering in the world's tropical forests. A Rapid Response Assessment. Arendal: UNEP and GRID-Arendal.

Nellemann, C., Henriksen, R., Kreilhuber, A., Stewart, D., Kotsovou, M., Raxter, P., Mrema, E., and Barrat, S. (eds.). 2016. *The Rise of Environmental Crime – A Growing Threat to Natural Resources Peace, Development and Security*. Nairobi: UNEP.

The New York Times. 2010. 'The bullet that keeps on killing', Editorial. 13 September.

The New York Times. 2015. 'The plunder of Myanmar', Editorial. 24 January.

The New York Times, 2016. 'Keeping the drillers from sacred grounds', Editorial. 20 November.

Olmo, del, R. 1987. 'Aerobiology and the war on drugs: a transnational crime', *Crime and Social Justice* 30, 28–44.

O'Sullivan, C., and Walters, R. 2016. 'Criminology, war and environmental despoliation', in *The Palgrave Handbook of Criminology and War*, edited by R. McGrary and S. Walklate. London: Palgrave Macmillan, 79–96.

Pala, C. 2015. 'Drama at sea: After a 110-day pursuit, a pirate fishing vessel sinks with its illegal haul', *Slate*, 6 April.

Palmer, B. 2015a. 'A silent victory: A federal judge stands up to the noisy navy for the sake of marine mammals', *On Earth: The Magazine of the Natural Resources Defense Council*, 1 April.

Palmer, B. 2015b. 'Please silence your sonar', *On Earth: The Magazine of the Natural Resources Defense Council*, 9 September.

Paulson, N., Zagorski, K. and Ferguson, D.C. 2015. 'On harm and mediated space: The BP oil spill in the age of globalisation', in *Environmental Crime and Social Conflict: Contemporary and Emerging Issues*, edited by A. Brisman, N. South and R. White. Farnham: Ashgate, 265–283.

Pearson, S. 2015. 'In Minnesota, fight between mining and environment gest personal', *Aljazeera America*, 23 August.

Perry, N. 2016. 'Air Force project threatened by climate change', *ClimateWire*, 19 October.

Plumer, B. 2014. 'How the oil boom could change U.S. foreign policy', *The Washington Post*, 16 January.

Prud'homme, A. 2011. 'Drought: A creeping disaster', *The New York Times*, 17 July.

Risen, J. 2010. 'U.S. identifies mineral riches in Afghanistan', *The New York Times*, 14 June.

Rodríguez Goyes, D. and South, N. 2016. 'Land grabs, bio-piracy and the inversion of justice in Colombia', *British Journal of Criminology* 56(3), 558–577.

Romans, B. 2014. 'More grizzly bear conflicts expected during special Grand Teton elk seasons', *Field & Stream*, 22 October.

Samson, C. 2016 'Civil liberties of indigenous people have long been suppressed at Standing Rock', *The Conversation*, 8 December.

Satterlee, L. 2016. 'Climate drones: a new tool for oil and gas air emission monitoring', *Environmental Law Reports* 46(12), 11069–11083.

Smith, M. and Humphreys, J. 2015. 'The poaching paradox: why South Africa's 'Rhino Wars' shine a harsh spotlight on security and conservation', in *Environmental Crime and Social Conflict: Contemporary and Emerging Issues*, edited by A. Brisman, N. South and R. White. Farnham: Ashgate, 1–38.

South, N. 2016. 'Review essay: blood oil: tyrants, violence and the rules that run the world', *Global Crime* 18(1), 70–75.

Taylor, P. 2015. 'Would grouse protections hurt national defense? Republicans think so', *E&E News*, 29 April.

Teasdale, A. 2017. 'The return of the grizzly', *Sierra Magazine* 102(1), 38–45.

United Nations. 2013. Report of the Secretary General on the Activities of the United Nations Regional Office for Central Africa and on the Lords Resistance Army affected areas. S/2013/297. New York.

Unruh, J.D. and Williams, R.C. (eds.). 2013. *Land and Post-conflict Peacebuilding*. London and New York: Routledge.

Vogel, C. and Raeymaekers, T. 2016. 'Terr(it)or(ies) of peace? The Congolese mining frontier and the fight against "conflict minerals"', *Antipode* 48(4), 1102–1121.

Waldholz, R. 2015. 'Halibut dumping stirs fight among fishing fleets in Alaska', National Public Radio (NPR) 5 June. Transcript available at: www.npr.org/templates/transcript/transcript.php?storyId=412237031 [accessed 18 October 2017].

Waldman, S. 2016. 'Arctic ice melt strains U.S.-Russia relations', *ClimateWire*, 19 October.

Wall, T. and McClanahan, B. 2015. 'Weaponizing conservation in the "heart of darkness": The war on poachers and the neocolonial hunt', in *Environmental Crime and Social Conflict: Contemporary and Emerging Issues*, edited by A. Brisman, N. South and R. White. Farnham: Ashgate, 221–238.

Watson, J. 2016. 'Navy carrier group powered partly by biofuel sets sail', Associated Press, 20 January.

Wells, J.C. 2006. 'National security and the endangered species act: A fresh look at the exemption process and the evolution of army environmental policy', *William & Mary Environmental Law and Policy Review* 31(9), 255–290.

White, R. 2008. 'Depleted uranium, state crime and the politics of knowing', *Theoretical Criminology* 12(1), 31–54.

White, R. 2014. 'Environmental insecurity and fortress mentality', *International Affairs* 90(4), 835–851.

Wittenberg, A. 2015. 'Army's eco-friendly quest breeds more deadly bullet', *Greenwire*, 15 June.

Wittenberg, A. 2015. 'Domestic oil, gas boom changes U.S. security posture – experts', *E&E News*, 26 June.

Wyatt, T. and Brisman, A. 2016. 'The role of denial in the "theft of nature": a comparison of biopiracy and climate change', *Critical Criminology* 25(3), 325–341.

3   Eco-mafia and environmental crime in Italy

Evidence from the organised trafficking of waste

Anna Rita Germani, Antonio Pergolizzi and Filippo Reganati

Introduction

Environmental crime is currently one of the most profitable forms of criminal activity and eco-mafia has become a big business in the waste sector in Italy, where organised criminal networks are involved in the illegal disposal of commercial, industrial and radioactive waste. Apart from diffusely high levels of corruption, there is often the problem of weak and inadequate enforcement of environmental laws. Waste trafficking is an emblematic example of such a problem that is, in turn, encouraged by a low degree of social perception.

In Italy, waste trafficking has become one of the fastest growing areas of crime and one of the most lucrative industries among organised criminal activities (National Antimafia Directorate 2015). Criminal groups have infiltrated both the Italian urban and hazardous waste management cycle, resulting in serious economic as well as environmental and social damage both for enterprises in general (affected by the unfair competition of those that make use of the illegal market) and for companies that deal specifically with the recycling and the recovery of materials (the latter being one of the leading sectors of the circular economy).

Despite the prevalence among the public of the simplistic view that organised crime is responsible for waste trafficking, Italian authorities (i.e. the National Anti-Mafia Directorate) have more recently emphasised that corporations with no mafia relations commit waste-related environmental crimes much more often (Roberti 2014; de Falco 2014). Environmental crime that involves the illegal production and distribution of goods and services is in the literature considered more an 'enterprise' crime than a 'mafia-type' crime (Hayman and Brack 2002; Roberti 2014).[1] Enterprise crime involves producers, processors, retailers and

---

1   The Italian Anti-Mafia Prosecutor Franco Robert, has tirelessly supported the view that waste related crimes more than mafia crimes are corporate crimes. This is also in line with the content of Europol report (2013) that highlights the relevant, autonomous and propulsive role of legal firms in environmental crime activities.

final consumers who demand and supply illegal goods or services in a free-market relationship.

In this chapter, we present our analysis of the determinants of the organised trafficking of waste (ex art. 260 of the Italian Environmental Code) using waste, economic and enforcement data in a panel analysis over the period 2002–2013. Given the high heterogeneity of economic, environmental and institutional characteristics, as well as the involvement of organised crime in waste-related management activities, Italy is a compelling case study.[2] Our main findings reveal that, in most Italian regions, enforcement activities do not exert significant deterrence on criminal behaviour; a negative relationship between enforcement and waste trafficking can be identified only if levels of enforcement efforts are very high. Moreover, we find that the major determinants of the rate of waste trafficking differ between Italy's northern-central and southern regions and this confirms the existence of regional dualism. In particular, while in the northern-central area the crime rate is positively related to level of education and negatively to the adoption of environmentally sound policies, in the southern regions organised waste trafficking activities are negatively related to the education attainment and positively to the endowment of waste management plants.

Understanding the network behind the illegal traffic of waste

How waste is treated depends on a kaleidoscope of choices that can make it end up on the right path, along with enhancement of its value, or on the wrong path, leading straight to the illegal market with the involvement of the mafia. Several factors influence actors' choices, such as malfeasance the model of waste governance and adopted economic policies (especially those related to municipal waste) the development models applied the quality of networks and social capital.

Eco-crimes related to waste are characterised by their markedly economic tract; waste not only produces illicit business when it is disposed of illegally (although the literature has so far focused only on this aspect) but it is also used to mask other illicit flows, such as those of weapons, drugs, human beings and for purposes such as money laundering, fraud, to fuel biomass power plants with contaminated organic matter, and to recover materials illegally. Waste is, therefore, the perfect example of regulatory processes in the management of services that can take changing forms and contents depending on the different contexts in which they are grounded.

Legitimate and illegal waste management sectors can be connected in several ways. The legitimate sector may be the victim, the facilitator, or even the beneficiary of illegal waste management (van Daele *et al.* 2007). Understanding

---

2 Italy is characterised by strong regional differences in terms of productive structures, infrastructure endowments, per-capita income, environmental governance models and public enforcement of laws efforts.

how institutional, economic and social networks interact is crucial to explain why in one specific territory waste is managed efficiently and legally, whereas only a few kilometres away, illegality and inefficiency seem to be persistent. For example, although the Campania region has the highest environmental crime rate in Italy and is sadly known worldwide for the disaster of the so-called 'Land of Fires', there are also provinces and municipalities where waste is properly managed, separate collection rates equal to 80 per cent and the criminal presence is limited (Legambiente 2015; Pergolizzi 2015).

The complexity and sometimes the contradictions of the Italian waste sector regulations themselves – accompanied by a diffuse and inadequate system of enforcement – generate criminogenic risk factors. Moreover, some EU and national policies are based on 'end-of-waste' criteria.[3] These criteria define specific types of materials and waste as by-products to be used in production processes and thereby excludes them from the waste legislation.[4] The EU end-of-waste policies, aimed at promoting the recycling of waste, are actually leading to more complex and confusing national rules that are easy to circumvent. At the same time, the policy creates a new market for secondary raw materials obtained from waste, which encourages black market illegal recycling (CIVIC 2016). However, if we want to identify vulnerabilities and loopholes in the waste governance models that facilitate the entry of (organised) crime in this sector of the economy, we need to look also at the complex supply chains that emerge from the legal framework and at the resulting market.

We must first distinguish between municipal (or urban) waste (hazardous and not hazardous) and special waste (hazardous and not hazardous). The first is about a quarter of the total amount of waste produced annually in Italy[5] (with similar percentages in other countries).[6] In 2013, the amount of special waste was 131.6 million tons of which 8.7 million tons concerned hazardous waste (ISPRA 2015).

For each type of waste, we first describe the supply chain as characterised by different technical and organisational structures, actors and their interactions. Second, based on investigations, official documents and interviews with enforcement agencies officers, we try to detect some specific vulnerabilities that might appear in the different links of the whole chain.

3 The end-of-waste criteria specify when certain waste ceases to be waste and obtains a status of a product (or a secondary raw material). According to Article 6 (1) and (2) of the Waste Framework Directive 2008/98/EC, certain specified waste shall cease to be waste when it has undergone a recovery (including recycling) operation and complies with specific criteria to be developed in line with certain legal conditions.
4 According to Law 152/2006, as amended in 2010, it is considered a by-product and not waste, within the meaning of Article 183, paragraph 1, letter a), any substance or object that fulfils all the following conditions: a) the substance or the object is originated from a production process, of which it constitutes an integral part, and whose primary purpose is not the production of such a substance or object; b) it is certain that the substance or the object will be used, in the course of the same or a subsequent production process or use, by the manufacturer or a third party; c) the substance or object can be used directly without any further processing other than

The urban waste supply chain

In Italy, management of municipal waste is under a public responsibility. Local authorities – individually or in a consortium – may decide to manage this service either directly or indirectly via outsourcing. Given the complexity of waste management, direct management usually takes the form of a public–private partnership where local authorities establish and participate in ad hoc in-house public companies regulated by private law. If local authorities decide to out-source their waste management obligations, a private company will be (sub)-contracted. Figure 3.1 presents the three stages of municipal waste management and the various actors involved, as well as vulnerabilities in terms of criminal behaviour.

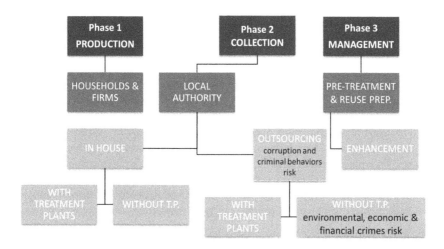

Figure 3.1 Urban household waste sector: actors and vulnerabilities
Source: Authors' own elaboration.

normal industrial practice; d) further use is lawful, i.e. the substance or object fulfils, for the specific use, all relevant requirements relating to products and health and environmental protection and will not lead to overall adverse environmental or human health.
5   In Italy, there are about 30 million tons of municipal waste produced in one year (ISPRA 2015).
6   The production of municipal waste amounted in 2010 to just under 32.5 million tons, pointing out a percentage increase of 1.1 per cent compared to 2009. The trend in the production of municipal waste appears, in general, consistent with the trend of socio-economic indicators such as gross domestic product and household expenses, even though, compared to what was observed for the latter, the growth of the production of waste is found, between 2003 and 2007, more sustained and the next contraction, between 2007 and 2009, less obvious (ISPRA 2012).

The first phase (i.e., waste production) concerns the production of waste. Here, the main actors are households, firms and similar actors.[7]

During the second phase, municipalities or associations of municipalities collect waste. As mentioned above, either companies established by the municipality or third-party companies may carry out this step. In the first case, the in-house companies may or may not have facilities for waste-treatment and/or enhancement. If they do, the chain of logistics does not involve other actors. If not, other private entities must be hired through single tendering procedures.

Third parties that collect waste usually have their own treatment facilities although it is also possible that they must subcontract some activities to other firms. They may hire subcontractors at their own discretion and this increases the risk of illegal or non-transparent practices.

The 1997 Ronchi Decree introduced an integrated system of collection and management of steel, aluminium, paper, wood, plastic and glass packaging-waste aiming to minimise the environmental impact of disposal of such packaging waste, through prevention, recovery and recycling. The non-profit organisation CONAI, the Italian National Packaging Consortium, mainly coordinates the process. The system operates on the basis of the polluter pays principle following the Extended Producer Responsibility as laid down in Directive 94/62CE on packaging of waste.[8] This mechanism – theoretically – ensures greater traceability and transparency and thus prevents illegal flows of waste.

The third phase comprises operational waste management and concerns pre-treatment (selection, separation and treatment operations) and preparation for reuse. This phase entails activities such as reuse, recycle, incineration without energy recovery, incineration with energy recovery, and disposal of waste to a landfill. The value of waste is not intrinsic, but depends on how it can be processed. After the phase of preliminary treatment, the waste may be enhanced through material and energy recovery[9] and sold on the market. As a final step, residual waste that cannot be recycled or enhanced further will be disposed of in landfills or incinerated. Enhancement may be energy or material related: energy recovery is operated by the State (in Italy, Manager Services Electric, GSE manages this) while material recovery is left to the free market.

7   As required by Legislative Decree. 152/2006, the 'urban' waste are primarily household waste, i.e. wastes 'from local and places used for residential purposes'. There are also wastes arising from some specific economic activities which are assimilated by the local municipalities to the urban wastes.

8   CONAI directs the activities and ensures the recovery results of six consortia of materials: steel (Recreate), aluminum (Cial), paper (Comieco), wood (Rilegno), plastic (Corepla) and glass (Coreve), ensuring the necessary connection between them and the public administration. The CONAI then collaborates with the municipalities on the basis of specific agreements governed by the Agreement national framework ANCI-CONAI and represents for citizens a guarantee that the materials from the collection is correctly managed through recovery and recycling processes.

9   Energy recovery from waste is the conversion of non-recyclable waste materials into useable heat, electricity or fuel through a variety of processes, including combustion, gasification, pyrolisation, anaerobic digestion and landfill gas (LFG) recovery. This process is often called waste-to-energy (WTE).

The special waste supply chain

The treatment of special waste is left essentially to the free market. In other words to producers of waste, on the one hand, and the companies that provide waste management services on the other. Economic convenience dictates management of special waste and this explains why many firms choose informal ways to reduce their costs of disposal. Furthermore, the requirement of urban proximity that applies to urban waste and prohibits disposal outside the region does not exist for special waste. This implies that the supply chain for special waste is likely to be longer, although some recent examples show that this is sometimes also true for urban waste. For a number of years for instance, both the Campania and Lazio regions sent household waste to Germany and the Netherlands (ISPRA 2015). Transfrontier shipments may result from inefficiencies and mismanagement, but also from criminogenic, if not criminal tout court, models of governance.

Figure 3.2 provides an overview of the phases relevant to the management of special waste, the various actors involved, the possible vulnerabilities and the risk of criminal behaviour. The first phase concerns the production of waste and the second phase refers to proper operational management. The company responsible for managing the waste usually has its own installations, but may also make use of facilities owned by other companies. Operating costs obviously depend by the complexity and the dangerousness of the waste to be managed. These costs also reflect the suitability of waste for its use after treatment as a secondary raw material with economic value. Because of a self-certification system in this phase, third party professionals such as chemical laboratories that oversee whether the process of treatment and recovery has been compliant with procedures provided by law may also play a role.

Vulnerabilities in the supply chain of the urban waste sector

During the second phase, when waste collection is entrusted to a specialised company, a vulnerability first appears during the public procurement procedure to contract a third party. Here, there exists the risk of criminal infiltration. Conglomerates of companies may, for example, exert influence, more or less legally, on the political and administrative apparatus to procure public contracts. They may also use informal contacts with corrupt officials to tailor specific tenders to the characteristics of the company and, thus, assure to win the bid. The types of crimes occurring in this second phase are mainly related to corruption, such as fraud, extortion,[10] associative crimes,[11] collusive tendering[12] and (ideological)

10 Art. 317–318 and 319 penal code and also art. 319 ter, 320, 321 and 322 penal code; for corruption between private parties, see art. 2635 penal code.
11 Art. 416 and 416 bis penal code.
12 Art. 353 penal code.

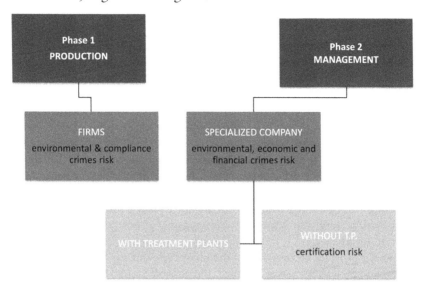

Figure 3.2 Special waste sector: actors and vulnerabilities
Source: Authors' own elaboration.

forgery of documents by a public official.[13] In general, corruptive agreements that materialise in this area are encouraged by: i) the failure to establish transparent links between different tiers of government and the interests of the private sector (mainly, powerful local private companies) who find new opportunities to seek illicit gain through pressuring local government officials;[14] ii) the complex bureaucratic-administrative system; iii) the weak system of control and verification; and iv) criminogenic criteria related to the assignment of contracts (for example, the requirement to award the contract to the lowest bidder tout court).

A second vulnerability in the urban waste management phase occurs when the contractor does not have its own treatment facilities and must therefore subcontract third parties for both material and operational waste management. Once again this may result in corruption and collusion scenarios leading to: i) increased costs; ii) lack of control, traceability and transparency of waste management operations; and iii) loss of the possibility to enhance waste. This is what happened in the City of Rome where the public company AMA (*Azienda Municipale Ambiente*) had to contract a private monopolist that owned the

13 Art. 476–479 penal code.
14 The existing legislation attributes jurisdiction to the public sector that in turn can subcontract or even directly assign the task to private firms. In such a case, it is likely that corruption and property crimes might arise.

treatment facility. This allowed the company to exploit its monopoly power by fixing higher prices.

The types of crimes committed in this phase are: i) environmental offences, in particular causing environmental disasters and pollution, that may result in death and personal injury; obstruction of inspections and failure to clean up pollution,[15] exceeding threshold values, illegal trafficking of waste,[16] illegal management of waste,[17] organised trafficking of waste,[18] transport in the absence of documents[19] (so-called *formulari*); ii) economic and financial crimes (fraud,[20] tax evasion and tax fraud,[21] money laundering[22]); and iii) associative crimes (criminal conspiracy and even mafia-type crimes[23]).

Vulnerabilities in the supply chain in the special waste sector

Special waste comprises the largest part (about 80%) of all waste generated and usually its disposal is more expensive and complex. The longer the travel distance between the places of waste production and management, the greater the risk of illegal practices comparable to other supply chains (Legambiente 2014). During the first phase of production, the nature of the hazardous waste must be made clear – as happens in the case of the urban waste sector – by the assignment of specific codes (so-called EWC – European Waste Catalogue) based on the characteristics and level of dangerousness of waste. Because this is a self-certification system, waste producers can falsify the codes to reduce the disposal costs and this is a widespread practice. Falsifying these documents is obviously a crucial step in the process and it can be done in various ways such as obtaining false analysis from corrupt chemical laboratories, forgery of loading/unloading records, and improper use of identifying codes assigned to the waste materials. For example, a toxic solvent that should be shipped to a landfill for hazardous waste can easily be 'transformed' into harmless urban waste. Because of this fraud, the toxic solvent is at best transported to a landfill for municipal waste or worse disposed into an illegal landfill or recovered as compost to be used in farmlands. In this phase, the frequently committed types of crime are primarily environmental offences foreseen by D.lgs. 152/2006 (illegal or unauthorised waste management, disaster and environmental pollution, transport in the absence of

---

15 Art. 452 bis, ter, quater, septies and terdieces penal code.
16 Art. 259 Dlgs 152/2006.
17 Art. 256 Dlgs 152/2006.
18 Art. 260 Dlgs 152/2006.
19 Art. 258 Dlgs 152/2006.
20 Art. 640 penal code.
21 Legislative Decree n. 74/2000 (in force since September 2011), as amended by L.D. 138/2011, and further adjusted by Decree n. 158/2015).
22 Art. 648 bis penal code.
23 Artt. 416 and 416 bis penal code.

documents, the so-called formulari, discharges and emissions in violation of Decree No. 152/2006,[24] illegal mixing of hazardous waste[25]).

In the second phase, the one consisting of the assignment and the operational management, documents (Fir) accompanying waste are vulnerable to manipulations such as the EWC code switch (the so-called '*giro bolla*') aimed at reducing the costs of disposal or at pretending that waste was treated when it actually was not. Here, vulnerabilities follow from the lack of plants for treatment, disposal and recovery at the territorial level, which impacts on the costs of disposal. The movement of waste from one system to another (storage, processing, enhancement) more easily allows the manipulation of codes and the weight of waste, because the procedures are based on self-certification and are hardly subjected to control.

Just as in the case of municipal waste, in the special waste sector a self-certification system is applied in which private bodies that certify the compliance with treatment and recovery procedures play a role, and also third party professionals such as chemical laboratories may be involved. In this phase we once again observe that the most frequent types of crime are: i) environmental offences (environmental disaster, environmental pollution, discharges and emissions in violation of maximum thresholds values, illegal traffic of waste, illegal waste management, illegal organised trafficking of waste, absence of documents; ii) economic and financial crimes (tax evasion, money laundering and fraud); and iii) associative crimes (criminal conspiracy and even mafia-type crimes).

24 In this regard, art. 133, as amended by Legislative Decree n. 46/2014 on administrative sanctions, reads: 'Whoever, unless the fact constitutes a crime and outside the cases sanctioned under Article 29-quattuordecies, paragraphs 2 and 3, in conducting a discharge exceeds the emission limit values set in the tables in Annex 5 to part Three of this decree, or the various threshold values established by the regions in accordance with Article 101, paragraph 2, or those set by the competent authority in accordance with Article 107, paragraph 1, or Article 108, paragraph 1, shall be punished by a fine from 3,000 euro to 30,000 euro. If a failure to respect limits drains discharging into protected areas of water resources for human consumption provided for in Article 94, or in bodies of water placed in protected areas established by the applicable legislation, apply the administrative penalty of not less than 20,000 euro'.
25 In particular, Article 187 of Legislative Decree 152/2006 prohibits the mixing of hazardous waste with different hazardous properties or hazardous waste with non-hazardous waste. Mixing shall include the dilution of hazardous substances. Although paragraph 2 allows some exceptions to this principle, if certain conditions are expressly provided for by the same provision of the law. In general, the reclassification of hazardous waste to non-hazardous waste may not be achieved by diluting or mixing the waste with the aim of lowering the initial concentrations of hazardous substances under the thresholds for defining the dangerous nature of the refusal (art. 184, par. 5-ter).

Organised trafficking of waste in Italy: some evidence

In the Italian legal system, offences regarding the protection of the environment are almost always qualified as misdemeanours that fall outside the Penal Code. In 2015 the Italian Parliament introduced environmental crimes into the Penal Code (Law 68/2015). In particular, five new crimes were introduced: pollution and environmental disaster (including aggravated penalties for death or public health damage), obstruction of controls, illegal transport and abandonment of radioactive materials and omitted remediation.[26] Among the few crimes that qualify as a felony there are organised activities in the context of waste trafficking.[27] First introduced in 2001 when art. 22 of the Law 93/2001 implemented the art. 53-bis of the d.lgs. 22/1997 (the so-called *decreto Ronchi*), in 2006 organised activities in the context of waste trafficking became part of the Environmental Code (EC). In particular, art. 260 EC sets a penalty of imprisonment from one to six years for any person who sells, receives, transports, exports, imports or otherwise improperly handles large quantities of waste in order to obtain an unfair profit through operations and preparation of means and continuing organised activities. If the waste is highly radioactive, a more severe sanction of three to eight years' imprisonment applies.

Figure 3.3 shows the annual number of reported cases of organised waste trafficking in Italy. It increased up to 2010 and fell off in the following years. It is worth noting that in 2010, investigations of organised trafficking of waste was brought under the responsibility of the DNA (National Antimafia Directorate) and its districts (DDA, *Direzioni Distrettuali Antimafia*).[28]

26 For example, as far as the illegal trafficking of waste is concerned, it was first introduced in Article 259 of the Environmental Code (D.Lgs. 152/2006) on the 'Illegal shipment of waste', which punishes '*whoever carries out a shipment of waste constituting illicit traffic according to Article 26 of the Regulation (European Economic Community) 1 February 1993, no. 259 or carries out a shipment of waste listed in the Annex II of the above-mentioned Regulation in violation of article 1, par. 3, a), b), c) and d), of the Regulation itself shall be punished with a fine from €1550 to €26000 and with arrest of up to two years. The penalty is increased in case of shipment of dangerous waste*'. Art. 256 of the Environmental Code punishes 'whoever carries out an activity of collection, transport, recovery, disposal, trade and brokerage of waste without the permit, registration or communication based on Articles 208, 209, 210, 211, 212, 214, 215 and 216 shall be punished by: a) arrest from three months to one year or fined from 2 600 to 26 000 Euro for non-dangerous waste; b) arrest from six months to two years and a fine from 2 600 to 26 000 Euro for dangerous waste'. It is an abstract endangerment offence punishing the exercise of activity out of the preventive control of the public administration. In particular, it is a misdemeanour and can be committed intentionally or negligently.

27 A recent law (Law 6/2014) was introduced into the Environmental Code Article 256 bis on the 'Illegal burning of waste', which punishes with imprisonment from two to five years whoever sets fire to waste abandoned or deposited in an uncontrolled manner in unauthorised areas.

28 The DNA comprises 26 Direzioni Distrettuali Antimafia (DDA), who are in charge of mafia investigations.

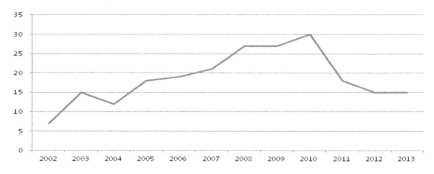

Figure 3.3 The total number of reported cases of organised illegal trafficking of waste by year

Source: Authors' elaborations on Legambiente database

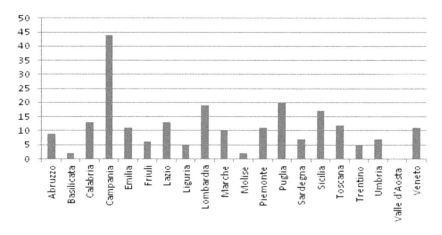

Figure 3.4 The total number of reported cases of organised illegal trafficking of waste by region (2002–2013)

Note: Data in the table represent all cases reported to the judicial authority between 2002 and 2013

Source: Authors' elaborations on Legambiente database

The shift of responsibility for the investigations to the DDA led to improved cooperation between investigators and this explains the reduction in the number of violations. Although exchange of knowledge and information was strengthened, this also generated some structural and organisational delays that have slowed down the investigation and enforcement process.

Figure 3.4 shows the distribution of cases according to the location of the investigation office (*Procura Distrettuale*). This makes clear that a small number of regions, including Campania, Apulia, Lombardy and Sicily, account for most cases. These four regions cover 44.6 per cent of the total number of investigations, and are also the regions where most environmental violations in the entire

Table 3.1 The number of regions involved in the investigations (2002–2013)

Number of regions	Number of investigations	%
One	111	49,6
Two	28	12,5
Three	25	11,2
Four	26	11,6
Five	13	5,8
Six	4	1,8
Seven	10	4,5
Eight	3	1,3
Nine	2	0,9
Ten	2	0,9
Total	224	100,0

Source: Authors' elaborations on Legambiente database

waste cycle have been detected.[29] However, as Table 3.1 illustrates, half of the investigations concern more than one region (111 out of 224); moreover, the 23.7 per cent of the reported cases concern up to three regions, the 19.2 per cent up to six regions and the remaining 7.6 per cent between seven and ten regions. Investigations spill beyond the region where they start, spreading out to a large part of the national territory. Waste trafficking is a crime with a long 'production chain' and it requires professional criminal skills linked by a network structure not limited to a specific region.

As the occurrence of crime usually depends on several factors, including the stringency of law enforcement, it is of special interest to analyse in detail the success of the police in enforcing environmental criminal law. Figure 3.5 shows the trends in the number of offenders charged and the number of offenders arrested for organised trafficking of waste. Similar to the number of reported crimes shown in Figure 3.3, we can see that the number of offenders arrested peaked in 2010 and dropped afterwards. Here, a possible explanation may also be the shift of responsibility for investigation to the DNA. The two curves demonstrate different trends over time: while the curve indicating the number of charges is quite erratic, the curve illustrating arrests is more regular, which could be attributed to the fact that the arrested offenders represent the hard core of the criminal organisations who, in order to execute their illegal activities, need only a minimal informal support structure. The average number of offenders arrested in each investigation varies between four and six, which is consistent with what investigators consider sufficient to set up an organisation to traffic waste.[30]

29 In particular, Campania is all along the region with the highest number (953 only in 2013) of detected environmental crime in the waste cycle (Legambiente 2014).
30 It is worth noting that, in order to conduct organised activity for the illegal trafficking of waste, there needs to be at least one entrepreneur operating in the waste sector, a transportation company, a chemical laboratory and one broker.

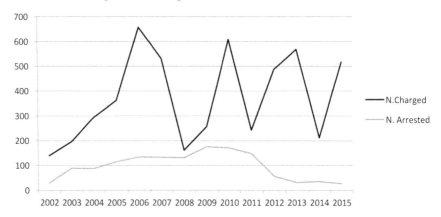

Figure 3.5 The total number of offenders charged and arrested
Source: Authors' elaborations on Legambiente database

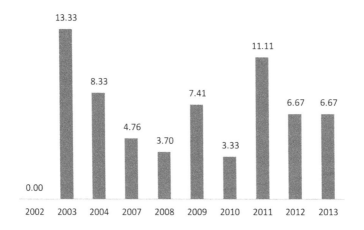

Figure 3.6 Percentage of cases in organised illegal trafficking of waste that have an
identified mafia connection, 2002–2013
Source: Authors' elaborations on Legambiente database

Another important feature is the degree of organised crime's involvement in waste trafficking. Looking at Figure 3.6, we see that mafia clans only had a marginal role. In the period between 2002 and 2013, according to Legambiente, only 6.7 per cent of reported cases involved mafia clans. This figure is similar to that provided by the DNA: between July 2012 and June 2013 only four cases out of 123 refer to the Mafia. The low degree of organised crime's involvement might be explained by the strong corporate nature of this type of crime as it involves entrepreneurs, transporters and brokers, all of whom aim to meet the demand and supply of waste (Roberti 2014; de Falco 2014). In other words, some waste producers are eager to dispose of their waste at low costs, and other firms are ready to earn money illegally by disposing of all types of waste.

Mafia clans indeed are just one of the actors involved. Data derived from our preliminary investigation confirms that entrepreneurs or economic players who have captured the large and easy economic opportunity offered by illegal waste management play the most important role. The Italian authorities have in fact left the waste management sector to private improvisation without any overall industrial point of view. Of all the Italian mafias, the Camorra syndicate was and still is involved most often.[31]

Theoretical background and hypotheses

To develop testable hypotheses that guide the empirical analysis, a range of determinants have been considered. This includes socio-economic, environmental and policy variables that might influence illegal behaviour in general (Ehrlich 1973; Cornwell and Trumbull 1994) and environmental offences in particular (Hamilton 1996; Helland 1998; Stafford 2002; Eckert 2004). Assuming that potential criminals are cynical profit-maximisers who base their decision on whether or not to commit a crime on calculation, it follows that they will comply with the law as long as the benefits of offending outweigh the costs of compliance. As such, polluters are expected to comply with environmental regulations when the probability of being apprehended and sanctioned, coupled with the penalty imposed, is sufficiently high. From this, we derived the following research hypotheses:

> Hypothesis 1: An increase in the enforcement effort results in, ceteris paribus, a lower number of violations; in other words, enforcement improves deterrence.

This hypothesis postulates that increasing enforcement efforts (i.e., judicial investigations, arrests) will lead to increased deterrence. Empirical studies (Cohen 2000) have shown that generally a high level of enforcement implies a high level of deterrence.

> Hypothesis 2: An increase in economic activity leads, ceteris paribus, to a higher number of violations of illegal trafficking of waste.

31 In particular, the *Casalesi*, a clan that took its name from a small town near Caserta, Casal di Principe. This clan is mostly responsible for the environmental disaster caused by the illegal waste dumped in the agricultural fields near the provinces of Caserta and Napoli ('Terra dei fuochi'). Last year, Domenico Bidognetti, the former *chief* of the Casalesi, was the first boss to be convicted for causing environmental disaster. For this eco-crime he was sentenced to 20 years in prison.

The level of economic activity might influence illegal trafficking of waste in two ways (Almer and Goeschl 2010): in terms of a scale effect and of an income effect. Both mechanisms predict a higher number of violations for higher levels of economic activity.

> Hypothesis 3: An increase in the legal income of the population leads, ceteris paribus, to less (more) violations of illegal trafficking of waste.

The literature on economics of crime has largely stressed the role of legal income opportunities in affecting the benefits and costs of crime. Theoretically, the relationship between the level and growth of income and crime is ambiguous. On the one hand, higher income opportunities may increase the chances for employment in the legal sector and therefore reduce the crime rate; on the other hand, higher income opportunities that improve the level of transferable assets in the community may potentially raise the revenues from crime.

> Hypothesis 4: An increase in the level of education leads, ceteris paribus, to less (more) violations of illegal trafficking of waste.

Another economic factor that may affect the decision to engage in criminal activities is education. Primarily, higher levels of educational attainment, being associated with higher returns in the labour market, may increase the opportunity cost of criminal behaviour. In addition, education may alter personal preferences in a way that affects decisions to engage in crime, bringing about a 'civilisation' effect.

> Hypothesis 5: An increase in the costs of treatment and disposal of waste lead, ceteris paribus, to more violations of illegal trafficking of waste.

Waste trafficking occurs when higher profits are expected compared to legal options of recycling or disposal, combined with regulatory or enforcement failure (Sigman 1998). Therefore, criminal behaviour is driven by an attempt to reduce the relatively high costs of legal treatment of waste, of legal disposal (i.e., landfill tax) and of transportation costs.

> Hypothesis 6: A more environmentally sound policy and an integrated system of waste management and disposal reduces, ceteris paribus, the incentive to illegally traffic waste.

The lack of adequate (and effectively enforced) waste management policies generates institutional and regulatory uncertainty, which fosters the illegal trafficking of waste. Mazzanti and Montini (2014) have shown that the heterogeneous waste management and disposal performances in Italy depend not only on the existence of a north–south division, but also on the quality of waste policy and idiosyncratic socio-economic factors.

Data description and empirical strategy

Data on the organised trafficking of waste were provided by the *Osservatorio Ambiente e Legalità* of Legambiente. The dependent variable is the crime rate i.e. the annual number of investigations related to organised waste trafficking activities (art. 260 of the Environmental Code) per 100,000 inhabitants in each region. In our empirical analysis, we use a set of explanatory variables divided into three groups: deterrence, waste market-related and socioeconomic. To address the deterrent effect on criminal behaviour, we use two variables: the charge rate and the arrest rate. The first is measured by the ratio of the number of offenders charged and the total number of recorded offenders and reflects the percentage of offenders the legal authorities identify. The second variable is defined as the ratio of the number of arrested offenders and the number of recorded offenders. This indicates the portion of offenders who have already received some kind of punishment, but do not reveal the certainty of their conviction. For both deterrence variables, we have also used their squared terms in order to control for a possible non-monotonic relation.

The group of waste related variables comprises the number of waste treatment plants in each region and the per capita recycling (or recovery) rate. The first variable is a proxy for the costs of treatment and disposal of waste, while the second indicates adoption of environmentally sound management policies at the regional level.

Finally, we have completed our dataset with socioeconomic variables that reflect the legal income opportunities of potential criminals. In particular, we have inserted into our model the Gross Domestic Product per capita at 2005 constant prices; the growth rate of the real GDP at 2005 constant prices; the male unemployment rate, and the share of the population that has enrolled in secondary school.[32] Table 3.2 provides some descriptive statistics of our sample.

Econometric methodology

Based on recent literature we implement in this section a simple model of environmental crime (Rickman and Witt 2007; Machin and Meghir 2004). It posits a relationship between annual reported crime in each region and region-level enforcement variables, plus some other control variables. The estimation equation takes the following form:

$$\ln crime_{it} = a_0 + \beta \ln crime_{it-1} + X'_{it}\gamma + \mu_i + year_t + \varepsilon_{it}$$

32 As there is great support in the general crime literature that different socioeconomic variables play an important role in explaining the amount of crime, we additionally tested the following list of variables: population density, value added of manufacturing sector, number of manufacturing firms, rate of irregular workers and income inequality. However, none of these seem to have a significant influence on environmental crime.

Table 3.2 Basic descriptive statistics

	Obs	Mean	St.Dev.	Min	Max
Crime rate	240	0.036	0.056	0	0.346
Charge rate	240	0.350	0.405	0	1
Arrest rate	240	0.153	0.256	0	1
GDP growth rate	220	0.011	0.023	−0.057	0.067
Average income	240	25014	6483	14063	35469
Education attainment	200	95.201	5.880	73	106.3
Male unemployment rate	240	7.132	4.261	1.6	21.4
Recycling rate	240	27.9	16.8	2.8	64.6
Number of plants	240	1.229	2.651	0	13

where the subscripts i and t represent the region and time period, respectively. The dependent variable ($\ln crime$) is the crime rate, while the explanatory variables are the lagged crime rate and a set (X) of socioeconomic and waste specific variables characterising the crime. The lagged crime rate in the previous year was inserted into the model in order to identify possible dynamics in crime. As a matter of fact, the economic crime literature has identified the possibility of criminal hysteresis or inertia (Sah 1991; Glaeser *et al.* 1996; Fajnzylber *et al.* 2002). In other words, higher crime today is associated with higher crime tomorrow. Crimes that were committed in the past may affect current criminal behaviour for several reasons. First, criminals can learn by doing, acquiring some level of adequate criminal know-how, which allows them to reduce expected cost of carrying out criminal acts (Case and Katz 1991).

Moreover, convicted criminals are likely to have less legal job opportunities, thus reducing their personal cost of participating in criminal activity and making the commission of crime more attractive. Variable μ_i is a region fixed effect to control for some time-invariant regional characteristics that were omitted from the model but had an impact on crime rates over years; $year_t$ is a time effect that captures the common variations in crime rates across regions and removes the correlation among regions; finally, ε_{it} stands for a well-behaved error term distributed IID $(0, \sigma^2)$.

The dependent variables and all explanatory variables, except for the number of incinerators, were natural logged to alleviate the problem caused by the skewed distributions of some variables. This also simplified calculating the percentage change of crime rates for a 1 per cent change in each explanatory variable (elasticity). The number of incinerators was not logged as the time series contained a substantial number of zeros.

We estimate our model using the first-differenced GMM procedure (Arellano and Bond 1991; Arellano and Bover 1995). This estimator allows controlling for (weak) endogeneity by using the instrumental variables, which consist of appropriate lagged values of the explanatory variables. Consistency of the GMM estimator crucially depends on the validity of the instruments. We address this issue by considering two specification tests suggested by Arellano and Bond (1991). The first is the Sargan test of over identifying restrictions, which tests the null hypothesis of the overall validity of the instruments used. Failure to reject the null hypothesis gives support to the model. The second test examines the hypothesis that the error term is not serially correlated. We test the null hypothesis that the differenced error term is first and second order serially correlated. Failure to reject the null hypothesis of no second-order serial correlation implies that the original error term is serially uncorrelated and the moment conditions are correctly specified.

Results

Table 3.3 provides the GMM estimates obtained using the Arellano–Bond methodology. Three statistics tests are reported: (i) the Sargan test of over-identifying restrictions; (ii) and (iii) the first and second order serial correlation tests.

In Columns (i) and (iv) of Table 3.3, the reported results do not control for socioeconomic and waste-specific variables. In particular, estimates show that there is no crime persistence, with the coefficient of the lagged dependent variable being negatively and statistically insignificant. Both charge and arrest rates are positive and statistically significant. This result is quite unexpected and differs from the majority of the existing literature, because the cost of breaking the law, as measured by the charge to arrest ratio, should reduce the crime rate. This result might imply that deterrence does not yet effectively prevent crime; if deterrence would be stronger, then one would expect to see reduction in the number of organised waste trafficking violations. It may be that arrests are an insufficient indicator for deterrence and the positive significant relationship might reflect this. This supports the suggestion of previous authors that criminals do not consider the likelihood of the negative consequences of committing a crime (Wilson and Herrnstein 1985). The results could also mean that criminal sanctions may not be the most effective solution, given the fact that waste traffickers are usually companies (with their own industrial plants and logistical resources) for which administrative sanctions and interdiction measures, such as the suspension or revocation of licences and concessions (i.e., administrative sanctions or measures that interrupt a company's business) tend to have a stronger deterrent effect than criminal sanctions.

However, the negative and significant coefficients of both squared terms reveal the existence of a hump shaped relation between organised waste trafficking and law enforcement efforts. In line with D'Amato *et al.* (2014), our result indicates that law enforcement can influence organised waste trafficking only up to a certain threshold and a deterrence effect on criminal behaviour cannot go beyond that level.

Columns (ii) and (v) report the results obtained when the economic-specific covariates are inserted into the model. Now, we find that the lagged crime rate

Table 3.3 The determinants of organised trafficking of waste in Italy

	(i)	(ii)	(iii)	(iv)	(v)	(vi)
Crime rate lagged	−0.068 (−1.57)	−0.184*** (−7.13)	−0.170*** (−6.15)	−0.060 (−1.58)	−0.164*** (−4.63)	−0.152*** (−3.96)
Charge rate	0.873*** (4.42)	0.654*** (4.41)	0.680*** (4.76)			
Charge rate^2	−2.138** (−2.90)	−1.511* (−2.44)	−1.585** (−2.69)			
Arrest rate				1.015*** (4.21)	1.042*** (3.83)	1.072*** (3.83)
Arrest rate^2				−2.232** (−3.22)	−3.119** (−3.14)	−3.236** (−3.20)
GDP growth rate		−4.787 (−0.67)	−5.511 (−0.69)		−4.584 (−0.69)	−5.421 (−0.72)
Average income		−0.040 (−0.40)	−0.016 (−0.15)		−0.039 (−0.37)	−0.031 (−0.27)
Education attainment		0.540*** (5.67)	0.533*** (5.10)		0.400*** (4.06)	0.412*** (3.56)

	(1)	(2)	(3)	(4)	(5)	(6)
Male unemployment rate	0.000 (0.04)	−0.005 (−0.32)	0.002 (0.13)		0.008 (0.50)	0.015 (0.72)
Recycling rate			−0.035 (−1.51)			−0.037 (−1.57)
Number of plants			−0.001 (−0.70)			0.002 (0.09)
Constant		0.002 (0.84)	0.003 (0.57)	0.002*** (3.96)	0.003 (1.41)	0.002 (0.52)
Observations	200	160	160	200	160	160
Wald's test (χ^2)	114***	276***	352***	127***	165***	271***
Specification tests(p-values)						
i) Sargan test						
ii) Serial correlation	0.452	0.433	0.682	0.398	0.722	0.591
First order	0.008	0.039	0.038	0.001	0.020	0.019
Second order	0.107	0.104	0.090	0.378	0.307	0.289

Note: Time dummies have been included but omitted here. t-values in brackets. *** $p<0.01$, ** $p<0.05$, * $p<0.1$

is negative and significant, meaning that this type of crime is not persistent over time in Italian regions. Also, the share of population that has enrolled in secondary school appears to be significantly and positively correlated with the crime rate. Similar to the results of previous studies the positive sign of this variable may be attributed to the fact that a higher level of education may reduce the cost of committing a crime or may raise the revenues of crime (Buonanno 2006). However, in this specific case, the positive relationship between levels of education and waste trafficking can be explained by the nature of the crime. Being a typical economic crime, it seems to involve mainly subjects with higher levels of education since the covert illegal mechanisms require high skills and resourcefulness. One of the most recent and important inquiries on waste trafficking concerned the Italian Emilia Romagna region. The region has scores highest on both per-capita income and children's level of education and is also one of the regions that fights eco-criminals more intensively. This is not surprising, since high levels of per-capita income and children's education push the economy to high productive performances, and these may offer more opportunities to waste traffickers, especially in the recycling sector. In fact, operating in this sector requires specific professional skills. It is important to know and understand the law and possible legal vulnerabilities but also the supply and demand mechanisms in the waste management market. The business also requires a dynamic economy able to support demand for illegally trafficked waste and facilitate the hiding of the illicit into legitimate flows. The coefficients on GDP per capita, GDP growth rate and male unemployment rate are not statistically significant.

Finally, columns (iii) and (vi) in Table 3.3 present regressions that include two different indicators of waste management activities. As we can see, results are qualitatively similar to those presented above and once again suggest that the only significant determinants of organised waste trafficking are the deterrence variables, the degree of educational attainment and the lagged crime rate.

With regard to the GMM specification tests, all regression models are supported by the Sargan test, which confirms the validity of the instruments used (i.e. the instruments are not correlated with the error terms). As expected, there is evidence for first-order serial correlation, but there is no indication of second-order serial correlation.

Territorial heterogeneity

In order to account for the structural and relevant differences between Italy's north and centre on the one hand and the south on the other, we estimated the crime equation for each of these territorial aggregations. For this we used panel datasets for the 12 regions belonging to the north and centre and for the remaining eight regions belonging to the south of Italy. Table 3.4 displays the coefficient estimates for the northern and centre regions.

With the exception of the model in column (iv), the lagged crime rate has a significant negative effect in all other models. This indicates the absence of any persistence in crime, but past crime seems to reduce current criminal behaviour. Furthermore, the results for both the charge rate and the arrest rate are uniformly positive and significant: an increase in both deterrence variables increases the crime rate. Only the squared term of the arrest rate is negative and significant. Our findings indicate that law enforcement variables do not lead to significant deterrence of criminal behaviour. Education attainment exhibits a positive and a significant effect on the crime rate indicating that as previously found, if the incidence of crime is higher then this is also true for the share of the population that has enrolled in secondary school. It is worth noting that our findings show that average income exhibits a negative and significant coefficient (columns v and vi). This means that, in the north-centre, improvements in the overall economic condition increases employment in the legal sector and reduces crime rates.

Finally, our results show that the crime rate in the north-centre area is also driven by the per capita recycling and recovery rate. In these regions, recycling and recovery policies seem to be the best instruments to prevent crime, because they drastically reduce the use of both landfills and waste transports across the country, two areas conducive to enabling organised crime. Empirical evidence shows that in those regions where waste management policy is more virtuous (i.e., Trentino, Friuli Venezia Giulia and Marche), the propensity to commit this type of crime is much lower. For example, in 2013 the above-quoted regions registered the lowest number of reported environmental crimes (Legambiente 2014).

The picture slightly changes when we consider empirical results for the southern regions, as displayed in Table 3.5.

First, lagged crime rate is not always statistically significant. In addition, as for the deterrence variables we find that in the southern Italian regions law enforcement measures related to the organised waste trafficking do not exert significant deterrence. In particular, both the charge rate and the arrest rate are positive and significant while their squared terms exert a negative and statistically significant effect on crime rates. In addition, in models (v) and (vi) the coefficient for education attainment is negative and significant, which indicates that higher educated people also have a higher moral stance or less time available to participate in illegal criminal activities, and this results in fewer crimes.

Finally, our proxy for the cost of waste disposal exhibits a positive and significant effect on crime rate, indicating that an increase in the incidence of crime coincides with a higher presence of waste treatment and recycling facilities in the region. In regions with a higher organised crime presence and levels of corruption of waste management policy, waste treatment plants are used to intercept waste demand and to channel it mainly towards illegal outlets. As police investigations also often show, landfills and waste treatment plants are used to mask illegal operations of waste management.

Table 3.4 The determinants of organised trafficking of waste in the North-Centre of Italy

	(i)	(ii)	(iii)	(iv)	(v)	(vi)
Crime rate lagged	-0.157* (-2.21)	-0.236*** (-3.34)	-0.242** (-2.61)	-0.124 (-1.73)	-0.144** (-2.59)	-0.152** (-2.61)
Charge rate	0.467** (2.76)	0.360* (2.33)	0.426** (3.27)			
Charge rate^2	-0.607 (-0.77)	-0.295 (-0.34)	-0.437 (-0.64)			
Arrest rate				0.821** (2.74)	1.152** (3.12)	1.109** (3.12)
Arrest rate^2				-2.180 (-1.56)	-4.666** (-2.82)	-4.432** (-2.83)
GDP growth rate		1.461 (0.32)	1.420 (0.24)		1.605 (0.24)	1.437 (0.22)
Average income		-0.093 (-1.80)	-0.024 (-0.36)		-0.125** (-3.22)	-0.100* (-2.54)
Education attainment		0.561*** (8.97)	0.460*** (5.69)		0.375*** (4.60)	0.352*** (4.05)

	(1)	(2)	(3)	(4)	(5)	(6)
Male unemployment rate	-0.000 (-1.00)	-0.003 (-0.26)	0.016 (1.02)		0.011 (1.10)	0.015 (1.02)
Recycling rate			-0.138** (-2.77)			-0.041 (-0.82)
Number of plants			-0.004 (-1.69)			-0.001 (-0.74)
Constant		0.002 (1.36)	0.016 (1.76)	0.001** (2.75)	0.001 (0.79)	0.007 (1.08)
Observations	120	96	96	120	96	96
Wald's test (χ^2)	629***	250***	231***	167***	278***	195***
Specification tests (p-values)						
i) Sargan test ii) Serial correlation	0.46	0.541	0.323	0.291	0.244	0.32
First order	0.012	0.034	0.058	0.008	0.013	0.012
Second order	0.133	0.160	0.136	0.615	0.210	0.167

Note: Time dummies have been included but omitted here. t-values in brackets. *** p<0.01, ** p<0.05, *p<0.1

Table 3.5 The determinants of organised trafficking of waste in the South of Italy

	(i)	(ii)	(iii)	(iv)	(v)	(vi)
Crime rate lagged	-0.083*** (-3.65)	-0.094*** (-3.98)	-0.195* (-2.10)	-0.194* (-2.18)	-0.138 (-1.81)	-0.117 (-1.92)
Charge rate	1.205** (3.19)		0.822** (2.80)	0.782** (2.87)		
Charge rate^2	-3.347*		-2.054*	-1.782*	-3.308*** (-3.57)	-3.347*** (-3.43)
Arrest rate^2		-3.041*** (-3.36)				
GDP growth rate			11.990 (1.43)	13.801 (1.59)	8.038 (0.97)	8.177 (1.05)
Average income			-0.696 (-0.83)	-0.831 (-1.06)	-0.204 (-0.27)	-0.204 (-0.32)
Education attainment			-0.525 (-0.66)	-0.403 (-0.57)	-1.111** (-2.60)	-1.101* (-2.46)

	(1)	(2)	(3)	(4)	(5)	(6)
Male unemployment rate	0.000 (0.90)		0.002 (0.09)	0.00378 (0.13)	−0.007 (−0.27)	−0.000 (−0.02)
Recycling rate				−0.031 (−1.33)		−0.032 (−0.85)
Number of plants				0.014* (2.10)		0.005 (0.79)
Constant		0.004*** (3.35)	0.017 (1.44)	0.006 (0.56)	0.016 (1.55)	0.016 (1.02)
Observations	80	80	64	64	64	64
Wald's test (χ^2)	77***	222***	32***	130***	264***	425***
Specification tests(p–values)						
i) Sargan test						
ii) Serial correlation	0.137	0.061	0.327	0.205	0.188	0.267
First order	0.045	0.081	0.077	0.025	0.089	0.077
Second order	0.160	0.227	0.211	0.143	0.109	0.211

Note: Time dummies have been included but omitted here. t-values in brackets. *** $p<0.01$, ** $p<0.05$, * $p<0.1$

Conclusions

This chapter can contribute to a better understanding of the possible determinants of a still empirically unexplored type of environmental crime, i.e. organised waste trafficking (art. 260, D.Lgs. 152/2006). We first explored a number of vulnerabilities in the waste management sector showing: i) that it may be used to commit financial and other types of crimes, and ii) the fact that it is not always clear at what stage the transition from legal to illegal activity occurs, due to the particular nature and complexity of the supply chains in the sector. Next, our empirical results revealed that in most Italian regions enforcement activities do not exert significantly deter criminal behaviour. Only very high levels of enforcement efforts reduce waste trafficking. Moreover, the outcomes show that the major determinants of the waste trafficking rate differ in Italy between northern-central and southern regions, confirming the existence of a regional dualism. In particular, while in the north-centre area the crime rate is positively related to the level of education and negatively to the adoption of environmentally sound policies, in southern regions the organised trafficking activities are negatively related to the education attainment and positively to the endowment of waste management plants.

In the North of Italy, the best plant equipment is linked to a better management of the entire waste cycle as shown by the higher standards of recycling rate, but in the south, the existence of various mafias and organised crime systems results in moving the waste management plants more towards personal interests and illegal practices. Therefore, we can argue that the presence of an adequate plant facility is important but not sufficient without effective policies to prevent and contrast organised crime and without the implementation of stronger social control processes at the local level.

Moreover, in the north the positive relationship between levels of education and waste trafficking is explained by the nature of the crime considered. This being a typical economic crime it seems to attract perpetrators with higher levels of education since the hidden illegal mechanisms require high skills and resourcefulness. Unlike other forms of trafficking, operators must know the legal market and its dynamics, the complex legislation and the weaknesses of the control systems to be able to operate effectively. Almost all the investigations completed so far (since 2002) show that the falsification of documentation (the so-called *formulari*) and of the results of chemical-physical analysis is a constant practice. In addition, other sophisticated types of crimes, such as corruption in the public procurement system, fraud in public procurements and money laundering activities are emerging; crimes that also require high skills and well-defined professional abilities.

Overall, our pilot study enriches our understanding on the determinants of waste trafficking and highlights the heterogeneity inherent in the Italian regions. From a policy perspective, the evidence obtained allows us to support the hypothesis that in Italy a better-integrated system of waste management and disposal coordinated with a long-term industrial strategy at the national level, should be urgently implemented in order to restrict the illegal flows of waste. One of the most emblematic cases is the disposal of tires that, with the introduction of a system that holds the manufacturer responsible for their discard, has eliminated illegal activities (CIVIC 2015). Moreover, the enforcement approach could be changed: even though organised crime plays a significant role in the waste management industry, particularly in the area of illegal dumping and international illegal trafficking of hazardous waste, organised mafia-like criminals are not the only players.

In light of the results obtained, our general conclusion is that in Italy waste-related policies should be rethought by addressing the dynamics behind demand as well as supply of (legal and) illegal markets; as long as free-market mechanisms create profit-making opportunities and, consequently, attract new entities into the markets, environmental police agencies will be destined to fail if not accompanied by a more integrated approach able to consider crime policy, environmental policy, economic policy and good governance. Tougher enforcement of existing laws may not be enough to combat environmental crimes if market oriented interventions are not adopted to influence the final equilibrium and outcomes. The identified vulnerabilities show that there is a potential that the waste management sector may diffusely generate high levels of criminal activity at several levels (environmental, economic and financial). Some of these vulnerabilities and the consequent risks of opening the door to criminal opportunities could be reduced only if policy makers will pay more attention to the actual governance models of waste, focusing on the causes of crimes beyond the legal economic structures and activities of waste management.

References

Almer, C. and Goeschl, T. 2010. 'Environmental crime and punishment: empirical evidence from the German penal code', *Land Economics* 86, 707–726.

Arellano, M. and Bond, S. 1991. 'Some tests of specification for panel data: Monte Carlo evidence and an application to employment equations', *Review of Economic Studies* 58(2), 277–297.

Arellano, M. and Bover, O. 1995. 'Another look at the instrumental variable estimation of error-components models', *Journal of Econometrics* 68(1), 29–51.

Buonanno, P. 2006. 'Crime and labour market opportunities in Italy (1993–2002)', *Labour* 20(4), 601–624.

CIVIC. 2015. *The Vulnerabilities in the Trade Chains of Plastic Waste and WEEE*. Corpo Forestale dello Stato, Agenzia delle Dogane e dei Monopoli, Legambiente. Available at: progettocivic.eu (accessed 22 August 2017).

CIVIC. 2016. *Common Intervention on Vulnerabilities in Chain*. Corpo Forestale dello Stato, Agenzia delle Dogane e dei Monopoli, Legambiente. Available at: progettocivic.eu (accessed 22 August 2017).

Cohen, M.A. 2000. 'Empirical research on the deterrent effect of environmental monitoring and enforcement', *Environmental Law Reporter* 30, 10245–10252.

Cornwell, C. and Trumbull, W. 1994. 'Estimating the economic model of crime with panel data', *The Review of Economics and Statistics* 76(2), 360–366.

D'Amato, A., Mazzanti, M., Nicolli, F. and Zoli, M. 2014. *Illegal Waste Disposal, Territorial Enforcement and Policy. Evidence from Regional Data*, SEEDS working paper series, 03/2014.

de Falco, G. 2014. 'Traffico illecito dei rifiuti: un approaccio giudiziario', *Gazzetta Ambiente* 4, 71–75.

Direzione Nazionale Antimafia (DNA). 2015. *Relazione annuale sulle attività svolte dal Procuratore nazionale antimafia e dalla Direzione nazionale antimafia nonché sulle dinamiche e strategie della criminalità organizzata di tipo mafioso nel periodo 1° luglio 2013 – 30 giugno 2014*. Rome: DNA.

Eckert, H. 2004. 'Inspections, warnings and compliance: The case of petroleum storage regulation', *Journal of Environmental Economics and Management* 47, 232–259.

Ehrlich, I. 1973. 'Participation in illegitimate activities: A theoretical and empirical investigation', *The Journal of Political Economy* 81(3), 521–565.

Europol. 2013. Threat Assessment 2013. Environmental Crime in the E.U., available at https://www.europol.europa.eu/publications-documents/threat-assessment-2013-environmental-crime-in-eu

Fajnzylber, P., Lederman, D. and Loayzab, N. 2002. 'What causes violent crime?', *European Economic Review* 6(7), 1323–1357.

Glaeser, E.L., Sacerdote, B. and Scheinkman, J.A. 1996. 'Crime and social interactions', *Quarterly Journal of Economics* 111(2), 507–548.

Hamilton, J.T. 1996. 'Going by the (informal) book: The EPA's use of informal rules in enforcing hazardous waste laws', in *Advances in the Study of Entrepreneurship, Innovation, and Economic Growth, Volume 7*, edited by G.D. Libecap. Bingley: Emerald Group Publishing, 109–155.

Hayman G. and Brack, D. 2002. *International Environmental Crime. The Nature and Control of Environmental Black Market*. London: The Royal Institute of International Affairs.

Helland, E. 1998. 'The revealed preferences of state EPAs: Stringency, enforcement, and substitution', *Journal of Environmental Economics and Management* 35, 242–261.

Istituto Superiore per la Protezione e la Ricerca Ambientale (ISPRA). 2012. *Rapporto rifiuti speciali. Edizione 2012*. Roma: ISPRA.

Istituto Superiore per la Protezione e la Ricerca Ambientale (ISPRA). 2015. *Rapporto rifiuti speciali. Edizione 2015*. Roma: ISPRA.

Legambiente. 2014. *Rapporto Ecomafia 2014*. Milan: Edizioni Ambiente.

Legambiente. 2015. *Rapporto Ecomafia 2015*. Milan: Edizioni Ambiente.

Machin, S. and Meghir, C. 2004. 'Crime and economics incentives', *Journal of Human Resources* 39, 958–979.

Mazzanti, M. and Montini, A. 2014. 'Waste management beyond the Italian north-south divide: Spatial analyses of geographical, economic and institutional dimensions', in *Handbook on Waste Management*, edited by T.C. Kinnaman and K. Takeuchi. Cheltenham: Edward Elgar, 256-285.

Pergolizzi A. 2015. *Analisi teorica ed empirica sulla determinazione dei costi e dei benefici sociali generati dalla gestione dei rifiuti. Tra reti sociali e illegalità, strumenti di governance e buone pratiche*. Camerino: University of Camerino. PhD Dissertation.

Rickman, N. and Witt, R. 2007. 'The determinants of employee crime in the UK', *Economica* 74, 161–175.

Roberti, F. 2014. *Audizione del Procuratore Nazionale Antimafia. Commissione parlamentare d'inchiesta sulle attività illecite connesse al ciclo dei rifiuti. XVII Legislatura*. Available at: camera.it/leg17/210?commissione=39&annomese=201411&view=filtered (accessed 9 September 2017).

Sah, R.K. 1991. 'Social osmosis and patterns of crime', *Journal of Political Economy* 99(6), 1271–1295.

Sigman, H. 1998. 'Midnight dumping: Public policies and illegal disposal of used oil', *The RAND Journal of Economics* 29(1), 157–178.

Stafford, S. 2002. 'The effect of punishment on firm compliance with hazardous waste regulations', *Journal of Environmental Economics and Management* 44(2), 290–308.

van Daele, S., Vander Beken, T. and Dorn, N. 2007. 'Waste management and crime – regulatory, business and product vulnerabilities', *Environmental Policy and Law* 37(1), 34–38.

Wilson, J.Q. and Herrnstein, R. 1985. *Crime and Human Nature.* New York: Simon and Schuster.

4 Supply and demand

Regulation and the trade in illegal wildlife

Amy Couper and Reece Walters

Introduction

The illegal wildlife trade (IWT) is a global 'industry' that causes extensive ecological destruction and irreplaceable loss to biodiversity (Herbig 2010, p. 125). It involves cruelty to animals, violence to humans and is one of the most significant threats to species survival with the trade currently threatening around one third of birds and mammals worldwide (Broad *et al.* 2003; Healy 2013; Lyons and Natusch 2013). Furthermore, it undermines legitimate economies and exacerbates official corruption (Rosen and Smith 2010). As the opening quotations from international headlines attest, it is a visibly thriving and openly accessible multi-billion euro market that devastates human lives and endangers protected and threatened global fauna and flora.

This booming trade has been examined with green criminological discourses and defined as 'poaching, smuggling and capturing endangered species or species whose trade is regulated by law', where endangered species are those that face a high risk of extinction in the foreseeable future (South and Wyatt 2011, p. 546). This includes domestic and international trade of wildlife and wildlife parts in violation of any laws or international agreements, such as CITES (Wyatt 2013, p. 132). Despite this, it is commonly argued that it is the second largest international illicit trade, to that of drugs (Rosen and Smith 2010; Sollund 2011). The financial turnover of blackmarket wildlife trade has been estimated between $5b to $20b each year (Healy 2013; Rosen and Smith 2010; Sollund 2013; Warchol 2007; Wellsmith 2010). The large discrepancies between estimated values can be attributed to low detection rates, leading to an unknown shadow figure (Wyatt 2009, p. 144). South and Wyatt (2011, p. 540), also suggest that estimates may be based on different values placed on wildlife and wildlife products, further explaining the discrepancies. Although the exact size of the trade cannot be known, Sollund (2013) argues that it is steadily increasing as a result of globalisation and the World Wide Web.

The need for the trade in wildlife and wildlife products to be regulated has long been acknowledged and changes in the political climate in the 1960s lead to the implementation of the Convention on International Trade in Endangered Species of Fauna and Flora (CITES) in 1975, following a review of the need to regulate the trade (IUCN 2000). CITES is a legally binding, international government agreement designed to protect endangered species against unsustainable harvest by using a globally cooperative approach. Under CITES species are listed on one of three appendices according to their rarity (Brown and Swails 2005). Signatory nations are required to create laws capable of upholding the requirements of CITES (Griffis 2010). In addition to CITES, nations implement federal or state legislations designed to regulate the trade of non-endangered species that have not been listed on the IUCN Red List.

Green criminology and the illegal wildlife trade

Green criminology has blossomed into a range of critical discourses examining environmental concerns within notions of power, harm and justice (Walters and Westerhuis 2013). In 2013, Nigel South and Avi Brisman compiled the first *International Handbook of Green Criminology*; in their introduction they describe it as a 'capacious and evolving perspective' where 'diversity is one of its great strengths'. They further add it includes a:

> . . . set of intellectual, empirical and political orientations towards problems (harms, offences and crimes related to the environment, different species and the planet). Importantly, it is also an 'open' perspective and framework, arising from within the tradition(s) of critical criminology; at the same time, it actively seeks inter- and multi –disciplinary engagement.
>
> (South and Brisman 2013)

Within Green Criminology there have been pioneering works focusing on crime and animals, namely in animal rights and welfare (Beirne 2009; Nurse 2013; Beirne and South 2007), and species justice and illegal trade in wildlife (Sollund 2013; Wyatt 2011). This chapter extends upon these important contributions by examining IWT utilising 'the Allee effect' and 'treadmill of production theory'. Therefore, it is worth exploring each of these theories in more detail to ask how supply and demand networks of illegal wildlife trade are facilitated by global markets and world trade?

The 'Allee effect' stems from the principles established by Warder Clyde Allee in the 1930s. Allee (1931) discussed the concept of 'inverse density dependence', which he used to refer to the demographic and life history traits of populations. These notions were further elaborated on by Odum (1953), but were referred to as the 'Allee Principles'. The concept of the 'Allee effect' did not have a clear definition until Stephens *et al.* (1999, p. 186) examined the initial principles and defined it as 'a positive relationship between any component of individual fitness and either numbers or density of conspecifics'. This means that when a population suffers from low density or population size, the fitness of individuals within the population declines (Courchamp *et al.* 2008). This, in turn, can lead to extinction.

There are numerous mechanisms that can produce the Allee effect within populations (Berec *et al.* 2007, p. 185). One of these mechanisms is known as the Anthropogenic Allee Effect. The Anthropogenic Allee Effect (AAE) is an economic theory developed by Courchamp *et al.* (2006) that emphasises commodity 'rarity' and the value of endangered wildlife. The rarer a species, the greater the value placed on its market price. As a result, consumer demand for endangered species can lead to exploitation, over supply and extinction (Angulo and Courchamp 2009). The demand for rarity also affects inconspicuous lesser-known species or, as Lyons and Natusch (2013, p. 283), suggest 'perceived rarity'. They suggest that perceived rarity, resulting from genetic abnormalities and colour mutations, is equally as desirable in IWT as actual species rarity. The AAE is a theory that is highly relevant to the discussion of the 'supply and demand' of IWT. This is because Berec *et al.* (2007) state that this mechanism of the Allee effect is evident in activities relating to the exotic pet trade, trophy hunting industry and other activities that are typical of the illegal trade in wildlife and wildlife products.

Lynch and Stretesky (2014, p. 139) argue that green crimes and environmental harms are perpetuated by modes of production that form an essential component of contemporary 'local and global political economies'. For Stretesky *et al.* (2014) ongoing economic growth and fiscal prosperity presented as an essential social good must be challenged. Central to ToP is that capitalism, with its expanding technologies, is intrinsically environmentally destructive. The treadmill is driven by a perpetual need to service consumer society, with the supply and demand of expanding markets and trade-oriented economic policies underpinning con-temporary globalised international relations and providing the fabric and essence of environmental despoliation. The ongoing commercialisation and commodi-fication of products, resources and global commons, for example, fuel the treadmill through expanding trade and consumption. As such, governing rationales premised on capitalist ideologies are, according to Stretesky *et al.* (2014), both responsible for environmental destruction and incapable of redressing ongoing harm. The inability to reverse environmental damage or the 'law of entropy' is crucial to their critique of ecological disorganisation. According to this critique, the commercial processes of production exploit and manipulate the natural environment for power and profit and as a result, disrupt, reorganise and disfigure the ecological balance that sustains environmental stability and development (*Cf* Johnson *et al.* 2015).

IWT: contexts, causes and constructs

The listing of a species as 'endangered' is a double-edged sword. On the one hand, it enhances conservation efforts, on the other, it may unwittingly promote consumer demand (Hall *et al.* 2008, p. 75). The demand for wildlife and wildlife products is greatest in developed countries in the Northern Hemisphere, while supply emanates from less developed countries in the South (Hayman and Brack 2002). The nation that leads the demand for the IWT is China, where the trades in traditional medicine and bush meat flourish. This is followed by the US and European Union due to the demand for exotic pets and collectors' items and the

Middle East, for the demand from the falconry trade (Wyatt 2013). Leading source areas for the IWT include Southern and Central Africa, South-East Asia and Central and Southern America, where biodiversity is high. However, countries like the US, Russia and Canada, where fauna and flora species are less diverse, are also known for attracting demand from the trade (Warchol 2007; Wyatt 2013).

The increase in IWT is attributed to low detection, enforcement and prosecution rates. Lowther *et al.* (2002), suggest that inadequate resourcing of those responsible for monitoring the trade as well as a lack of expertise in identifying endangered species is responsible for the low detection rates in the United Kingdom. This is supported by Alacs and Georges (2008), who state that IWT is treated as a low priority crime in Australia, leading to a large number of cases remaining undetected. Furthermore, when crimes are detected the subsequent punishments are usually fines or very minimal prison sentences (Alacs and Georges 2008). According to Warchol *et al.* (2003), the potential profits of successfully trading endangered wildlife vastly exceed the likely penalties. This, combined with poor enforcement and small conviction rates, results in illegal wildlife traders seldom being deterred by the threat of apprehension (Schneider 2008; Wyatt 2009). Finally, the autonomous and clandestine nature of IWT, combined with modern digital technologies, makes it exceedingly difficult to even identify offenders (Stoner 2014). According to Stoner (2014), modern digital technologies allow for online trading forums that enable individuals, who would otherwise not exist in criminal circles to operate from their homes, therefore, making it easier for individuals to become involved in the IWT. These online trading forums are subject to decreased monitoring and regulations and provide increased opportunities for traders to use clandestine advertising methods to evade detection. For example, Stoner (2014) reports that traders use common guises to evade detection, such as the use of 'ox bone' to describe ivory in the illegal ivory trade.

The IWT is fuelled by the demand for a vast array of endangered species used for such things as traditional medicine, ornaments, clothing apparel and food (Broad *et al.* 2003). Rhinoceros horns, pangolin scales, tiger bones and genitals, leopard pelts and paws, and bear paws and gallbladders are all highly prized for use in traditional medicine (TRAFFIC 2008; Warchol *et al.* 2003). Moreover, the bush meat trade targets a large number of endangered species with tortoises and freshwater turtles among the most highly prized species for their meat. Furthermore, shells and preserved insects are kept as curios (Haweswood and Callister 1991; Nijman and Nekaris 2014), while pelts and ivory are used for furniture, wall hangings and ornaments (Warchol *et al.* 2003). Live wildlife is traded for private collections, the exotic pet market, the game industry and biomedical labs and circuses (Warchol *et al.* 2003). Birds, due to their colourful plumage and mimicry capability (Wright *et al.* 2001, p. 718) and reptiles for their low maintenance costs and ability to be easily concealed during transportation (Alacs and Georges 2008) are both highly prized in the black market as exotic pets (Herrera and Hennessey 2007).

As mentioned, the demand for endangered wildlife is a key driver in IWT. Sollund (2011) and Schneider (2008) argue that endangered species are the most valued and highly sought after by international consumers because their rarity increases their desirability. TRAFFIC (2008) suggests that local villagers are predominantly responsible for illegally harvesting reptiles for IWT, with their main motivation being to obtain enough money to survive. These are opportunistic criminals who will target all species (Natusch and Lyons 2012), however, are less likely to encounter highly valued endangered species in their everyday lives than intentional poachers (Pires and Clarke 2011). This means that neither of these types of offenders is as harmful to species survival as intentional poachers in that they are targeting the most abundant species.

Transport company employees are also linked to IWT through legitimate business that permits access to the mechanisms required to transport animals across international borders (Wyatt 2013). Finally, organised crime groups run high volume/high value trafficking. One example of this is the organised trafficking of falcons into the Middle East for the falconry trade (South and Wyatt 2011). This trade is facilitated by Syrian and Lebanese students studying at Russian universities, who operate with hunters and inhabitants of taiga settlements on behalf of organised crime syndicates. In addition, there are correlations between the organised trafficking of wildlife and zoo chains in the United States, who purchase large volumes of expensive species from lucrative markets of organised crime (Sollund 2011). For example, one of America's leading exotic animal distributers, United States Global Exotics, was found to be involved in the illegal trafficking of thousands of individuals of various exotic species for intended distribution to American zoo chains (Sollund 2013).

The various methods involved in all stages of IWT, from obtainment of the wildlife to the final consumer, help to explain the mechanisms required to commit wildlife smuggling offences. Some of these include foreigners hiring local poachers (Warchol 2007), to villagers using domestic animals to attract wild animals for capture (Sollund 2011). Another technique that foreign traders employ is to pose as researchers in order to gain information on where to locate and subsequently harvest wildlife (Herbig 2010). Furthermore, IWT is often run parallel to other illicit trades allowing it to utilise the same smuggling routes. Hayman and Brack (2002) explain how organised smuggling gangs have combined narcotics, weapons and parrots when illegally crossing international borders. Wyatt (2013) supports this, referring to correlations between the illegal trade of abalone meat and methamphetamines.

Offenders typically use falsified documentation to smuggle wildlife rather than physical concealment (Wyatt 2013). Legitimate captive breeding farms also provide opportunities for smugglers to launder wildlife into the legal wildlife trade. In South-east Asia, legitimate breeding farms play a substantial role in laundering wild-caught green pythons, sugar gliders (Lyons and Natusch 2011, 2012) and other species of reptiles and amphibians (Natusch and Lyons 2012; Lyons *et al.* 2013) into the legal pet trade. Beastall and Sherpherd (2013) and Sherpherd (2013) both report claims of captive breeding that is unfeasible for one reason or another, suggesting the existence of laundering. Finally, Halstead (1994) discusses how reported captive breeding success of Australian parrots commonly coincides with local, wild population availability, suggesting that laundering wild caught animals into the legal trade also takes place in Australia.

There is a vast array of techniques used to conceal wildlife and wildlife products in the smuggling process. Common techniques include packing reptiles into cassette cases or placing illegal specimens under legal specimens of venomous species in order to deter inspections (Herbig 2010). Smugglers often paint ivory to make it appear as wood or marble and conceal birds within hollowed out books, prosthetic legs, ceramic garden gnomes or plastic tubes (Rosen and Smith 2010; South and Wyatt 2011). However, bird eggs are increasingly preferred by smugglers to live birds because they are easily concealed in hidden vests (Alacs and Georges 2008). Finally, smugglers in the IWT have been reported to use rental or stolen cars, which can be easily abandoned if they are detected (Tailby and Gant 2009) and use speciality vehicles such as ambulances, to avoid suspicion (Cao Ngoc and Wyatt 2013).

Case study: Australia's response to IWT

Australia continues to play a leading role in the international effort to prevent the illegal trade in endangered wildlife. Australia, through its Federal Department of Environment, is the Chair of the Coalition Against Wildlife Trafficking, an alliance of 'like-minded governments and organizations', formed in 2005 to improve law enforcement, to reduce demand for the supply of illegal trade and raise political and public awareness (CAWT 2016, p. 1). It also has one of the first and most progressive dedicated environmental courts, namely the New South Wales Land and Environment Court, established in 1979 (White 2013). It is a country that proudly boasts its environmental assets and recently had its Federal Environment Minister awarded the inaugural 'Best Minister in the World' at the World Government Summit (ABC News 2016). In 2014, it appointed a national *Threatened Species Commissioner* to 'bring a new national focus and effort to secure our threatened flora and fauna' (Department of the Environment 2015, p. 1). This was followed by the appointment of an 'Ambassador for the Environment' in 2016 to lead developments with the UN Framework Convention on Climate Change and 'promote Australia's interests on international environmental issues, including climate change policy, world heritage, whaling, illegal wildlife trafficking, blue economy and oceans' (Bishop 2016). It has also initiated innovative endeavours and networks with auction houses and cruise ship operators to raise awareness with potential buyers of the ecological harms and international penalties (UNEA 2014). While the penalties for IWT in all Australian states and territories have increased significantly in recent years, native birds and reptiles continue to be routinely targeted on global illegal markets for sale as 'rare and exotic' pets (Muller 2014). As such, Australia works collaboratively with its regional neighbours to combat the illegal trade in wildlife (Topsfield 2016).

Given Australia's international leadership role in IWT and its ongoing interest as a 'target nation' for smugglers, the intention here was to examine in detail the policies and practices of this jurisdiction's detection, enforcement and prosecution processes. The Australian Customs and Border Protection agency is responsible for detecting and enforcing wildlife trade. In 2004–2005 there were 3,904 reported seizures and this figure increased to 7,533 during 2006–2007 'perhaps because of increased screening at airports (including incomings and outgoings) indicating more success at detection rather than an increase in trafficking' (Wyatt 2013:4). In 2009–2010 customs conducted 4,104 seizures of plants and animals (Barry 2011); and recent figures for January to August 2015 reveal 858 seizures (Department of Environment 2015). Such are the latest official reports from the Australian Government. As Wyatt (2013) succinctly notes, these statistics identified in the annual reports of the relevant Australian government department reveal little about the policies and practices of regulation and law enforcement. There are no government explanations of the reporting process, for example, nor is there a definition of 'seizure' or items confiscated, nor details or profiles of offenders apprehended. Indeed, the authors attempted on three occasions throughout 2015–2016 to access more detailed data from the Department of Environment through the Australian *Freedom of Information Act* (1982), and were informed that no consolidated national Australian database exists that distinguishes between items seized, offence type and offender profile. Moreover, there is no database for prosecutions and court outcomes. Instead, the Federal Department of the Environment publishes 'media releases' identifying the details of specific court cases. It has also recently begun to publish summaries of court cases in its annual reports. For example, from the 858 seizures mentioned above for 2015 only three matters were referred to court, and all three in the Magistrates Court (lower court).

In an attempt to gather qualitative information about offence type, offender profile and the extent to which treadmill of production theory and the Anthropogenic Allee Effect provide useful analytical insights into IWT, this research sought to construct a series of case studies utilising official court transcripts involving IWT cases in Australia. However, IWT case prosecutions in Australia are most commonly dealt with by the lower courts (Magistrates and District) and as a result, are not reported on court databases that provide judgements and judicial rulings. As mentioned above, attempts to elicit prosecution and non-compliance outcomes from the relevant government authority were unfruitful. Therefore, a dataset of the Wildlife Seizures Office (WSO) media releases for all reported court cases were collated for the years 2006–2016. During this period the regulatory authorities in Australia dealt with more than 10,000 reported cases of illegal trafficking in wildlife. It must be remembered that Australia's six states and two territories operate as separate and independent jurisdictions for compliance and enforcement of Federal or Commonwealth legislation, namely *The Environment Protection and Biodiversity Conservation (EPBC) Act* (1999) with a maximum penalty of 10 years imprisonment per offence or a fine of up to AUD$110,000. There is no national database in Australia that coordinates the regulatory activities of these eight jurisdictions. Moreover, each jurisdiction provides differing and only partial information of their activities.

As mentioned, this research managed to extract some enforcement and prosecutorial activities through repeatedly applying through *Freedom of Information Act* (1982), however, it was apparent that individual jurisdictions did not catalogue or report specific cases of prosecution. The media releases of the WSO and subsequent Lexis Nexis, Austli and Westlaw legal database searches, revealed less than two dozen cases resulting in successful prosecution. We have selected four of the more serious prosecutions with outcomes involving imprisonment.

Case One

The case of *R v Petersen* ([2009] NSWDC 282) was heard in the New South Wales District Court. The accused was charged with the attempted export of native fauna under the Australian *EPBC Act* (1999). Petersen attempted to illegally export 44 native specimens, although none were listed as endangered. The majority, notably reptiles, were Shingleback Lizards (*Tiliqua rugosa*), which currently remain 'unassessed' by the IUCN Red List. The individual value of each specimen was approximately AUD$5,000 on the international black market (IBM) (Kaow 2010). The accused also attempted to export an albino Darwin carpet python from Australia's Northern Territory. Overall, the total estimated value of the seizures was AUD$200,000 (€130,000). This case highlighted the blackmarket appeal for exotic and colourful reptiles as well as the demand for rarity, as is the case for the albino Darwin carpet python. The relative ease in both capture and transportation of shingleback lizards provides smugglers with a lucrative AUD$5,000 (€3,500) per specimen, while the Darwin carpet python attracts AUD$20,000 (€14,000) for its perceived rarity due to its unique colour mutation.

Petersen, an electrician at the time of the offence, was a reptile enthusiast. He had previously volunteered at and been employed by a local pet store earlier in his life. This led him to gain access to specific social circles of reptile enthusiasts. Furthermore, his girlfriend, who lived in Shanghai, regularly met with him in Phuket, Thailand. These two factors led him to be approached by a third party who is labelled in the transcript as Mr X. Mr X, who he knew from his interest in reptiles, offered to pay for his flights to Thailand and provide spending money in exchange for Petersen smuggling native reptiles in his luggage. Petersen agreed to the exchange in which Mr X would meet him at the airport and fill his luggage with reptiles.

In sentencing, the judge took many factors into account. Those that favoured a harsher sentence were that the offender seemed remorseful for reasons other than the wrongfulness of the offence and that he was aware of the amount of cruelty involved, having previously worked in a pet store. Factors that favoured a light sentence were that none of the species were endangered, he was otherwise of good character, he admitted guilt early in the process and assisted in the investigation. Although there was discussion about not sentencing Petersen to imprisonment, failure to imprison would not act as a strong enough deterrent for future offenders. Petersen was sentenced to 18 months imprisonment, to be released at 12 months into a good behaviour bond.

Case Two

In the Appeal case of *Henri Robert Morgan v R* ([2007] NSWCCA 8), the offender attempted to export the eggs of three Australian native species of birds to South Africa in a cummerbund. Two of these species were the Sulphur-crested Cockatoo and Galah; and the third, a Major Mitchell; a species endemic to Australia with a highly regulated trade. Preliminary searches for these species in the online South African pet trade revealed that increasing demand has significantly increased the value of this species for suppliers (Kleinbosch Birds 2014). Therefore, although this species is not rare in terms of species abundance, it is rare in that the demand in the South African pet trade is greater than the legal supply.

Morgan was intercepted at the Sydney Kingsford Smith Airport with 24 native bird eggs concealed underneath his clothing. He had a first class return flight to Johannesburg that was due to return exactly one week later. Morgan stated in the trial that he came to commit the offences through being repeatedly propositioned by his neighbour to smuggle native bird eggs to South Africa. He stated that although he had continuously declined to partake in the offence, his personal circumstances changed at the time of this offence, which led him to agree to act as a courier. He stated that he was planning to create a helicopter bungee jumping business in South Africa, and the money and flights offered to him in return for his involvement would facilitate this plan. The judge, however, elected not to accept this factor of the trial on the basis of insufficient evidence. Despite this, it was agreed that his role in the offence was as a courier only and he was not involved in the capture or sale of the eggs.

The initial sentence in this case was two years' imprisonment for the offence of attempted wildlife trafficking. The primary factors that the Judge of Appeal took into account were the nature and extent of the offender's role and his motivations in committing the offence. It was determined that Morgan was a courier for profit only. Second, it was determined that the offender was aware of the criminal nature of the offence, which was demonstrated by the fact that he attempted to smash all the eggs upon detection. It was also considered that this act caused irreversible damage to what would otherwise have been 24 viable specimens. The final factors that weighed against the offender were the potential harms associated with the offence, in terms of potential disease risk and species decline. Factors that were considered in favour of the offender were his inferior health, long-standing employment, his demonstration of remorse and his role in assisting his drug-dependent daughter. Overall, the Judge of Appeal did not amend the initial sentence and Morgan was sentenced to two years' imprisonment for the offence of attempted wildlife smuggling. However, he was only to serve one year on the condition of being released into a 12-month good behaviour bond at the end of the first year.

Similarly to Case 1, Case 2 also involves the attempted export of several Australian native species. In this case, Morgan targeted Major Mitchell Cockatoos, Sulphur-crested Cockatoos and Galahs. Parrots are desirable in the international pet trade due to their colourful plumage and mimicry capability (Wright *et al.* 2001). They are also easily concealed at the egg stage, which contributes to their desirability as targets for smugglers. All of these factors contribute to their disproportionate presence in IWT with parrots, alongside reptiles, being most commonly intercepted by ACBPS between 2000 and 2007 (Alacs and Georges 2008, p. 147).

Each of these three species of parrot is listed as 'of least concern' on the IUCN Red List. Despite this, both Sulphur-crested Cockatoos and Galahs are listed on Appendix II of CITES, meaning that the increased need to have their trade heavily regulated has been internationally acknowledged. Furthermore, although only two of these species are listed on CITES Appendix II, they are all heavily regulated by Australian legislation.

Case Three

In *Phillips v State of SA* ([2007] SASC 279) the Supreme Court of South Australia heard on appeal the illegal harvest and sale of native species. This case involved the attempted trade of the blacklip abalone. The IUCN Red List has not currently assessed this species' conservation status. Furthermore, it has been removed from species protected under the *EPBC Act* (1999), meaning that it's trade is now regulated through Fisheries legislation (Routh 2010). McShane (1998) suggests that it is incredibly difficult to assess the sustainability of abalone stocks and that harvest size is not a sufficient indicator. However, the level of sustainability has slowly decreased since 1989, with a steep decline in species abundance observed between 2006 and 2009, around the time that the offence was committed (Stobart *et al.* 2013). In addition, the total allowable commercial catch in South Australia decreased by 30 per cent between 2004 and 2005 and a further 18 per cent in the following year due to increasing concern about the health of the population (Mayfield *et al.* 2006, p. 4). Therefore, the declining population around the time of the offence and the heavy regulations surrounding its trade did temporarily increase its rarity.

The offender's trade in the abalone meat did not involve a high level of sophistication. In each instance, the offender was caught selling the meat from the boot of a car. In this case, the offender was charged with four separate offences each of the four times they were caught illegally trading abalone meat. According to the relevant legislation, the maximum penalty for each of these offences is a AUD$60,000 (€39,000) fine as well as or alternately imprisonment for up to two years. Phillips was initially sentenced to 20 months imprisonment with a non-parole period of 12 months and fines totalling AUD$14,000 (€9,100). Mitigating factors that were considered in the initial sentencing were that Phillips was the primary carer for his mentally ill partner, had three young children and had sought rehabilitation for his drug use. However, the aggravating factors in this case were that the offender had previously been given the benefit of a suspended sentence for similar offences and had had the suspension revoked. Overall, the Judge of Appeal concluded that the initial sentence was appropriate and the appeal was dismissed.

Case Four

In *R v Degelder* ([2006] VSCA 249) the accused was charged with the offence of taking a commercial quantity of a priority species, contrary to s111B of the Fisheries Act (1995).

The species targeted in this case was greenlip abalone, which currently remains unassessed by the IUCN Red List of threatened species. However, the Department of Environment and Primary Industries (DEPI) (2014) suggest that Victoria, where this offence occurred, has one of the only remaining sustainable wild-harvest abalone stocks. However, factors such as a uniquely short harvest period and increasing demand from the global market can mean that the demand is greater than the legitimate supply (DEPI 2014). Therefore, although the local population of abalone was not 'officially' endangered at the time of the offence, it was considered to be rare in that the global demand is greater than the legal available supply.

Degelder was the only offender in this case and demonstrated advanced knowledge and skill in the method he used to commit the offence. It was determined that he had arrived at the beach at approximately 1:30 am on the morning of the offence. He had unloaded his diving gear before relocating his car up the road. He returned from the beach at 4 am with his diving gear and two dark plastic bags, which he loaded into his car. Degelder was then stopped at a road block approximately 25 minutes later at which he was found to have wet diving gear, commercial abalone harvesting equipment and an abalone harvest bag that smelled of abalone meat. Although he did not have any abalone meat on his person at this time, officers later found two bags of freshly shucked abalone meat on the roadside prior to the roadblock. It was determined that Degelder had dumped them there because no other cars had used the road that day.

At the time of the offence Degelder was serving a suspended sentence, which was subsequently breached by his offending. The initial sentence that Degelder received was two years' imprisonment for his breach of section 111B of the *Fisheries Act* (1995), which has a maximum penalty of five years' imprisonment. This was ordered to be in conjunction with his continued sentence for previous offences. Overall, he was ordered to serve a total of 25 months' imprisonment with a non-parole period of 13 months. In addition to this, the Magistrate ordered the forfeiture of the property seized in the offence including diving equipment, abalone equipment, meat and clothing. Degelder was also prohibited from boarding any licensed fishing vessels in Victoria and being found on or in Victorian waters without a lawful reason.

The grounds for the appeal were that the initial sentence under the *Fisheries Act* (1995) was too excessive and that the restored sentenced should not be served cumulatively. The Judge of Appeal allowed the appeal on the basis of a discretionary error surrounding the breach of the suspended sentence. Factors that were considered were the offender's life-long recreation as a diver, his personal troubles at the time of the offence and his history of similar offences. Overall, the sentence was lowered to 17 months' imprisonment for the fisheries offence and a further three months for the restored sentence with a non-parole period of 10 months fixed.

Treadmills, global IWT and the Allee effect

The four cases discussed in detail above all point to the significance of 'rarity', and 'supply and demand' in the motivations of offenders, the attraction to global markets, the decisions to prosecute and the impact on sentencing. While the overwhelming majority of IWT cases in Australia result in warnings or minor fines, there are occasions, when courts will both incarcerate and sanction with significant fiscal penalties. The more serious sentencing practices are seen in New South Wales (including two of the cases discussed above) where a dedicated land and environment court has operated for more than three decades. It is also in this jurisdiction where courts have ruled that 'the more serious the lasting environmental harm the more serious the offence and, the higher the penalty'.[1] Here we observe the Anthropocentric Allee Effect's on policy and subsequent enforcement. The rarity of a species and its population decline increases its global value; or it also increases the perceived seriousness of the offences in countries, such as Australia, where dedicated courts operate to adjudicate such wildlife crimes.

The treadmill of production and sale underpins the ongoing lucrative nature of the global IWT industry here the most endangered species return the greatest profits for criminal enterprises. The above cases also allude to the significance of species harm in the decisions of the court; however, the number of cases being prosecuted in Australia, a reported leader in the fight against IWT, remains very low. This research concludes that a lack of coordinated data and joined-up strategy across Australian states plays a significant role in regulatory disparity and policy inconsistency. By its own admission the Department of the Environment has recently endorsed this view stating; 'The effectiveness of the Department of the Environment's regulation of wildlife trade under Part 13A of the *EPBC Act* (1999) has been undermined by the absence of appropriate and tailored policy and procedural guidance, functional IT support systems and a risk-based approach to monitoring compliance'. (DoE, 2016:1) This position is not aided by the various lower court jurisdictions in which IWT is processed. We believe that

---

1   Camilleri Stock Feeds Pty Ltd v Environmental Protection Authority (1993) NSWLR 683.

jurisdictional harmony and consolidation is required to alleviate judicial disparity and aluminate government policy consistency, efficiency and transparency. To this end, a specialist environmental jurisdiction within Australia's Federal Court would be beneficial. The *EPBC Act* (1999) is a Commonwealth or Federal piece of legislation. This Act provides the largest penalties for IWT and it is this legislation under which offenders are charged. To hear EPBC criminal matters in one consolidated setting with specialist advocates and judicial officers serves to emphasise the seriousness of this offence while co-ordinating prosecutorial processes for policy and practice enhancement.

There has been a steady growth in both developed and developing countries of specialist environmental frameworks, which often include specialist Environmental Courts or Tribunals. It is reported that some 350 ECTs operate across 41 countries, facilitating various forms of environmental due process and justice (Hamman *et al.* 2015). The growth of ECTs can be attributed to 'continual [pressure] worldwide for effective resolution of environmental conflicts and/or expanding recognition of the need for procedural and substantive justice vis-à-vis environmental matters' (White 2013, p. 268). These burgeoning fora for settling environmental disputes can inculcate both civil and criminal jurisdictions and resolve a variety of claims from more administrative matters, such as planning permits, to serious prosecutions involving environmental contamination. The diversity and complexity of environmental cases increasingly requires innovative approaches based on 'problem-solving' before judicial officers with specialised knowledge (White 2013). Australia already has a well renowned specialist environmental court, namely the New South Wales Land and Environment Court (Walters and Westerhuis 2013) and others have called for dedicated environmental judicial settings in other state jurisdictions (Hamman *et al.* 2015). A specialist environmental court provides the necessary jurisdictional consolidation and 'joined up thinking' (Elliot 2009) to tackle the expanding organised criminal networks associated with IWT.

References

ABC News. 2016. 'Greg Hunt wins inaugural Best Minister in the World award at Dubai summit', 10 March.

Alacs, E. and Georges, A. 2008. 'Wildlife across our borders: a review of the illegal trade in Australia', *Australian Journal of Forensic Sciences* 40(2), 147–160.

Allee, W.C. 1931. *Animal Aggregations. A Study in General Sociology*. Chicago: University of Chicago Press.

Angulo, E. and Courchamp, F. 2009. 'Rare species are valued big time', *PLoS ONE* 4(4), 1–5.

Barry, C. 2011. 'Australia's wildlife blackmarket trade', *Australian Geographic*, 3 March.

Beastall, C. and Shepherd, C.R. 2013. 'Trade in 'captive bred' echidnas: claims of captive breeding warrant further investigation as efforts to produce second-generation short-beaked echidnas over the last 100 years fail', *TRAFFIC Bulletin* 25(1), 16–17.

Beirne, P. 2009. *Confronting Animal Abuse: Law, Criminology and Human-Animal Relations*. New York: Rowman and Littlefield.

Beirne, P. and South, N. (eds.) 2007. *Issues in Green Criminology*. Cullompton: Willan Publishing.

Bishop, J. 2016. 'Ambassador for the Environment', *Department of Foreign Affairs and Trade, Media Release*, 29 February.

Broad, S., Mulliken, T. and Roe, D. 2003. 'The nature and extent of legal and illegal trade in wildlife', in *The Trade in Wildlife: Regulation for Conservation*, edited by S. Oldfield. London: Earthscan Publications, 39–77.

Brown, D. and Swails, E. 2005. *Convention of the International Trade in Endangered Species (CITES)*. London: Verifor Case Studies.

Cao Ngoc, A. and Wyatt, T. 2013. 'A green criminological exploration of illegal wildlife trade in Vietnam', *Asian Criminology* 8(2), 129–142.

Coalition Against Wildlife Trafficking (CAWT). 2016. *Partners in the Global Flight Against Illegal Wildlife Trade*. Available at: cawtglobal.org (accessed 1 March 2016).

Courchamp, F., Angulo, E., Rivalan, P., Hall, R.J., Signoret, L., Bull, L. and Meinard, Y. 2006. 'Rarity value and species extinction: The Anthropogenic Allee Effect', *PLoS Biology* 4(12), 2405–2410.

Courchamp, F., Berec, L. and Gascoigne, J. 2008. *Allee Effects in Ecology and Conservation*. Oxford Scholarship Online.

Department of the Environment. 2015. *Threatened Species. Commissioner Report to the Minister for the Environment*. Canberra: Department of the Environment.

Department of the Environment. 2016. *Performance Audit Managing Compliance with the Wildlife Trade Provisions of the Environment Protection and Biodiversity Conservation Act 1999. Report for the Auditor-General ANAO*. Report No.7, 2015–16. Canberra: Department of the Environment.

Department of Environment and Primary Industries (DEPI). 2014. *Victorian Wild Harvest Abalone Fishery Management Plan*. Melbourne: Victorian Government.

Elliot, L. 2009. 'Combatting transnational environmental crime: joined up thinking about transnational networks', In *Eco-Crime and Justice. Essays on Environmental Crime*, edited by K. Kangaspunta and I. Haen Marshall. UNICRI, 55–78.

Griffis, C. 2010. 'Convention on International Trade in Endangered Species', in *Encyclopedia of the U.S. Government and the Environment: History, Policy, and Politics*, edited by M. Lindstrom. Santa Barbara, CA: ABC-CLIO, 248–250.

Hall, R.J., Milner-Gulland, E.J. and Courchamp, F. 2008. 'Endangering the endangered: The effects of perceived rarity on species exploitation', *Conservation Letters* 1(2), 75–81.

Halstead, B. 1994. *Wildlife Legislation in Australia: Trafficking Provisions*. Canberra: Australian Institute of Criminology.

Haweswood, T. and Callister, D.J. 1991. 'Collection and export of Australian insects: an analysis of legislative protection and trade to Europe', *TRAFFIC Bulletin* 12(3), 41–48.

Hayman, G. and Brack, D. 2002. *International Environmental Crime: The Nature and Control of Black Markets*. London: Royal Institute of International Affairs.

Healy, J. 2013. *Threatened Species*. Thirroul: The Spinney Press.

Herbig, J. 2010. 'The illegal reptile trade as a form of conservation crime: A South African criminological investigation', in *Global Environmental Harm: Criminological Perspectives*, edited by R. White. Devon: Willan Publishing, 110–131.

Herrera, M. and Hennessey, B. 2007. 'Quantifying the illegal trade in Santa Cruz de la Sierra, Bolivia, with emphasis on threatened species', *Bird Conservation International* 17(4), 295–300.

IUCN. 2000. *Trade Measures in Multilateral Environmental Agreements*. Gland, IUCN Report (09/11/00).

Johnson, H., South, N. and Walters, R. 2015. 'The commodification and exploitation of fresh water: Property, human rights and green criminology', *International Journal of Law, Crime and Justice* 44, 146–162.

Kaow, J. 2010. Border Security Australia Frontline S08E10 – Wildlife Trafficking (documentary).

Kleinbosch Birds. 2014. 'Major Mitchell's Cockatoo'. Available at: kleinboschbirds.co.za (accessed 10 August 2017).

Lowther, J., Cook, D. and Roberts, M. 2002. *Crime and Punishment in the Wildlife Trade*. Wolverhampton: University of Wolverhampton.

Lynch, M. and Stretesky, P. 2014. *Exploring Green Criminology: Toward a Green Criminological Approach*. Surrey, UK: Ashgate Publishing Ltd.

Lyons, J.A. and Natusch, J.D.J. 2013. 'Effects of consumer preferences for rarity on the harvest of wild populations within a species', *Ecological Economics* 93(1), 278–283.

Lyons, J.A. and Natusch, D.J.D. 2012. 'Over-stepping the quota: the trade in Sugar Gliders in West Papua, Indonesia', *TRAFFIC Bulletin* 24(1), 5–6.

Lyons, J.A. and Natusch, D.J.D. 2011. 'Wildlife laundering through breeding farms: illegal harvest, population declines and a means of regulating the trade of green pythons (Morelia viridis) from Indonesia', *Biological Conservation* 144(1), 3073–3081.

Lyons, J.A., Natusch, D.J.D. and Shepherd, C.R. 2013. 'The harvest of freshwater turtles (Chelidae) from Papua, Indonesia, for the international pet trade', *Oryx* 47(2), 298–302.

Mayfield, S., Carlson, I.J. and Chick, R.C. 2006. *Central Zone Abalone (Haloitis leavigata and H. rubra) Fishery*. West Beach SA: South Australian Research and Development Institute.

McShane, P.E. 1998. 'Assessing stocks of abalone (Haloitis spp.): methods and constraints', in *Proceedings of the North Pacific Symposium on Invertebrate Stock Assessment and Management*, edited by G. Jamieson and A. Campbell. Ottawa: National Research Council of Canada, 41–48.

Muller, G. 2014. 'Australian reptiles and birds targeted for illegal trade', *ABC News*, 2 March.

Natusch, D.J.D. and Lyons, J.A. 2012. 'Exploited for pets: the harvest and trade of amphibians and reptiles from Indonesian New Guinea', *Biodiversity and Conservation* 21(11), 2899–2911.

Nijman, V. and Nekaris, K.A.I. 2014. 'Trade in wildlife in Bali, Indonesia, for medicinal and decorative purposes', *TRAFFIC Bulletin* 26(1), 31–36.

Nurse, A. 2013. *Animal Harm: Perspectives on Why People Harm and Kill Animals*. Farnham: Ashgate.

Odum, E.P. 1953. *Fundamentals of Ecology*. Philadelphia: W.B. Saunders Company.

Pires, S. and Clarke, R.V. 2011. 'Are parrots CRAVED? An analysis of parrot poaching in Mexico', *Journal of Research in Crime and Delinquency* 49(1), 122–146.

Rosen, G.E. and Smith, K.F. 2010. 'Summarizing the evidence on the international trade in illegal wildlife', *Ecohealth* 7(1), 24–32.

Routh, N. 2010. *Environment Protection and Biodiversity Conservation Act 1999: Amendment of List of Exempt Native Specimens*. Commonwealth of Australia, EPBC303DC/SFS/2010/04.

Schneider, J.L. 2008. 'Reducing the illicit trade in endangered wildlife: the market reduction approach', *Journal of Contemporary Criminal Justice* 24(3), 274–295.

Sollund, R. 2013. 'Animal trafficking and trade: abuse and species injustice', in *Emerging Issues in Green Criminology: Exploring Power, Justice and Harm*, edited by D. Westerhuis, R. Walters and T. Wyatt. Basingstoke: Palgrave Macmillan, 72–92.

Sollund, R. 2011. 'Expressions of speciesism: the effects of keeping companion animals on animal abuse, animal trafficking and species decline', *Crime, Law and Social Change* 55(5), 437–451.

South, N. and Brisman, A. 2013. 'Critical green criminology, environmental rights and crimes of exploitation', in *New Directions in Crime and Deviance*, edited by S. Winlow and R. Atkinson. London: Routledge, 99–111.

South, N. and Wyatt, T. 2011. 'Comparing illicit trades in wildlife and drugs: an exploratory study', *Deviant Behavior* 32(6), 538–561.

Stephens, P.A., Sutherland, W.J. and Freckleton, R.P. 1999. 'What is the Allee Effect', *Oikos* 87(1), 185–190.

Stobart, B., Mayfield, S., Dent, J. and Matthews, D.J. 2013. *Western Zone Blacklip Abalone (Haliotis rubra) Fishery (Region A)*. West Beach: South Australian Research and Development Institute.

Stoner, S. 2014. 'Tigers: exploring he threat from illegal online trade', *TRAFFIC Bulletin* 26(1), 26–40.

Tailby, R. and Gant, F. 2009. 'The illegal market in Australian abalone', in *Environmental Crime: A Reader*, edited by R. White. Devon: Willan Publishing, 399–411.

Topsfield, J. 2016. 'Australian tip-off leads to online wildlife trafficking sting in Indonesia', *The Sydney Morning Herald*, 17 March.

TRAFFIC. 2008. *What's Driving the Wildlife Trade?* Washington, DC: World Bank.

United Nations Environment Assembly (UNEA). 2014. 'Statement by Australia During the High-Level Segment on Illegal Wildlife Trade: 26 June 2014'.

Walters, R. and Westerhuis, D. 2013. 'Green crime and the role of environmental courts', *Crime, Law and Social Change* 59(3), 279–290.

Warchol, G.L., Zupan, L. and Clarke, W. 2003. 'Transnational criminality: an analysis of the illegal wildlife market in Southern Africa', *International Criminal Justice Review* 13(1), 1–26.

Warchol, G.L. 2007. 'The transnational illegal wildlife trade', *Criminal Justice Studies* 17(1), 57–73.

Wellsmith, M. 2010. 'The applicability of crime prevention to problems of environmental harm: a consideration of illicit trade in endangered species', in *Global Environmental Harm: Criminological Perspectives*, edited by R. White. Devon: Willan Publishing, 132–149.

White, R. 2013. 'Environmental crime and problem-solving courts', *Crime, Law and Social Change* 59(3), 267–278.

Wright, T., Toft, C.A., Enkerlin-Hoeflich, E., Gonzalez-Elizondo, J., Albornoz, M., Rodríguez-Ferraro, A., Rojas-Suárez, F. *et al.* 2001. 'Nest poaching in neotropical parrots', *Conservation Biology* 15(3), 710–720.

Wyatt, T. 2009. 'Exploring the organization in Russia far east's illegal wildlife trade: two case studies of the illegal fur and illegal falcon trades', *Global Crime* 10(1–2), 144–154.

Wyatt, T. 2013. *Wildlife Trafficking: A Deconstruction of the Crime, the Victims and the Offenders*. New York: Palgrave Macmillan.

Part II

Corporations, environmental violations and the money

5 The 'Dieselgate' scandal
A criminological perspective

Toine Spapens

Introduction

In September 2015, the 'Dieselgate' scandal surprised the world. It transpired that Volkswagen (VW), a company respected for its technological prowess and quality cars, had installed software – a so-called 'defeat device' – in its turbocharged diesel engine passenger cars. The software detected emissions test situations and then automatically scaled down the settings of the engine to reduce nitrogen oxide (NO_x) levels to far below the output generated during normal use. The VW group includes Audi, Porsche, Seat and Skoda, and its cars share many components, including engines and the software that controls them. Thus, the defeat devices had been installed in at least 11 million cars worldwide.

Undoubtedly the affair is one of the major environmental crime cases that have recently come to light. In terms of harm, in the EU alone air pollution of all kinds was responsible for over 400,000 premature human deaths in 2010, not counting damage to flora and fauna (European Commission 2013). NO_x is particularly dangerous. In 2012, NO_x emissions contributed to a total of approximately 72,000 premature deaths in the EU (Gieseke and Gerbrandy 2017, p. 26).

Ironically, VW had pursued diesel technology in passenger cars not only for economic reasons, as diesel engines are more fuel efficient than petrol engines, but also to claim environmental friendliness. VW was originally founded by the Nazi regime in the 1930s to provide the German people with an affordable car – and from which would emerge the VW Beetle after the war (Rankin 2015). Notwithstanding this tainted past, the company acquired a 'progressive' image in the 1960s particularly in the USA. The Beetle was completely different in size and luxury compared to the standard American car of the time and choosing to drive one was a statement against the mainstream (Burnett 2002). The VW Bus even became a hippie icon, often painted with peace and love symbols, and for instance the legendary singer Janis Joplin owned a Porsche – then basically a more technically advanced, better looking and much faster Beetle – which was also custom painted in psychedelic colours.

Later on, in the 1990s, VW boasted that it was leading in ensuring environmental protection and social awareness. For example, the company was one of the first to draw up binding principles to protect the environment and resources in its Environmental Policy Statement of May 1995 (Kopp and Richter 2006, p. 204). In the 2000s many American customers who bought a VW-diesel car did so because it emitted less CO_2 and thus helped to lessen global warming. However, they were not aware of their cars' excess emissions of NO_x.

Recently the Dieselgate scandal has been analysed from, for instance, health, business ethics and corporate governance perspectives (Krall and Peng 2015; Bovens 2016; Rhodes 2016; Siano *et al.* 2016). Here I will look at the affair from a criminological viewpoint. After a brief sketch of a general framework of analysis in the next section, I will summarise events in the third section. Subsequently, I will analyse the case from three different perspectives: the behaviour of the CEO's who headed VW since the 1990s; company characteristics and state-corporate crime. Finally, the last section offers a brief conclusion regarding the financial impact of the affair.

The chapter is based on a literature review and official reports, biographies and media publications. Because of the complexity of the case, and restrictions of space, I will mainly focus on the affair itself and not compare it to findings of studies of other major corporate crime cases within the automotive industry or in other sectors.

Framework of analysis

In this chapter, I adopt a theoretical framework developed by Vaughan (2007), who seeks explanations for corporate crime at the individual, organisational and systemic levels and, more importantly, in how these interact.

To begin with, we may scrutinise the personal characteristics of those responsible for the wrongdoing. In this chapter, I limit myself to looking at VW's CEOs. It was of course not possible to diagnose them, and thus the description is limited to their visible behaviour. In the VW case, hurting the company was clearly not the objective of those involved, despite the consequences. Whether the defeat devices were developed by rogue engineers or ordered by the company executives is still unclear. However, the role of top managers is considered highly important in explaining corporate crime. After all, their decisions and behaviour may have substantial influence on corporate culture; the people at the top set an example and the people below them follow. Case examples show that corporate deviance is often supported by the senior management and that decisions on malpractice were taken at the highest corporate levels (Punch 1996, p. 57; Clinard and Yeager 1980). Research into the relationship between executives' personalities and fraud has been scarce (Rijsenbilt and Commandeur 2013).

At the personal level Punch (1996), for example, points at aspects of depersonalisation, in other words to what extent managers within corporations may feel cut off from the consequences of their actions ('win at all costs') and at the way in which they are able to neutralise the harm or negative impact of particular actions. Burke (2012) points at the fact that in many corporate crime cases, the perpetrators had huge egos. Rijsenbilt and Commandeur (2013) for example found a positive relation between CEO narcissism and fraud.

From a rational perspective, we may assume that CEOs who put high pressure on their staff and set almost impossible goals may invoke rule breaking. Generally, the feeble and the soft hearted do not survive long in this environment. It may urge personnel to cut corners if complying with regulatory requirements means not being able to reach targets, especially when top managers tend to break a rule or two themselves, or (give the impression) that they approve of such behaviour. Furthermore, over-demanding managers often define business in terms of combat and war, in which competitors are the enemy who need to be defeated. Constant pressure, feelings of stress, and the perception of being in a 'battle' can lead to 'combat fatigue', which lessens restraint in decision making (Punch 1996).

Second, explanations for corporate crime are sought at the organisational level. It is assumed that company characteristics and culture explain corporate crime. Features of a company's internal structure – economic, legal, organisational and normative – play a role in generating criminal activity within the system, independent at least to some degree from the criminal's personal motives (Apel and Paternoster 2009, p. 20). Corporate culture may be influenced by CEOs, but part of it is also in the 'DNA' of a company and difficult to change in the short run. In terms of structure, the size and complexity of organisations can produce circumstances in which oversight and control are difficult (Punch 1996). In this chapter, I will look at VW's organisational and management structure as well as its internal compliance systems.

Third, the outside world is an important element in how corporations behave. Critical criminologists have stated that capitalism itself must be taken into account when explaining corporate crime (Slapper and Tombs 1999). Some even argue that all business is inherently criminogenic (Punch 1996). If we take a less radical approach, we may look at opportunity structures and market characteristics, for instance, those shaped by the nature of the business and competitors' success or failure. Regulatory restrictions or taxes may also produce criminogenic incentives. Here, I approach the question from a state corporate crime perspective. It provides a framework for studying forms of organisational deviance created or facilitated by the intersection of political and economic institutions (Kramer and Michalowski 2006). The concept is defined as 'illegal or socially injurious actions that result from a mutually reinforcing interaction between 1) policies and/or practices in pursuit of the goals of one or more institutions of political governance and 2) policies and/or practices in pursuit of the goals of one or more institutions of economic production and distribution' (Aulette and Michalowski 1993). The question therefore is whether national governments (and the European Commission) did indeed facilitate VW's emission fraud, either by failing to draw up adequate regulations or by not enforcing them.

As mentioned above, criminogenic risk factors at these three levels interact and may be intertwined to the extent that it is difficult to attribute them to the individual, the corporation or its environment. For instance, if a CEO decides to openly take risks and bend the rules to achieve results, lower-ranking managers and staff may probably want to do the same (or find another job). Generally, macro-institutional forces outside of organisations become visible in organisational settings, and thus affect individual decisions and actions (Vaughan 2007, p. 4).

The Dieselgate case: a summary

Diesel engines and defeat devices

The impetus for the development of diesel engines for passenger cars came from rising prices for petrol since the early 1970s, a trend that was accelerated by the oil crisis of 1973. Diesel engines had the advantage of being as powerful as petrol engines, while being more fuel efficient. Diesel was also cheaper than petrol. The downside was that early diesels were noisy, did not run very comfortably, and needed to warm up before they reached full performance. In 1989, VW developed the Turbocharged Direct Injection (TDI) engine, which solved most of these problems. The engineer responsible for this new engine was Ferdinand Piëch, who then worked for the Audi division of VW (Fürweger 2011). This success would make VW a leader in diesel engine technology and help Piëch to become CEO of the VW group in 1993. He held the position until 2002 when he turned 65, but he continued as chairman of the supervisory board until 2015.

Because passenger vehicles added substantially to air pollution, especially in the inner cities, ever-stricter emissions regulations were imposed from the 1970s onwards, with the USA as a frontrunner (EPA 1971). This resulted in increasing pressure on car manufacturers to balance the costs of reducing the cars' emissions against performance and affordability. In the 1990s, rapid developments in computer technology led to engine control systems that made the cars more environmentally friendly. However, computerisation also presented opportunities for fraud, not in the least because emissions were measured in laboratory situations with a standard test cycle. This combination led to sophisticated defeat devices that 'sensed' when the vehicle was being tested – for instance because the wheels were moving but the steering stayed stationary – and made emissions remain within parameters (Kostlow 2015).

Already in the 1990s, it had become clear that car manufacturers had indeed used this type of 'smart' software to circumvent emissions regulations. In 1993 for instance, the American Environmental Protection Agency (EPA) discovered that a Cadillac emitted thrice as much carbon monoxide when they diverted from the pre-defined test cycle. In the 1990s, road-testing equipment was still too heavy for passenger cars, but it was applied for testing trucks and vans. In 1997, defeat devices were discovered in heavy truck engines, resulting in settlements with the manufacturers for 1 billion dollars (Ewing 2017, pp. 71–73). However, for the EPA testing diesel passenger cars was not a high priority because almost all vehicles in the USA ran on petrol.

In the early 2000s, VW had started to work on a new common rail type diesel engine, designated as EA189, which was to succeed the TDI. With this engine, VW hoped to increase its market share in the USA, particularly by emphasising its environmental friendliness. However, engineers were struggling with keeping emissions within limits without increasing the price of the car too much. Regarding NO_x, they could choose from three emission reduction technologies: lean NO_x traps, exhaust gas recirculation and Selective Catalytic Reduction (SCR) systems, which applied a urea based chemical substance to break down NO_x into harmless components. The more expensive car brands sometimes used all three systems simultaneously in order to meet with USA regulations. However, VW focused on the less affluent customer so for them this was not an option.

In 2002, Bernd Pischetsrieder became the new company executive. He wanted to equip the EA189 engine with a SCR-system. The technology would have to be bought from Daimler in the shape of BlueTec, because VW had not yet developed its own version (Rauwald 2017a). The decision was not received well with the company's engineers, let alone with Piëch. After all, they considered themselves the cutting edge of diesel technology and were not keen on using equipment developed by another car manufacturer (Ewing 2017). In addition, the chemical solution needed to be refilled every few months because the special tank was rather small. Installing a bigger one was not considered an option because it would 'reduce cargo space'. The issue had not been solved when Pischetsrieder's term as CEO was cut short in 2007.

Under the new boss, Martin Winterkorn, the BlueTec plan was quickly dismissed. Unfortunately, it left VW engineers with an emission problem they were unable to solve. The Audi division had installed a defeat device in their 3.0 litre common rail diesel engine that was already on the market. VW engineers accidently stumbled on it when they had examined the engine for their own design process. In November 2006, a software engineer was tasked with adopting the code for the EA189 (Ewing 2017, p. 120).

That same month the plan was presented to the people responsible for engine development and engine electronics, some 15 in total. The presentation lead to intense debate: some attendees morally objected to the device, which was clearly breaking the law, whereas others expressed fears of getting caught. In the end Rudolf Krebs, then head of motor development at VW, simply ordered the defeat device to be built, but he strongly advised not to get caught (Hummel 2016). Later on, Krebs claimed he had no recollection of the event. In any case the risks were considered to be limited, because Audi's device had already been in use for a number of years without anyone noticing.

By 2012 VW had developed its own SCR-system called BlueMotion, which also used a urea based chemical substance, trademarked as AdBlue. The system worked so well that it no longer required a defeat device. However, there was still the small-tank problem. Instead of putting in a larger tank or making it easier to refill, VW developed a second defeat device. This time it reduced the rate at which the AdBlue was consumed by simply turning off the system most of the time, but of course not in test situations.

Catching the perpetrator

Environmental experts in the EU were pondering over the fact that emission standards had been tightened for a few decades already, whereas corresponding reductions in pollution levels failed to materialise. In 2007, staff working at the European Commission asked the Joint Research Centre (JRC) – a EU organisation that carries out studies on behalf of the Commission – to measure emissions in real-life conditions. For this purpose, the JRC developed a portable device known as the Freeway Performance Measurement System (PeMS). The tests quickly revealed that NO_x emissions from diesel passenger cars were much higher under road conditions than in the laboratory. Results were published in a journal in 2008 and also brought to the attention of the European Commission (Becker 2016). Unfortunately, as will be discussed in more detail below, the Commission took no further action, and the report did not draw public attention either.

However, this was not the end of the story. A few years later Peter Mock, the European managing director of the International Council on Clean Transportation (ICCT) – an informal network of regulators – pointed out the issue to his American counterpart John German and advised him to do some testing in the USA as well. Mock specifically mentioned the emissions of the diesel VW Passat and VW Jetta (Neate 2015).

German approached West Virginia University (WVU) to carry out field tests. WVU already had experience with emissions testing of larger vehicles on the road and was therefore a logical choice. They used a version of the PeMS that the JRC had developed. WVU also cooperated closely with the California Air Resources Board (CARB), which was highly interested in the study because NO_x levels were a big problem in that state's cities. Because the ICCT could only provide limited funding, doctoral students carried out the testing with a rented BMW and a VW Jetta, and with a borrowed VW Passat of the 2012 model. The latter had the BlueMotion system whereas the Jetta was equipped with a lean NO_x trap.

Testing was done in 2012 and it transpired that the emission control systems of the BMW mostly worked, but that the VWs indeed performed awfully and even in normal driving conditions emitted up to 35 times more NO_x than regulations allowed. Curiously, both cars performed fine under lab testing conditions. Yet, the WVU researchers later said that they did not think of deliberate wrongdoing, but assumed that technical flaws in the emission control system explained their findings (Ewing 2017, pp. 166–172). The test results were reported in a paper that was published in May 2014 on the ICCT website. Once again it did not attract much attention, but this time an enforcement body had been involved that was willing to show its teeth.

Immediately after the publication, Bernd Gottweis, VW's head of product safety, wrote a memo to Winterkorn in which he warned that the CARB intended to do additional research that would inevitably reveal the defeat devices. Furthermore, he thought that VW would not be able to find a simple fix for the problem (Ewing 2017, p. 177). Later, Winterkorn denied having read the memo. In any case it failed to set off alarms.

Towards the CARB, VW chose to go into denial. When the regulators started further testing and discussed the outcomes with VW's engineers, the latter challenged the quality of the testing and came up with 'alternative facts', but failed to satisfy the regulators (Ewing 2017, p. 182). To show goodwill, VW recalled the diesel cars for a software update that was to solve the problem. It did indeed reduce emissions somewhat, but far from enough, and the update left the defeat device intact. In June 2015, the regulators put some updated VWs through non-standard test cycles, which showed that the fix had not solved the problem.

The CARB now had had enough and demanded the software code for inspection, including the engine software of earlier models, threatening that it would refuse to approve the new 2016 VWs for California. VW finally woke up and hired a Washington DC law firm to explore the company's options and the possible legal and financial consequences of getting caught. The lawyers thought that it would cost VW a maximum of around 100 million dollars, which did not seem too bad. However, they had based their estimate on the treatment of firms that had chosen to cooperate with the authorities from the moment they had started to ask questions. So far, VW had done nothing of the kind (Ewing 2017, pp. 195–197). Finally, in August 2015 the head of VW's Environmental and Engineering office admitted to the head of the CARB that the company had used defeat devices. Logically they were furious about VW's deliberate obstructions.

The affair hits the headlines

On 18 September 2015, the EPA held a press conference that broke the story to the public. It caused an outcry, not in the least with people who had bought a VW for environmental reasons. Winterkorn stated that he was shocked by the events and claimed that he never knew about the defeat devices. However, as the responsible chief executive he saw no other option than to resign, doing so five days later (Farrell and Ruddick 2015).

In the USA, legal and financial consequences of corporate crime may be massive. For instance, CEOs run the risk of being sentenced to lengthy prison terms, even though in practice these are seldom imposed. Fines may add up to billions of dollars. More importantly, victims may start class action lawsuits and the American courts are notorious for awarding huge sums in damage compensation. And there was a lot of damage, for instance with car owners who saw the value of their vehicles drop substantially; car dealers who were left with stock they were unable to sell, at least not at the original price; and competitors who claimed that VW had held an unfair advantage over them for years. A first settlement was reached in June 2016 and amounted to a maximum of 14.7 billion dollars. Apart from fines, the biggest part of this sum was reserved for buying back cars from owners at a fixed price, but costs would of course be less if they decided to keep their cars. In January 2017, the company also settled for 4.3 billion dollars with the U.S. Justice Department. At the time of writing eight persons have been charged with criminal offences. This was only the beginning, because further cases are pending in the USA and in other parts of the world. I will limit the remainder of this summary to events in the EU.

The situation in the EU

Not surprisingly, the affair also caused uproar in Europe, but the legal and financial consequences of Dieselgate are less likely to be as serious as in the USA. First, the company faces lower potential criminal penalties and financial compensations in most of the Member States, and second, EU emissions regulations contained a massive loophole, which will make it more difficult to prove criminal intent.

In the EU, emission standards are set in Regulation (EC) No 715/2007 and its annexes.[1] In the Union, such a Regulation is directly enforceable as law. However, the Member States remain responsible for setting adequate penalties and for enforcement. Of course, this creates differences and in many countries maximum (financial) penalties are low. For example, in the Netherlands violating environmental regulations qualifies as an economic offence for which the maximum fine is 1 million euro. Although for natural persons a maximum prison term of six years applies, corporate environmental criminals are rarely sent to jail. In a number of Member States VW now faces proceedings for violating administrative and/or criminal laws, for instance in France, Italy, Germany, Switzerland, Spain, the Netherlands, the Czech Republic and Romania. Particularly in Germany, the authorities hit hard on VW as well as on Audi. So far, they have indicted 47 persons in different cases (including double entries) (Riering 2017). At the time of writing all are still under investigation or pending in court.

However, customer response in the EU at first seemed less aggressive than in the USA. A first explanation might be that Europeans prefer diesel more for economical than for environmental reasons, and it quickly became clear that almost all diesel cars were just as 'dirty' as the VWs, which in fact caused even less pollution than most other brands (Poelert 2015; Archer 2016). Second, already in October 2015 VW had recalled cars for a fix, which may have helped to restore trust, although some drivers complained the changes seriously affected their car's performance and safety (Brignall 2017). Finally, in Europe, going to court with damage claims will not result in compensations anywhere near to what is awarded in the USA, and most EU Member States do not allow class action lawsuits. The United Kingdom is one of the exceptions and by March 2017, 35,000 car owners had already joined in a case against VW (Laville 2017).

Apart from this, investigators (and lawyers) in the EU face a more complex situation, because the EU Regulation leaves a lot of room for defeat devices. It does forbid their use in normal driving circumstances, but it allows defeat devices for engine protection. Both terms are not defined. Accordingly, most car manufacturers have a rather broad definition of situations that require avoiding

---

1   Official Journal of the European Union, L171/1, 29.6.2007.

damage to the engine. Cold weather is for instance an important reason for tuning down emission control systems, but for some cars 'thermal protection' is apparently needed in temperatures up to 17 degrees Celsius (Archer 2016, p. 23) – in other words, during most of the year in North-Western European climates. The 'dirtiest' diesel cars manufactured by over 20 different companies all used this escape route to exceed emissions standards (Archer 2016, pp. 11–14).

The European Parliament's Commission of Enquiry

In the European Parliament (EP) focus was on the regulators and the question why they had obviously failed to do their jobs. In March 2016, the EP installed a Commission of Enquiry (CoE) to find out. When the CoE presented its report in March 2017, the findings were devastating (Gieseke and Gerbrandy 2017). According to the CoE 'the [European] Commission lacked the political will and decisiveness to act upon the seriousness of the high NO_x emissions and to give priority to the protection of public health that was at stake' (Gieseke and Gerbrandy 2017, p. 6). The CoE concluded that the Commission's non-actions amounted to maladministration on several counts, for instance because it had ignored the JRC study that had pointed at 'strange' emission behaviour already in 2008. Individual Member States were also lectured for sloppy enforcement and for the fact that most of them had not adopted 'an effective, proportionate and dissuasive penalty system, notably in relation to the illegal use of defeat devices'.

In January 2016, the European Commission had already drafted a proposal for a 'Regulation on the approval and market surveillance of motor vehicles, Real Driving Emissions (RDE) testing and other relevant regulatory developments', which was approved in May 2017.[2] Regulations now require the manufacturer to allow access to the car's software protocols. Combined with RDE testing, this is believed to make it very difficult to circumvent emission requirements.

The proposal also included a range of other measures, not in the least enabling the Commission to impose penalties on car manufacturers and technical services of up to 30,000 euros per vehicle. Cars that were already on the market would be re-tested periodically. In the Netherlands for instance, road tests conducted in 2016 revealed that 13 out of 23 cars that had been certified there did not comply with emission standards, but only Suzuki and Jeep were suspected of using unlawful defeat devices (van der Aa and Nieuwenhuizen 2017).

Yet, far more trouble for German car manufacturers may be on the way. In July 2017, *Der Spiegel* wrote that Volkswagen, BMW, Daimler, Porsche and Audi had been involved in large-scale illegal price-fixing since the 1990s (Domen and Hawranek 2017). Allegedly about 200 staff of the companies had been directly involved. The cartel included cost-sharing, technologies, business strategies and emissions. According to *Der Spiegel* it had also been one of the important factors

---

2   COM (2016) 31 final, Brussels, 27.1.2016.

that led to the emissions fraud scheme. For example, the fact that VW did not want to install a bigger tank for the AdBlue had had nothing to do with 'cargo space' but everything with an agreement between the companies on its size, allegedly to keep the price down. If this and other allegations prove to be true, it will be the biggest corporate fraud case that has ever come to light in Germany. Because the EU is hitting hard on cartels, the German automakers could face fines in the billions and in the USA, class action lawsuits are already in preparation. So far, the companies have not commented on the allegations, although BMW did claim that agreements on the AdBlue tank had been necessary to allow development of a standardised refilling system, but had had nothing to do with emissions (Manager Magazin 2017).

The role of VW's top management

The rest of this chapter focuses on explanations for the Dieselgate scandal. VW's own assessment of the causes of the affair was that these were the misconduct and shortcomings of individual employees; weaknesses in some processes and a mindset in some areas of the company that tolerated breaches of rules (Crête 2016, p. 19). This section starts with looking at the role of VW's top managers. Three risk factors are discussed here: imposing high pressure on personnel; promoting taking risks and bending rules and chief executives with huge egos.

Imposing high pressure on personnel

Obviously, Piëch and Winterkorn were notorious for putting high pressure on VW's lower managers and engineers (although Piëch was more sentimental towards the factory workers who often stayed with VW from one generation to another). Both CEOs are described as 'a nightmare for their underlings' by being overly demanding and micro-managing the tiniest details. Under Piëch's and Winterkorn's rule, the price of failure was dismissal or demotion (Milne 2015). In addition, both Piëch and Winterkorn were known for intimidating behaviour and for leaving other managers in constant uncertainty about their jobs. Piëch for instance sometimes attended meetings without saying a word, which left other attendees in total confusion (Ewing 2017, p. 91). During business trips, senior managers who annoyed him received a ticket for a flight home in their hotel rooms without any explanation. One VW senior manager said: 'he is completely insane and utterly unreliable' (Hoeks 2015). Nevertheless, the same person also stated that he was 'very happy to have him around'. Winterkorn would express himself loudly, yelling at anything that displeased him and he was also physically intimidating. Every Tuesday top VW managers were gathered in Wolfsburg and received relentless criticism from Winterkorn in front of their peers. Managers who were favourites one week could fall from grace the next. Sometimes they had to read in the media about being demoted or even dismissed (Ewing 2017, p. 157).

Taking risks and bending the rules

A second risk factor is the framing of top managers in terms of winners, champions, peak-performers and risk-takers whose gambles paid off (Punch 1996). Although VW had a code of conduct stating that employees had to follow local and international rules, regulations and treaties top managers themselves clearly did not live up to these standards and did not set much of an example.

Here, Piëch seems to qualify more than Winterkorn. To begin with Piëch broke internal rules when he worked at Audi, where he actually developed the TDI engine behind the back of his superiors, assuming they would not approve of what he was doing. More seriously were two major scandals that happened under Piëch's watch: the López affair, which was one of the biggest examples of corporate espionage of the past decades, and the labour leader scandal.

In the 1980s, López, a Spanish national, was the star purchasing manager of General Motors (GM), a big competitor of VW. In 1993, Piëch managed to persuade him to step over to VW. However, López also took along seven members of his team and, allegedly, boxes full of highly sensitive company information (Kurylko and Crate 2006). GM was infuriated and filed lawsuits in the USA and Germany against López, Piëch and Volkswagen for corporate espionage. Piëch responded by stating that Volkswagen was 'at war' with GM 'in which anything was permitted'. Even the German Minister of Economic Affairs intervened, and urged both companies to exercise restraint and to refrain from phrases such as war, battle and slaughter (Punch 1996, p. 30). GM sought as much as 4 billion dollars in damages, but VW eventually settled in 1997 for 100 million dollars. In Germany, the criminal case against López was dropped, and in the USA, it ground to a halt because Spain refused extradition. Piëch himself was never put on trial.

In 2005, the labour leader scandal hit the headlines. The core of the affair was that during Piëch's days as CEO VW had maintained a secret fund to pay for bordello visits and prostitutes for union officials. Moreover, the head of VW's *Betriebsrat* (worker's council) had received large special bonuses and his Brazilian mistress was given a job at the company that paid her over 400,000 euros a year (Spiegelonline 2011). The affair was apparently explained by the fact that in Germany worker's councils are powerful bodies, and workers also hold half of the seats in companies' supervisory board (see below).

Company executives with huge egos

Many individuals implicated in major fraud cases have huge egos and seem almost larger than life (Burke 2011, p. 28). Indeed, VW's top managers were treated as 'gods' with staff for instance exiting elevators to make way for top brass, and lunches in the executive dining room delivered under gleaming silver domes (Rauwald and Reiter 2016). Again, Piëch in particular treated VW as his personal possession. As a member of the Porsche family he indeed was the co-owner of the company, even if he had started out as a modest engineer.

'For Piëch what is important is power, not money' according to a former senior executive (Milne 2015). Already being a millionaire by heritage, he could afford to take career chances that people with mortgages might not dare (Ewing 2017, p. 40). An indication of his huge ego was how he explained why he had 12 children – with four different wives. He claimed that it would improve the chance that his 'unique qualities' be transferred to future generations (Hoeks 2015).

Although VW's strength lay in affordable mid-ranged cars, Piëch personally preferred more expensive vehicles. It allegedly inspired him in 1998 to acquire Bentley, Lamborghini and Bugatti, three companies that made cars on the extreme end of luxury and/or performance, but only at modest profits. He also personally initiated the development of the VW Phaeton – which was also a pet project of Winterkorn – which was to compete with the more expensive Mercedes and BMW models, and also with Audi. It turned out to be a commercial disaster (Cremer 2015). The target group simply did not want to be seen in a VW, no matter how technically advanced it was. According to some, with the Phaeton Piëch finally crossed the line between genius and megalomania (Ewing 2017, p. 89). However, as long as VW continued to grow and create jobs there was no threat to his dominance.

Company characteristics

The next question is whether VW's company characteristics may help to explain the scandal. Looking at how the organisation developed, it is clear that it grew very rapidly from a rather provincial car maker that until the second half of the 1960s had a catalogue of some five models, to a genuine multinational including seven different brands and offering tens of car models. And although Piëch and Winterkorn were extreme examples, they were also the product of a company culture that had existed for a long time and that proved hard to break.

VW's centralised organisational structure and 'engineering culture'

Soon after the war VW was back in business. The first post-war CEO was Heinrich Nordhoff, who stayed in office from 1948 to 1967. He was the driving force behind the success of the Beetle. Nordhoff introduced a traditional command and control management model and organised the company in an almost military style (Ewing 2017, p. 59). Being an engineer, he focused on engineering. VW even had its own 'politburo', the Product Strategy Committee, which lorded over every aspect of development and settled disputes between financial, sales and engineering teams, usually in favour of the latter (Rauwald and Reiter 2016).

Any CEO that was to follow would primarily be respected for succeeding in technical innovation. Piëch for instance earned his kudos for developing the TDI. Kurt Lotz, who succeeded Nordhoff in 1971, was credited for introducing the successful new model of the VW Golf, and the technology of a water-cooled front-mounted engine and traction. Its engineering focus is also visible in VW's spending on research and development, amounting to 13.1 billion euros in 2014, which was more than any other car-manufacturer invested in R&D (*The Economist* 2015). VW was basically controlled by a small cadre of executives whose background was in engineering with ties going back decades (Ewing 2017, p. 216).

By contrast, managers who tried to modernise VW's organisational structure and management style fared less well, particularly if they were 'outsiders'. The first example was Carl Hahn, who became CEO in 1982. Although a child of the company, he was a cosmopolitan with vast international experience, including a term as head of VW North America. He was a consensus builder and favoured a more diplomatic management style (Meiners 2006). Under Hahn VW expanded into a global player and opened factories in China, Spain, Portugal and, after the fall of the Iron Curtain, in former Eastern Germany, the Czech Republic, Slovakia, Poland and Hungary. In 1986 VW acquired Seat, and in 1990 Skoda. Hahn understood that these developments also called for a change in the company's organisation and management style. Whether he gained much progress is unclear, but in any case, whatever he did achieve would be quickly reversed by his successor, Piëch.

Another top manager who tried to change VW was Pischetsrieder. He had joined VW only in 1999 and when he became CEO in 2002, he set about promoting that employees take more responsibility and initiative. The labour leader scandal further convinced him that VW's management culture needed to be changed. Pischetsrieder for instance installed ombudsmen to whom employees could report corruption on a confidential basis (Kopp and Richter 2007). However, as a CEO he did not last long, because he came into conflict with the workforce representatives after he announced plans to cut down on labour costs, and was forced to leave VW in 2007 (Dalan and Seidlitz 2006). His successor was Winterkorn, and once again it was back to the old ways of doing things.

It is difficult to assess whether a centralised command and control corporate culture is a criminogenic risk factor per se, because in a decentralised setting compliance may also be difficult to manage. In the case of VW, however, it was clear that leaving almost all decision power in the hands of just a few Primadonnas had contributed to Dieselgate and earlier scandals. The next CEO Müller started to shift decision-making away from Wolfsburg (Rauwald 2017b). In addition, VW wanted its board of directors to become more international and diverse. However, the *Vorstand* is still dominated by middle-aged engineers who were all born in Germany, except for one (Rauwald 2017b). There is also only a single female on the board. Her predecessor, also a woman, quit after only a year (Der Spiegel 2017). Apparently, it is still difficult for outsiders to find their way and changing the company's management culture is obviously a long-term process.

Composition of the supervisory board

Both Piëch and Winterkorn were insatiable in striving for growth (*The Economist* 2015). Although their desire for size was probably to a large extent caused by personal ambitions, it was also related to a combination of two organisational characteristics. One was the large workforce and low productivity rate and the other the fact that the workers and the State of Lower Saxony had a majority in the supervisory board and would halt any attempts at reducing labour costs by cutting jobs. The power of the workers also helps to understand the labour leader scandal. Piëch always did his utmost to accommodate the worker representatives, because they were an important source of his own power (Ewing 2017, p. 45). Perhaps VW's management simply went a bit too far in its efforts to keep relationships cosy (*The Economist* 2005).

A central tenet of Rhineland capitalism is a cooperative relationship between workers and management. This is expressed for instance in the fact that workers hold half the seats in supervisory boards. Furthermore, at VW the State of Lower Saxony owned 20 per cent of the shares that gave it two seats. This lead to the peculiar situation that the two parties combined could veto any major decision. When it came to guaranteeing employment, they typically voted together (Jung and Park 2017).

This had serious consequences for the company, because it was notably overstaffed. VW employed about 80 per cent more people than Toyota to produce roughly the same number of vehicles (Rauwald and Reiter 2016). This seriously affected profitability. In 2015, the profit margin on every VW that left the dealer was only 2 per cent (*The Economist* 2015). There were two options to increase the productivity rate: cutting jobs or increasing sales without expanding the workforce. Piëch and Winterkorn chose the second strategy, whereas Pischetsrieder found his Waterloo opting for the first. It helps to explain why VW had to keep expanding, and why some corners had to be cut in the process. Only after the scandal became public did the *Betriebsrat* finally accept that cutting jobs was inevitable and agreed to a reduction of 30,000 people by 2020, which would cut costs by 3.7 billion euros (Rauwald and Reiter 2016).

Internal compliance systems

VW was obviously ill equipped to cope with stricter regulations in the field of safety and emissions that increasingly confronted the auto industry. Regulatory pressure ever more called for setting corporate standards and internal compliance systems. However, in this respect the company lagged behind competitors (Ewing 2017, p. 64). Either VW's compliance systems failed to prevent lower ranking staff from breaking the rules, or were unable to rein in top executives.

Over the years VW had seen various cases in which employees had been able to violate internal and external regulations without anyone noticing. At least, that is what the top management claimed even though affairs had the scent of their (quiet) approval. For example, in the labour leader scandal low-ranking managers had apparently been able to set up a secret fund and spend millions of euros without anyone noticing; at least Piëch vehemently denied that he had known about it. In the Dieselgate affair top managers too consequently denied any wrongdoing and Winterkorn dismissed knowing about the defeat devices

(Matussek and Rauwald 2017). An internal investigation carried out by a law firm concluded that the entire scheme had been the work of individual employees. Nine, including the head of quality control, were suspended (Ewing 2017, p. 223).

Of course, theoretically this line of events could be plausible. It had happened before that engineers developed new technology behind the backs of their superiors. Piëch himself had done it when designing the TDI. Furthermore, the software programming of the first VW defeat device was ordered by the head of motor development at the end of 2006, and not by chief executive Pischetsrieder, although this does not rule out his consent.

However, most observers find it hard to believe that lower level managers and staff had been solely responsible for the cheat. Winterkorn habitually interfered in even the smallest design issues, and although engine software might not have been as 'sexy' to him as a visible part of the car, it is difficult to accept that he did not oversee what his staff was cooking up in order to 'comply' with something as important as environmental regulations (Matussek and Rauwald 2017). Certainly, attorney general Eric Schneiderman, who is prosecuting VW in the State of New York did not believe Winterkorn had been ignorant (Neate 2016). In any case he could and should have known about the defeat devices after Bernd Gottweis had handed in his memo in May 2014, and even after that he had done nothing to promote that VW come clean with the CARB, for example.

The State-corporate crime perspective

From a state-corporate crime perspective, the all-important question in the Dieselgate case is why it took so long before the fraud was discovered. Did governments and the EU indeed facilitate the defeat devices? Here I will look at two issues: whether VW's economic power and political clout helped to influence regulations and to what extent it explains the apparent lack of enforcement that occurred in the EU.

Economic power and political clout

Economic power generates political influence, and this certainly helps a company that wants to resist tighter regulations (Punch 1996). Volkswagen was the world's 14th largest corporation at the end of 2014 and if it had been a nation state it would have a bigger GDP than countries such as Finland, Chile, Pakistan or Ireland (Rhodes 2016). Clearly, the auto industry is of huge importance in Germany, but also in the EU in general. The EU automotive industry directly employs around 3 million people in manufacturing jobs and another 9 million in related jobs. In Germany, it is the biggest industry sector and in 2015 around 792,500 people were working in car manufacturing alone (GTAI 2016). Furthermore, cars are the country's biggest export product. It is no surprise that this ensured having the ear of the highest government levels and via them of the EU's Commissioners.

The car manufacturers' influence on regulations was visible in the debate on the testing of emissions in the EU. Already in 2007 it was clear that the standard laboratory emission test was completely inadequate because, apart from being predictable, it asked so little of the engine that defeat devices were not even necessary to pass the test. The European Commission had been tasked with developing real driving emission testing (RDE) to replace it. However, the process took eight years and even then, temporary so-called conformity factors (exemptions) had been included, which allowed car makers to exceed emission norms by up to double the standards until 2021.

The CoE was extremely critical about how the European Commission had managed the working group that had been responsible for making the changes as well as to how the Member States had operated in it. To begin with, next to civil servants from the Member States, over half of the working group consisted of experts from the car industry (Gieseke and Gerbrandy 2017, p. 6). Usually, the role of 'industry representatives' in such meetings is restricted to the status of observers. This does not mean that they need to keep silent, but they are not allowed to take part in debates among government representatives. In this case, they were apparently not bound by such protocol and constantly delayed the work by re-opening topics that were considered clarified or even decided upon (Gieseke and Gerbrandy 2017, pp. 6–8). This may perhaps have also been caused by the fact that just six Member States participated actively in the discussions, although others did voice criticisms of the Commission's proposals.

Some of the Member States favoured less stringent testing methods and no less than 11 – but not including Germany (!) – objected to relatively strict conformity factors proposed by the Commission and voted for less stringent measures (Gieseke and Gerbrandy 2017, p. 7). However, the Germans had been busy to guard their car industry's interests in a more covert way. When it became clear to 'Berlin' that stopping RDE testing was a no-go, they had started to advocate conformity factors that temporarily allowed to exceed norms up to a certain level. The German government had already struck a deal with the Commission on a figure of 1.4 when just a day before the decision was to become final, the German Association of the Automotive Industry (VDA) protested. The VDA wanted the factor to be set between 2.5 and 3.0. At the last minute Prime Minister Angela Merkel herself renegotiated with the Commission's President Jean-Claude Juncker, and the conformity factor was set at 2.1 (Gude *et al.* 2015).

The Commission's behaviour may not have come as a surprise when we take into account that already in 2008 it had received the JRC-report that revealed the emissions problem. However, even in 2016 the Commission continued to deny it had known about illegal practices. According to a spokesperson 'no concrete evidence on the use of defeat devices or of the failure of a Member State to act was ever brought to the attention of the Commission' (Becker 2016). Technically this was not a lie, because the JRC-report was not the result of criminal investigation or court ruling, but the Commission could not deny that it had received strong indications that something was wrong.

According to documents obtained by *Der Spiegel*, a memo was circulated at the Commission in 2010 stating that the discrepancy between laboratory and road tests was caused by 'an extended use of certain abatement technologies in diesel vehicles' (Becker 2016). In the summer of 2012, the Commissioner for Enterprise and Industry was informed – both by letter and in a personal meeting – about software manipulations being undertaken by automobile manufacturers, when a parts supplier of VW blew the whistle. In 2014, the issue even led to an argument within the Commission when the head of DG Environment sent a letter to his counterpart at DG Enterprise and Industry demanding him to do his job (Becker 2016). The documents contain repeated references to the exertion of influence on the Commission, including by the automotive industry.

Apart from the Commission, individual Member States were also well aware of possible emissions manipulation long before the VW scandal hit the headlines. *Der Spiegel's* documents show that the issue had been discussed for years between the Commission and Member State governments (Becker 2016). The conclusion of the CoE was clear: 'The delays were also due to choices of political priorities, lobby influence and constant pressure from the industry that directed the focus of the Commission and the Member States to avoiding burdens on industry in the aftermath of the 2008 financial crisis' (Gieseke and Gerbrandy 2017, pp. 33–34).

Lack of enforcement

Although partly intertwined with economic power, the attitude of regulators towards companies that violate regulations, particularly if corporations are 'too big to fail', can be seen as a separate problem. First line enforcement of environmental regulations is almost always the responsibility of administrative agencies. Criminal law enforcement is usually restricted to the most serious cases, often meaning that the (deadly) damaging effects of violations are immediately visible because they have resulted in major accidents, spills or other disasters.

Administrative enforcement agencies tend to 'look forward' and focus on how to prevent further violations and if possible, repair the damage that was done in the past. They are less interested in 'looking backward' and to punish for what has happened in the past. This attitude often invokes criticism from criminal law enforcement agencies as well as from the general public, because it creates the impression of being overly lenient, or even outright corrupt (Spapens 2012). In the case of VW too, inspectors clearly had no interest in destroying the industry and relationships were cordial (Ewing 2017, p. 68).

A specific problem in the context of enforcement of emission standards was how the approval procedure for new models was organised in the EU. A car manufacturer could until the recent modification of the Regulation, apply for approval in any Member State, and if it was granted the permit was, because of the principle of mutual recognition, valid for the entire EU (Gude *et al.* 2015). This enabled car manufacturers to shop and apply for certification in countries that were not too critical. In Germany, the Federal Motor Transport Authority had a reputation for this, particularly with its own car industry. An example was the immediate approval of the simple software fix VW offered to its customers directly after the scandal became public. Perhaps they should have done more serious testing, since the fix allegedly also seriously affected the cars' performance, and some customers complained that the engine had stalled without warning, causing dangerous situations (Brignall 2017).

At VW, lack of enforcement may have created the impression that they would be able to get away with the fraud, and if not, that consequences would be limited. According to some, VW has a legacy as a quasi-state entity that has long steamrolled regulators (Smith and Parloff 2016). Indeed, a large corporation has the means to hire the most expensive law firms and thereby often manages to avoid convictions, whereas the costs of financial settlements may be passed on to the customers, or may even be tax deductible (Spapens 2012). Most certainly, VW's trickery had not been a total secret, not for its competitors and parts suppliers, and not for the EU countries' environmental ministries and EU institutions. If the latter had done their job, VW would have been exposed for cheating as early as 2008.

Concluding remarks

This chapter has demonstrated how a combination of characteristics from persons, the organisation and its environment created the Dieselgate scandal. With regard to the latter we must even look beyond VW, because other car manufacturers clearly enjoyed similar 'privileges'. If the company had not been such a powerful economic entity, the affair would probably have been stopped in its tracks within a year after the first defeat device was developed. If the car industry as such would not have been so important, non-standard emission testing and RDE-testing could have been introduced much earlier, and might have even prevented the entire affair. We can conclude that the wrongdoing was indeed state facilitated. In this respect, it is telling that even Angela Merkel considered it *Chefsache* to defend the German car industry against regulatory requirements aimed at reducing the number of premature deaths in the EU. This also helps us to understand why Dieselgate was exposed in the USA, because in that country VW had far less political influence, although there too Merkel personally complained a few times about emission standards being too tight.

Because other car manufacturers cheated too, it is more difficult to point at specific characteristics of the CEOs and the organisation to explain what happened. It would require a comparative study of companies to gain more insight. Some observations, however, can be made. Internally, Piëch and Winterkorn may have been bullies who set goals that were (almost) impossible to achieve, perhaps because they simply wanted to be the biggest in the business, but their behaviour is to some extent also explained by the unique composition of VW's board of supervisors. However, they could have taken another route: the centralised structure and command and control culture, as well as the inadequate internal compliance systems may have been difficult to break, but it would not have been impossible if it had been done consequently. Now, CEOs who tried to change VW's organisation and culture, were succeeded by company executives who quickly undid whatever was achieved.

Finally, a few words must be said about the financial impact of the scandal. Clearly, VW took a huge financial risk when it applied the defeat devices. By June 2017 the scandal had already cost the company 22.6 billion euros in fines, repairs and other penalties (Rauwald 2017b). And this is by far not the end, as lawsuits are still pending. However, VW's liquidity position was and is excellent and the company has so far not been threatened by bankruptcy.

The main effect on VW was the need to cut costs in order to cope with the financial consequences of Dieselgate. This did in fact increase the company's profitability. In 2016, VW also finally surpassed Toyota as the world's biggest automaker. On the downside, sales in the USA increased only less than 1 per cent and in Europe they even dropped by 4 per cent. Growth depended mainly on China, which is now VW's biggest market. Surprisingly, in 2016 the number of employees also increased, even when plans for reducing the size of the workforce had already been agreed upon.

However, prospects in the longer term are highly uncertain, not in the least because the storm clouds of a potentially much more harmful affair – the car industry cartel – are building. More interestingly, the Dieselgate scandal has started affecting the entire car industry, instead of just VW. In the USA and the EU, customers are clearly turning away from diesel (Jung and Park 2017). In 2016, the share of diesel cars sold in Germany decreased from 47 to 43 per cent and is expected to continue to drop. The trend may accelerate because cities in different EU countries are preparing a total ban on diesel cars. Furthermore, the affair, combined with the Paris agreement on climate change, has accelerated the speed at which countries plan to make a full transition to electric cars. France and the UK announced a ban on the sale of new petrol and diesel cars by 2040, and a total ban by 2050. Norway, a major oil producer by the way, wants to make the transition by 2025. Some expect that market developments may outpace the regulators and electric cars will be the norm much sooner than the deadline set in France and the UK, for instance.

In 2016, VW, in its future vision, announced it would focus on electric cars, albeit without disregarding its core business of building petrol and diesel cars (Tovey 2016). However, VW started to invest in research and development of electric cars only recently and clearly runs behind its competitors. Time will tell if VW's engineers will be able to make up the difference.

References

Aa, van der, E. and Nieuwenhuis, M. 2017. 'Ook Suzuki haalde trucjes uit met sjoemelsoftware', *Brabants Dagblad*, 11 July.

Apel, R. and Paternoster, R. 2009. 'Understanding 'criminogenic' corporate culture: what white-collar crime researchers can learn from studies of the adolescent employment – crime relationship', in *The Criminology of White-Collar Crime*, edited by S. Simpson and D. Weisburd. New York: Springer, 15–33.

Archer, G. 2016. *Dieselgate: Who? What? How?* Transport and Environment.

Aulette, J. and Michalowski, R. 1993. 'Fire in Hamlet: A case study of state-corporate crime', in *Political Crime in Contemporary America*, edited by K. Tunnell. New York: Garland, 171–206.

Becker, M. 2016. 'EU Commission has known for years about manipulation', *Spiegel online*, 15 July.

Bovens, L. 2016. 'The ethics of Dieselgate', *Midwest Studies in Philosophy* XL, 262–283.

Brignall, M. 2017. 'Up in smoke: the VW emissions 'fix' has left our car undriveable', *The Guardian*, 25 March.

Burke, R. 2011. 'Crime and corruption in organizations', in *Crime and Corruption in Organizations: Why It Occurs and What To Do About It*, edited by R. Burke, E. Tomlinson and C. Cooper. Farnham: Gower Publishing Ltd., 3–65.

Burnett, D. 2002. *From Hitler to Hippies: The Volkswagen Bus in America*. The University of Texas at Austin, Master thesis.

Clinard, M. and Yeager, P. 1980. *Corporate Crime*. New York: Free Press.

Cremer, A. 2015. 'VW refuses to give up on failed $1 billion luxury car', *Businessinsider.com*, 28 January.

Crête, R. 2016. 'The Volkswagen scandal from the viewpoint of corporate governance', *The European Journal of Risk Regulation* 1, 25–31.

Dalan, M. and Seidlitz, F. 2006. 'Die wundersame Welt von Wolfsburg', *Die Welt*, 12 November.

Der Spiegel 2017. 'Einzige Frau verlässt VW-Vorstand', 26 January.

Domen, F. and Hawranek, D. 2017. 'Das geheime Kartell der deutschen Autobauer', *Der Spiegel*, 21 July.

The Economist 2005. 'Together they stand. Germany's "co-determination" rules should go', 14 July.

European Commission 2013. *Commission Staff Working Document. Executive Summary of the Impact Assessment.* SWD 2013 532 final. Brussels.

Ewing, J. 2017. *Faster, Higher, Farther. The Inside Story of the Volkswagen Scandal.* London: Transworld Publishers.

Farrell, S. and Ruddick, G. 2015. 'Volkswagen CEO Martin Winterkorn quits over diesel emissions scandal', *The Guardian*, 23 September.

Fürweger, W. 2011. *Ferdinand Piëch: Der Automanager des Jahrhunderts.* Vienna: Ueberreuter.

Gieseke, J. and Gerbrandy, G-J. 2017. *Report on the inquiry into emission measurements in the automotive sector 2016/2215INI.* European Parliament, Committee of Inquiry into Emission Measurements in the Automotive Sector, A8–0049/2017.

GTAI 2016. *The Automotive Industry in Germany.* Berlin: Germany Trade and Invest Gesellschaft für Außenwirtschaft und Standortmarketing mbH.

EPA 1971. 'Hearings Set on Automobile Pollution Control', *Press release*, 4 March.

Gude, H., Hawranek, D., Traufetter, G. and Wüst, C. 2015. 'The German government's role in the VW scandal', *Spiegel online*, 6 November.

Hoeks, L. 2015. 'President Volkswagen is een genadeloos patriarch', *Financieel Dagblad*, 13 April.

Hummel, M. 2016. 'VW-Abgasskandal: Welche Mitarbeiter sind schuld?', *HNA*, 27 April.

Jung, J. and Park, S.B. 2017. 'Case study: Volkswagen's diesel emissions scandal', *Thunderbird International Business Review* 59(1), 127–137.

Kopp, R. and Richter, K. 2007. 'Corporate social responsibility at Volkswagen Group', in *Corporate Ethics and Corporate Governance*, edited by W. Zimmerli, K. Richter and M. Holzinger. Berlin/Heidelberg: Springer-Verlag, 201–210.

Kostlow, T. 2015. 'VW emissions scandal will impact future engine controls, testing', *SAE International*, 5 October.

Krall, J. and Peng, R. 2015. 'The Volkswagen scandal. Deception, driving and deaths', *Significance*, 12 December.

Kramer, R. and Michalowski 2006. 'The original formulation', in *State Corporate Crime: Wrongdoing at the Intersection of Business and Government*, edited by R. Michalowski and R. Kramer. New Brunswick NJ: Rutgers University Press, 18–26.

Kurylko, D. and Crate, J. 2006. 'The López Affair', *Automotive News Europe*, 20 February.

Laville, S. 2017. 'Thousands join UK legal case against VW over emissions scandal', *The Guardian*, 20 March.

Manager Magazin 2017. ' "5er-Runde" unter Kartellverdacht, VW ruft Krisensitzung ein', 24 July.

Matussek, K. and Rauwald, C. 2017. 'Ex-VW CEO Winterkorn deflects blame for emissions cheating', *Bloomberg*, 19 January.

Meiners, J. 2006. 'Volkswagen's Carl Hahn: An early global visionary', *Automotive News Europe*, 9 January.

Milne, R. 2015. 'Ferdinand Piëch's influence seen everywhere at Volkswagen', *Financial Times*, 19 October.

Neate, R. 2015. 'Meet John German: the man who helped expose Volkswagen's emissions scandal', *The Guardian*, 26 September.

Neate, R. 2016. 'Volkswagen sued in three US states over diesel emissions cheating', *The Guardian*, 19 July.

Poelert, E. 2015. 'Liefde voor VW blijft', *De Volkskrant*, 18 November.

Punch, M. 1996. *Dirty Business. Exploring Corporate Misconduct*. London: Sage Publishing.

Rankin, J. 2015. 'From Hitler to Herbie and hubris – how Volkswagen was brought low', *The Guardian*, 26 September.

Rauwald, C. and Reiter, C. 2016. 'At Volkswagen, engineering change in the eye of the diesel storm', *Bloomberg*, 8 December.

Rauwald, C. 2017a. 'How a top-secret deal could have stopped VW's diesel scandal', *Bloomberg*, 13 January.

Rauwald, C. 2017b. 'VW aims for greater diversity to keep cheaters in check', *Bloomberg*, 26 June.

Rhodes, C. 2016. 'Democratic business ethics: Volkswagen's emissions scandal and the disruption of corporate sovereignty', *Organization Studies* 37(10), 1501–1518.

Riering, B. 2017. 'Staatsanwaltschaft sieht erste Urteile noch in diesem Jahr', *Automobilwoche*, 1 April.

Rijsenbilt, A. and Commandeur, H. 2013. 'Narcissus enters the courtroom: CEO narcissism and fraud', *Journal of Business Ethics* 117, 413–429.

Siano, A., Vollero, A., Conte, F. and Amabile, S. 2016. 'More than words. Expanding the taxonomy of greenwashing after the Volkswagen scandal', *Journal of Business Research* 71, 27–37.

Slapper G. and Tombs, S. 1999. *Corporate Crime*. Harlow: Longman.

Smith, G. and Parloff, R. 2016. 'Hoaxwagen: Scandal will haunt VW for years', *Fortune*, March 15.

Spapens, T. 2012. *De complexiteit van milieucriminaliteit*. The Hague: Boom Lemma uitgevers.

Spiegelonline 2011. 'Ex-Betriebsratschef Volkert vorzeitig entlassen', 2 September.

The Economist, 2015. 'A mucky business. Systematic fraud by the world's biggest carmaker threatens to engulf the entire industry and possibly reshape it', *The Economist*, 26 September.

Tovey, A. 2016. 'Volkswagen bets on electric cars after 'dieselgate' scandal', *The Telegraph*, 17 June.

Vaughan, D. 2007. 'Beyond macro- and micro-levels of analysis, organizations, and the cultural fix', in *International Handbook of White-Collar and Corporate Crime*, edited by H. Pontell and G. Geis. New York: Springer, 3–24.

6 Environmental responsibility and firm value

Nadja Guenster and Jakob Koegst

Introduction

An extant empirical literature analyses the effects of environmental performance on financial performance (Horvathova 2010; Endrikat *et al.* 2014; Friede *et al.* 2015). Friede *et al.* (2015) find more than 2,000 studies, dealing with the ESG and financial performance link. The majority of these studies points towards a positive environmental–financial performance relation. Although there is a huge amount of studies on this topic, one question remains difficult to answer: what is the direction of causality between environmental performance and financial performance? It is unclear whether environmental performance increases corporate value or if higher corporate value leads to better environmental performance. The second direction of causality has its origin in the slack resource theory. Firms with a good financial performance have more available resources, which they can invest in environmental responsibility (Waddock and Graves 1997). For example, Barnea and Rubin (2010) conjecture that managers invest in CSR, because it has a warm-glow effect and improves their personal reputation. For the first direction of causality, the literature provides different arguments why environmental performance can both increase revenues and cut costs (Porter and van der Linde 1995; Klassen and McLaughlin 1996). Russo and Fouts (1997) base their argumentation on the resource-based view and state that environmental responsibility can be an intangible resource, which can increase sales among customers with ecological awareness. Porter and van der Linde (1995) argue that a higher level of environmental performance can increase firms' innovation capacity. These innovative production technologies have the ability to increase resource efficiency. Walley and Whitehead (1994) disagree with the aforementioned studies by arguing that benefits from sustainability are unlikely to outweigh the high costs of installing eco-efficient systems.

We contribute to a better understanding of the direction of causality by focusing on different components of firm value and analysing how each component is affected by the firm's environmental performance. The value of a firm can be computed as the free cash flows of the firm discounted with its financing costs. We follow this approach and split corporate value into its components profitability and financing costs. We start by investigating the environmental performance–profitability link. The literature points towards a positive relation between environmental performance and overall profitability as measured by return on assets (ROA) (Hart and Ahuja 1996; Russo and Fouts 1997; King and Lenox 2002; Guenster *et al.* 2011). Because we cannot infer the direction of causality from these regression studies, we decompose profitability into its components: revenue and cost. Revenue can be enhanced by price premia and larger purchase quantities. Several empirical studies with different methodologies document price premia for green products. This finding is consistent for food (Loureiro *et al.* 2002; Loureiro and Lotade 2005; Aguilar and Vlosky 2007; Olesen *et al.* 2010; Norwood and Lusk 2011) and non-food products (Bjørner *et al.* 2004; Casadesus-Masanell *et al.* 2009). A positive side effect of being sustainable is the customer's higher brand loyalty (Koller *et al.* 2011). The empirical evidence on higher price premia and brand loyalty supports the idea that causality goes from environmental performance to revenue and not vice versa. Unfortunately, there is to our knowledge no evidence on purchase quantities. There is only case study evidence for the impact of environmental performance on costs (Shrivastava 1995; Nidumolu *et al.* 2009). From these case studies it seems that investments in sustainability can pay off.

The second driver of corporate value is financing costs. The empirical results reveal that cost of equity is higher for companies with a low level of environmental performance (El Ghoul *et al.* 2011; Chava 2014). Yet, environmental strengths are not rewarded with a decline in the cost of equity (Chava 2014). The analysis of Chava (2014) shows that firms with more environmental concerns have less institutional ownership. This finding directly relates to the theoretical model of Heinkel *et al.* (2001), which indicates that the smaller investor base of polluting companies leads to a higher cost of equity. The higher cost of equity therefore seems to be a consequence of shunning by institutional investors. Reverse causality is very unlikely here: a higher cost of equity would not chase away but attract investors. Similar to the results for the cost of equity, firms with environmental concerns have to bear a higher cost of debt. Firms with environmental strengths are not rewarded with a lower cost of debt. Nandy and Lodh (2012) show that firms with better environmental management get better bank loan contracts in terms of deal size and maturity. The causality issue for cost of debt cannot be answered as clearly as for the cost of equity. However, the argumentation that a higher cost of debt induces firms to lower environmental performance does not sound convincing. Therefore, we conjecture that a better environmental performance leads to a lower cost of debt, and not vice versa.

The vast majority of studies point out that environmentally conscious firms have a higher valuation (Konar and Cohen 2001; King and Lenox 2002; Guenster *et al.* 2011). This is consistent with our analysis of the mechanism that drives the relation between environmental performance and firm value. By conducting a fine-grained analysis of the drivers of corporate value, we obtain a deeper understanding of why and how environmental performance links to financial performance. Overall, the evidence on the different mechanisms supports the idea that better environmental performance has a positive impact on corporate value.

Environmental responsibility and profitability

In this section we examine how environmental performance and profitability are related to each other. We split profitability into its two components, revenues and costs. First, we scrutinise the effect of environmental performance on revenues. Subsequently, the existing literature about the environmental performance–cost link is reviewed. Lastly, we briefly summarise the existing literature about the impact of environmental performance on overall profitability, measured as return on assets (ROA), and compare the results to our expectation from the analysis of revenues and costs.

Revenue effects

The environmental performance of a company can affect revenues through various channels. Consumer preferences for green goods could result in a higher willingness-to-pay, higher sales volume, and greater customer loyalty. Russo and Fouts (1997) presume that eco-sensitive customers buy more goods from companies with a good environmental reputation. Klassen and McLaughlin (1996) argue in the same vein and propose that sustainability can lead to market share gains. Additionally, they propose that environmental certifications can be used as a differentiation strategy. The differentiation strategy allows firms to circumvent price competition and thereby charge higher prices.

Several scholars elicit the willingness-to-pay for green products. Survey-based evidence shows that price premia exist for a large variety of green products, e.g. eco-labeled apples (Loureiro *et al.* 2002), certified wood products (Aguilar and Vlosky 2007) and coffee (Loureiro and Lotade 2005). A shortcoming of survey-based studies is the lack of incentives. Without incentives people have a tendency to overstate their willingness-to-pay, because their answers have no implications for their wealth. Casadesus-Masanell *et al.* (2009) overcome this issue by using real purchase data from the outdoor brand Patagonia. They study the impact of a change from conventionally grown cotton to organic cotton on the sales of the Patagonia flannel shirt. Their analysis reveals an average price premium of 10 per cent for the organic shirt. The authors interpret their result as an additional willingness-to-pay for environmental friendliness. Bjørner *et al.* (2004) analyse real purchase data for eco-labeled toilet paper, paper towels and detergents. The products are labelled with the 'Nordic Swan', which is a Scandinavian environmental label. Their results show an average price premium for eco-labeled toilet paper of 13–18 per cent. There is no evidence of a price premium for eco-labeled paper towels and eco-labeled detergents. They argue that the results for detergents are confounded with a consumer test report, which was issued at the same time and showed a large market impact. The authors conjecture that eco-friendly customers do not buy paper towels at all and instead use reusable substitutes, e.g. the dishcloth. Therefore, they fail to find a price premium.

Having reviewed studies with real purchase data that focus on non-food products, we now move on to experimental evidence for food products. Olesen *et al.* (2010) show in an experiment that consumers are willing to pay higher prices for organic and Freedom Food salmon.[1] Consumers had to choose between different price scenarios. Because they subsequently had to buy the fish according to their choice, they were incentivised to expose their true willingness-to-pay. The study finds an average price premium of 15 per cent for organic and Freedom Food salmon compared to conventional salmon. Norwood and Lusk (2011) show in an experimental setting that people have a willingness-to-pay for animal wellbeing. The study focuses on the production of eggs and pork chops. In an experimental setting, consumers can choose between animal farming in an aviary or pasture system and a cage or crate system. In the aviary and pasture systems the animals have a lot more space than in a cage and crate system. Consumers are willing to pay $0.95 more for a dozen eggs and $2.02 more two pounds of pork chops raised in the aviary or pasture system. Overall, the evidence based on real purchase data and experiments consistently shows that consumers are willing to pay price premia for green products.

Another channel for increasing revenues is customer loyalty and brand reputation. Higher customer loyalty and brand reputation are associated with a decreasing price elasticity of demand. Koller *et al.* (2011) survey 228 car users and find that sustainability is an important criterion for car users. Sustainability influences the functional, emotional and social values, which then positively impact brand loyalty. Choi and Ng (2011) explore the effect of economic and environmental sustainability on company evaluation and purchase intent for tile producing companies using a survey. They survey people, who frequently buy building materials or renovated their home in the last two years. The final data set consist of 219 valid responses. An example for economic sustainability is the engagement in preserving the employment, whereas one example for environmental sustainability is the usage of recycled materials in the production process. Their results show that economic and environmental sustainability have a positive influence on the purchase intent and on the evaluation of a company. Customers displayed a stronger reaction to the companies' sustainability shortcomings than to its strengths. Environmental sustainability shortcomings of a company had a higher negative impact on consumer response than economic sustainability shortcomings.

All in all, studies point towards a price premium for green products. Besides the price premium, ecological sustainability enhances customer loyalty and brand reputation. The findings speak in favour of the hypothesis that high environmental performance can increase revenues.

Cost efficiency

Just based on the aforementioned studies, we cannot infer whether companies can boost their profits by adopting an eco-friendly strategy because we have not

---

1   Freedom Food (now RSPCA) is labeling animal farming standards by taking into account different dimensions of animal wellbeing (health, diet, environment, care). For more information: www.rspcaassured.org.uk/

scrutinised the effect of environmental sustainability on costs. The increase in costs could well outweigh the additional willingness-to-pay and thus lead to an overall decline in profitability. To investigate this possibility, we evaluate the findings of the empirical literature on the environmental performance–cost link in this section.

Shrivastava and Hart (1992) argue that pollution can be interpreted as inefficiency in the manufacturing process. They describe pollution as an ineffective usage of materials. In addition to that, Porter and van der Linde (1995) propose that environmental responsibility results in more efficient use of resources through process innovation. This increase in production efficiency leads to lower costs resulting in higher profitability. There are two different approaches to reduce emissions: proactive policies and end-of-pipe clean-up procedures. Proactive policies comprise the redesign of production and service delivery processes, which result in better resource efficiency and lower production costs (Russo and Fouts 1997). In addition to that, Russo and Fouts (1997) argue that the installation of eco-friendly technologies increases the firm's knowledge about pollution prevention and reduces the risk of environmental accidents, which decreases legal and clean-up costs. The win-win situation of increasing environmental sustainability and cutting manufacturing costs is critically discussed by Walley and Whitehead (1994). The authors emphasise the enormous costs of environmental programmes, which are likely to outweigh the benefits. The second method to reduce emissions is the end-of-pipe clean-up procedure, which is best described as simply cleaning up waste after producing it. This approach is expected to bear only costs and no benefits (Bhat 1999). One caveat is the weaker incentive for companies to produce less waste. The existence of a system, which deals with the produced waste, reduces the motivation to care about waste (King and Lenox 2002).

While scholars have come up with a lot of theoretical arguments on the relation between costs and environmental performance, empirical evidence is scarce. To our knowledge, it is limited to a couple of case studies and one survey. Shrivastava (1995) analyses the environmental technology of 3M Corporation. 3M is a conglomerate, which is producing specialty chemicals, polymers, industrial and consumer goods. The firm has increased its earnings by reducing costs through the adaptation of eco-friendly technologies. Their technologies aim to minimise the use of virgin materials and instead use recycled materials. They are designed to be cost saving by increasing energy and production efficiency. As the ability to redesign the production process differs between industries and companies, it is hard to generalise Shrivastava's findings about 3M. Nidumolu *et al.* (2009) analyse several large US companies and their change towards an environmentally friendly company (e.g. HP, Wal Mart, FedEx, Cisco, P&G, Clorox, Waste Management). They recommend the introduction of one global standard for environmental performance, which avoids the separate managing of sourcing, production and logistics for each market. This standardisation can result in economies of scale and optimised supply chain operations. Rao and Holt (2005) surveyed Southeast Asian companies about their supply chain management. They find empirical evidence that the greening of supply chains can improve competitiveness and economic performance. The effect of environmental performance on costs cannot be conclusively evaluated given the current state of literature. There are some convincing arguments for a decrease in costs related to an eco-friendly strategy, but there is little empirical evidence.

Aggregate profitability effects

In this section, we concentrate on the environmental performance–profitability link. The vast majority of studies examine data from the US. Those studies have some similarities, e.g. in regulatory settings, which eases the comparison. First, we deal with studies, which point towards a positive environmental performance–profitability link. Second, we discuss studies, which show confounding evidence. Lastly, we compare the US with international evidence. International evidence regarding the environmental performance–profitability link is scarce. Moreover, the difference in regulatory settings and measures of environmental performance make these studies hardly comparable to US studies. Studies measure environmental performance either with environmental scores (Russo and Fouts 1997; Guenster *et al.* 2011; Kim and Statman 2012; Lioui and Sharma 2012) or with pollution data (Hart and Ahuja1996; King and Lenox 2002; Horvathova 2012; Jo *et al.* 2013). The advantage of using pollution data is its high objectivity. Its disadvantage is its narrow focus. Environmental scores cover multiple sustainability dimensions, but the final score assessment is not fully traceable and contains subjective choices.

Positive link

Hart and Ahuja (1996) scrutinise the effect of emission reduction on ROA for firms engaged in manufacturing, mining and other types of production. Environmental performance is measured as the percentage change in an emissions efficiency index from 1988 to 1989. Their analysis reveals a significant positive relation between emission reduction and profitability. This positive relation is confirmed by Russo and Fouts (1997) with environmental ratings from the Franklin Research and Development Corporation (FRDC) for the years 1991 and 1992. They also find that the effect is stronger for firms operating in high-growth industries. King and Lenox (2002) focus on the performance effect of the different waste management methods, specifically waste prevention and waste treatment. The empirical results reveal that waste prevention has a positive effect on ROA, whereas waste treatment has no significant effect on ROA. Given these results, King and Lenox (2002) conclude that investments in pollution prevention are profitable and recommend this investment opportunity to managers.

Guenster *et al.* (2011) analyse the effect of eco-efficiency on profitability for a more recent and longer time period. The study uses monthly Innovest eco-efficiency ratings for the period from 1996–2004. The rating ranges from 0 (worst) to 6 (best). Innovest rates companies relative to their industry peers by taking quantitative and qualitative information into account. The score is

Table 6.1 Overview profitability studies

Study	Sample	Period	Environmental proxy	Effect on ROA
Hart and Ahuja (1996)	US stock market	1988–1989	TRI (pollution)	Positive effect from emission reduction; high polluters gain most from emission reduction
Russo and Fouts (1997)	US stock market	1991–1992	FRDC ratings	Positive; industry growth as a moderating factor
King and Lenox (2002)	US stock market	1991–1996	TRI (pollution)	Lower emissions and waste prevention increase ROA; waste treatment has no significant effect
Guenster et al. (2011)	US stock market	1996–2004	Innovest's eco-efficiency score	Positive; differential between good and bad environmental performers is driven by underperformance of bad performers
Kim and Statman (2012)	US stock market	1992–2000	KLD score	Positive and negative changes increase ROA
Lioui and Sharma (2012)	US stock market	1991–2007	KLD score	Strengths and concerns have a negative effect
Jo et al. (2013)	International sample; 30 countries (Asia Pacific, Europe, North America)	2002–2011	Trucost (external costs of polluting)	Positive effect from emission reduction; largest effect for firms in North America followed by Europe and Asia Pacific region
Horvathova (2012)	Czech companies	2004–2008	European Pollutant Release and Transfer Register	Negative short-term effect; positive long-term effect

Note: This table summarises the findings of studies relating environmental performance to profitability, measured as return on assets (ROA).

based on more than 60 criteria. It covers environmental liabilities from past accidents, current environmental risk exposures and strategies, and environmental profit opportunities. Broadly, Guenster *et al.* (2011) results show that a one-point increase in eco-efficiency rating results in a 0.09 increase in ROA, which is 2.2 per cent of the average sample ROA. They also analyse, if the effect is more pronounced for good or bad environmental performers. Companies, which have an eco-efficiency score ≤ 1 are considered as the least eco-efficient firms, whereas firms with an eco-efficient score ≥ 5 are classified as the most eco-efficient firms. The findings suggest an asymmetric relation. For industry-adjusted ROA the worst firms underperform by 0.32, which amounts to 8.4 per cent of the sample average ROA. However, the best firms only outperform by 0.11, which is only 3.6 per cent of sample average ROA. Thus, it seems that the environmental-financial performance link is more driven by the operational underperformance of the least eco-efficient companies.

Confounding evidence

In contrast to the aforementioned studies, Kim and Statman (2012) and Lioui and Sharma (2012) do not find a positive link between environmental performance and profitability. Kim and Statman (2012) hypothesise an inverse u-shaped relation between environmental and financial performance. Increases in environmental performance raise profitability only up to a certain point. Beyond the optimal point, further improvements in environmental performance lead to lower profitability. The authors use KLD data and examine whether positive or negative changes in KLD ratings increase or decrease profitability. KLD rates companies on five indicators of environmental strengths and six indicators for concerns.[2] Each indicator can have the value zero or one. The final score is calculated as the number of strengths minus the number of concerns. The empirical results show that managers choose the level of environmental performance to maximise profitability. Lioui and Sharma (2012) also rely on KLD scores. They hypothesise that environmental concerns have a negative impact on financial performance, because weak environmental performers are more likely to face costs from regulation. This mechanism is undisputed among scholars.[3] Interestingly, they also expect environmental strengths to have a negative effect on profitability. From their point of view, an engagement in environmental responsibility is time and resource consuming and therefore results in a decreased profitability. Their empirical results confirm both. The

2 The five potential environmental strengths are beneficial products and services, pollution prevention, recycling, alternative fuels and communications. The six potential environmental concerns are: hazardous waste, regulatory problems, ozone depleting chemicals, substantial emissions, agricultural chemicals and climate change.

3 The negative effect from environmental performance on financial performance was already shown by Hart and Ahuja (1996), Russo and Fouts (1997) and Guenster *et al.* (2011).

results imply that managers should optimally choose a medium level of environmental performance, which is neither evaluated as a strength nor as a concern.

International evidence

Jo *et al.* (2013) conduct an international study. The samples consist of Europe, North-America and the Asia-Pacific region. Instead of using the polluted amount per company (Hart and Ahuja 1996; King and Lenox 2002) they use the dollar value of the external costs arising from companies pollution provided by Trucost, because it clearly indicates the monetary damage to the environment. The monetary damage is computed by multiplying the firm's emissions and waste by the estimated marginal environmental costs of an additional ton of emissions. Their results show that it takes two years for pollution reduction to lead to higher operating performance, measured by ROA. After one year no significant relation was detected. The two-year lagged effect is stronger in North America and Europe compared to the Asia-Pacific region. The authors suspect that the differences occur due to the country-specific recognition of environmental problems among corporate executives and customers. Overall the results point towards a positive effect of environmental performance on ROA worldwide with a different intensity. Another non-US study is conducted by Horvathova (2012). Her sample consists of Czech firms' emissions. The analysis shows that the effect of environmental performance on profitability is negative with a one-year lag, but positive with a two-year lag. She concludes that increasing environmental performance is costly in the short-term, but pays off in the long-term.

The empirical evidence points towards a positive effect of environmental performance on profitability, which is consistent with the findings presented on revenues and cost. A serious issue is causality: in the evidence based on regressions it is unclear whether environmental performance leads to higher operating performance or vice versa. However, when we combine the evidence from the profitability regressions with the literature on revenue and costs from above, we can conclude that causality is likely going from environmental performance to financial performance. Reverse causality does not seem to be driving the relation between environmental performance and revenue. Consumers' willingness-to-pay for green products is not likely to be influenced by the companies' revenues. In addition to that, we find case study evidence that environmental performance can decrease costs, which is also not likely to be affected by reverse causality. Putting together the evidence on these different components of profitability, we conclude that most likely environmental performance leads to higher profitability.

Environmental responsibility and cost of capital

Cost of equity

In traditional finance models investors only care about risk and return. However, in the *Global Sustainable Investment Review* 2014 it was reported that 30.2 per cent of professionally managed assets are managed sustainably in some way.[4] The two most common strategies are ESG integration and negative screening. ESG integration is defined as choosing and investing in firms with a high level of environmental, social and governance performance. Negative screening is the shunning of firms with poor environmental performance by investors. Heinkel, Kraus and Zechner (2001) derive theoretically the impact of sustainable investing on the cost of equity. If polluting firms are shunned by green investors and these investors are a substantial fraction of the market, the non-green investors face a lack of risk sharing. Due to this lack in risk sharing idiosyncratic risk of shunned firms becomes priced and, consequently, these firms have a higher cost of equity. The model of Heinkel, Kraus and Zechner (2001) arrives at conclusions similar to the well-known model of Merton (1987) for the specific aspect of environmental performance. Parameterising their model, Heinkel, Kraus and Zechner (2001) find that the cost of equity capital of polluting firms increases relative to non-polluting firms if there are more than 25 per cent of green investors in the market. Comparing this number to the 30.2 per cent of sustainably managed assets, we expect a negative relation between environmental performance and the cost of equity capital.

The studies of Chava (2014) and El Ghoul *et al.* (2011) empirically analyse the effects of environmental performance on the cost of equity. Both studies apply the implied cost of capital (ICC) approach to measure ex ante expected stock returns. The ICC approach uses analysts' earnings forecasts and current stock prices to determine the cost of equity. Its main advantages are that one does not need to rely on noisy historical returns and a specific asset-pricing model (Gebhardt *et al.* 2001). The time period of both studies is 1992–2007 and they measure environmental performance using the KLD data. It is not surprising that both studies arrive at similar results. El Ghoul *et al.* (2011) use the net environmental score as an indicator of environmental performance. It is calculated as the number of strengths minus the number of concerns. The results indicate a negative relationship between environmental performance and cost of equity. Chava (2014) confirms this finding. In addition, he investigates separately the impact of environmental strengths and concerns on cost of equity. His findings show that environmental concerns are related to a higher cost of equity, whereas environmental strengths are not rewarded with a decline in the cost of equity. To provide an explanation for these findings, Chava (2014) analyses the relation between environmental strengths and concerns, and institutional ownership. He makes the notable finding that firms with more environmental concerns have less institutional ownership. In line with the theoretical argument made by Heinkel *et al.* (2001), this shunning could explain the higher cost of equity of environmental sinners.

While the previous studies were all US based, El Ghoul *et al.* (2014) investigate the environmental performance–cost of equity link in an international sample of

---

4   The report is available at: www.ussif.org/Files/Publications/GSIA_Review.pdf

30 countries. The study measures environmental performance as the external costs of pollution provided by Trucost for the period 2002–2011. It uses a methodology similar to the earlier US-based paper (El Ghoul *et al.* 2011). The results confirm the negative environmental–financial performance link internationally.

Cost of debt

Chava (2014) posits that social responsibility, lender liability laws and reputation risk can be reasons for not lending funds to firms with environmental concerns. He analyses how environmental performance affects firms' bank loans. The results for bank loans are similar to his findings for the cost of equity. Better environmental performance is associated with a reduction in the cost of debt when using the net environmental score. Again his results indicate that concerns are related to the higher cost of debt, while strengths do not have a significant impact. By investigating the lender structure in the loan syndicate, Chava (2014) finds that firms with environmental concerns have fewer lenders. This can be interpreted as empirical evidence for shunning in the debt market. Chava (2014) analyses whether environmental performance is proxying for default risk. He investigates the effect of environmental performance on bankruptcies, covenant violations and credit rating downgrades. He detects no significant relation between environmental performance and one of the above-mentioned default risk proxies. A conservative interpretation is that default risk is not solely influencing the environmental performance–cost of debt link. Concentrating on loan contract characteristics, Nandy and Lodh (2012) find that companies with a high level of environmental performance have lower bank loan spreads, a bigger deal size, a longer maturity and more collaterals. Both studies arrive at the result that environmental friendly firms get better bank loans than firms with environmental concerns.

Similar to Chava (2014), Hoepner *et al.* (2014) examine the effect of environmental sustainability on bank loan spreads in 28 different countries for the period 2005–2012. The authors use Oekom ratings, which provide sustainability scores for the environmental and social dimension at the firm and country level. They hypothesise that environmental sustainability at both the firm and country level decrease the cost of debt. Contrary to Chava (2014) their empirical findings do not indicate that better sustainability on the firm level is related to a lower cost of debt. However, their analysis shows that a high environmental sustainability on a country level significantly decreases bank loan spreads.

Overall, the studies point towards a negative relation between environmental performance and cost of debt. The studies on the cost of equity consistently point in the same direction: financing costs decrease with a higher level of environmental performance. This effect should be a strong incentive to invest in better environmental performance. In particular, the results of Chava (2014) show that environmental concerns can lead to significantly higher financing cost.

Environmental responsibility and valuation

The studies reviewed so far indicate that better environmental performance increases profitability and decreases cost of capital. As firm value is comprised of these two components, we expect to find a positive effect of better environmental performance on valuation.

Konar and Cohen (2001) investigate the effect of pollution and environmental litigation on firm value for manufacturing firms for the year 1989. Pollution is proxied with the aggregated emission of toxic chemicals scaled by revenue. The number of environmental lawsuits is used as the environmental litigation variable. Like most studies in this area, Konar and Cohen (2001) use Tobin's q as an indicator of corporate value. Tobin's q can be interpreted as a measure of the intangible value assigned to a firm by financial markets. It is defined as the market value of the firm's assets divided by their replacement value. Higher pollution is associated with a significant decrease in firm value. This relation was stronger for companies operating in high polluting industries. Although the effect of environmental litigation on firm value was statistically significant, it is economically small. King and Lenox (2002) confirm the results of Konar and Cohen (2001) regarding pollution and firm value for a longer and more recent time period (1991–1996). Additionally, they analyse the effect of waste prevention and waste treatment on Tobin's q. Their results show that waste treatment does not influence q significantly, whereas waste prevention leads to higher values of q. The authors recommend managers to invest more in waste prevention instead of onsite waste treatment.

Guenster *et al.* (2011) confirm the aforementioned studies and detect a positive environmental performance–firm value link. Supplementary to previous studies, they account for a broader perspective of environmental performance through employing the Innovest eco-efficiency ratings. The results show that the effect is mostly driven by the market's punishment of low eco-efficient companies. Furthermore, by splitting the sample in two periods it appears that the valuation differential in subperiod 2 (2001–2004) is twice as large as in subperiod 1 (1997–2000). They conclude that investors change their attitude towards eco-efficiency in a positive way over time. The change of investor preferences over time was confirmed by Chava (2014), with expected stock returns. He splits up his sample in two periods 1992–1999 and 2000–2007. Similar to Guenster *et al.* (2011), in the latter period concerns had a more pronounced effect on the expected return of stocks than in the first period.

Kim and Statman (2012) find that both increases and decreases in environmental performance relate to a higher Tobin's q. Thus managers choose the level of environmental performance according to maximise q. This is a similar result as they find for the relation between environmental and operating performance discussed above. A distinction the reviewed literature points out is that Guenster *et al.* (2011) recommend managers to improve environmental performance, while Kim and Statman (2012) provide evidence that managers choose the optimal level of environmental performance to maximise the firm value.

Conclusion and discussion

Our main research question was whether environmental performance affects firm value. By looking at the regression studies in a previous section, one cannot infer causality. To overcome this issue, we concentrate on the drivers of firm value, namely profitability and the cost of capital.

We start by discussing the influence of environmental performance on profitability. We conduct a fine-grained analysis of the environmental performance effect on the potential drivers of profitability: revenues and costs. Evidence from experiments and real-purchase data shows that customers are willing to pay more for environmentally friendly products. Unfortunately, we did not find any study, which dealt with the effect of environmental performance on the quantity of goods sold. There are valid arguments for a negative relation of environmental performance and costs. A number of case studies support this proposition. However, given the current state of literature we cannot reach a definite conclusion. Studies succeed in showing a positive link between environmental performance and overall profitability. By taking the results from the revenue section and the convincing arguments from the cost section into account, we conclude that the higher profitability of green companies is driven by their environmental performance.

The empirical evidence in the third section shows that companies with environmental concerns have to pay a higher cost of equity. Companies with environmental strengths do not benefit from a lower cost of equity. Chava (2014) shows that this result can be explained by institutional investors shunning firms with environmental concerns. This finding is in line with the theoretical predictions of Heinkel *et al.* (2001). The evidence for the cost of debt points in the same direction. Thus, environmental performance has a negative effect on the cost of capital, which increases firm value. As the underlying explanation for the effect is shunning by institutional investors, it seems unlikely that reverse causality plays an important role.

By disentangling different mechanisms, we are able to obtain a deeper understanding of the drivers of the environmental performance–firm value relationship. Looking at each mechanism in isolation, we can conclude for the respective mechanism that the effect goes from environmental to financial performance. Putting the pieces together, these insights allow us to conclude that also at the aggregate level environmental performance has a positive impact on firm value.

Given these findings, it is remarkable that there are still so many companies that have a poor environmental record. The literature offers several explanations as to why managers forego profitable investments in sustainable technologies. Decanio (1993) proposes management myopia as one possible explanation. Managers are not likely to undertake investments in sustainability when they are expected to pay off only far in the future. Furthermore, he considers the principal-agent problem in his analysis. Managers are exposed to company risk to a higher degree than diversified shareholders. Even, if an environmental project increases firm value, managers refrain from investing, if it is too risky from their perspective. Another potential explanation is top management's focus on market share expansion rather than on energy saving projects (Decanio 1993). Consequently, top management is overlooking cost saving sustainability projects. Another explanation is that investment decisions are dependent on the overall macro-economic situation. Delmas and Pekovic (2015) point out that firms do not invest in resource efficiency strategies in economic downturns. Their survey of French firms reveals that only 10 per cent of firms invest in times of economic downturn compared to 46 per cent in steady or growing market conditions. To overcome this underinvestment issue, Martin *et al.* (2012) recommend the installation of an environmental or energy manager. In their UK survey, they find firms with an environmental or energy manager to have better energy efficiency. Boyd and Curtis (2014) confirm in a US sample that good environmental management, particularly lean production, is associated with higher energy efficiency. To sum up, it seems that the dominant explanation for a firm's bad environmental record is not value maximisation but poor management and agency problems. There is a need for further research into why managers miss sustainability profit opportunities and how shareholders can direct the managers' attention towards them. Furthermore, better incentive schemes to overcome the principal-agent problem and managerial myopia regarding environmental responsibility have to be developed. As Berrone and Gomez-Mejia (2009) show that more long-term CEO incentives promote pollution prevention, in particular in 'dirty' industries.

References

Aguilar, F.X. and Vlosky, R.P. 2007. 'Consumer willingness to pay price premiums for environmentally certified wood products in the US', *Forest Policy and Economics* 9(8), 1100–1112.

Barnea, A. and Rubin, A. 2010. 'Corporate social responsibility as a conflict between shareholders', *Journal of Business Ethics* 97(1), 71–86.

Berrone, P. and Gomez-Mejia, L.R. 2009. 'Environmental performance and executive compensation: An integrated agency-institutional perspective', *Academy of Management Journal* 52(1), 103–126.

Bhat, V.N. 1999. 'Does it pay to be green?', *International Journal of Environmental Studies* 56(4), 497–507.

Bjørner, T.B., Hansen, L.G. and Russell, C.S. 2004. 'Environmental labeling and consumers' choice – an empirical analysis of the effect of the Nordic Swan', *Journal of Environmental Economics and Management* 47(3), 411–434.

Boyd, G.A. and Curtis, E.M. 2014. 'Evidence of an 'Energy-Management Gap' in US manufacturing: Spillovers from firm management practices to energy efficiency', *Journal of Environmental Economics and Management* 68(3), 463–479.

Casadesus-Masanell, R., Crooke, M., Reinhardt, F. and Vasishth, V. 2009. 'Households' willingness to pay for 'green' goods: evidence from Patagonia's introduction of organic cotton sportswear', *Journal of Economics & Management Strategy* 18(1), 203–233.

Chava, S. 2014. 'Environmental externalities and cost of capital', *Management Science* 60(9), 2223–2247.

Choi, S. and Ng, A. 2011. 'Environmental and economic dimensions of sustainability and price effects on consumer responses', *Journal of Business Ethics* 104(2), 269–282.

DeCanio, S.J. 1993. 'Barriers within firms to energy-efficient investments', *Energy Policy* 21(9), 906–914.

Delmas, M.A. and Pekovic, S. 2015. 'Resource efficiency strategies and market conditions', *Long Range Planning* 48(2), 80–94.

El Ghoul, S., Guedhami, O., Kwok, C.C. and Mishra, D.R. 2011. 'Does corporate social responsibility affect the cost of capital?', *Journal of Banking & Finance* 35(9), 2388–2406.

El Ghoul, S., Guedhami, O., Kim, H. and Park, K. 2014. 'Corporate environmental responsibility and the cost of capital: international evidence', *KAIST College of Business Working Paper Series* (2014–008).

Endrikat, J., Guenther, E., and Hoppe, H. 2014. 'Making sense of conflicting empirical findings: A meta-analytic review of the relationship between corporate environmental and financial performance', *European Management Journal* 32(5), 735–751.

Friede, G., Busch, T. and Bassen, A. 2015. 'ESG and financial performance: aggregated evidence from more than 2000 empirical studies', *Journal of Sustainable Finance & Investment* 5(4), 210–233.

Gebhardt, W.R., Lee, C. and Swaminathan, B. 2001. 'Toward an implied cost of capital', *Journal of Accounting Research* 39(1), 135–176.

Guenster, N., Bauer, R., Derwall, J. and Koedijk, K. 2011. 'The economic value of corporate eco-efficiency', *European Financial Management* 17(4), 679–704.

Hart, S.L. and Ahuja, G. 1996. 'Does it pay to be green? An empirical examination of the relationship between emission reduction and firm performance', *Business Strategy and the Environment* 5(1), 30–37.

Heinkel, R., Kraus, A. and Zechner, J. 2001. 'The effect of green investment on corporate behavior', *Journal of Financial and Quantitative Analysis* 36(4), 431–449.

Hoepner, A.G., Oikonomou, I., Scholtens, B. and Schröder, M. 2014. 'The effects of corporate and country sustainability characteristics on the cost of debt: An international investigation', *ZEW-Centre for European Economic Research Discussion Paper* (14–100).

Horvathova, E. 2010. 'Does environmental performance affect financial performance? A meta-analysis', *Ecological Economics* 70, 52–59.

Horvathova, E., 2012. 'The impact of environmental performance on firm performance: Short-term costs and long-term benefits?', *Ecological Economics* 84, 91–97.

Jo, H., Kim, H., Lee, B.S. and Park, K. 2013. 'Corporate environmental responsibility and financial performance around the world', *KAIST College of Business Working Paper Series* (2013–2017).

Kim, Y. and Statman, M. 2012. 'Do corporations invest enough in environmental responsibility?', *Journal of Business Ethics* 105(1), 115–129.

King, A. and Lenox, M. 2002. 'Exploring the locus of profitable pollution reduction', *Management Science* 48(2), 289–299.

Klassen, R.D. and McLaughlin, C.P. 1996. 'The impact of environmental management on firm performance', *Management Science* 42(8), 1199–1214.

Koller, M., Floh, A. and Zauner, A. 2011. 'Further insights into perceived value and consumer loyalty: A 'Green' perspective', *Psychology and Marketing* 28(12), 1154–1176.

Konar, S. and Cohen, M.A. 2001. 'Does the market value environmental performance?', *Review of Economics and Statistics* 83(2), 281–289.

Lioui, A. and Sharma, Z. 2012. 'Environmental corporate social responsibility and financial performance: Disentangling direct and indirect effects', *Ecological Economics* 78, 100–111.

Loureiro, M.L. and Lotade, J. 2005. 'Do fair trade and eco-labels in coffee wake up the consumer conscience?', *Ecological Economics* 53, 129–138.

Loureiro, M.L., McCluskey, J.J. and Mittelhammer, R.C. 2002. 'Will consumers pay a premium for eco-labeled apples?', *Journal of Consumer Affairs* 36(2), 203–219.

Martin, R., Muûls, M., de Preux, L.B. and Wagner, U.J. 2012. 'Anatomy of a paradox: Management practices, organizational structure and energy efficiency', *Journal of Environmental Economics and Management* 63(2), 208–223.

Merton, R.C., 1987. 'A simple model of capital market equilibrium with incomplete information', *The Journal of Finance* 42(3), 483–510.

Nandy, M. and Lodh, S. 2012. 'Do banks value the eco-friendliness of firms in their corporate lending decision? Some empirical evidence', *International Review of Financial Analysis* 25, 83–93.

Nidumolu, R., Prahalad, C.K. and Rangaswami, M. 2009. 'Why sustainability is now the key driver of innovation', *Harvard Business Review* 87(9), 56–64.

Norwood, F.B. and Lusk, J.L. 2011. 'A calibrated auction-conjoint valuation method: valuing pork and eggs produced under differing animal welfare conditions', *Journal of Environmental Economics and Management* 62(1), 80–94.

Olesen, I., Alfnes, F., Røra, M.B. and Kolstad, K. 2010. 'Eliciting consumers' willingness to pay for organic and welfare-labelled salmon in a non-hypothetical choice experiment', *Livestock Science* 127(2), 218–226.

Porter, M.E. and van der Linde, C. 1995. 'Green and competitive: ending the stalemate', *Harvard Business Review* 73(5), 120–134.

Rao, P. and Holt, D. 2005. 'Do green supply chains lead to competitiveness and economic performance?', *International Journal of Operations & Production Management* 25(9), 898–916.

Russo, M.V. and Fouts, P.A. 1997. 'A resource-based perspective on corporate environmental performance and profitability', *Academy of Management Journal* 40(3), 534–559.

Shrivastava, P. 1995. 'Environmental technologies and competitive advantage', *Strategic Management Journal* 16(1), 183–200.

Shrivastava, P. and Hart, S. 1992. 'Greening Organizations', *Academy of Management Proceedings* 1992, 185–189.

Waddock, S.A. and Graves, S.B. 1997. 'The corporate social performance-financial performance link', *Strategic Management Journal* 18(4), 303–319.

Walley, N. and Whitehead, B. 1994. 'It's not easy being green', *Harvard Business Review* 72(3), 46–51.

7 Too big to deter, too small to change?

Profitability and environmental compliance in the waste and chemical industry in the Netherlands

Karin van Wingerde and Marieke Kluin

Introduction

Even though the financial costs of corporate environmental crime are often very difficult to measure precisely, it has long been recognised that environmental crime has impact far beyond financial losses. Losing wildlife, depleting national resources and damaging the natural environment are just some of the disastrous consequences of environmental crime. At the same time, however, environmental crime is also one of the most profitable forms of corporate crime, not only generating income by the sale of illegal or environmentally unfriendly goods and products, but also because companies may reduce production costs by not investing in mandatory measures to prevent environmental damage. The United Nations Environment Programme (UNEP) and INTERPOL (2016) have estimated the value of environmental crime at 3 billion US dollars, which exceeds the amount of money spent on the prevention of it by 10,000 times. Environmental crime has also been vastly increasing and is now estimated to be the world's fourth largest crime sector (Nellemann *et al.* 2016, p. 7).

Yet, the prevention and deterrence of corporate environmental crime are very difficult to achieve. In his book *Too Big To Jail. How Prosecutors Compromise With Corporations* Garrett (2014, p. 1) has characterised prosecuting corporate crime as a 'battle between David and Goliath' where the prosecution symbolises David and the corporation the giant Goliath.[1] Garrett (2014, p. 149) found that

---

1 One of the editors of this book kindly reminded us that as David won this battle, this metaphor is often used inaccurately. What Garrett presumably means however, is to illustrate the fight of a weak prosecution against some of the most strong, powerful and multinational corporations in the world. In this light, the prosecution might be better symbolised by Goliath: bureaucratic, inflexible and hampered by a lack of resources, strict rules of conduct, and a lack of political or cultural support for the blameworthiness of violations of the law it must enforce. Parker (2006) characterised the latter as the 'compliance trap' of regulatory enforcement.

47 per cent of the deferred prosecution agreements that he analysed between 2001 and 2012 (in total 2,262 companies), did not include criminal penalties. Moreover, 23 per cent of the convicted companies paid no fine at all. Garrett argues that some firms simply are 'too big to jail' emphasising power asymmetries between these large firms and governments and regulatory bodies on the other.

Criminological and socio-legal research has long recognised the potential pitfalls in combating corporate crime. In his seminal book *Where the Law Ends* (1975), Christopher Stone already described the paradox that the largest and most powerful corporations in the world require more efforts from regulatory and enforcement agencies to limit violations, yet it is very difficult to accomplish that due to complexities of these firms, their often international character and their value for the economy. Ever since, there is a large and growing body of literature devoted to understanding how to best influence the behaviour of large business firms (Sutherland 1980; Simpson 2002; Hertz 2003; Snider 2010; Parker and Lehman Nielsen 2011) and if and how we can deter it (Braithwaite and Makkai 1991; Thornton *et al.* 2005; Schell-Busey *et al.* 2016; van Wingerde 2012, 2016). The literature shows, however, that there is not much support for the idea that deterrence works, especially when larger, more powerful corporations are involved: '[these, actors] are sanctioned less often and less stringent than smaller firms' (Yeager 2016, p. 446). As large and powerful corporations are often able to negotiate the terms of the penalty or prosecution agreement, have greater resources to fight back in court, and as a result of the complexity of offences and the multitude of different actors involved, it is often more difficult to prove their involvement in committing these crimes. For example, in one of the major corporate environmental scandals of the last decade, the Probo Koala case, van Wingerde (2015, pp. 266–267) shows that there was a lot of ambiguity about the composition and toxicity of the waste dumped, and consequently about the causality between the waste and the health problems of the people affected by the waste dump. Moreover, there were many actors involved in different countries making it difficult to distinguish who was ultimately culpable and which authority had jurisdiction for enforcement. In many cases, these ambiguities are used by corporate actors to exclude or limit liability, often with success. Yeager (2016: 446) emphasises that this leads to an uneven distribution of enforcement outcomes and he characterises deterrence of corporate crime as 'elusive'. The above description seems to suggest that there is no incentive whatsoever for large corporations to comply with environmental laws and regulations. Strongly put, environmental crime is profitable without running the risk of detection and strict legal action.

On the other hand, however, environmentally friendly activities and operations have become increasingly more important for firms. Many firms nowadays report about environmental compliance and participate in Global Sustainability Indices. Also, investments in, for example, sustainable products and services can have a positive effect on the firm's public image, which in turn could make it easier to recruit well-trained employees, to renew the firm's environmental licence, and to receive governmental approval on new developments or new activities. In other words: investing in the environment might be good for business in the future by enhancing the firm's social licence to operate, which refers to the degree of approval of society for business activities and the perception of stakeholders that the firm's operations are legitimate (Joyce and Thomson 2000; Gunningham *et al.* 2003, 2004; Lynch-Wood and Williamson 2007). Moreover, larger and more profitable firms are of course also better suited to invest in environmental compliance and protection, which in turn could provide them with reputational and competitive advantages. Economic incentives and constraints therefore drive firms' abilities to invest in environmental compliance measures, to adopt alternative measures that are more sustainable, or to take measures beyond what has been required by formal, legal regulations (Porter and van der Linde 1995; Prakash 2000; Gunningham *et al.* 2003, 2004).

In sum, firms' size and profitability may both enable firms to invest in environmental compliance measures *and* create serious problems for the enforcement of environmental crimes. This chapter explores how very large and profitable firms deal with environmental compliance by presenting a qualitative case study in two highly visible, environmentally important, capital-intensive and scrutinised industries in the Netherlands: the waste industry and the chemical industry. Using data on ten firms in these industries we will analyse: 1) the financial revenues of these firms, 2) how these firms can be characterised in terms of their responsivity towards compliance with the law, and 3) the ways in which environmental violations have been dealt with.

The next section first discusses the existing literature on what has been conceptualised as the economic licence of business firms. The approach and data will then be described followed by three subsections presenting the results of the study, focusing first on the profitability of these firms and thereafter on their compliance with environmental regulations, and on the enforcement of violations. The final section summarises and discusses the findings and sets out the implications.

Firm size, profitability and the economic licence

In their seminal work on corporate environmental compliance, Gunningham, Kagan and Thornton (2003, pp. 35–36) have conceptualised the various external pressures that drive firms toward improving environmental compliance as conditions or requirements of a 'license to operate', which includes a regulatory, social and economic licence. The regulatory or legal licence refers to the firm's legal obligations; the social licence expresses the demands and expectations from the firm's social and local environment; and the economic licence refers to the financial situation of business firms and/or the economic situation in the market that either constrains or enables firms to invest in environmental compliance measures. Of course, these licences do not influence compliance behaviour independently, but they interact (Gunningham *et al.* 2003, 2004). For example, penalties imposed by a public regulator may trigger community reactions. Moreover, legal obligations of business firms may also empower social stakeholders to monitor firms' environmental performance. Finally, the extent to which a firm is able to meet the demands of the legal and social licence also depends on the financial situation. The economic licence may therefore operate as a brake on or an accelerator for environmental measures and improvements (Gunningham *et al.* 2003, p. 37).

While the economic licence is undeniably important, the empirical evidence on *how* it influences firm behaviour and/or enforcement is far from conclusive. Whether and to what extent the economic licence influences the compliance behaviour of business firms depends on the field of research, the type of methods and data utilised, the type of industry studied, and the type and size of the firms involved.

One important strand of literature – business management studies, see for an overview the contribution of Guenster and Koegst in this volume – is concerned with how corporate value, share prices and – more broadly – profitability influence investments in the environment, sustainability, human rights and vice versa: how environmental investments influence the value of corporations (Hamilton 1995; Russo and Fouts 1997; Konar and Cohen 2001; Mill 2006; Scholtens 2006; Orlitzky 2009; Guenster *et al.* 2011). In other words, it aims to empirically investigate the links between profitability and environmental performance. These studies generally come to the conclusion that 'it pays to be green' (Russo and Fouts 1997, p. 534). For example, in a study on the environmental performance of 243 listed firms, Russo and Fouts (1997) found that environmental performance and profitability are positively linked and this effect was even strengthened by industry growth. In addition, research has shown that by investing in more sustainable techniques and processes, for example pollution control techniques, firms can reduce operating and compliance costs in the long term and even increase their market value. For example, in their study on the emissions of toxic chemicals by listed companies, Konar and Cohen (2001) found that the amount of toxic chemicals emitted had a significant and negative impact on the value of the firm. More strikingly, they found that a 10 per cent reduction in emissions of toxic chemicals would result in a $34 million increase in market value. Finally, this type of research has shown that stock market prices may be affected by transparency about firms' environmental performance (Shane and Spicer 1983; Hamilton 1995; Karpoff *et al.* 2005).

Another body of literature deals with the relative importance of economic factors compared to social and legal factors in influencing firms to comply with the law. These – mainly socio-legal – studies often use case study data to investigate how and under what circumstances the economic licence can be relevant to influence firms' environmental compliance. In their study on pulp and paper mills, Gunningham *et al.* (2003, pp. 86–89) found that mills operated by larger and more profitable firms did have lower absorbable organic halides emissions and better pollution control technology than less profitable firms, as long as one takes into account that it takes time before profit makes its way into improved environmental performance (p. 87). They compared data about firms' profits from the beginning of the 1990s with emission data from the end of that decade. At the same time however, Gunningham *et al.* (2003) show that in such a highly visible and closely regulated industry as the pulp and paper mills industry, the pressures from the social and legal licence were far more important catalysts for long term change. The economic licence merely limited firms on how much they could invest in environmental compliance measures. This has led researchers to investigate the licensing framework in smaller, less visible industries. For example, in a study that was originally designed to explore the impact of the social license on small and medium sized firms, Lynch-Wood and Williamson (2007) found that for these firms, market pressures generated by consumers and customers are the most important drivers that set the conditions of the social licence. Similarly, in their study on the trucking industry, a highly competitive market, with many small companies, Thornton *et al.* (2008, 2009) show that these firms are almost entirely driven by their economic licence. Finally, in one of the first quantitative tests of the licensing framework of Gunningham et al., Rorie (2015) discovered that the only external pressure that did not have any impact on corporate environmental crime was the economic licence.

In sum, while the opportunity to increase profits or to reduce costs may be a strong motivator for compliance and overcompliance behaviour, the economic licence also seems to serve 'as a brake' (Gunningham *et al.* 2003) on costly compliance measures and seems to be of particular importance to smaller and medium-sized firms. In the remainder of this chapter, we will analyse how ten companies in two highly visible industries can be characterised in terms of their profitability and their responsivity towards environmental compliance, and how violations have been dealt with. The next section first discusses our approach and data.

Approach and data

Approach

This chapter presents the results of a case study of ten companies in the waste industry and chemical industry in the Netherlands between 2010 and 2014. These are two industries that are dominated by large and powerful commercial corporations who increasingly operate across national borders. For example, in 2012, the chemical industry's estimated annual turnover was 77 billion euros, representing 19 per cent of all Dutch export (Kluin 2014, p. 17). The annual turnover of the Dutch waste industry is estimated at 7 billion euros. Similarly, the 25 largest waste firms in the Netherlands all have an annual turnover of 25 million euros and the five largest firms together achieve an annual turnover of 2.1 billion euros (Noordhoek 2014). At the same time, both the waste industry and the chemical industry have often been described as industries that are vulnerable to environmental crime (Huisman 2016). In both industries, toxic and dangerous substances are produced, processed, stored and transported on a daily basis. These substances are generally considered to be highly vulnerable to manipulation and therefore create opportunities for environmental crime. For instance, van Daele *et al.* (2007, pp. 35–36) point to the problem of so-called 'mirror entries'. This means that certain substances are only defined as 'hazardous' when the concentration exceeds certain levels. Corporations can keep the concentration of hazardous substances under these limits and thus remain outside the scope of law enforcement authorities. Moreover, the hazardous nature of these activities has resulted in several serious incidents and chemical disasters in both industries in the past. Most companies in the waste and chemical industry in the Netherlands are located in densely populated areas raising community concerns about potential disasters and these firms are under intense scrutiny of regulatory bodies and the general public. These characteristics make chemical and waste industries a good case study for analysis in this project.

The analysis is based on three sources: two detailed case studies on the waste industry (van Wingerde 2012) and the chemical industry (Kluin 2014) focusing on environmental compliance; and analysis of the financial revenues of ten firms in the waste and chemical industry in the Netherlands.

In depth case studies in the waste and chemical industry

The study in the waste industry was originally designed to analyse how important general deterrence is in motivating firms in the waste industry in the Netherlands to comply with the law (van Wingerde 2012, 2016). It used 70 in-depth interviews with environmental managers, directors and public and private regulators of 40 firms in the waste industry in the Netherlands, observations of environmental practices at these firms, document analysis of annual reports, legal permits and inspection reports, and the media coverage of these firms in all national and regional newspapers since 2000 was analysed using *Lexis Nexis*.

The study in the chemical industry was designed to understand to what extent, how and why law enforcement influences compliance of 15 chemical companies with Seveso regulations (Kluin 2014, 2015). The data used in this study was collected through a trend analysis of all health and safety and environmental violations of 15 companies between 1999 and 2011, participant observations of 19 on-site inspections, and a questionnaire among chemical corporation employees.

The methods are described more fully in the original reports (van Wingerde 2012; Kluin 2014). Both studies, however, shed light on compliance with environmental laws and regulations and on the enforcement of environmental violations of these firms.

Analysis of financial revenues and self-reported violations and environmental issues

Merging the two sets of companies, yields a total of 55 companies. For these corporations we then sought to collect original data on the financial revenues between 2010 and 2014 through the online database *Company.info*. This database – accessible through the library of Erasmus University Rotterdam – contains annual reports, historical information about boards of directors and shareholders, and information about bankruptcies. We checked all 55 companies against this database for the annual reports with information about their net turnover, net profits, environmental investments and environmental issues and violations in the years 2010 through 2014. In addition, we checked company websites for annual reports that were missing in our database.

It proved to be extremely hard to collect data for all the firms in our dataset and for all the years that we were interested in. For 14 firms we hardly found any data about annual turnovers and profits. This was either the result of the fact that these corporations were bankrupt and no longer existed, or because these companies were rather small and simply did not provide any information about their revenues on their website. For another 14 companies we did find data for some of the years, but not for all. We excluded these 28 companies from the analysis. This resulted in information of the financial revenues of 27 companies.

Yet, at this point our data still had some limitations. Most prominently, our financial data – that we collected specifically for this contribution – was more recent than our qualitative data. We have tried to overcome this by collecting additional information about the environmental compliance situation of these firms. We analysed the number and type of violations and enforcement actions that companies had self-reported in their annual statements and we collected media content about environmental compliance issues about these firms. However, we were not able to find new information for all the 27 firms in our sample. Consequently, we decided to select ten companies in total (five waste companies, five chemical firms) for which we had the most detailed information about their financial situation and their compliance histories. Therefore, this contribution is limited to a mere description of the profitability of these ten firms, their responsivity towards compliance and the enforcement of environmental violations by these firms.

Data

This study reports on five companies in the chemical industry and five in the waste industry in the Netherlands. Table 7.1 shows that almost all firms are privately owned. One waste company is owned and operated by municipalities. This is rather common in the waste industry in the Netherlands due to the public interests involved in the treatment and processing of waste (public hygiene, environmental concerns, quality of life) (van Daele *et al.* 2007; van Wingerde 2012). With regard to the number of employees, the data includes five medium-sized firms (up to 200 employees) and five large firms (more than 200 employees).

Altogether, the above approach and data allowed for a detailed understanding of the profitability of firms in the waste and chemical industry in the Netherlands and their environmental compliance. In the description below, we will use the following identifiers for the firms studied: W = waste, C = chemical; L = large (200+ employees), M = medium-sized (50–200 employees); Pu = public firm, Pr = private firm.

Table 7.1 Overview of the data: characteristics of ten firms

Type of firm	Chemical facility	Waste company
Ownership	5	5
Public		1
Private	5	4
Size based on number of employees		
Small: < 50	0	0
Medium: 51–200	2	3
Large: >200	3	2

Results

Profitability

How profitable are firms in the waste and chemical industry in the Netherlands? Table 7.2 presents the average net turnover of the ten companies in our sample. It demonstrates that, despite the global economic downturn, these firms managed to sustain their annual turnover at a continuously high and consistent level, with an average of 3.1 billion euros per year.

While net turnover is a measure of a business's success and growth, net profit reflects its revenues after all expenses. In other words: net profit is the actual money in the bank after paying all other expenses. Table 7.3 presents the net profit of the firms in our sample. At first glance, it shows a somewhat different picture. In 2012 and 2014, average net profits were negative, meaning that in these years costs exceeded revenues. However, this was almost entirely the result of one company that had negative profits in all years analysed. In 2012, W1Mpr had a negative profit of 65 million euros and in 2014 its negative balance sheet had increased to 549 million euros. According to its annual financial report this

Table 7.2 Average net turnover in euros (x 1.000)[a]

	2010	2011	2012	2013	2014
Waste	312,327	352,374	371,580	330,700	323,218
Chemical	5,339,445	6,117,963	6,338,711	5,935,571	5,725,729
Average	2,825,886	3,235,169	3,355,145	3,133,136	3,024,474
	Range 48,513– 14,640,000	Range 58,163– 15,697,000	Range 54,664– 15,390,000	Range 53,678– 14,590,000	Range 52,713– 14,296,000
	Std 5,007,716	Std 5,601,244	Std 5,723,639	Std 5,400,574	Std 5,331,809

Note:
a Std is unbiased.

Table 7.3 Average net profit in euros (x 1,000)

	2010	2011	2012	2013	2014
Waste	–808	–7.211	–19.814	–1.894	–135.699
Chemical	217.805	158.764	–362.763	127.726	47.856
Average	108,499	75,777	–191,289	62,916	–43,922
	Range –22,000– 837,000	Range –25,000– 541,000	Range –2,106,000– 147,984	Range –104,209– 661,000	Range –549,288– 600,000
	Std 275,563	Std 183,115	Std 713,972	Std 225,714	Std 322,884

was due to investment activities abroad that will lead to increased profits in the future. All years considered though, our sample shows that the average net profit of these firms was 2.4 million euros.

Table 7.2 and 7.3 also show that the chemical firms in our sample reported much higher annual turnovers and profits than the waste companies. What is more, the waste companies reported negative net profits in all years considered. This corresponds to general developments in both markets. After setbacks in 2009, due to the economic downturn, both markets continued to grow, rising quickly above levels of 2007, before the start of the global economic crisis. At the same time, however, the macroeconomic situation has been particularly unfavourable to the waste industry. Not only did the global economic crisis impact the economic situation more in general, it also resulted in declining waste volumes. Combined with the overcapacity in the market for waste incineration, this has led to lower profit margins and price pressures in the waste industry. Most firms, however, did establish higher turnover rates and described their economic situation as 'successful', 'doing fine', and 'solid'. For example, according to their annual reports, W1Mpr 'managed to maintain its market share and achieved customer growth', W2Lpr 'has managed to respond to market changes', and W11Mpr has proven itself 'resilient against market headwinds'. At the same time, also the chemical industry experienced setbacks due to the volatility of prices for raw materials, such as oil, metals and gases. As a result, C24Lpr in 2012 and C26Lpr in 2013 and 2014 also reported negative profits. Yet, in a report about the future of the chemical industry in the Netherlands, the Association of the Dutch Chemical Industry (VNCI) envisioned substantial economic growth for the industry and expected the Netherlands to 'remain a world leader in the chemical industry' (Deloitte Netherlands 2012, p. 1). In sum, waste management and processing chemical products remain 'big business'. Despite the economic pessimism of the past few years, the above findings suggest that the economic licences of firms in the chemical and waste industry provide them with enough leeway to invest in environmental compliance. The next paragraph therefore describes what efforts these firms have taken to comply with environmental regulations.

Environmental management style and environmental compliance

Rationally, firms that are more profitable should be able to invest more in environmental compliance measures to prevent violations and to better organise their compliance process than firms that are economically more restrained. Drawing on our qualitative data, we therefore analysed how the environmental management styles of these firms could be characterised into a typology. Are these firms responsive towards compliance with environmental rules and regulations, and do they indeed invest in environmental improvements?

In their study on pulp and paper mills, Gunningham *et al.* (2003) constructed five types of firms based on the managerial attitude towards environmental problems, the firm's actions and implementation efforts to meet specific demands, and the explanations for those actions (2003, pp. 8, 96–102). The five types include:

Environmental Laggards are not committed to compliance with environmental standards and their management is not committed to develop open dialogues with regulators and the social environment. They will only comply with regulations to avoid the high costs of enforcement actions.

Reluctant Compliers aim to meet minimum regulatory standards, but they are looking to cheat unless monitored closely. Similar to environmental laggards, they are not fully committed to establish open relationships with regulators and their social environment.

Committed Compliers aim to meet their legal obligations but they do so even when there are possibilities to cheat. They are willing to make substantial environmental investments but only if these contribute to future profits. They aim to establish open relationships with their legal and social environment, but predominantly see their legal license as most important.

Environmental Strategists and *True Believers* are more forward looking and see a strong environmental performance and investing in compliance measures beyond what is required by law as good for business. Environmental strategists are however afraid of the misinterpretation of information about their activities and therefore carefully manage their relationships with their legal and social environment and they are not fully transparent. In contrast, *true believers* aim to establish an open dialogue with their legal and social environment and are transparent about the environmental impacts of their activities.

As Gunningham *et al.* (2003) explain, each type shows a greater commitment to compliance, a greater interest in exploring environmental possibilities, more responsiveness to regulators and environmental activists, and the development of routines for environmental measures. Our qualitative data allowed us to apply this typology to the firms in our sample. In each category we sought to include two companies, one waste company and one chemical firm.

Environmental laggards

The management in these companies clearly holds a general aversion to environmental rules and to monitoring and supervision by regulatory authorities. This translates into constant differences of opinion between inspectors and the companies about the interpretation of rules and regulations. According to the management of these companies, regulatory authorities are too rigid in their interpretation of certain norms and fail to understand the practical problems that often occur in the waste and chemical industry where what is considered to be good environmental conduct changes very frequently. This attitude towards environmental compliance is particularly apparent at companies that have started out as family businesses with a relatively limited number of activities and since then have developed into large companies covering a wide range of activities. The management styles of W2Lpr and C24Lpr are typical examples of environmental laggards. W2Lpr is a large private company responsible for the collection and processing of household and industrial waste. The company has had continuous compliance issues throughout the past two decades. For example, in 2001 the company received a fine of 50,000 euros for the illegal export of contaminated timber. In the years thereafter, inspectors reported many environmental violations for which the company was fined each time. While the company had an average net profit of 4.1 million euros between 2010 and 2014, it does not seem to have changed its attitude towards compliance. In 2016, the company received a fine of 36,000 euros for inadequate safety protocols as a result of which an employee lost his hand. The company is not committed to an open dialogue with inspectors and its social environment. It is not transparent about its environmental performance and investments. For example, in its annual report there is no mentioning whatsoever about any of the environmental issues that took place. At the same time, however, the company tries to build its public image by providing financial support to a number of local initiatives such as various football clubs, a skate team and a healthcare institution. This 'impression management' (Goffman 1967), however, does not extend to the situation that the company involves the regulator or the local community in an open dialogue about its environmental policies and performance.

C24Lpr produces metal alkyls, chlorine and hydrogen and has been in existence for more than 40 years. Even though this company, by far, is the most profitable firm in our sample, with an average net turnover of 1.5 billion euros, it has a long history of environmental violations, including explosions on the premises, leakages of chemicals, fractures in pipelines and illegal emissions (Kluin 2014, pp. 145–149). Kluin recorded a total of 110 environmental violations and almost 60 health and safety violations between 1999 and 2011. Inspectors characterised the company as 'reactive', because it has shown no responsibility whatsoever for environmental compliance. The company deliberately avoided costs to comply with regulations and it had failed to do proper maintenance. An investigation into one of the violations showed that the corporation had not carried out routine maintenance services for a couple of years. The company received numerous enforcement actions over the years, including administrative and criminal fines and temporary shutdowns.

Reluctant compliers

The reluctant compliers in our sample, W14Mpr and C26Lpr, have started relatively late with environmental compliance as an integrated part of their business operations. W14Mpr for example, specialised in the demolition of construction waste, was founded in 1919 when regulation and enforcement were largely absent and was located in what back then was a rural area. Over the years, not only did regulation and enforcement practices increase, but also the surroundings developed, thus the company had to deal with a new regulatory and social environment. While the firm has an average net profit of 1.8 million euros per year, it still has difficulty with the demands and expectations of its legal and social environment and is rather reactive in responding to these demands. Its management believes that many of these demands are unfair because the company 'was there much longer' (van Wingerde 2012, p. 219). Over the years this has led to many arguments with regulators and its neighbours.

According to C26Lpr's annual reports, public safety and the environment are top priorities for the firm. Yet, Kluin (2014, p. 155) reported that C26Lpr had a total of 309 environmental violations between 1999 and 2011. During an inspection in 2012, a serious violation in an explosive area was detected and the company requested the inspectors not to mention it in their final report. Although the company seeks to meet the minimum standards, its management is particularly reluctant towards regulators and is reactive in dealing with environmental issues.

Committed compliers

W1Mpr and C25Mpr, both medium-sized, private companies are typical committed compliers. W1Mpr specialises in the treatment and processing of industrial waste and operates several land fill sites, which are located near very densely populated areas. In the past the company has been subject to scrutiny from their local environment, mainly for odour and dust nuisance. As a result, the company tried to present itself as a committed complier, by taking its legal obligations seriously and by trying to improve its environmental performance. Nonetheless, W1Mpr reported compliance issues in all years analysed. What makes it a committed complier though, is their drive to solve these issues and the fact that they have been extremely transparent about these compliance issues in their annual reports. Because of its previous experiences with the social environment however, it remains somewhat hesitant towards creating an open dialogue with their social stakeholders.

C25Mpr is a producer of industrial gases and is located in an industrial area in the Rotterdam harbour. Similar to W1Mpr, the company is relatively open to discuss its compliance issues with the environmental regulator. It has regular meetings with the regulatory authorities about its approach to environmental compliance and, although its investments in the environment are primarily seen as costs, it recognises the long-term benefits to the environment. Moreover, with only 40 violations since 1999 it is one of the best compliers in our sample (Kluin 2014, pp. 149–151).

Environmental strategists and true believers

As mentioned above, the environmental strategists and true believers are the most 'forward-looking' in their approach to environmental compliance. W11Mpr can be characterised as a strategist that is extremely aware of its public image that has been fragile over the years. The company has had many environmental compliance issues in the past. In 2007, the company was convicted for several environmental crimes and in 2010 the public prosecutor started a new investigation into the company. In addition, the company faces many odour complaints from the nearby residential area. One the one hand, this has led the company to invest a lot of money in environmental compliance measures and maintenance. For example, between 2012 and 2014, it invested on average 12.7 million euros in environmental compliance measures. On the other hand, the company is extremely sensitive towards its public image. Because of the fear that information is misinterpreted, the flow of information about the environmental performance of the company is carefully controlled. For example, its annual environmental report includes only aggregated data of all business units of the company, separate locations are not visible. Moreover, the company registers compliance issues as 'to do's' in its compliance management system because this sends a more positive message to regulators and the public (van Wingerde 2012, pp. 295–296).

Also C22Mpr, which transports, stores and handles containers with dangerous substances, had issues with environmental compliance in its early years. After investments in environmental compliance measures and the hiring of better-qualified personnel, it took considerable steps to ensure that it was in compliance with regulatory requirements. Since 1999, the company had only 24 environmental violations, all of which were handled through warnings (Kluin 2014, p. 118). On the other hand, C22Mpr generally does not spend money on the environment because 'it is the right thing to do'. It approaches environmental issues as normal business decisions and only invests in the environment if it helps reaching business success.

The two companies that come close to being true believers at least in terms of its environmental attitude, are W9Lpu and C23Lpr. What distinguishes these firms from the others in our sample is their approach towards environmental investments. These are not solely seen as costly investments, but doing good for the environment is seen as an integrated part of its business success and these firms frequently invest in environmental measures that go beyond what is required by law. For example, C23Lpr invested a little over 10 per cent of its turnover in 2014 in environmental safety measures. And W9Lpu created business success by being the first company to develop innovative recycling techniques, which make it possible to completely reuse certain materials that otherwise would have gone to waste. Both companies do not fully resemble true believers though – which according to Gunningham *et al.* (2003, pp. 102, 116) might not even be achievable in the real world – as they were still fined for environmental violations. Kluin (2014, p. 132), however, concludes that of the 15 companies analysed in her study, C23Lpr had the lowest number of violations and the company turned out to be very responsive, proactive and transparent in reaction to enforcement actions. Also W9Lpu reported violations in all years analysed, but these were relatively minor offences, leading to relatively small fines.

In sum, the above description of our ten companies shows that their attitude towards environmental compliance varies widely. While all these companies are rather profitable, the analysis has shown that in most cases environmental compliance is perceived as a 'burden' and not yet seen as a part of the success of the business. Moreover, all companies reported environmental violations throughout the years analysed. This is due to historical developments, previous negative experiences with regulators and their social environment, and the managerial attitude towards environmental compliance. Let us now see how the environmental violations have been dealt with.

Enforcement

Previous research has suggested that while large and complex companies are involved in illegalities quite frequently, only a relatively small number of cases result in criminal prosecution. Most cases are dealt with through civil or regulatory proceedings (Sutherland 1980). For example, Clinard and Yeager (1980) found that only 1.9 per cent of the cases that they analysed resulted in criminal sanctions. In her study into cases handled by the *Securities and Exchange Commission (SEC)*, Shapiro (1984, 1985) found that only 11 per cent of the cases resulted in criminal prosecutions and more than 50 per cent of the 526 cases that she analysed were dealt with informally, not resulting in any sanction whatsoever. More recently, Beckers (2017, pp. 263–296) analysed the extent to which the 237 largest corporations in the Netherlands had criminal records and focused on the ways in which the offences were dealt with. His research shows that almost 80 per cent of these firms did not have a criminal record (pp. 266–267). Those firms that did have a criminal record (N=50) were mainly involved in environmental offences. Even though these 50 firms can be characterised as exceptionally large in terms of the average number of employees (12,741) and their annual profits (average: 294.5 million euros) (p. 268), the penalties for these crimes were rather low. The average fine constituted 5,059 euros (p. 285). Moreover, Beckers shows that in the majority of cases the public prosecutor holds a preference for out-of-court settlements. In sum, even though rule violations are widespread among the largest and most powerful companies, criminal enforcement is rare and even when companies are convicted penalties are relatively lenient.

Consistent with these findings, the self-reported violations and enforcement actions in the annual reports show that a lot of violations are left untouched and that the sanctions are insignificant compared to the profits of most of these firms. For example, W1Mpr reported compliance issues in all years considered and received fines for almost all violations. In 2011, the firm received 13 fines for several health and safety and environmental violations. The total amount paid constituted 19,961 euros. In total, the company paid 109,159 euros in fines for four years of violations. Moreover, W9Lpu reported violations in all years, but it only received a fine of 6,750 euros and a fine of 9,000 euros for two accidents, including one fatal, on the premises.

Two companies reported about criminal penalties in their annual reports. In 2012, W11Mpr was criminally prosecuted and convicted because the company had made a profit out of its environmental violations almost a decade earlier. While the prosecutor had demanded a fine of 17.5 million euros, the court imposed a fine of 7 million euros, roughly 8 per cent of its net turnover. Two years later, the company was convicted because it had failed to report an environmental incident at its premises. The fine imposed was 35,000 euros. At the same time however, the regulators left over 12 violations untouched. Also W14MPr had failed to report an environmental incident at its premises. The penalty imposed was 2,000 euros.

Interesting enough, though, the reported issues and violations can be entirely attributed to the annual reports of waste companies. Logically, this does not lead to the conclusion that chemical companies are better compliers than waste firms. In her earlier work, Kluin (2014, p. 107) showed us that all 15 companies in her study were involved in environmental crimes: she reported a total of 1,916 environmental violations in the period between 1999 and 2011. It does, however, suggest that waste companies are more transparent in disclosing environmental issues. This may be due to the fact that waste companies – compared to chemical firms – have been subject to intense public scrutiny in the past (van Wingerde 2012). By disclosing environmental issues, even if those are unfavourable to the firm, companies may set the tone of the debate and may influence public perceptions about the industry (e.g. Arena *et al.* 2015).

In sum, enforcement appeared to be extremely lenient, which is consistent with previous research and our own observations in these industries (van Wingerde 2012; Kluin 2014). When criminal law is being used, however, companies expect that it concerns serious violations by calculating offenders. These relatively small penalties only communicate the message that the violation in itself is rather insignificant, undermining the potential deterrent effect the sanction may have and the legitimacy of the public regulator (van Wingerde 2012, 2015, 2016; Yeager 2016).

Conclusion

This chapter reports the results of a qualitative case study of ten companies in the waste and chemical industry in the Netherlands designed to explore how profitable these firms really are and how these companies deal with environmental compliance. As a case study of only ten firms this chapter cannot provide definitive answers to the question how profitability and compliance are related to one another. This study does shed some light, however, on environmental compliance of these firms and the factors explaining individual firm differences.

One key finding of this chapter is that waste and chemical companies in the Netherlands are rather profitable with an average net profit of 2.4 million euros per year. At the same time, all these firms had compliance issues in the years analysed and we have observed that most violations are met with financial penalties that are rather insignificant, thus confirming the idea that these firms are indeed too big to deter, while being too 'small' to take environmental compliance seriously. This questions the proposition that is often posed in the business management literature that industry growth and environmentally friendly behaviour can coincide (Stretesky *et al.* 2013).

Yet, this study also shows that the attitude towards compliance varies greatly among these firms. Using the environmental management styles constructed by Gunningham *et al.* (2003), we have presented profiles of these firms' attitude towards environmental compliance. It shows that profitability or a lack thereof does not necessarily serve as a 'brake' on environmental investments. In fact, the most profitable company in our sample, C24Lpr, can be characterised as an environmental laggard. Therefore, profitability in itself does not fully explain individual firm differences (Gunningham *et al.* 2003; Lynch-Wood and Williamson 2007; Thornton *et al.* 2008; Rorie 2015). The different responses to environmental compliance seem to be far more dependent on historical interactions with the regulatory and social environment and the managerial attitude towards compliance. Moreover, we have observed a clear difference in our data between violations reported by the waste firms and the chemical corporations in our sample. Based on the annual reports analysed, we could only find violations reported by waste companies; chemical firms did not publicly report the environmental issues that they were confronted with while research by Kluin (2014) showed that all companies had been involved in environmental violations. This suggests that waste companies are more transparent in reporting environmental matters than chemical firms. As discussed previously, this is due to the fact that the waste industry has had a much longer history being under public scrutiny than the chemical industry in the Netherlands, which has only been in the public eye since 2011 when a series of major incidents took place.

Finally, this study also has some limitations. As mentioned before, it proved to be extremely hard to collect data for all the companies in our sample and for all the years that we were interested in. Moreover, self-reports are often biased. As firms aim to present themselves as positive as possible in their annual statements, it might be convenient to try to fit facts and figures about compliance into their own objectives, which often makes it difficult to assess the value of the materials collected. As a result, this chapter cannot present causal links between profitability and environmental compliance. In order to do that, longitudinal data is necessary about environmental performance of firms, for example data on emissions or violations, and sanctions. However, one of the key differences between the Anglo-Saxon countries and the Netherlands is that this data is largely unavailable in the Netherlands. Since its inception in the early 1970s, for example the United States Environmental Protection Agency has kept comprehensive data on the nature, scope and results of their inspections, about emissions, and about compliance (Cohen 2000). In the Netherlands, however, the registration and management of such data is still in its infancy. This chapter therefore demonstrates the need for regulators to keep better records and for making this data available to regulatory agencies and academic researchers. Only then will we be able to gain more insight into the compliance records of firms over time and provide more definitive answers to the question of how profitability and compliance are related to one another.

References

Arena, C., Bozzolan, S. and Michelon, G. 2015. 'Environmental reporting: transparency to stakeholders or stakeholder manipulation? An analysis of disclosure tone and the role of the Board of Directors', *Corporate Social Responsibility and Environmental Management* 22, 346–361.

Beckers, J. 2017. Between Ideal and Reality. An empirical study of the criminal justice approach to organisational criminality in the Netherlands. (Tussen Ideaal en Werkelijkheid. Amsterdam: Uitgeverij Bijzonder Strafrecht.nl.

Braithwaite, J. and Makkai, T. 1991. 'Testing an expected utility model of corporate deterrence', *Law & Society Review* 25, 7–39.

Clinard, M.B. and Yeager, P.C. 1980. *Corporate Crime*. New York: Free Press.

Cohen, M.A. 2000. 'Empirical research on the deterrent effect of environmental monitoring and enforcement', *Environmental Law Reporter* 30(4), 10245–10252.

Daele, S. van, Vander Beken, T. and Dorn, N. 2007. 'Waste management and crime: regulatory, business, and product vulnerabilities', *Environmental Policy and Law* 37(1), 34–38.

Deloitte Netherlands 2012. *The Chemical Industry in the Netherlands: World Leading Today and in 2030–2050.*

Garrett, B.L. 2014. *Too Big to Jail. How Prosecutors Compromise with Corporations.* Cambridge: Harvard University Press.

Goffman, E. 1967. *Interaction Ritual: Essays on Face-to-Face Interaction*. New York: Anchor Books.

Guenster, N., Bauer, R., Derwall, J. and Koedijk, K. 2011. 'The economic value of corporate eco-efficiency', *European Financial Management* 17(4), 679–704.

Gunningham, N., Kagan, R. and Thornton, D. 2003. *Shades of Green. Business, Regulation, and Environment.* Stanford: Stanford University Press.

Gunningham, N., Kagan, R. and Thornton, D. (2004). 'Social license and environmental protection: why businesses go beyond compliance?', *Law & Social Inquiry* 29, 307–341.

Hamilton, J.T. 1995. 'Pollution as news: media and stock market reactions to the toxics release inventory data', *Journal of Environmental Economics and Management* 28, 98–113.

Hertz, N. 2003. *The Silent Takeover – Global Capitalism and the Death of Democracy.* Amsterdam: Pandora Pockets.

Huisman, W. 2016. 'Criminogenic organizational properties and dynamics', in *The Oxford Handbook of White-Collar Crime*, edited by S. van Slyke, M. Benson and F. Cullen. New York: Oxford University Press, 435–462, section B on Autonomy and responsibility.

Joyce, S.A. and Thomson, I. 2000. 'Earning a social license to operate: social acceptability and resource development in Latin America', *The Canadian Mining and Metallurgical Bulletin* 93 (1037), 49–52.

Karpoff, J.M., Lott, J.R. and Wehrly, E.W. 2005. 'The reputational penalties for environmental violations: empirical evidence', *Journal of Law and Economics* 48(2), 653–675.

Kluin, M.H.A. 2014. *Optic Compliance. Enforcement and Compliance in the Dutch Chemical Industry*. Ridderkerk: Ridderprint.

Kluin, M.H.A. 2015. 'The perception of Seveso regulation and inspection in chemical corporations', in *The Routledge Handbook of White-Collar and Corporate Crime in Europe*, edited by J. van Erp, W. Huisman and G. Vande Walle. Oxford: Routledge, 486–511.

Konar, S. and Cohen, M.A. 2001. 'Does the market value environmental performance?', *Review of Economics and Statistics* 83, 281–289.

Lynch-Wood, G. and Williamson, D. 2007. 'The social license as a form of regulation for small and medium enterprises', *Journal of Law & Society* 34 (3), 321–341.

Mill, G.A.J. 2006. 'The financial performance of a socially responsible investment over time and a possible link with corporate social responsibility', *Journal of Business Ethics* 63, 131–148.

Nellemann, C., Henriksen, R., Kreilhuber, A., Stewart, D., Kotsovou, M., Raxter, P., Mrema, E. and Barrat, S. 2016. *The Rise of Environmental Crime – A Growing Threat to Natural Resources Peace, Development and Security*. Nairobi: UNEP.

Noordhoek, F.K. 2014. *Afval! Jaarboek 2013 [Waste! Yearbook 2013]*. Utrecht: Noordhoek Publishers.

Orlitzky, M. 2009. 'Corporate social performance and financial performance: a research synthesis', *The Oxford Handbook of Corporate Social Responsibility* (online). DOI:10.1093/oxfordhb/9780199211593.003.0005.

Rorie, M. 2015. 'An integrated theory of corporate environmental compliance and overcompliance', *Crime, Law and Social Change* 64(2), 65–101.

Parker, C. 2006. 'The compliance trap: the moral message in responsive regulatory enforcement', *Law & Society Review* 40(3), 591–622.

Parker, C. and Lehmann Nielsen, V. (eds.) 2011. *Explaining Regulatory Compliance. Business Responses to Regulation*. Cheltenham: Edward Elgar.

Porter, M.E. and Linde, van der, C. 1995. 'Green and competitive: ending the stalemate', *Harvard Business Review* 73, 120–134.

Prakash, A. 2000. *Greening the Firm. The Politics of Corporate Environmentalism*. Cambridge: Cambridge University Press.

Russo, M.V. and Fouts, P.A. 1997. 'A resource-based perspective on corporate environmental performance and profitability', *Academy of Management Journal* 40(3), 534–559.

Schell-Busey, N., Simpson, S.S., Rorie, M. and Alper, M. 2016. 'What works? A systematic review of corporate crime deterrence', *Criminology & Public Policy* 15(2), 387–416.

Scholtens, B. 2006. 'Finance as a driver of corporate social responsibility', *Journal of Business Ethics* 68(1), 19–33.

Shane, P.B., and Spicer, B.H. 1983. 'Market response to environmental information produced outside the firm', *Accounting Review* 52, 521–538.

Shapiro, S.P. 1984. *Wayward Capitalists: Targets of the Securities and Exchange Commission*. New Haven, CT: Yale University Press.

Shapiro, S.P. 1985. 'The road not taken: The elusive path to criminal prosecution for white-collar crime', *Law & Society Review* 19, 179–217.

Simpson, S.S. 2002. *Corporate Crime, Law, and Social Control*. New York: Cambridge University Press.

Snider, L. 2010. 'Framing e-waste regulation: the obfuscating role of power', *Criminology & Public Policy* 9(3), 569–577.

Stone, C.D. 1975. *Where the Law Ends: The Social Control of Corporate Behavior*. New York: Harper & Row.

Stretesky, P., Long, M. and Lynch, M. 2013. 'Does environmental enforcement slow the treadmill of production? The relationship between large money penalties and toxic releases within offending corporations', *Journal of Crime and Justice* 36, 235–249.

Sutherland, E.H. 1980. *White Collar Crime. The Uncut Version*. New Haven: Yale University Press.

Thornton, D., Gunningham, N.A. and Kagan, R.A. 2005. 'General deterrence and corporate environmental behavior', *Law & Policy* 27(2), 262–287.

Thornton, D., Kagan, R.A. and Gunningham, N. 2008. 'Compliance costs, regulation, and environmental performance: Controlling truck emissions in the US', *Regulation & Governance* 2(3), 275–292.

Thornton, D., Kagan, R.A. and Gunningham, N. 2009. 'When social norms and pressures are not enough: environmental performance in the trucking industry', *Law & Society Review* 43 (2), 405–436.

Wingerde, van, C.G. 2012. *De afschrikking voorbij: Een empirische studie naar afschrikking, generale preventie en regelnaleving in de Nederlandse afvalbranche. (Beyond Deterrence: Deterrence, Prevention, and Compliance in the Dutch Waste Industry)*. Nijmegen: Wolf Legal Publishers.

Wingerde, van, C.G. 2015. 'The limits of environmental regulation in a globalized economy. Lessons from the Probo Koala case', in *The Routledge Handbook of White-Collar and Corporate Crime in Europe* edited by J.G. van Erp, W. Huisman and G. Vande Walle. Oxford: Routledge, 260–275.

Wingerde, van, C.G. 2016. 'Deterring corporate environmental crime. Lessons from the waste industry in the Netherlands', in *Environmental Crime in Transnational Context. Global Issues in Green Enforcement and Criminology*, edited by T. Spapens, W. Huisman, and R. White. Oxford: Routledge, 193–207.

Yeager, P.C. 2016. 'The elusive deterrence of corporate crime', *Criminology & Public Policy* 15(2), 439–451.

8 Waste crime from three criminological perspectives

Implications for crime control and harm prevention

Lieselot Bisschop and Wim Huisman

Introduction

A rising world population and increased production and consumption generate ever higher quantities of waste. By 2050, the approximately 9 billion people on the planet will produce an estimated 13.1 billion tonnes of waste per year (Hoornweg and Bhada-Tata 2012; Zoi Environmental Network and GRID-Arendal 2012). The use of chemicals in product manufacturing has also contributed to a higher toxicity of waste (Pellow 2007). From the 1960s, the Global North became increasingly concerned about the potential environmental and health hazards in these higher quantities and toxicities of waste. These concerns led to the creation of many laws and regulations about waste recovery, disposal and transport. Answering to these legal requirements of environmentally sound waste treatment implied a much higher cost. This resulted in the waste industry becoming a sector of high economic importance (Mathews *et al.* 2012; Rucevska *et al.* 2015).[1]

Waste trade happens for several reasons such as the recovery of secondary materials, the proximity of recycling facilities across borders and the existence of specific treatment facilities in few locations. The search for cheaper ways to treat and/or dispose of waste is, however, the most important reason behind the trade. The financially most interesting option is often located across borders (European Environment Agency 2012). Both legal and illegal enterprises are keen to pocket those high profits (Ruggiero and South 2010). In fact, the transition from legal to illegal can occur at several stages of the waste process such as national and cross-border transport, in collection or disposal (Passas 1999).

---

1   This chapter is an adaptation of the following article: Bisschop, L. and Huisman, W. (2016). 'Afvalcriminaliteit vanuit drie criminologische perspectieven. Implicaties voor preventie en controle'. *Cahiers Politiestudies*, Vol.38 (Special Issue: Groene Criminologie en Veiligheidszorg), pp.111–137. Printed with permission of the publisher.

Illegal waste disposal is one of the first topics that was defined as environmental crime (Block and Scarpitti 1985; Szasz 1986) and thus became part of 'green criminology' research (South 1998a, 1998b). Long before the emergence of this sub-discipline, waste crime was studied from other criminological perspectives. The criminogenic opportunities of waste as a product and as a sector are abused by both corporations and criminal organisations; making waste crime the topic of corporate and organised crime research.

Studying a phenomenon within a specific criminological research tradition impacts its framing – and therefore the way in which the phenomenon is defined and characterised. This influences theoretical explanations about the nature and causes of the phenomenon, which in turn impacts the crime prevention or control policy and thus the ways in which police and other security services address it. A clear example of this is the conclusion of the Dutch Organised Crime Monitor that organised crime happens in social networks, which resulted in a crime control strategy of targeting offenders that occupy crucial 'nodes' in these networks (Kleemans and Kruissink 1999; Kleemans 2014a). Of course, police work is more often informed by forms of crime that affect and concern citizens directly and visibly. Organised and corporate crime does not seem to be high on civilians' lists of concerns (Devroe and Ponsaers 2015). However, we consider it a responsibility of criminologists to translate scientific insights about crime to implications for policy making.

In this chapter, we therefore aim to explicitly connect theory to practice. Our central question is which implications different criminological approaches to the waste-crime nexus and their respective etiological explanations hold for crime control and harm prevention. To answer this question, we build on three criminological perspectives on waste crime: waste as organised crime, waste as corporate crime and waste from a green criminology perspective. For each of these three perspectives, we discuss what consequences the theories – and views on the role of illicit gains of waste crime – have for controlling and preventing waste crime and whether the contemporary regulation and enforcement answers to these requirements.

Besides drawing from existing criminological studies on waste crime, this chapter builds on the findings of our own studies on the Dutch waste sector (Huisman 2001; van Erp and Huisman 2010; Huisman and van Erp 2013) and the Belgian trade in e-waste (Bisschop 2015). We also pay attention to how these three criminological perspectives are reflected in reports and recommendations on waste crime by NGOs and international governmental organisations. For each of the three perspectives, we discuss a couple of prominent cases of waste crime that reflect the framing of the nature and the causes of the theoretical perspectives.[2]

---

2 We do not claim to assess the causal relationship between the framing and the criminological perspective: were cases analysed from that respective perspective or did the cases result in the framing of this type of waste crime from a specific perspective?

In the following part of this chapter, we discuss what waste crime is and how waste as a sector and product creates criminogenic opportunities for illicit gain. Next, we discuss the involvement of organised crime groups in waste crime, after which we turn to a review of the role of legitimate companies in waste crime. Then we analyse waste crime from a green criminological perspective. In the discussion, we discuss how these three perspectives relate to each other and propose an integrated strategy for the prevention and control of waste crime.

Waste and crime

Whenever there is no further purpose for a product or substance, be it in production or consumption, waste is generated. Waste treatment is the process that changes the characteristics of the waste to facilitate its handling, to make recovery of secondary raw materials possible or to reduce the quantity and hazardous nature (Williams *et al.* 2013). Waste disposal is the final phase, which can refer to landfill, incineration and dumping. Waste can refer to a variety of materials such as glass, metal, paper, textiles, plastic or organic material (or a mix thereof). It can also be classified based on sectors of everyday life, such as households, agriculture, mining, energy production, manufacturing and construction. Also illicit activities such as drug production generate waste. When substances create extra risks for harming the environment and human health, such waste may be labelled as toxic or hazardous waste. This brings challenges for ecologically sound treatment, which usually also means extra costs.

Waste crimes refer to the trade, treatment or disposal of waste in ways that breach international or domestic environmental legislation and cause harm or risk to the environment and human health. This can refer to administrative/ regulatory violations (e.g. in the case of non-compliance with licence requirements) as well as breaches of criminal law (e.g. deliberately causing harm). Many cases of non-compliance with waste regulation are, in fact, dealt with by regulatory agencies and might not even come to the attention of police or justice officials. Moreover, many violations of waste regulation do not require specific actions; they are often violations exactly because required actions to adhere to regulatory requirements were not taken (Huisman and van Erp 2013). Many waste crimes thus equal crimes of omission, albeit often with very conscious inaction. Some waste crimes do require specific actions such as in the dumping of hazardous waste and constitute crimes of commission. Further, illegal trafficking of waste often includes fraudulent activities, such as falsifying loading bills or lab reports.

A number of sector and product specific characteristics help explain the connection between waste and crime. The criminogenic character of waste relates, in part, to the development of the sector and the regulatory framework. Today, the waste sector is heavily regulated, but prior to the 1980s there were hardly any laws about the management of and trade in (hazardous) waste. Around that time, disasters such as Three-Mile Island (1979) and Chernobyl (1986), both of which involved radioactive waste, and the Love Canal case (mid 1970s), where a neighbourhood was built on land formerly used as an industrial chemical dumpsite (see Levine 1982 for details), raised public concern about (hazardous) waste generation and disposal in industrialised nations. Once the waste sector within industrialised nations was more strictly regulated, the export of hazardous waste to countries with lower environmental standards and therefore lower costs for treatment and/or disposal became commonplace. When several disturbing cases of toxic waste exports from industrialised to developing countries were exposed, these hazardous waste exports were criminalised in international law.[3] The increased regulation of the industry made the prices for environmentally sound waste treatment skyrocket. The globalised waste marked, however, continued to provide opportunities for both legal and illegal profits (Pellow 2007). The rapid growth and international character of the sector allowed a diversity of actors to work in the waste industry, with brokers and subcontractors involved at different stages (Szasz 1986). In collection, transport and treatment, multiple smaller companies try to compete with the few big ones (Vander Beken 2007). Combining that with high profit margins and a small chance of getting caught, this is a breeding ground for cutting corners and exploiting legislative loopholes. This is especially true because regulation and enforcement has not kept pace with this global market space (Tompson and Chainey 2011).

The waste sector is an un-level global playing field, with asymmetries between countries in laws, politics, culture, knowledge and awareness. These asymmetries are criminogenic because they foster the demand for illegal goods or services, are an incentive to participate in illegal markets and hamper the ability of authorities to control (Passas 1999, p. 402). Whereas many countries have ratified and implemented the international legal framework for (hazardous) waste trade, many others have not, which results in legal and law enforcement asymmetries, and consequently in jurisdiction (s)hopping in search of the most favourable (illegal) agreement or for the space between the laws (Clapp 2002; Heckenberg 2010). This goes hand in hand with asymmetries in knowledge and awareness about the dangers of substandard treatment and disposal of (hazardous) waste. Moreover, there are economic asymmetries between regions of the world, which can lead countries to accept financially interesting waste transports into their country despite an absence of facilities for treatment or disposal (Bisschop 2012). Those harmed by this illegal trade often do not have the economic means nor political power to oppose the polluters (Mohai and Saha 2007).

3   1989 Basel Convention on the Control of Transboundary Movements of Hazardous Wastes and their Disposal; 1998 Bamako Convention on the Ban of the Import into Africa and the Control of Transboundary Movement and Management of Hazardous Wastes within Africa; 1989 Lomé IV Convention; 1994 Ban Amendment; Montreal Protocol on Substances that Deplete the Ozone Layer; International Convention for the Prevention of Pollution from Ships (MARPOL); 2001 OECD Decision on Control of Transboundary Movements of Wastes Destined for Recovery Operations, the 2001 Stockholm Convention on Persistent Organic Pollutants, the 1985 Vienna Convention for the Protection of the Ozone Layer, and 1992 Rotterdam Convention on the Prior Informed Consent Procedure for Certain Hazardous Chemicals and Pesticides in International Trade.

We have explained why the waste sector is considered to be crime-facilitative, but also waste as a product is criminogenic (Gobert and Punch 2003). Waste allows for fairly easy disguises by mixing it up with less hazardous waste, mislabelling it or selling it as second-hand commodities (Gibbs *et al.* 2010). Recyclable material is for instance used to hide hazardous waste or household waste is mixed with hazardous waste and then dumped. Other fraudulent techniques used are the falsification of customs forms by using non-hazardous waste or product codes to classify hazardous waste. Traders under- or over-invoice to disguise waste shipments. An increasing number of containers, containing hazardous waste, are also abandoned in ports throughout the world (Rucevska *et al.* 2015). Expensive environmentally sound waste treatment means an inverse incentive structure for waste. In contrast to many other industries, waste treatment companies are paid before they incur any costs for treatment and/or disposal. This makes it very tempting to limit the costs and maximise the profits without regard for regulation (Huisman 2001). This makes waste crime a low risk and high profit phenomenon (Rucevska et al. 2015).

As illustrated above, waste as a global sector and as a product creates ample criminogenic opportunities and incentives for illicit gain. In what follows, we analyse waste crime from three criminological perspectives: organised crime, corporate crime and green criminology. For each perspective, we pay attention to the theories used, take note of a couple of prominent cases and discuss implications for crime prevention and control.

Waste and organised crime

Organised crime theory and waste

Organised crime is one of those types of crime that does not easily lend itself to a clear definition as illustrated by the multitude of existing definitions in scientific literature and policy documents (Von Lampe 2017). Over the years these definitions have shifted between *who* and *what* notions of organised crime and are now often settling on a combination of the two. The former notion refers to stable partnerships of criminals who systematically engage in crime (organised crime groups), whereas the latter refers to serious criminal activities in more loosely organised structures (Paoli and Vander Beken 2014). Organised crime can involve many types of crime (fraud, embezzlement, money laundering, racketeering, extortion, human trafficking, drug trafficking, etc.) and many types of actors who on their own do not constitute a criminal organisation, but do so in interaction (Finckenauer 2005). Organised crime is often defined as complex criminal organisations that aim to control illegal markets – and even branch out to legal markets – and attain control by means of violence and/or corruption. However, it changes with new criminal opportunities arising and its definition thus requires flexibility (Von Lampe 2008). Moreover, differentiating between organised crime and corporate crime is not always easy, because there are many interfaces between the two (Ruggiero 1996). Organised crime is inextricably intertwined with legal activities and companies and is socially embedded (Kleemans and van de Bunt 2008; van de Bunt *et al.* 2014). In the case of bigger corporations, the corporate crime argument is usually quite clear, but much smaller corporate entities might have been created with criminal intentions. In (Dutch) practice, police investigations concerning environmental crime often focus on small, almost marginal, companies (Huisman and van Erp 2013). When defining waste crime as organised, this refers to perpetrators who systematically commit these offences and who created their organisation or cooperation with that criminal intent. Illicit activities are their primary raison d'être and these waste crimes go hand in hand with forgery, tax fraud, money laundering, corruption, extortion, etc.

Definitions and theories concerning organised crime therefore need to be dynamic in order to account for new developments in society (Kleemans 2014b). Recent criminal policy often uses organised crime in combination with serious crime. Also environmental crime cases often involve serious crime and have demonstrated the interconnectedness of organised crime groups with legal actors. Distinctions between these activities and labels are therefore not always clear-cut.

Although this chapter provides examples of organised crime involvement in waste crimes, it is necessary to keep in mind that different countries have different conceptualisations. Using a fairly narrow definition of organised crime, referring strictly to organised crime groups as Mafia-like organisations, Italy only reports organised crime group involvement in environmental crime if it concerns the mafia. Germany, using the definition of the *Bundeskriminalamt* (BKA) reports seven cases in 2011 and eight in 2012 (environmental crime overall, not specific to waste). During those same years, the Netherlands reports 34 and 42 prosecutions of environmental organised crime cases (EnviCrimeNet 2014, p. 18).[4]

> Whereas the term organized crime still has strong evocative power, which undoubtedly explains its political success, the many different criminal actors and activities that have been subsumed under this make it a vague umbrella concept, as a basis for empirical analyses, theory-building or policy-making.
>
> (Paoli and Vander Beken 2014, p.13)

These conceptual difficulties render assessments of the scope of organised crime involvement in waste crimes (and other environmental crimes) and cross-country comparisons difficult.

Cases

Many official reports conclude that organised crime plays an important role in the illegal trade and dumping of (hazardous) waste (Europol 2015; IMPEL-TFS

---

4   It is unclear to what extent these reported cases also answer to the official definition of organised crime that is in use in the Netherlands since the Parliamentary Inquiry of 1996 (Kleemans 2014a).

2012; Interpol 2009; UNODC 2013). The connection between waste and organised crime is not new. To the contrary, this has been discussed for decades, especially related to the United States and Italy (Ruggiero 1996; Szasz 1986). We discuss these two countries because they can be considered prominent cases. Afterwards, we broaden the scope to other countries.

In the United States of the 1970s and 1980s, organised criminals virtually monopolised the collection and disposal of waste, especially in the states of New Jersey and New York (Block 2002; Szasz 1986). Disguised as legitimate firms (e.g. *USA Waste*; *Waste Management*), organised crime groups dominated the solid waste industry. These criminal waste practices ranged from predatory pricing, over mixing of hazardous and non-hazardous waste, to dumping of toxic waste. A parliamentary inquiry demonstrated the relationships of these waste firms with public officials. Regulators failed to effectively deal with the overcharging by the waste collectors, amounting to double or triple the prices of other major US cities, and they also failed to address the systemic corruption. These organised crime groups even resorted to vandalism, violence and threats towards their customers and potential competitors to establish and uphold their monopoly, including two murders (Jacobs *et al.* 1992). Similar waste hauling racketeering happened in other US cities such as Boston and Chicago, which were later settled in anti-trust cases (Block 2002). The connection of the waste industry and organised crime in the United States is not merely something of the past. In a 2013 US Federal District Court case, 32 people – member of La Cosa Nostra families – were indicted for crimes in the garbage hauling industry (Department of Justice 2013; Rashbaum and Goldstein 2013).

Similar to the US, the involvement of organised crime in the Italian waste industry has long been recognised (Massari and Monzini 2004). An estimated 20,000 tonnes of hazardous waste disappear every year, either dumped at sea or illegally transported and dumped outside of Italy's borders (Alessio D'Amato *et al.* 2014). One modus operandi is the invoice switch (*giro bolla*) in which hazardous waste goes from the producer to a temporary storage facility, which changes the documents from hazardous to non-hazardous without actually treating the waste (Alessio D'Amato and Zoli 2011). The trade in waste is allegedly controlled by 'Ndrangheta, La Cosa Nostra and Camorra, that ship it to Eastern European or West African countries, dumping the waste in construction sites or landfills or selling it as fertilizer' (Liddick 2009; Eman 2013; Legambiente 2014). Italy also has about 5,000 illegal landfill sites, especially in the region of Campania, which hardly produces any waste (Senior and Mazza 2004). Corruption of local authorities helps these illegal organisations to continue their business largely undisturbed (Alessio D'Amato and Zoli 2011; Past 2013).

Many academic publications and government reports refer to the US and Italy when discussing organised crime involvement in waste crimes. Reports about other countries rarely mention specific cases. The Interpol Pollution Crime Working Group (Interpol 2009; INTERPOL Pollution Crime Working Group 2009) reported about the illegal import and export of waste, ozone-depleting substances and e-waste, and about the illegal dumping of hazardous waste. They report that the complexity of the waste legislation makes it difficult to clearly delineate legal and illegal activities. Also Europol identified the illegal trade in waste as an important threat for European member states and stresses the importance of proactive approaches because criminal markets and methods are flexible (Europol 2011, 2015). Both organisations refer to business-like structures and loosely organised involvement of organised criminals, who work together for specific criminal opportunities and then form new groups, rather than hierarchically structured organised crime. Some of these more loosely organised networks do have international connections and try to assume power over legal waste treatment or transport companies.

In November 2011, *EnviCrimeNet* was created in Europe, under the auspices of Europol. One of EnviCrimeNet's activities has been an *Intelligence Project on Environmental Crime* focused on intelligence gathering about the involvement, vulnerabilities and threats of organised crime groups in environmental crime. Their first report (EnviCrimeNet 2014) links environmental crimes to money laundering, fraud, forgery, corruption and even terrorism and drug trafficking. It states that the threat and extent of environmental crime is overall under-estimated, partially due to a lack of information about the involvement of organised crime groups. As mentioned earlier, the Netherlands prosecuted several organised environmental crime cases in recent years. These concerned illegal collection, (international) trade, storage and dumping of hazardous waste and e-waste (EnviCrimeNet 2014). Several of the criminal groups were inter-twined with legal companies through money laundering, illegal construction and corruption. In a couple of cases there was a connection to drugs and human trafficking. The Southern part of the Netherlands for instance has several cases of dumping of chemical waste resulting from the production of synthetic drugs. Environmental criminals who used to work alone, get together in criminal groups. Another analysis of Dutch waste crime police investigations found no connection to drugs, human or weapons trafficking (Neve 2013). For the illegal export of waste from Belgium to African countries, there is often some degree of organisation with the so-called 'waste tourists', evident from their falsified passports and interconnections (Bisschop 2012).

Organised crime is an area that comes with mythical numbers and attempts to criticise them might be perceived as a way to claim the topic is not important (Calderoni 2014). While the various reports by governmental and non-governmental organisations mainly present the assumption that the waste industry is vulnerable to organised crime, empirical research and the available cases mainly show waste crime that is committed by mostly licit companies in the waste industry (see below). Organised crime in the traditional interpretation of mafia-like stable criminal organisations might not be the primary type of crime involved in the waste business, with the American and Italian cases as the well-known exceptions. Instead, more flexible cooperation focused on the illicit activities, often intertwined with corporate forms of organised crime, have taken their place (Carter 1999). The interconnectedness of illegal trade with the legal economy is obvious and often it concerns fraud and tax evasion (serious crime) rather than organised crime in the strict sense of the word. The involvement of organised crime groups is therefore not always apparent.

Implications for crime prevention and control

Labelling waste crime as organised crime implies that the governance response is one of traditional crime control, policing of illegal markets and trying to eliminate and deter perpetrators. Police organisations, whether working within national borders or cooperating internationally, are challenged in their reporting about organised crime. As discussed above, the differences in definitions of organised crime, make a systematic comparison across countries and regions difficult. This is even more true for environmental crime, because it often receives low-priority on policy agendas. This is especially difficult when there is a suspicion of government authorities being involved in the waste crime, either directly or by facilitating it. A policy analysis in the region of Campania (Italy) has for instance shown that the lack of effective responses to the waste issue goes hand in hand with a failure of democracy (Burgalassi *et al.* 2010). This refers to a lack of involvement of locals in decision-making processes despite these locals being the first to be affected by the waste crisis in the region.

Waste as organised crime implies a high priority for crime control, especially compared to corporate crime (see below). Organised crime is often investigated from a 'follow the money' point of view (Kleemans 2014a). This can also be relevant for waste crime. Money laundering investigations can be an inspiration. A recent evaluation of financial investigation in Dutch environmental crime cases stressed the potentiality of such an approach (Neve and van Zanden, this volume). This is currently put in practice in one Belgian police district that assigned environmental crime investigations to (chief) investigators with financial investigation expertise.[5]

Moreover, contemporary crime investigations and strategic analyses increasingly focus on intervening in the logistical processes of organised crime and on removing situational opportunities (Bullock *et al.* 2010; Spapens 2011). Considering waste crime as organised provides the possibility to apply these approaches, even though the first practical experience with them has delivered few specific leads for new crime control or prevention strategies (Huisman and van Erp 2013; Neve 2013). Script analysis can be useful to identify modus operandi and involved actors (both legal and illegal) (Sahramäki *et al.* 2016). However, challenges remain in implementing this in enforcement practice because it also requires policy makers and enforcement agencies to analyse how they might (un)consciously facilitate (undermining) criminal activities (Kolthoff and Khonraad 2016).

The involvement of organised criminals in waste crime is not always clear, as has been explained earlier. A partial explanation lies in the limited reporting and

5   Personal correspondence by first author.

investigation of waste trafficking, which results in few to no criminal groups being identified (Eurojust 2014). Remaining challenges are cross-border cooperation in investigating and prosecuting waste crime (Eurojust 2014; Spapens and Huisman 2016). The few cases prosecuted in countries where waste trafficking is discovered often rely on judicial proceedings in countries of origin. This is usually a lengthy process and countries do not always keep each other posted (Bisschop 2015). The EU's Environmental Crime Directive requires member states to install 'effective, proportionate and discouraging sanctions' for environmental crime. In practice, prosecution rarely occurs and sanctioning even less (Eurojust 2014). There are several reasons for this. The use of special investigative techniques for waste crimes is impossible in many countries because they are classified as too low to be considered serious crime. Too little high-quality information is gathered to result in meaningful intelligence. Witness statements from countries of destination of the waste are often not considered admissible in court. Often the shipper, successfully, claims he did not know about the legislation and criminal intent cannot be proven. An absence of technical expertise is also common. As a consequence, police and justice officials often prosecute for the 'traditional' crimes and not the environmental ones.

Waste and corporate crime

Corporate crime theory and waste

In their landmark study on crimes committed by America's 70 largest corporations, Clinard and Yeager defined corporate crime as 'any act committed by corporations that is punished by the state, regardless of whether it is punished under administrative, civil or criminal law' (Clinard and Yeager 1980, p. 16). Criminologists disagree on whether the definition should be limited to breaches of criminal law or rather not be limited to law breaking at all. There is also disagreement about whether the corporation itself or corporate managers should be seen as perpetrators, resulting in the development of alternative definitions of corporate crime. Despite these differences, scholars generally agree that corporate crimes are primarily committed for the corporate benefit in contrast to other forms of white-collar crime, which benefit the individual. Although the distinction between organised and corporate crime has been criticised, the former is mostly seen as an informal organisation of people working together with the sole purpose of committing crimes, while corporate crime involves formal organisations without an organisational goal to commit crimes that commit crimes to achieve these goals (Friedrichs 2010). While corporate crimes are sometimes portrayed as victimless, or as merely producing economic harm, many types also produce physical harm. According to Friedrichs (2010, p. 65), corporate contributions to poisoning the environment may well be the most common form of such 'corporate violence'.

As discussed above, waste is the inevitable by-product of production and consumption processes of economies on the rise. Waste problems can be traced back to Ancient Rome, but waste became particularly problematic after the nineteenth-century industrialization and for many developing economies it is increasingly cumbersome today (Hoornweg and Bhada-Tata 2012). Hazardous waste dumping has always been harmful, but it only became a *crime* problem when the production, transport and treatment of waste was regulated more strictly.

Corporate waste crime comes in two types: waste production and waste treatment. Crime in waste production occurs when corporations dump types or quantities of waste in breach of the requirements of their licence or when they dispose waste in absence of a licence. This can concern wastewater, air pollution or other (hazardous) waste streams resulting from industrial processes. Case studies show that many of these corporations either knew or should have known the inherent risks in dumping hazardous waste, but still opted for dangerous low-cost methods of disposal. Furthermore, they typically resisted changing these practices until forced to do so and actively lobbied against environmental legislation outlawing these practices (Friedrichs 2010, p. 66).

Besides industries producing waste and getting rid of it in an illegal manner, companies in the collection, transport and processing of waste produced by others can be involved in environmental crimes. As explained above, the waste industry is highly regulated in many industrialised countries because of the potential environmental risks of – especially hazardous – waste processing. The legal obligation to process waste in an environmentally responsible manner created a market for the services of waste hauling and processing companies. In the 1980s, the costs for the legal processing of hazardous waste were approximately 2,500 USD per tonne, whereas many developing countries accepted this waste for maybe 3 USD per tonne, making it more cost efficient to ship waste to the Caribbean than shipping it 60 kilometres within state borders (Rosoff *et al.* 2007, p. 166). In some cases, the profit opportunity, just by collecting waste, seems to be the sole business strategy (Huisman and van Erp 2013). In corporate crime cases, business activities are often seemingly designed for proper handling of waste, but once the waste is collected – and the money is in the pocket – the temptation of cheap substandard treatment or outright dumping is high. Criminological handbooks on corporate and white-collar crimes are not the only ones that consider corporations as the main culprits for waste crimes. Also environmental NGOs such as Greenpeace or the Basel Action Plan often label corporations as waste criminals, for instance related to the illegal disposal of e-waste (Kuper and Hojsik 2008).

So, while the waste industry was meant to prevent environmental harm, it is seen as vulnerable for corporate and organised crime (Vander Beken 2007). As discussed above, the waste industry in Italy and the United States has been associated with organised crime. In contrast, studies have associated the waste industry in the Netherlands with corporate crime. The 1980s and 1990s witnessed several high-profile criminal cases against waste processing companies such as *Tanker Cleaning Rotterdam*. While the Netherlands is not alone in having corporate waste crime cases, it is quite unique that it resulted in parliamentary inquiries and subsequent criminological studies. The parliamentary inquiry charged the research team Fijnaut with investigating the alleged infiltration of the waste sector by organised crime (given the Italian and American examples). Instead, the studies showed that established companies in the waste industry were committing crimes and that several characteristics of the waste industry facilitated environmental crime (van Vugt and Boet 1994; Bruinsma 1996; van den Berg 1995; van den Anker and Hoogenboom 1997). The first characteristic is the previously discussed reversed incentive structure. However, van Wingerde (2012, p. 85) claimed this to be largely a thing of the past as waste processing firms nowadays often have long-term contracts with waste producing companies. Second, the waste regulations are complex, fail to regulate the entire market and have trouble keeping up with the dynamic character of it. Third, some firms hold monopoly positions while others control many or all segments of the disposal chain (Vander Beken 2007). Recent mergers and up-scaling have increased this problem. Hence, effective industry monitoring is even harder to achieve whereas illegal practices are easily covered up. This combination of factors offers ample opportunity to commit violations with impunity (van de Bunt and Huisman 2007).

Cases

Among the best-known cases of corporate pollution is the Love Canal case. Throughout the 1920s, 1930s and 1940s, a canal near Niagara Falls (New York) served as a municipal dumpsite and later as an industrial dumpsite for the Hooker Chemical Company (Levine 1982). About 20,000 tonnes of metal drums filled with highly toxic chemical waste were dumped there. After the closure of the dump site, near the end of the 1950s, the land was sold for US$1 to the city who later built a school and residential neighbourhood for over 1,000 families on it. For years, residents complained of odours and substances bubbling up near houses or playgrounds, unaware of the toxic waste under their feet. A health study later confirmed the serious health problems residents and school children had been suffering for decades (cancer, birth defects, miscarriages, etc). Eventually hundreds of families were evacuated form the area and about 70 acres of land were fenced off. The company was compelled to pay US$20 million to former residents (Friedrichs 2010). In the aftermath, the US created the so-called *Superfund* to clean up hazardous waste dumpsites.

A more contemporary illustration is that of the 2006 toxic waste dumping, which was connected to *Trafigura* and the ship *Probo Koala* they chartered (van Wingerde 2015). The waste was a residue of a process of upgrading low quality coker naphta to fuel oil by treating it with caustic soda, which was carried out on board the vessel. The coker naphta came from Mexico and was transported over land to the US where it started its journey aboard the *Probo Koala*. Trafigura decided to move the operation to a ship when the Tunisian refinery *Tankmed* refused to carry out further washings after workers complained of terrible smells. The upgrading process on board the Probo Koala resulted in 554 tonnes of hazardous slops. Finally, in Ivory Coast the slops were loaded onto 12 trucks and dumped in 18 locations near the city of Abidjan. Around 108,000 people needed medical attention and 15 people died, although Trafigura vehemently denied these figures as well as causality. There were several failed attempts to dispose of the waste in other countries (Malta, Italy and Gibraltar) (van Wingerde 2015). On route for Estonia to load a gasoline cargo, *Trafigura* asked for a quote from *Amsterdam Port Services* (APS) in the Netherlands to treat the slops. The quote based in *Trafigura*'s description of the contents as 'gasoline slops' that resulted from regular operation of the ship was €27 per m3 but after taking samples and finding out what the slops were actually composed of APS significantly increased the quote (€1,000 per m3), which *Trafigura* rejected. They attempted to unload the waste in Nigeria but eventually ended up in Ivory Coast despite an absence of suitable treatment facilities in that country. In Ivory Coast, *Compagnie Tommy*, a company that had a license (since one month) but neither the facilities nor the human resources to handle this type of waste, was contracted to deal with the 'slops' for €30 per m3. After the vessel had offloaded the waste in Ivory Coast, the Probo Koala set sail for Estonia, after which it was blocked by Greenpeace and court cases started in Ivory Coast, the United Kingdom, the Netherlands and France. In 2007, Trafigura (and its Ivory Coast subsidiary *Puma Energy*) received immunity from criminal prosecution in Ivory Coast following a financial settlement of €152 million but without admitting liability (Greenpeace and Amnesty International 2012; van Wingerde 2015). In 2009, Trafigura reached a settlement in British courts, agreeing to pay approximately 950 GBP to each of the 30,000 claimants. In 2012, after several years of criminal investigations, court proceedings and appeals, Trafigura and the Dutch prosecution office reached a settlement of €1 million. This is undoubtedly a case of illegal trade and dumping of hazardous waste, in a complex construction of several companies (*Trafigura, its subsidiaries* and companies they hired) and countries (Mexico, USA, the Netherlands, Ivory Coast). This has even been called a state-corporate crime given the failure of the Ivory Coast authorities to respond (MacManus 2012). The Probo Koala case illustrates 'that legal and economic complexities can make it difficult to effectively enforce and prosecute corporate environmental crime' (van Wingerde 2015, p. 265).

Another type of industrial waste, albeit a very different one, is discarded end-of-life vessels. Approximately 12,000 vessels become obsolete each year, because they are no longer sea-worthy, because they no longer answer to the requirements (e.g. double hull) set by the *International Maritime Organization* (IMO) or because the economic context makes it more profitable to dismantle the ships for parts and secondary raw materials than to keep it in business (NGO Shipbreaking Platform 2013). The shipbreaking industry reclaims the valuable steel and other metals, but also has to deal with toxic substances such as asbestos, lead, mercury, residual oil and polychlorinated biphenyls (PCBs). When handled in unsafe ways by beaching the ships, these toxins affect the health of the workers and leak into the coastal and marine environment (Neşer *et al.* 2008). By beaching these vessels in developing countries, the shipping industry flouts international regulations on hazardous waste although those regulations long ignored this particular aspect of the waste trade and there are many loopholes to exploit (Rousmaniere and Raj 2007). Most of those vessels change owners in the last years and months of travel and use flags of convenience to arrive at their final destinations (India, Pakistan, Bangladesh), thereby disguising the original owner. Part of the responsibility for these waste crimes thus lies with the shipping industry and original owners of the vessels, who neglected to check where their vessels eventually end up. Shipbreaking by beaching is the result of a complex criminogenic interplay of economic actors (shipping lines, financial institutions, cash buyers, classification companies, shipping yards) and political actors (port states, flag states, tax havens) on national as well as international level (Claeys 2017).

We explained earlier how waste collection and processing in the United States has historic connections to organised crime groups, but the waste management corporations that took their place after the crackdown on organised crime do not have flawless track records either. They 'possess extensive histories of chronic violations of environmental law, as well as convictions for antitrust violations such as restraint of trade, price-fixing, and bid-rigging' (Carter 1999, p. 24). These same companies have been charged with and sometimes convicted for bribing public officials. In other words, their activities are very similar to those of their mafia-predecessors.

Illegal waste shipments are sometimes classified as shipments of products in an attempt to evade waste regulations. A 2001 case involved the discovery of two leaking containers in the port of Rotterdam with paperwork indicating chemicals (legal trade), not the 300 tonnes of mixed expired hazardous waste (illegal trade) that it actually was (EPA 2006, cited in Rucevska *et al.* 2015). The origin of these containers was a US storage facility that had illegally stored chemicals, which the US EPA had ordered to the clean up. The storage company then attempted to trade the chemical waste illegally by sending 29 containers to Nigeria, for dumping purposes. In transit in the port of Rotterdam, customs discovered that the buyer in Nigeria did not exist and started an investigation, discovering the illegal trade.

In a study into the illegal trade in electronic waste between Belgium and Ghana (Bisschop 2012), there was a connection to corporate crime in the waste sector. Several stages of the waste process held potential for illegal trade and dumping. The practices of some refurbishment companies and collectors of e-waste fed into illegal e-waste trade. Scrap metal dealers are intermediaries in the collection of e-waste and facilitate the waste fraud. This is consistent with findings by the Interpol Enigma operation, which resulted in criminal investigations into 40 companies for illegal e-waste trade (Interpol 2013). Some shipping agents also facilitate the smuggling or hinder law enforcement by obscuring the paper trail. With the increasing importance of the online marketplace, there are also companies selling e-waste online (e.g., Craigslist, Marketplace, Kapaza, Alibaba, ScrapMetalForum, eBay, etc.).

Several illegal waste practices – whether in collection, processing or disposal – are intertwined with legal waste and transport activities, taking advantage of lacking regulation and enforcement. Even some prominent waste companies with ISO certification who advertise sustainable practices are involved in waste fraud (Rucevska *et al.* 2015). Legal entities sometimes outsource their waste treatment and disposal, later claiming they did not know about the illegal dumping practices or substandard treatment, albeit that the cheap prices offered for treatment could have been cause for suspicion (Bisschop 2015). Overall, this makes clear that waste crime is undoubtedly connected to corporations and therefore a corporate crime.

Implications for crime prevention and control

Labelling waste crime as corporate crime implies that the governance response is one of regulating legal markets and monitoring compliance (Huisman 2014). Contrary to organised crime, part of the corporate waste crimes are crimes of omission (see above): the environmental regulations require companies to take action to avoid harmful substances polluting the environment. Rule compliance requires the investment of time and money; non-compliance saves time and money. In order to prevent and detect violations, regulatory agencies are required to (pro-)actively enforce these rules. Studies have shown repeatedly that environmental law enforcement knows many practical difficulties (Hawkins 1984; Hutter 1997). Even though computerisation has facilitated information exchange among regulatory agencies, the interpretation of waste regulations and the systematic monitoring of compliance remain problematic (Kluin 2014).

Since the 1980s, environmental governance in general, and for waste in particular, is partially entrusted to corporations (Huisman 2001; van Wingerde 2012). Self-regulation is often financially interesting for corporations, it helps to protect the company's reputation or it helps to ward off more intrusive regulation or anticipate a future tightening of rules (Bartley 2007; Gunningham *et al.* 2003). Studies have shown that self-regulation can work (de Bree 2011), but it does not necessarily encompass the entire waste market from collection over treatment to disposal. In a situation of self-regulation, governments are often meta-regulators, who check the companies before granting licences and also check their functioning afterwards, albeit often sporadically. This system is often visualised by means of a pyramid of responsive regulation, persuading companies to compliance when the 'slippery slope will inexorably lead to a sticky end' (Braithwaite 2008, pp. 93–94), which means revoking licences or applying criminal justice in case of serious or repeat violations. However, a recent study of the general deterrent effect of sanctioning in the waste industry in the Netherland showed that it only works for those companies that least need it: only those firms that are already actively managing compliance are receptive to the normative signals send by punitive sanctions (van Wingerde 2012). Corporate waste crime thus remains an issue of active and unwavering prevention and control.

Waste from a green criminological perspective

Green criminological theory and waste

When approaching waste crime from a green criminological perspective, a first concern is the definition of crime. Although it would take us too far out of the scope of this chapter to discuss the details about defining environmental crime and harm, it means that a mere judicial definition of environmental crime is too narrow as much environmentally harmful behaviour escapes the boundaries of national legislation. Therefore, environmental harm should be the core focus, no matter whether it is officially classified as a regulatory infringement (Halsey and White 1998; South 1998a). This refers to immediately noticeable or measurable harm, but also harm that only manifests itself after a longer period of time or that is harmful across borders (White 2011). Victims can refer to people but also animals, plants or ecosystems (Hall 2015). This for instance refers to the effect that pollution – a type of waste – has on the air, water or soil quality, even when this concerns only minimal quantities that cause damage only after prolonged exposure. Studying victimisation from a green criminology perspective is therefore not limited to an antropocentric perspective but is ecocentric (White and Heckenberg 2014).

A second topic of importance is the causes of waste crime. Because green criminology is inspired by critical criminology, the role of the powerful in the emergence of environmental harm is studied and empirical causality is inextricably linked to normative questions about responsibility. A green criminology view on corporate crime implies that corporations are explicitly named as culprits and not merely individuals within those corporations. This refers to companies that collect, treat and produce waste but do not bother much about the rules for environmentally sound waste handling. However, a green criminology is not so much interested in the criminogenic characteristics of corporations that violate environmental laws. Such corporations are viewed as being part of a political-economic system that produces ecological disorganisation. Especially the concept of the 'treadmill of production' describes how environmental harms are the direct result of the process of economic production, economic growth and capital accumulation under the capitalist mode of production (Lynch *et al.* 2013). This also refers to the influence of those same powerful actors on policy making and environmental regulation, which guarantees the continued existence of their polluting practices (Mol 2013). These same powerful economic actors are also the ones most likely to influence international treaties and policy making and enforcement in developing countries (Michalowski and Kramer 1987). Waste from a green-criminology perspective can also include an analysis of how informal waste collection and recycling is criminalised (Brisman 2010; Groombridge 2013). Especially the power imbalance between developing countries and multinational companies – whose gross national revenue regularly exceeds that of developing countries – is relevant. Such a perspective invites to look at the responsibility for environmental crime throughout the entire supply chain. Both the cheap treatment and recycling and the (wasteful) production and product engineering contribute to the illegal trade and dumping of e-waste. Producers for instance actively choose to produce products with shorter life cycles that are virtually impossible to fix in order to guarantee continued sales (planned obsolescence) (Brisman and South 2013). The responsibility for waste crime and by extension pollution lies also with the consumers, who generate massive amounts of waste. Consumers often do not realise how much waste (air pollution, waste water, etc.) is generated for each product. Many of those costs are hidden and externalised (White 2011).

A green criminological perspective implies that harm and crime are approached through an (environmental) justice lens. This pays attention to how the most vulnerable groups in society are disproportionately harmed by environmental crime. For waste crimes this refers to the contrast between rich and poor, developing and industrialised countries and within industrialised countries (Clapp 2001; Mohai and Saha 2007; Pellow 2007). The global South is especially vulnerable due to their often weak regulatory system and government, but also their precarious socio-economic situation, causing them to accept illegal but financially interesting (hazardous) waste shipments, no matter whether they originate in corporate or organised crime constructions. Moreover, the political situation might also be one where environmental concerns are not high on the agenda. As a consequence, waste traders can shop around for the lowest costs for waste disposal and offer officials in poor countries attractive prices or bribes for accepting the (toxic) waste into their lands. Also minorities in industrialised countries (e.g. USA) are disproportionately exposed to environmental harm resulting from waste fraud (McDowell 2013; Ozymy and Jarrell 2015; Stretesky and Lynch 1998). These activities are not necessarily illegal, but definitely harmful (awful but lawful). A green criminological approach thus allows us to pay attention to these differences between the Global North and South, rich and poor, powerful and powerless, with waste generally produced by the former and ending up with the latter.

Within a green criminology perspective, studies about waste crime are also closely related to those about pollution. This refers to pollution caused by the political-economic system – the treadmill of production – which accepts harm as 'inevitable' to sustain production and consumption processes (Lynch *et al.* 2013). This for instance refers to waste and pollution – environmental harm – resulting from activities of the oil and gas industry (Carrington *et al.* 2014; Jarrell and Ozymy 2012; Opsal and Connor 2014; Smandych and Kueneman 2010). Another topic that is commonly seen as pollution but actually concerns waste is the plastic islands and micro plastics in our oceans (Eriksen *et al.* 2013). Of course, it is hard to name the culprit for this harm, similar to many other topics on the green criminology radar (e.g. climate change) (White 2015).

Cases

A green criminology perspective on waste crime considers diverse types of harm affecting flora, fauna and vulnerable groups. A green perspective on waste crime allows for a more radical critique of the political economy in explaining and preventing environmental crime (Ruggiero and South 2013). The following provides a couple of examples.

A first example is that of pollution (or waste production) that arises from oil extraction such as that in the Nigerian Niger Delta. Oil extraction is a lawful activity that can still result in pollution incidents and major environmental harm. For decades, multinational oil companies, through local subsidiaries, have been extracting raw oil from the Niger delta. With 550 oil spills in 2014 alone (Amnesty International 2015), the Niger Delta is faced with chronic environmental and health damage to one of the most bio-diverse wetlands of Africa and to one of the most densely populated areas of Nigeria. Water, air and soil degradation together with light and noise pollution by gas flaring irreparably harmed biodiversity and habitats (Nurse 2016). Local fishing and farming – a source of livelihood for the majority of the impoverished population – collapsed (Izarali 2015). This case answers to several of the characteristics of corporate waste crimes, but the added relevance of a green perspective lies in the attention for the diversity of harms and the attention for systemic causes. The oil production, pollution and degradation of the environment went hand in hand with a more general disruption of the region through conflict, military violence, human rights abuses and lack of investment in education and health care (Bisschop and Janssens 2016). Understanding the causes of the environmental harm in the Niger Delta requires an examination of the broader political and economic environment that facilitates these harms. About 80 per cent of Nigeria's state revenue comes from oil and gas extraction and many people work for the oil industry. Even though the Nigerian economy is Africa's biggest (World Bank 2015), it is ranked very low on the UN's Human Development Index (UNDP 2015). Oil revenue ends up with political elites and does not benefit all citizens (Omgba 2015). The oil industry is also linked to several human rights violations, aside from the environmental harm. Legal action in Nigeria is difficult because many laws are not publicly available and because of the lack of transparency in the legal system (UNEP 2011). In 2009, Shell did make a 'compassionate' payment of 15.5 million USD to people in Ogoniland, without admitting liability for the deaths of several local environmental and human rights activists. Several victims, with support of ENGOs, continue to seek redress, but then abroad. A court case by relatives of Ogoni environmental and human rights activists, which started in 2002, made it to the US Supreme Court in 2012 where it was dismissed because of a lack of connection to the USA. The same plaintiffs, however, recently started a court case in the Netherlands (de Bruyne 2017). Friends of the Earth, together with four Nigerian farmers, also sued the Dutch headquarters of Shell, for oil pollution in three villages inflicted by subsidiary Shell Nigeria. In 2015, the Dutch judiciary found the case to be admissible, but the court case about the role of Shell in the oil pollution is still ongoing in appeal (rechtspraak.nl 2015). This case illustrates that the causes of environmental harm can be very diverse and are often also of a systemic nature. The capitalist dependence on oil as a resource, extracting the oil at virtually any cost, is fundamentally at odds with the wellbeing of nature (Stretesky *et al.* 2014). This not only rings true in developing countries, but was also demonstrated for the US (Greife and Stretesky 2013, p. 165) where state legislation is more likely to be favourable to oil discharges (pollution) when state revenue relies on the oil industry, when more production takes place and when political resistance is low.

An example of waste treatment is the earlier mentioned trafficking of e-waste (Bisschop and Vande Walle 2013). A lot of e-waste, disguised as second hand products, is shipped to developing countries (West Africa and South East Asia) where a large share is (immediately) dismantled to recuperate secondary raw materials. This dismantling is done by vulnerable groups (e.g. poor, minors, religious minority) and without any means to protect themselves from the toxins,[6] which are released when burning the waste (Eidgenössische Materialprüfungs- und Forschungsanstalt EMPA 2009; Sepúlveda *et al.* 2010). E-waste smuggling also causes economic harm because it unfairly competes with the legal waste market and because less secondary raw materials are being recycled. As such, it also undermines environmental policy and law enforcement (Quadri 2010).

Implications for crime prevention and control

A green criminology view on waste crime considers the systemic causes (e.g. politics, economy) and pays attention to harm and inequality, which also has implications for its approach to crime prevention and control strategy, which is in line with that of critical criminology. This means that green criminologists focus on exposing and changing the criminogenic nature of political and economic systems as well as on specific offenders or crime opportunities.

A green criminological perspective on crime prevention and control would stress the relevance of the interconnectedness of public and private actors (Hall, 2015). Such a perspective builds on the approach to waste as organised and as corporate crime, as discussed earlier. It adds to that a discussion about possible systemic causes in everyday life. This starts out with the definition of what crime is, which in the case of waste fraud has to be interpreted beyond the legal definition. It also implies that harm is not limited to human victims but also includes the environment. Moreover, in addition to a criminal law or administrative approach, solutions for waste crime are sought earlier on in the entire supply chain (producing less waste, consuming fewer products). This means that solutions are found way beyond the realm of criminal justice. 'Action taken outside of the criminal law to address such harms, particularly by way of civil claims, is potentially more effective in achieving redress than the limited punishment-based approach of the criminal law' (Nurse 2016, p. 148). A green perspective inevitably brings us to a questioning of the capitalist system with its focus on surplus value in disregard for potential environmental consequences (Lynch *et al.* 2013; Stretesky *et al.* 2013). It also means the inclusion of the actual

---

6   E-waste often contains lead, flame retardants, beryllium and mercury.

costs of production in the price of product, both in terms of water usage and recycling costs once the product is discarded (White and Heckenberg, 2014). This approach to prevention and control of waste crime is in line with campaigns of several ENGOs (e.g. Greenpeace Guide to Greener Electronics; 350.org). Several companies also invest in internalising the costs and limiting waste (e.g. fair phone).

The question of best practices in prevention and control is partly answered by looking at efforts by NGOs and other social movements. This includes campaigns to deal with climate change (e.g. 350.org, sing for the climate) or with the harm resulting from oil and gas extraction (keystone XL, fracking) (Bradshaw 2015; White and Kramer 2015). Sometimes this leads to action research, sometimes including judicial procedures, to counter polluters (Jarrell and Ozymy 2010). A green criminology perspective to preventing and controlling waste crime inevitably involves a diverse mix of strategies, critically eying the political, social and economic context, which shapes environmental crime and its governance. Law enforcement plays a secondary role and even then restorative justice is preferred over retribution.

Tackling complex waste crimes

The above analysis makes clear that waste crime is diverse. It involves corporations who pollute more than their licence allows for. It includes sub-standard treatment of waste. Sometimes criminal organisations are involved when they illegally trade or dump waste. They falsify documents and abuse legal commercial structures. Sometimes waste crime also involves governments who fail to (effectively) regulate environmental issues. Finally, also consumers are responsible. Thinking about the control and prevention of waste crime thus requires us to take into account a diversity of potential perpetrators and responsibilities. It is important to include all links in the waste chain from production until final disposal.

In the inherently global context of the waste industry, waste crime requires agencies to work together across institutional and national boundaries (Spapens and Huisman 2016). Transit of hazardous waste remains most difficult to police (EnviCrimeNet 2014). Traffic police regularly stop trucks and confiscate leaking barrels of battery acid or other chemical substances. However, there is limited judicial follow-up and the authorities often end up paying for disposal. Oftentimes it is simply treated as an administrative offence and therefore not registered in crime statistics (Eurojust, 2014). Licences and inspections are the responsibility of regulatory agencies whereas trade is regulated by customs. Data exchange between these agencies is a challenge, despite the fact that much of the policy on waste is directed by the EU (Bisschop 2014). This requires a mix of administrative and criminal approaches, which increasingly takes place within nation states but will require considerable effort to achieve on an international level.

The British *Environment Agency* has intensely focused on waste fraud over the last decade and has successfully prosecuted over 30 cases involving companies and their directors (Rucevska *et al.* 2015). They implemented an intelligence led policing approach to reduce illegal exports of hazardous waste (*Securing Compliant Waste Exports Project*) (Gibbs *et al.* 2015). This project was successful in implementing this policing strategy, despite the challenges inherent to policing environmental crime (Biermann and Pattberg 2008). By linking enforcement and regulatory information they guided intelligence and addressed environmental crime on the national level. As this intelligence led policing project evaluation showed, combining regulatory and enforcement data can guide better intelligence gathering and result in successful prosecution (Gibbs *et al.* 2015). This was successful on the national level, but application in other countries (with different geographic, political and economic conditions) would require adaptations. Applying this on an international level brings specific challenges that are typical for international cooperation, such as insufficient resources, exchanging information and guarantees for the security of that intelligence or the challenge of cooperating across jurisdictions. The globalisation of business practices – in the waste sector and others – makes smart regulation a challenge (Gibbs *et al.* 2010). The analysis and governance of waste crime on mere national level clashes with the international character of the waste industry. A better harmonisation of waste policy and especially its implementation might result in better insights into who is involved in waste crime and how better to prevent and control it. In addition to that, there are challenges that are typical for environmental crime such as a traditionally more compliance rather than crime control oriented regulatory strategy (Pink 2013; Pink and White 2015). Another challenge is that nation states are often faced with opposition when they want to regulate business (Rothe 2010).

Given the inherent limitations of dealing with waste crime through retributive justice, a focus on prevention is crucial. A theoretical model that is popular with policy makers in dealing with traditional crimes is the situational crime prevention model (Clarke 1992). Recently, this model was applied to organised crime and corporate crime (Benson and Madensen 2007; Bullock *et al.* 2010). Even though this model is successful in dealing with illegal poaching, it has not yet resulted in promising prevention strategies for waste crime (Huisman and van Erp 2013).

The prevention and control of waste crime holds opportunities for cooperation among different actors (companies, governments, NGOs). There is reason to be hopeful, especially about more community oriented approaches to waste crime, next to the more formalised ones. Slovenia for instance saw an increase in detection of environmental crime in 2009, which can most likely be explained by a national NGO campaign that invited citizens and authorities to report cases of illegal waste dumping (Eman 2013). A Greenpeace report revealed that the electronics originating from Dutch companies were dumped in Ghana, after which the Dutch Environmental Inspectorate attempted to trace the companies that had disposed of the equipment to sanction them. In this case, the attempts were unsuccessful, but by using Greenpeace's information, the Inspectorate sent a signal that it is willing to cooperate with NGOs and to back up NGO monitoring actions with law enforcement (van Erp and Huisman 2010). Also, fieldwork in Ghana about the (il)legal trade in e-waste (Bisschop 2015) made clear that NGO campaigns can positively influence awareness of both authorities and citizens about the harms resulting from substandard dismantling and burning of electronics.

Conclusion

Waste can be more cheaply dealt with by illegal enterprises who disregard environmental regulations as well as by legal companies who treat waste they are not licensed for with potential partnerships between the two (Ruggiero and South 2010). The term 'organised crime' for labelling waste crime might indeed be less accurate than the concept 'illegal enterprise', where businesses, authorities and organised criminals interact (Ruggiero and South 2010; Chambliss 1978). Labelling waste crime as either corporate or organised crime has significant crime control and prevention consequences. Corporate crime is mostly dealt with by better regulating and monitoring companies in legitimate markets, whereas organised crime is mostly countered by using criminal law to target entrepreneurs operating in criminal markets. From a policy perspective, organised or corporate makes a whole world of difference. Waste as corporate crime brings with it a range of regulatory options. Waste as organised crime mandates the international police organisations to make it a priority. The challenge is in bridging those two approaches. Waste crime as environmental crime prioritises the environment no matter who bears responsibility for the harm, whether these are corporations, organised crime groups, governments or consumers. This also explicitly talks about the inequality between the Global North and South, rich and poor, powerful and powerless. This implies that avoiding environmental harm requires structural and cultural changes of mentality and behaviour. The challenge lies in finding a strategy for the prevention and control of waste crimes that incorporates these three perspectives.

References

Amnesty International. 2015. 'Nigeria: Hundreds of oil spills continue to blight Niger Delta', press release, 19 March.

Anker, van den, M. and Hoogenboom, B. 1997. *Schijn bedriegt: overheid, bedrijfsleven en gelegenheidsstructuren voor criminaliteit op de hergebruikmarkt.* The Hague: Vuga.

Bartley, T. 2007. 'Institutional emergence in an era of globalization: the rise of transnational private regulation of labor and environmental conditions', *American Journal of Sociology* 113(2), 297–351.

Benson, M. and Madensen, T. 2007. 'Situational crime prevention and white-collar crime', in *International Handbook of Corporate and White Collar Crime*, edited by H. Pontell and G. Geis. New York: Springer, 609–626.

Berg, van den, E. 1995. *De markt van misdaad en milieu; deel II.* The Hague: WODC.

Biermann, F. and Pattberg, P. 2008. 'Global environmental governance: taking stock, moving forward', *Annual Review of Environment and Resources* 33(1), 277–294.

Bisschop, L. 2012. 'Is it all going to waste? Illegal transports of e-waste in a European trade hub', *Crime, Law and Social Change* 58(3), 221–249.

Bisschop, L. 2014. 'How E-waste challenges environmental governance', *International Journal for Crime, Justice and Social Democracy* 3(2), 82–96.

Bisschop, L. 2015. *Governance of the Illegal Trade in E-Waste and Tropical Timber. Case Studies on Transnational Environmental Crime*. Farnham: Ashgate.

Bisschop, L. and Janssens, J. 2016. 'Ecocide en milieu(on)veiligheid: miskenning of erkenning?', *Orde van de Dag* December, 33–45.

Bisschop, L. and Vande Walle, G. 2013. 'Environmental victimization and conflict resolution. A case study of e-waste', in *Debates in Green Criminology: Power, Justice and Environmental Harm*, edited by T. Wyatt, R. Walters, and D. Westerhuis. Basingstoke: Palgrave Macmillan, 34–54.

Block, A. 2002. 'Environmental crime and pollution: wasteful reflections', *Social Injustice* 29(1–2), 61–81.

Block, A. and Scarpitti, F. 1985. *Poisoning for Profit: The Mafia and Toxic Waste in America*. New York: W. Morrow.

Bradshaw, E. 2015. 'Blockadia rising: rowdy greens, direct action and the keystone XL Pipeline', *Critical Criminology* 23(4), 433–448.

Braithwaite, J. 2008. *Regulatory Capitalism: How it Works, Ideas For Making it Work Better*. Cheltenham: Edwar Elgar.

Bree, de, M. 2011. 'Ontwikkelingen in systeemtoezicht', in *Managementsystemen en toezicht*, edited by M. de Bree. Rotterdam: Erasmus Universiteit, Erasmus Instituut Toezicht and Compliance, 51–60.

Brisman, A. 2010. 'The indiscriminate criminalisation of environmentally beneficial activities', in *Global Environmental Harm: Criminological Perspectives*, edited by R. White. Cullompton: Willan Publishing, 161–192.

Brisman, A. and South, N. 2013. 'Conclusion: the planned obsolescence of planet earth? How green criminology can help us learn from experience and contribute to our future', in *Routledge Handbook of Green Criminology*, edited by N. South and A. Brisman, London and New York: Routledge, 409–417.

Bruinsma, G. 1996. 'De afvalverwerkingsbranche', In *Inzake opsporing: enquêtecommissie opsporingsmethoden, Deel II onderzoeksgroep Fijnaut: branches*, edited by G. Bruinsma and F. Bovenkerk. Den Haag: SDU, 261–310.

Bruyne, de, M. 2017. 'Nigeriaanse weduwes beginnen zaak tegen Shell', *NRC Handelsblad*, 29 June.

Bullock, K., Clarke, R. and Tilley, N. 2010. *Situational Prevention of Organised Crimes*. Cullompton: Willan Publishing.

Bunt, van de, H., and Huisman, W. 2007. 'Organizational crime in the Netherlands', *Crime and Justice. A Review of Research* 35, 217–260.

Bunt, van de, H., Siegel, D. and Zaitch, D. 2014. 'The social embeddedness of organized crime', in *The Oxford Handbook of Organized Crime*, edited by L. Paoli. Oxford: Oxford University Press, 13–31.

Burgalassi, D., D'Alisa, G., Healy, H. and Walter, M. 2010. 'Conflict in Campania: waste emergency or crisis of democracy', *Ecological Economics: The Transdisciplinary Journal of the International Society for Ecological Economics* 70(2), 239–249.

Calderoni, F. 2014. 'Mythical numbers and the proceeds of organised crime: estimating mafia proceeds in Italy', *Global Crime* (March 2015), 37–41.

Carrington, K., Donnermeyer, J. and DeKeseredy, W. 2014. 'Intersectionality, rural criminology, and re-imaging the boundaries of critical criminology', *Critical Criminology* 22(4), 463–477.

Carter, T. 1999. 'Ascent of the corporate model in environmental-organized crime', *Crime, Law and Social Change* 31(1), 1–30.

Chambliss, W. 1978. *On the Take: From Petty Crooks to Presidents*. Bloomington: Indiana University Press.

Claeys, J. 2017. *Europese schepen op Zuid-Aziatische stranden: een state-corporate crime? De criminogene rol van overheden en bedrijven bij shipbreaking*. Unpublished Master Thesis in Criminology, Ghent University, Belgium.

Clapp, J. 2001. *Toxic Exports: The Transfer of Hazardous Wastes from Rich to Poor Countries*. Ithaca: Cornell University Press.

Clapp, J. 2002. 'Seeping through the regulatory cracks: the international transfer of toxic waste', *SAIS Review* 22(1), 141–155.

Clarke, R. 1992. *Situational Crime Prevention*. New York: Harrow and Heston.

Clinard, M. and Yeager, P. 1980. *Corporate crime*. New York: Free Press.

D'Amato, A. and Zoli, M. 2011. *Bureaucrats vs the Mafia: Corruption, Extortion and Illegal Waste Disposal*. Available at: siecon.org/online/wp-content/uploads/2011/04/DAmato-Zoli1.pdf [accessed 7 October 2017].

D'Amato, A., Mazzanti, M., Nicolli, F. and Zoli, M. 2014. *Illegal waste disposal, territorial enforcement and policy. Evidence from regional data*. SEEDS working papers, 3/2014.

Department of Justice. 2013. '32 Individuals Charged In Manhattan Federal Court in Connection with Alleged Organized Crime Scheme to Control the Commercial Waste Disposal Industry', press release, 16 January.

Devroe, E. and Ponsaers, P. 2015. 'Evidence based beleid en praktijk bij de politie in Nederland en België?' *Tijdschrift voor de Politie* 76(10), 20–25.

Eidgenössische Materialprüfungs- und Forschungsanstalt (EMPA). 2009. *Ewasteguide.info: Hazardous Substances in e-Waste*. Switzerland.

Eman, K. 2013. 'Environmental crime trends in Slovenia in the past decade', *Varstvoslovje – Journal of Criminal Justice and Security* 15(2), 240–260.

EnviCrimeNet. 2014. *Intelligence Project on Environmental Crime – Preliminary Report on Environmental Crime in Europe*, The Hague.

Eriksen, M., Maximenko, N., Thiel M., Cummins, A., Lattin, G., Wilson, S., Hafner, J., Zellers, A. and Rifman, S. 2013. 'Plastic pollution in the South Pacific subtropical gyre', *Marine Pollution Bulletin* 68(1), 71–76.

Eurojust. 2014. *Strategic Project on Environmental Crime*, The Hague.

European Environment Agency. 2012. *Movements of waste across the EU's internal and external borders*. EEA Report No 7/2012, Luxembourg: Office for Official Publications of the European Union.

Europol. 2011. *OCTA 2011 – EU Organised Crime Threat Assessment*. The Hague: European Police Office.

Europol. 2015. *Exploring Tomorrow's Organized Crime*. The Hague: European Police Office.

Erp, van, J. and Huisman, W. 2010. 'Smart regulation and enforcement of illegal disposal of electronic waste', *Criminology and Public Policy* 9(3), 579–590.

Finckenauer, J. 2005. 'Problems of definition: What is organized crime?', *Trends in Organized Crime* 8(3), 63–83.

Friedrichs, D. 2010. 'Integrated theories of white-collar crime', in *Encyclopedia of Criminological Theory*, edited by F. Cullen and P. Wilcox. Thousand Oaks CA: Sage Publications, 480–487.

Gibbs, C., McGarrell, E. and Axelrod, M. 2010. 'Transnational white-collar crime and risk. Lessons from the global trade in electronic waste', *Criminology and Public Policy* 9(3), 543–560.

Gibbs, C., McGarrell, E. and Sullivan, B. 2015. 'Intelligence-led policing and transnational environmental crime: A process evaluation', *European Journal of Criminology* 12(2), 242–259.

Gobert, J. and Punch, M. 2003. *Rethinking Corporate Crime*. London: Reed Elsevier.

Greenpeace and Amnesty International. (2012). *The Toxic Truth. About a Company Called Trafigura, a Ship Called Probo Koala and the Dumping of Toxic Waste in Cote d'Ivoire*. London/Amsterdam.

Greife, M. and Stretesky, P. 2013. 'Crude laws: Treadmill of production and state variations in civil and criminal liability for oil discharges in navigable waters', in *Routledge International Handbook of Green Criminology*, edited by N. South and A. Brisman. London: Routledge, 150–166.

Groombridge, N. 2013. 'Litter, criminology and criminal justice', in *Routledge International Handbook of Green Criminology*, edited by N. South and A. Brisman. London: Routledge, 394–408.

Gunningham, N., Kagan, R. and Thornton, D. 2003. *Shades of Green: Business, Regulation and Environment*. Redwood City, CA: Stanford University Press.

Hall, M. 2015. *Exploring Green Crime: Introducing the Legal, Social and Criminological Contexts of Environmental Harm*. Basingstoke: Palgrave Macmillan.

Halsey, M. and White, R. 1998. 'Crime, ecophilosophy and environmental harm', *Theoretical Criminology* 2(3), 345–371.

Hawkins, K. 1984. *Environment and Enforcement: Regulation and the Social Definition of Pollution*. Oxford: Clarendon Press.

Heckenberg, D. 2010. 'The global transference of toxic harms', in *Global Environmental Harm: Criminological Perspectives*, edited by R. White. Collumpton: Willan Publishing, 37–61.

Hoornweg, D. and Bhada-Tata, P. 2012. *What a Waste. A Global Review of Solid Waste Management*. Washington DC.

Huisman, W. 2001. *Tussen winst en moraal: Achtergronden van regelnaleving en regelovertreding door ondernemingen*. Den Haag: Boom Juridische Uitgevers.

Huisman, W. 2014. 'Compliance and corporate crime control', in *The Encyclopedia of Criminology and Criminal Justice*, edited by D. Weisburd and G. Bruinsma. New York: Springer, 489–496.

Huisman, W., and Erp, van, J. 2013. 'Opportunities for environmental crime: a test of situational crime prevention theory', *British Journal of Criminology* 53(6), 1178–1200.

Hutter, B. 1997. *Compliance: Regulation and Environment*. Oxford: Oxford University Press.

IMPEL-TFS. 2012. *IMPEL – TFS Enforcement Actions III Project Report Enforcement of the European Waste Shipment Regulation*. Brussels.

Interpol. 2009. *Electronic waste and organized crime. Assessing the links. Phase II report for the Interpol Pollution Crime Working Group*. Interpol.

Interpol. 2013. 'Interpol operation targets illegal trade of e-waste in Europe and Africa', press release, 25 February.

Izarali, M. 2015. 'Human rights and state-corporate crimes in the practice of gas flaring in the Niger Delta, Nigeria', *Critical Criminology* 24(3), 1–22.

Jacobs, J., Friel, C. and Radick, R. 1992. *Gotham Unbound: How New York City Was Liberated from the Grip of Organized Crime*. New York: New York University Press.

Jarrell, M. and Ozymy, J. 2010. 'Excessive air pollution and the oil industry: fighting for our right to breathe clean air', *Environmental Justice* 3(3), 111–115.

Jarrell, M. and Ozymy, J. 2012. 'Real crime, real victims: environmental crime victims and the Crime Victims' Rights Act (CVRA)', *Crime, Law and Social Change* 58(4), 373–389.

Kleemans, E. 2014a. 'Organized crime research: challenging assumptions and informing policy', in *Applied Police Research: Challenges and Opportunities*, edited by E. Cockbain and J. Knuttson. New York: Routledge, 57–67.

Kleemans, E. 2014b. 'Theoretical perspectives on organized crime', in *Oxford Handbook of Organized Crime*, edited by L. Paoli. Oxford: Oxford University Press, 32–52.

Kleemans, E. and Kruissink, M. 1999. 'Korte klappen of lange halen? Wat werkt bij de aanpak van de georganiseerde criminaliteit', *Justitiële Verkenningen* 25(6), 99–111.

Kleemans, E. and Bunt, van de, H. 2008. 'Organised crime, occupations and opportunity', *Global Crime* 9(3), 185–197.

Kluin, M. 2014. *Optic Compliance: Enforcement and Compliance in the Dutch Chemical Industry*. Delft: TU Delft.

Kolthoff, E. and Khonraad, S. 2016. 'Ondermijnende aspecten van georganiseerde criminaliteit en de rol van de bovenwereld', *Tijdschrift voor Criminologie* 58(2), 76–90.

Kuper, J. and Hojsik, M. 2008. *Poisoning the Poor. Electronic Waste in Ghana*. Amsterdam: Greenpeace International.

Lampe, von, K. 2008. 'Organized crime in Europe: conceptions and realities', *Policing* 2(1), 7–17.

Lampe, von, Klaus. 2017. *Definitions of Organized Crime*. Available at: organized-crime.de/organizedcrimedefinitions.htm [accessed 23 August 2017].

Legambiente. 2014. *Ecomaffia: Le storie e i numeri della criminalita ambientale*, Milan.

Levine, G. 1982. *Love Canal: Science, Politics, and People*. Lexington MA: Lexington Books.

Liddick, D. 2009. 'The traffic in garbage and hazardous wastes: an overview', *Trends in Organized Crime* 13(2), 134–146.

Lynch, M., Long, M., Barrett, K. and Stretesky, P. 2013. 'Is it a crime to produce ecological disorganization? Why green criminology and political economy matter in the analysis of global ecological harms', *British Journal of Criminology* 53(6), 997–1016.

MacManus, T. 2012. *Toxic Waste Dumping in Abidjan*. Available at: statecrime.org/testimonyproject/ivorycoast [accessed 7 October 2017].

Massari, M. and Monzini, P. 2004. 'Dirty businesses in Italy: A case-study of illegal trafficking in hazardous waste', *Global Crime* 6(3–4), 285–304.

Mathews, G., Ribeiro, G. and Vega, C. 2012. *Globalization from Below. The World's Other Economy*. London/New York: Routledge.

McDowell, M. 2013. 'Becoming a waste land where nothing can survive: resisting state-corporate environmental crime in a 'forgotten' place', *Contemporary Justice Review* 16 (March 2015), 394–411.

Michalowski, R. and Kramer, R. 1987. 'The space between laws: the problem of corporate crime in a transnational context', *Social Problems* 34(1), 34–53.

Mohai, P. and Saha, R. 2007. 'Racial inequalities in the distribution of hazardous waste: a national-level assessment', *Social Problems* 54, 343–370.

Mol, H. 2013. 'A gift from the tropics to the world': Power, harm, and palm oil' in *Emerging Issues in Green Criminology*, edited by R. Walters, D. Westerhuis and T. Wyatt. Basingstoke: Palgrave Macmillan, 242–260.

Neşer, G., Ünsalan. D., Tekoğul, N. and Stuer-Lauridsen, F. 2008. 'The shipbreaking industry in Turkey: environmental, safety and health issues', *Journal of Cleaner Production* 16(3), 350–358.

Neve, R. 2013. *Geglobaliseerde afvalcriminaliteit. Illegale praktijken in de afvalstromen naar Afrika en China Verslag van een onderzoek voor het Nationaal dreigingsbeeld 2012.* Zoetermeer.

NGO Shipbreaking Platform. 2013. *Problems and Solutions.* Available at: shipbreakingplat form.org/problems-and-solutions/ [accessed 7 October 2017].

Nurse, A. 2016. 'Cleaning up greenwash: a critical evaluation of the activities of oil companies in the Niger', in *Hazardous Waste and Pollution*, edited by T. Wyatt. Switzerland: Springer, 147–161.

Omgba, L. 2015. 'Why do some oil-producing countries succeed in democracy while others fail?', *World Development* 76, 180–189.

Opsal, T. and O'Connor, T. 2014. 'Energy crime, harm, and problematic state response in Colorado: a case of the fox guarding the hen house?', *Critical Criminology* 22(4), 561–577.

Ozymy, J. and Jarrell, M. 2015. 'Corporate environmental crime and environmental victimization: exploring new legal precedents for securing recognition and restitution for environmental justice communities', *Environmental Justice* 8(2), 47–50.

Paoli, L. and Vander Beken, T. 2014. 'Organized crime: a contested concept', in *The Oxford Handbook of Organized Crime*, edited by L. Paoli. Oxford: Oxford University Press, 13–31.

Passas, N. 1999. 'Globalization, criminogenic asymmetries and economic crime', *European Journal of Law Reform* 1(4), 399–423.

Past, E. 2013. ' "Trash Is gold": documenting the ecomafia and campania's waste crisis', *Interdisciplinary Studies in Literature and Environment* 20(3), 597–621.

Pellow, D. 2007. *Resisting Global Toxics: Transnational Movements for Environmental Justice.* Cambridge, MA: MIT Press.

Pink, G. 2013. *Law Enforcement Responses to Transnational Environmental Crime: Choices, Challenges and Culture.* Canberra: Transnational Environmental Crime Project – Working Paper 4/2013.

Pink, G. and White, R. 2015. *Environmental Crime and Collaborative State Intervention.* Basingstoke: Palgrave Macmillan.

Quadri, S. 2010. 'An analysis of the effects and reasons for hazardous waste importation in India and its implementation of the Basel Convention', *Florida Journal of International Law* 22(3), 467–495.

Rashbaum, W. and Goldstein, J. 2013. 'FBI arrests nearly 30 with ties to waste industry', *The New York Times*, 16 January.

Rechtspraak.nl 2015. 'Nederlandse rechter bevoegd in proces tegen Shell over olielekkages Nigeria', 18 December.

Rosoff, S., Pontelland, H. and Tillman, R. 2007. *Profit Without Honor: White-Collar Crime and the Looting of America* (4th ed.). Upper Saddle River, NJ: Pearson Prentice Hall.

Rothe, D. 2010. 'Global e-waste trade. The need for formal regulation and accountability beyond the organization', *Criminology and Public Policy* 9(3), 561–567.

Rousmaniere, P. and Raj, N. 2007. 'Shipbreaking in the developing world: problems and prospects', *International Journal of Occupational and Environmental Health* 13(4), 359–368.

Rucevska, I., Nellemann, C., Isarin, N., Yang, W., Liu, N., Yu, K., Sandnæs, S., Olley, K., McCann, H., Devia, L., Bisschop, L., Soesilo, D., Schoolmeester, T., Henriksen, R., and Nilsen, R. 2015. *Waste Crime: Low Risks – High Profits. Gaps in Meeting the Global Waste Challenge. A Rapid Reponse Assessment.* Nairobi and Arendal: UNEP and GRID-Arendal.

Ruggiero, V. 1996. *Organized and Corporate Crime in Europe: Offers that Can't Be Refused*. Aldershot: Dartmouth Publishing.

Ruggiero, V. and South, N. 2010. 'Green criminology and dirty collar crime', *Critical Criminology* 18, 251–262.

Ruggiero, V. and South, N. 2013. 'Green criminology and crimes of the economy: theory, research and praxis', *Critical Criminology* 21, 359–373.

Sahramäki, I., Favarin, S., Mehlbaum, S., Savona, E., Spapens, T. and Kankaanranta, T. 2016. *Crime Script Analysis of Illicit Cross-Border Waste Trafficking*. Tampere/Milan/ Tilburg: Project BlockWaste.

Senior, K. and Mazza, A. 2004. 'Italian 'triangle of death' linked to waste crisis', *Lancet Oncology* 5(September), 525–527.

Sepúlveda, A., Schluep, M., Renaud, F., Streicher, M., Kuehr, R., Hagelüken, C. and Gerecke, A. 2010. 'A review of the environmental fate and effects of hazardous substances released from electrical and electronic equipment during recycling: Examples from China and India', *Environmental Impact Assessment Review* 30(1), 28–41.

Smandych, R. and Kueneman, R. 2010. 'The Canadian-Alberta tar sands: a case study of state-corporate environmental crime', in *Global Environmental Harm*, edited by R. White. Cullompton: Willan, 87–109.

South, N. 1998a. 'A green field for criminology: a proposal for a perspective', *Theoretical Criminology* 2(2), 211–233.

South, N. 1998b. 'Corporate and state crimes against the environment: foundations for a green perspective in European Criminology', in *The New European Criminology: Crime and Social Order in Europe*, edited by V. Ruggiero, N. South, and I. Taylor. London and New York: Routledge, 443–461.

Spapens, T. 2011. 'Barrières opwerpen voor criminele bedrijfsprocessen', *Justitiële Verkenningen* 37(2), 10–22.

Spapens, T. and Huisman, W. 2016. 'Tackling cross-border environmental crime: a "wicked problem."', in *Environmental Crime in Transnational Context: Global Issues in Green Enforcement and Criminology*, edited by T. Spapens, R. White, and W. Huisman. Farnham (UK)/Burlington (USA): Ashgate, 27–42.

Stretesky, P. and Lynch, M. 1998. 'Corporate environmental violence and racism', *Crime, Law and Social Change* 30(2), 163–184.

Stretesky, P., Long, M. and Lynch, M. 2014. *The Treadmill of Crime: Political Economy and Green Criminology*. London and New York: Routledge.

Szasz, A. 1986. 'Corporations, organized crime, and the disposal of hazardous waste: an examination of the making of a criminogenic regulatory structure', *Criminology* 24(1), 1–27.

Tompson, L. and Chainey, S. 2011. 'Profiling illegal waste activity: using crime scripts as a data collection and analytical strategy', *European Journal on Criminal Policy and Research* 17(3), 179–201.

UNEP. 2011. *Environmental Assessment of Ogoniland*. Nairobi: United Nations Environment Programme.

UNODC. 2013. *Transnational Organised Crime in East Asia and the Pacific. A Threat Assessment*. Bangkok.

Vander Beken, T. 2007. *The European Waste Industry and Crime Vulnerabilities*. Antwerpen: Maklu.

Vugt, van, G. and Boet, J. 1994. *Zuiver handelen in een vuile context: over (grensoverschrijdende) afvalstromen, milieucriminaliteit en integer handelen in het openbaar bestuur*. Arnhem: Gouda Quint.

Wingerde, van, K. 2012. *De afschrikking voorbij: Een empirische studie naar afschrikking, generale preventie en regelnaleving in de Nederlandse afvalbranche*. Nijmegen: Wolf Legal Publishers.

Wingerde, van, K. 2015. 'The limits of environmental regulation in a globalized economy', in *The Routledge Handbook of White-Collar and Corporate Crime in Europe*, edited by J. van Erp, W. Huisman, G. Vande Walle and J. Beckers. London and New York: Routledge, 260–275.

White, R. 2011. *Transnational Environmental Crime. Towards an Eco-Global Criminology*. New York: Routledge.

White, R. 2015. 'Climate change, ecocide and crimes of the powerful', in *The Routledge International Handbook of the Crimes of the Powerful*, edited by G. Barak. Abingdon and New York: Routledge, 211–222.

White, R. and Heckenberg, D. 2014. *Green Criminology: An Introduction to the Study of Environmental Harm*. Abingdon and New York: Routledge.

White, R. and Kramer, R. 2015. 'Critical criminology and the struggle against climate change ecocide', *Critical Criminology* 23(4), 383–399.

Williams, E., Kahhat, R., Bengtsson, M., Hayashi, S., Hotta, Y. and Totoki, Y. 2013. 'Linking informal and formal electronics recycling via an interface organization', *Challenges* 4(2), 136–153.

World Bank. 2015. Gross domestic product 2015. Retrieved from Washington, D.C. Available at: databank.worldbank.org/data/download/GDP.pdf [Accessed 12 August 2016].

Zoi Environmental Network and GRID-Arendal. 2012. *Vital Waste Graphics 3*. Geneva.

Part III

Financial regulation and enforcement

9 Green with envy

Environmental crimes and black money

Michael Levi

Introduction

The aim of this chapter is to explore the varieties of money laundering that are connected to a range of environmental crimes – especially illegal logging – how much we know about those areas and national and international anti money laundering (AML) control efforts within them (for example, in Global North/Global South relations), and what are the implications of these findings for theory and for harm control practices.

Neither money laundering nor environmental crimes have clear boundaries, nor do practitioners or scholars use the terms consistently. Despite the successful efforts of the Financial Action Task Force to approximate or homogenise legal definitions and institutions globally, the discourse surrounding the term 'money laundering' ranges from anything that is done with the proceeds of *any* crime (under UK and much EU MS legislation) to its popular image of complex financial transactions to hide the criminal origins of funds so that they can appear respectable – what is usually referred to as 'integration' within the conventional though outdated money laundering typology of placement-layering-integration. 'Environmental crimes' – the plural here being deliberate to avoid artificial homogenisation and confusion from ambiguity – range from national and transnational trafficking of exotic wildlife and timber, through allegedly intended (Volkswagen 'dieselgate' and others) regulatory deception and pollution, to unintended if careless or reckless corporate pollution, to intentional toxic waste dumping in unapproved sites.[1] The lowly place occupied by any of these sub-types on the European serious crime agenda may be noted in two ways:

---

1 See White (2014), Brisman and South (2017), Hillyard and Tombs (2017) and Walters (2017), for some radical conceptual discussions of the boundaries of environmental 'crime' and 'harm', one implication of which for this chapter is that every act (whether currently illegal or not) that profits from damage to any component of 'the environment' – broadly construed – should be included within this review of money laundering. That may be a desirable approach at some stage, but it is not one that will be adopted in this more conventional chapter, which takes the broad criminal construct of money laundering as its baseline for empirical analysis. I suggest that readers consider what would *not* count as environmental harm under the broadest approaches, and consider whether this is a good application of the term 'crime'.

1   In the EU Serious and Organised Crime Threat Assessment 2013, environmental crimes are not regarded as 'key threats' but as 'emerging threats' (Europol 2013, p. 39) and then are categorised as 'threats' but not as 'priority threats' (Europol 2017).[2]

2   In the European Union's Seventh Environment Action Programme, approved in November 2013 and in force until 2020, no reference at all was made to environmental crime nor to the criminalisation of actions that can damage the environment. More recently the EU Draft Council Conclusions, on countering environmental crime, made no mention of money laundering, but a significant emphasis on financial investigation (Council of the EU 2016). The EU Action Plan Against Wildlife Crime pressed member states to 'review ... legislation on money laundering to ensure that offences connected to wildlife trafficking can be treated as predicate offences and are actionable under domestic proceeds of crime legislation' (European Commission 2016a, p. 21). In support of this, in December 2016, the European Commission issued a proposal for a directive on money laundering instructing that member states should consider all offences set out in Environmental Crime Directive 2008/99/EC as predicate offences (European Commission 2016b, 2017, p. 13). This proposal is currently under discussion by the European Council and Parliament.

Eurojust (2016) reveals that there has been only one coordination meeting, no Joint Investigation Teams, and 16 cases spread evenly in the period 2014–2016. This is despite a Strategic Project on Environmental Crime (Eurojust 2014), which notes (p. 36) that 'a stronger focus on money laundering aspects could be considered during the investigation and prosecution of illegal waste shipments, trafficking in endangered species and surface water pollution to enhance the efficiency of the fight against environmental crime', though we should note that any such strategies may take some years of intelligence development to feed in noticeably.

One issue for reflection about the role of anti-money laundering (hereafter, AML) in combating environmental crimes and harms is that irrespective of any penalties imposed, the harm done to 'the environment' may be very much greater than the initial profits – if any – made from committing the crimes, and this has implications for what control strategies may be most likely to impact on those harms. Such calculations are also complex because, especially in the industrialised countries (excluding 'organised crime' in wildlife and suchlike trafficking), environmental crimes are often crimes of omission. Companies save money by not complying with expensive environmental legislation: proceeds of crime can be more difficult to calculate or to define. (The term 'effectiveness' raises questions

2   Environmental crime and trafficking of endangered species are not a priority within the current EU Policy Cycle; waste trafficking as an emerging crime was on the 'watch list' for the Europol SOCTA 2017.

about what impacts on behaviour, cultural awareness of/opposition to environ-mental harms, and so on, one is seeking to achieve). Furthermore, some smaller firms may have insufficient assets to repay the damages that are caused by their misconduct, and that too is relevant to controllability by any *ex post facto* mechanism, criminal or administrative, once the damage is done: so early intervention is especially critical. In addition, by the time criminal, regulatory or civil action is taken against them (if it ever is), 'criminal firms' (set up to commit crime and/or serve as fronts for crime) and/or wealthy individuals may have moved the proceeds of environmental crime beyond the jurisdiction of the courts and/or may have spent the profits on lifestyle.

When evaluating the evidence base on what happens to the money from this very broad range of activities and how they are financed, we need to consider both (a) the 'crime scripts'[3]– in particular how (un)evenly distributed the proceeds and profits[4] are along the crime chain; and (b) the extent to which financial investigators have unravelled systematically the money trail in those cases they have investigated (the representativeness of which is unknown, but the author's observation is that they are likely to be the easiest *or* the most dramatic cases). In corporate cases like pollution, there may be no specifically *criminal* money trail as such – any profits simply merge into the licit business accounts; but where waste has been sub-contracted for disposal illicitly (whether with or without the provable knowledge of the contractor), there may be a money trail for the subcontractor and perhaps for the contractors themselves. Likewise for timber and (dead or alive) wildlife that are sold with counterfeit or corruptly obtained provenance certificates, and/or by dummy companies set up in secrecy havens, which has been described as 'timber laundering' (Nellemann 2012), a term also used extensively for various wildlife crimes (UNODC 2016). This is a reasonable extension of the laundering concept to mean anything that hides the illicit nature of the activity, not just the financial rewards thereof, though in my interpretation, the deception is a sufficient predicate to mean that all proceeds become money laundering too, if the mental element of crime can be proven. The latter may be difficult when the goods pass through intermediaries, allowing the claim that they were purchased in good faith. Goods sold without paperwork – real or fake – require a different methodology for detection and investigation, and may be impossible to track *ex post facto* without help from inside informants unless there is some forensic linkage such as photographic footage or prints.

In principle, all countries now support anti money laundering (AML) and countering the financing of terrorism (CFT) policies and, thanks to both the soft and economic power efforts of the Financial Action Task Force, these are

---

3   Crime scripts are often illuminating ways of breaking down the necessary and sufficient conditions for offending, but often this is merely a modern term for old-fashioned criminalistics.
4   Proceeds are different from profits because profits are net of the expenses of running the criminal activity.

increasingly all-crime laws that enhance the formal coverage of environmental *criminal* (though not administrative) legislation. However, such commitments are not self-implementing and though environmental crimes may have upscaled rhetorically around the world (except in the US in the Trump era and the UK in the May era), a finite modest total amount of financial investigation resource in law enforcement and environment agencies has to be distributed according to real priorities, not just abstract ones. Indeed, this resourcing reflects both the (usually implicit) priorities and the cultural history of enforcement agencies, including the environment agencies themselves. The intersection between the typically more 'regulation-focused' actions of non-police agencies and the police (including Interpol and Europol, which have no direct arrest powers) is an intriguing feature here. In the UK, there has been central encouragement of a proceeds of crime focus in environmental crime, but many obstacles of low standing of financial investigation in policing culture/practices and ranking of environmental crimes in the competition for scarce financial investigation resources stand in the way, as they did in the early stages of proceeds of drugs and other crime work by the police (Levi and Osofsky 1995).

Action against the financing and proceeds of environmental crimes is affected by the domestic and international political economy considerations surrounding enforcement in the Global South as well as in the financial centres and import markets of the Global North. To the extent that illegal logging is conducted directly or with the support of powerful interests and that those interests have effective control of enforcement and/or prosecution agencies, neither police, regulators, nor the domestic Financial Intelligence Unit is likely to take significant action or to cooperate well with foreign investigators. There has as yet been no national AML evaluation in the third or current (fourth) FATF round that has focused on environmental crimes, though some aspects are the focus of much NGO and IGO activity.[5] However, there have been regional 'typologies' reports from Asia Pacific and from East and Southern Africa that highlight – if not always illuminate – the laundering component of illegal logging and wildlife trafficking trades (APG 2008; ESAAMLG 2016).[6] These start in the now conventional way with 'estimates' of the size of the trades and often quite *a priori* analyses of how the funds are (or rather, might be) transferred, often to the Global North, and how they in some ways finance terrorism. However, one sophisticated risk assessment of African wildlife crimes in the context of a money laundering typologies review noted that:

> despite the case studies indicating a lucrative business with significant financial gains in trading wildlife products such as ivory, almost all ESAAMLG member countries could not provide details on financial flows such as methods and techniques used to fund poaching activities in cases investigated. This is

5   See, for example, the Chatham House portal (illegal-logging.info/).
6   A further intensively researched typology on wildlife trafficking from the APG was published in 2017.

compounded by the fact that most ESAAMLG member countries' economies are predominantly cash based. Additionally, the study could not obtain data and information related to methods used to pay for the wildlife and wildlife products by end users and/or kingpins of the organized criminal syndicates, in the consumer countries.

(ESAAMLG 2016, para 14)

Despite being an official study, the Eastern and Southern African Anti-Money Laundering Group was able to obtain only very limited information from Asian countries. The report added (p. 16) that 'most wildlife authorities were unaware of the existence of an FIU [Financial Intelligence Unit] in their respective jurisdictions and the value FIUs could add to their combative efforts'. Of the 13 countries that responded to the questionnaire it sent out, 11 had received no intelligence reports relating to illegal trade in rhino horns and elephant tusks or parts of other vulnerable wildlife (p. 66).

Some attempt was made to estimate the volume and value of wildlife direct and indirect losses. However (p. 34) the one (anonymous) national risk assessment report analysed showed that the trafficking of wildlife and its products was only ranked 15th out of 16 offences in terms of the volume of proceeds laundered: $350,000 out of the total $1.8 billion estimated to be laundered. Taking the region as a whole, it was believed that most payments for poaching and corruption services were paid in cash at the point of delivery, which by inference implies access to money service businesses in the formal and/or informal sectors. Maguire and Haenlein (2015) indicated cause for scepticism about the wildlife-terrorism linkage often used to enhance the priority given to wildlife protection and many other activities (for a review of such claims in the Global North, see Levi 2010). For an excellent analysis of wildlife crime and the role that follow-the-money methods have played and have the potential to play, see Haenlein and Keatinge (2017).

Finally, one of the questions that we must consider is the extent of variations globally in issues such as 'illegal logging', industrial pollution, and so on, which presents challenges to the easy tropes about globalisation. Routine activities approaches (Felson 2006) require us to consider motivations, situational opportunities and capable guardianship in accounting for crime rates, and although this construct is often used in a less sophisticated way than is useful, in a comparative context, it could illuminate differences between countries and regions in the nature and level of 'criminal trades', because their criminal 'ecosystems' have important variations. In short, there is a local as well as a global context of the organisation of serious crimes (Levi 2012; Edwards 2016; Edwards and Levi 2008).

Illegal logging in Asia and its policy context

A decade ago, Dorn and Levi (2008) explored the ways in which political, cultural and economic differences and relations between the South East Asian and European regions shape their countries' priorities in and understandings of AML and CFT. Different nuances in policy priorities were traced through three broad economic fields in which AML and CFT are of concern: logging, which is of special interest to some Asian countries and global NGOs, although then approached cautiously by Western countries; 'informal' value transfer services including so-called Alternative Remittance Systems, where regulation seeks to exclude funds from crime and/or for terrorism, while aiming to facilitate transfer/repatriation from North to South of small amounts at low cost (see CGD 2015; Levi 2018, for unanticipated negative effects of regulation); and security, in relation to seaways, the trade in small arms, WMD proliferation and terrorism. The analysis illustrates how the varying emphases placed by countries and regions in relation to AML and CFT reflect how important politically and economically are the various substantive fields of activities in which financial flows originate.

Dorn and Levi's starting point was the context for AML/CFT policy in political and trade relations between Asian and European Union countries, as reflected in an inter-regional forum, the Asia-Europe Meeting (ASEM).[7] Anti-laundering policies are discussed within ASEM in the contexts of its 'economic pillar' and of its 'political pillar' (which includes security issues): the Asia Pacific Group on Money Laundering (APG) is the FATF-Style Regional Body that serves as an umbrella for this, in collaboration with the EU External Service. In 2005 the ASEAN Secretariat and the APG Secretariat concluded an agreement to enhance the coordination, technical assistance and training in relation to Anti-Money Laundering and Combating Terrorist Financing (APG 2005). Within this context, Dorn and Levi were asked to conduct research, some of the less technical and sensitive aspects of which are updated here.

Political, security, economic and development policy context

The EU is an important trading partner, and ASEAN has been growing dynamically though unevenly. Prior to 2005, Asian countries generally did not see the EU as a credible regional security partner. In the aftermath of the 2005 tsunamis and the spirit of reconciliation evoked by them, EU peace monitors joined with five regional countries in monitoring the ceasefire between the Indonesian government and GAM in Aceh, but there were and still are many differences of emphasis, whose logic can be understood in terms of the two regions' linked but differing histories of economic and political development (see Dorn and Levi 2008), which continues in an often fractious dialogue. For example, a report of the NGO Environment Investigation Agency (2017) criticising corruption in Vietnam's non-implementation of illegal logging controls

---

7   In 2017, ASEM is made up of 21 Asian countries, plus 30 European States, the European Union and the ASEAN Secretariat. This is a significant rise from its original membership.

was released on the eve of a meeting that concluded the negotiations for a Voluntary Partnership Agreement between the EU and Vietnam within the EU's global Forest Law Enforcement, Governance and Trade (FLEGT) Action Plan (Chatham House 2017). That appears to be the standard method of NGOs aiming to stimulate the conditions for changing policy and action.

In 2005 ASEM 'looked forward to enhanced cooperation between Europe and Asia' on AML (European Commission 2005). Other justice and home affairs initiatives include action against corruption; combating trafficking in women and children; combating the sexual exploitation of children; ministerial conference on cooperation for the management of migratory flows Europe-Asia; and law enforcement cooperation generally. All of these have gradually become seen as having a money-laundering component, at least in principle.

How AML/CFT become policy concerns

Money laundering has become a taken-for-granted component of the crime control scene, beginning with the Presidential Commission on Organized Crime (1984) and expanding into a catch-all category encompassing an ever-larger number of predicate crimes, evaluated by a global mechanism of dispersed regulators that has recently shifted from a fairly ritualistic assessment of laws and institutions closer to a Problem Oriented Policing model, at least in theory (Halliday *et al.* 2014; Levi *et al.* 2017). Even within the older framework, there was an element of negotiation in the setting of policy agendas. Some AML-related issues – for example intellectual property rights, safeguarding multilateral investments and opening up markets to full competition within a regulatory framework familiar to Western firms (e.g., in money transfer services) – were more energetically put on the AML agenda by the Europeans. Other issues, for example illegal logging and the international trade in small arms (related to regional insecurity), were brought to the table by Asian partners in the ASEM process and by NGO pressure, with the European side being slower to act.

There is a danger of taking an orientalist perspective, whether on AML or on terrorism, prioritising the interests of the Global North.[8] Bearing this in mind, one summary might run as follows:

AML/CFT concerns arising around insecurity at sea, the trade in small arms, Weapons of Mass Destruction (WMD) proliferation and terrorism. Here, action is supported by all countries, albeit with different nuances, interpretations and priorities in practice.
AML/CFT concerns arising from within illegal logging and closely related corruption and financing, illustrating a situation in which what were domestic issues within producer Asian countries have been accepted in principle as

---

8   For discussions of 'Southern criminology' and its salience to Green Criminology, see Carrington *et al.* (2016), White (2018) and Brisman and South (2017).

being international issues. However, practical action is slow and seems (though to a diminishing extent in the last decade) to let Western countries 'off the hook' when it comes to implementing AML measures, though NGOs regularly put pressure on the Global North over its role in paying bribes and laundering the proceeds of Grand Corruption. Action is inhibited also in some Asian (and African and Latin American) countries, where high-level corruption aligns with illicit logging, for example, though this can shift over time as regimes rise and fall, or need international aid.

AML/CFT concerns arising in relation to informal value transfer channels, including Alternative Remittance Systems, where the Western countries have urged action on less developed countries, reinforced by the private sector 'de-risking' in the Global North of accounts with 'high risk' correspondent banks and Money Service Businesses in the Global North and South, some of which will have gone 'underground' or merged with other firms to reduce scrutiny.

Illegal logging, corruption and financing issues

Over the past decades illegal logging, the international trade in tainted timber, the corruption that allows it and the money laundering that results from it have come onto the international policy agenda, particularly in the Asian region (Ant-Lkbn Antara news service 2005, and subsequently). Though sceptics may not find their methodology convincing, estimates by a variety of concerned bodies put the proportion of logging that is illegal at about one-fifth of the total for some Asian countries and up to 90 per cent for others (Tacconi *et al.* 2003, see table on p. 8; see material on illegal-logging info for contemporary case studies). The EU and US are sizable customers, and China has become a much more significant final destination during this century. European timber users have introduced and/or reinforced responsible purchasing policies and are exploring methods of reducing use of tainted supplies via Voluntary Participation Agreements: there is no evidence from any period that any nation is relying on anti-money laundering efforts alone. Illegal logging and its related ills have been propelled onto the policy agenda following alliances between governments and anti-corruption agencies in the region (Defensor and Fathoni 2005) and the EU; in other cases, IFIs such as the IMF and World Bank have emphasised action against corruption and illegal logging as part of loan conditions, both implicitly and explicitly (Levi *et al.* 2007).

However, there is a continuing economic incentive to take more timber than is permitted by regulations, a vibrant international demand for timber and some bank-related aspects (Setiono and Barr 2003). Despite Sharia obligations to examine the environmental impact of loans, the fact that the banks in Islamic countries continue to finance an industry that requires six times the amount of legally harvested timber is a very clear indication of how they are contravening the credit extension regulations (ibid.). Since then, there have been many laws and regulations covering these sectors in Indonesia (Sinaga *et al.* 2015) and elsewhere. Thus, when a bank finances an Indonesian timber concession company, it should obtain information on the company, including ultimate beneficial owners, and monitor transactions as it would with any other account. If there are suspicions of money laundering from illegal timber trading, it should file a suspicious transaction report (though in Indonesia, as elsewhere in the world, there are no legal requirements for public authorities to do anything about these reports). If a bank fails to make a suspicious transaction report, it may theoretically be liable criminally and perhaps civilly (depending on increasingly harmonised legislation around the world). These issues have been debated in meetings in the region. For example, an early joint presentation between an (anonymised) NGO and the head of Indonesia's AML agency looked at transfer pricing mechanisms used for concealing proceeds of illegal logging (also an issue that concerns GAFISUD due to illegal deforestation of the Amazon, which persists despite remote surveillance technologies). It also described existing AML powers and made recommendations to the banking industry, calling for cooperation:

> Banks should categorize forestry businesses as high-risk businesses; banks should create a list of high risk customers in the forestry sector; banks should report STR on customers reported by NGOs and the media as being implicated in forestry crimes; the police should begin to investigate the financial backers of illegal logging, by using the AML law; using international AML regimes for curtailing forestry and environment crimes.
>
> (Setiono and Husein 2005, p. 12)

Several Europe-wide meetings involving Financial Investigation Units from member states too place, leading to better understanding of the prospects for suspicious activity reports to FIUs and for AML action in the European context. In relation to the UK specifically, it was noted that:

> Based on legal advice, it appears that there is a basis for UK anti-money laundering legislation to be used as a tool against both trade in illegally harvested timber and also financing investments that lead to illegal logging. However, in practice there are several constraints to effective implementation.
>
> (Speechly 2004, p. 8)

These constraints include the low level of awareness within UK enforcement agencies of illegal logging issues, the need to establish clearly a parallel offence in UK domestic law (since 'illegal logging' is not specified as a criminal offence in the UK), limited experience within the enforcement agencies of investigation of similar cases, and the political reality that 'the Crown Prosecution Service has [other] priorities, for example, drug trafficking, people trafficking, arms trafficking and terrorism' (ibid.). This has not changed significantly since 2004. Similar observations were made in this period of the UK (and some other developed countries) by the OECD in relation to the inadequate legislation and low resources available to act against transnational bribery, though the Bribery Act 2010 transformed the UK's reputation in that respect.

The EU Action Plan for a Forest Law Enforcement, Governance and Trade agreement (FLEGT) initially explored several possibilities for action, including the development of assurances of origins of timber (European Commission 2003). Somewhat ironically, one predictable and no-doubt unintended consequence of the EU refusal to accept incoming timber unless the shipment has been legally certified would be to make EU importers almost immune to legal action under money laundering laws since they could use these to negate suspicions. Illegally harvested product requires certification in the exporting countries. That could increase the pressure for corruption among the certifying agencies – while providing to EU importers, their banks and others connected with the trade the defence they need against allegations of money laundering. So much depends on the operation and supervision of the FLEGT criteria, which are consistently heralded by the diplomatic process as an ongoing process (what anti-crime measures are not?) (ASEAN *et al.* 2016).

Questions might be raised about whether, given the entrenched nature of the trade, certification is a practical control mechanism; and whether companies should be allowed to enter the certification process without first having gained a 'clean bill of health' about their past activities. Some Asian NGOs wanted vetting of firms and also possibly land reform to be implemented before certification was introduced (Tacconi *et al.* 2004, pp. 24–25). However, certification within countries of origin, with a chain of custody through to the end user, was found politically feasible. Thus, while AML action has a future in relation to forestry markets, that future may be more imminent within the Asian and other 'countries of origin' than within the EU. Meanwhile, official investigations and charges laid in several countries in the region show that there are entrenched interests at all level of commercial life and government agencies (Haseman and Lachica 2005; Environmental Investigation Agency 2003, 2017).

The fact that illegal logging is seemingly closely integrated into international, regional and local legal trades in timber makes a drugs trafficking analogy inappropriate. Even the broader term 'corruption' seems to lose much of its force in this context, since connivance in the illegal timber trade is so bound into economic and regulatory routines. Without readier source identification (along the lines of the Kimberley diamond process), it is difficult to show that the timber is the product of illegal export, although in principle, by reference to their declared/known income and wealth, investigators should be able to determine whether assets in the possession of businesspeople or public officials are plausibly the product of legitimate activity, whether in Asia or elsewhere.

A thoughtful EU-focused evidence and policy review by Gregory (2015, pp. 3–4) concluded that

> while action on money laundering can in theory play a significant part in helping to preserve the world's forests, there are numerous obstacles:

Making illegal logging a predicate offence under the AML Directive would be unlikely to change bank behaviour or make it easier to bring AML illegal logging cases to court.

FIUs [Financial Intelligence Units] are overwhelmed by the quantity of 'suspicious transaction reports', and they do not have the resources to investigate more than a tiny proportion – mainly in their priority areas of drug dealing and serious organised crime. In this context, it is unlikely that illicit dealings related to illegal logging will receive much attention.

FIUs are reluctant to investigate AML in other jurisdictions unless requested by authorities in those jurisdictions. This means that EU-based FIUs, for instance, would be unlikely to investigate money laundering in the major timber-producing countries.

Illegal logging is difficult to detect merely by looking at cash flows, as illegal transactions look remarkably like legal ones.

Finally, there is little evidence that revenues from illegal logging flow to Europe on a significant scale, making it more difficult to make a case for reforming EU money laundering procedures. Illegal logging and money laundering remain important issues, which can and must be tackled, but it is doubtful that linking the two would be a very effective way forward, although there are clear cases where it has worked.

As the report put the argument in greater detail (Gregory 2015, pp. 25–26):

The problem with the timber trade is that illegal transactions look remarkably like legal ones. Illegal logging tends to be an "inside job". Companies with timber concessions log in places they are not supposed to or otherwise break the terms of their permits. This is hard to pick up simply by examining money flows going through accounts. A common scenario for money laundering is a criminal gang attempting to conceal the illegal nature of the proceeds of crime. This may be the pattern for certain types of environmental crime – poaching and wildlife trafficking, for example – but it is not typical of illegal logging. Forestry is generally an industrial operation. A tree trunk is not something that can be easily hidden and smuggled unlike, say, an elephant tusk or rhino horn. The most likely scenario for large-scale illegal logging is not a criminal gang that enters a forest to 'steal' trees but rather a legitimate operator who has some tree felling operations that are legal and others that are not. In these circumstances, transactions relating to the criminal and non-criminal sides of the business may look similar, which means there may not be any obviously anomalous patterns of financial activity for bank investigators staring at computer screens thousands of miles away to pick up as indicators of money laundering. However, theft of extremely high-value and rare species of trees of the type covered by the CITES Convention – rosewood, for example – may involve outside criminal gangs, whose efforts to hide the proceeds do fit the classic money laundering mode.

Environmental crimes in the Global North

Although it is correct that anti-money laundering and proceeds of crime confiscation have received substantial high level attention, they are not heavily used in practice against environmental crimes that originate in the G20 countries. One useful Australian report by Bricknell (2010) about the control of environmental crimes there did not mention either laundering or proceeds of crime confiscation. Much European analysis in recent times discusses large corporations generating chemical leaks into the water table (Kluin 2016; Kluin and Jagtman 2016), other forms of pollution, or waste dumping. The general thrust of this literature shows how little financial investigation is used as a tool in dealing with environmental crimes. This may be partly because these violators are not unknown members of organised crime networks who need to be traced or proven to be connected with the violation but are rather otherwise licit corporations. However, the shading between licit and illicit commerce may be difficult to discern in the case of SMEs and individuals targeted by the Scottish Environmental Protection Agency (SEPA) and, to a lesser extent, the UK Environment Agency, whose activism in using proceeds of crime provisions against local offenders is modest.

Thus, SEPA obtained in 2015–2016 confiscation orders for £2,356; £41,131; £28,538; and – its largest ever – £345,558.43 under the Proceeds of Crime (Scotland) Act 2002 (SEPA 2016). In one other case, there was a fine of £200,000. The most powerful Scottish gangs were undercutting legitimate operators by ignoring environmental standards or avoiding tax by mixing high-harm waste – that attracts higher rates of taxation for dumping – with low-risk rubbish.

In England and Wales, proceeds of crime orders were made in 106 Environment Agency cases 2011–2014 for a total of £9,725,956 averaging £91,754.[9] Subsequently, there have been other cases, some of which show the disparity between modest identified saved assets that have been confiscated and huge profits from crime already spent or hidden away (Environment Agency 2017). The latter case had a press notice, which does not indicate this disparity, but bravely stresses the lifetime burden of millions of pounds that are due if those convicted come into assets subsequently. This in turn depends on the surveillance of such offenders, which, being environment offenders, is not likely to be as high as drugs traffickers. The Environment Agency does not have the power to impose any civil penalties or reach any settlements with offenders in relation to money laundering offences. It can only take forward a prosecution of a money laundering offence in conjunction with another predicate environmental offence, as the absence of an environmental aspect to the allegations leaves it without legal *vires* to pursue money laundering alone. This is on account of the Environment Agency's founding principles that are set out in Section 4 of the Environment Act 1995, namely that:

---

9   Data supplied by the Agency.

It shall be the principal aim of the Agency (subject to and in accordance with the provisions of this Act or any other enactment and taking into account any likely costs) in discharging its functions so to protect or enhance the environment, taken as a whole, as to make the contribution towards attaining the objective of achieving sustainable development mentioned in subsection (3) below.

The absence of an environmental aspect to a case means that it falls outside of the ambit of Section 4 Environment Act 1995. So, as with the earlier examples of environmental crime in the Global South, much depends on the availability of *timely* financial investigation and the willingness to pursue such issues.

Conclusions

Historically, environmental crime issues have not played an important role in the genesis or maintenance of the AML 'movement' and, though some individual high profile cases have generated high perceptions of harm to which AML measures are one among several responses, AML/CFT considerations need to be reconciled with other issues of interest for the international and regional communities. What this underlines is that, in order to have sufficient leverage to provide impetus to wider policies, AML/CFT needs to be quite politically and commercially sensitive, as well as being technically informed. The present situation seems not so balanced in relation to ML and some other markets, notably forestry products profiled in this study, where the self-regulatory regimes at international and country levels would place primary responsibility on checks in countries of origin.

Where Western countries strong in international banking tend to see unregulated systems such as Alternative Remittance Systems as not only a big ML/TF risk, but also as unfair price competition, Asian partners and those prioritising development goals stress the benefits of secure and cheap remittance systems and the resulting incoming investment at grassroots level. This arguably stimulates local economic development, which is inhibited by restrictions on correspondent banking and official remittance mechanisms brought about by defensive de-risking by international banks (CGD 2015; Artingstall *et al.* 2016). Finally, though this is an evolving space, the focus of AML in the Global North has been the protection of their personal and financial security interests, albeit that since the Great Powers and their associated corporate sectors have economic and political interests around the globe, what happens overseas to risk their interests is also seen as their business. Whereas all parties display concern over the accelerating diminution of natural habitats resulting from illegal logging, the EU has not seen fit to give teeth to controls that might adversely affect financers, importers or end-customers of timber products – preferring to rely on voluntary and potentially-manipulable certification schemes.

The implications are fairly clear. As long as strong 'demand pull' exists in international markets for certain products, it will be difficult for the Asian (and

Latin American) region to eliminate or even reduce ML related to corruption and to the markets which stimulate it. This difficulty eventually became well understood in relation to ML/TF and drug trafficking, leading to a 'balanced approach' in relation to AML measures as well as in relation to the physical trade. Such balance is also accepted in relation to human trafficking and related AML. Strong advocacy of follow-the-money approaches continues to be made as a way of tackling under-controlled environmental harms (Haenlein 2017). Whether any particular set of measures is *realistic* would be as much political judgement as a technical one: however, clearly there are risks related to the impending policy (im)balance. To combat that risk, work on corruption and on illegal timber deserve fullest practical support, alongside efforts to combat the other forms of globalised illicit wildlife sectors including illegal fishing and poaching competing for scarce environmental protection resources (see Gregory 2015; Haenlein 2017; Haenlein and Keatinge 2017). The extent of that corruption may vary in different regions, but regional NGOs may not always reflect such nuances, seeking to motivate powers in the Global North to do something to reduce the ills. The urgency and remediability of harms have been incorporated in a recent action framework being promoted by EnviCrimeNet at a Brussels workshop (March 2017).

While there may be technical barriers to improved international cooperation against ML/TF, the bigger impediments may be economic and political sensibilities on both sides. Tensions over real world implementation of policies reflect differential priorities. Reflecting economic interests and cultural factors, the EU has a tendency to emphasise products and services originating in Asia as posing risks, and to locate responsibilities for monitoring and control as falling within Asia – a tendency reciprocated by Asian partners. As for the future, as the international balance of trade shifts, with Asia increasingly supplying finished goods to the West and increasing its influence in international fora, such as the Financial Action Task Force and OECD, so the issues for AML/CFT – including pressures for 'level playing fields' among ASEM/APG countries – can be expected to evolve. The impact of 'real world evaluation' in the FATF (2012, 2017) revised recommendations and methodology remains to be seen (Levi *et al.* 2017), as does the issue of whether these will include any or all of those 'environmental crimes' that violate criminal law: but the broader constructions of environmental crime contained in the radical harm literature will certainly not be included in these AML or anti-corruption frameworks, since the latter rest upon criminalisation, which is a dynamic process that can but not always does include 'conflicts of interest' among political figures. Law matters.

The ever-changing patterns of consumer electronics produce the need to eliminate e-waste, and advanced economies are likely to generate continued incentives to misrepresent the nature of these and other chemical products to save on disposal costs. Some of these environmental offences are in essence frauds, though they may not be prosecuted as such, if at all. The broader constructions of 'eco-crime' may, however, form part of an environmental preservation and harm prevention framework. If the all-crime framework generates anxiety about the costs of prevention, these broader ecological considerations will certainly do so.

Finally, 'follow the money' approaches are often attractive in offering the hope for transformations in control, but almost invariably fall short. This does not mean that there are no individual cases that give reason to hope for impact. An investigation by Thailand's Anti-Money Laundering Office in 2014 into a syndicate trafficking illegal wildlife, such as tigers and pangolins, and illicit rosewood resulted in the seizure of $37m in assets from the gang. One of the main clues in the investigation was the use of a zoo as a front operation, based in a remote part of Thailand where there are few tourists and so made no economic sense (Newman 2015). There are other individual successes and some more strategic ones, reviewed thoughtfully by Haenlein and Keatinge (2017). However, it is difficult to calculate the impact that any given increase in AML or proceeds of crime efforts might have, and where/in which jurisdictions those resources might best be placed for maximum effect. Impacts may be difficult where offender networks are linked to Grand Corruption, which can control FIU/criminal justice efforts and international cooperation. Some successful prosecutions, civil suits and more strategic changes in risks and opportunities for offenders send signals to offenders that they run greater risks than in the past; and actions in the Global North may reduce the impunity of corrupt elite and 'organised crime' actors in the Global South for their criminal wealth even if not for their personal criminal liabilities. (The latter often depends on US commitment and extra-territorial efforts).

Commitment and passion inflamed by environmental injustices made more visible by analysis and media-covered NGO activities *may* lead to rises in the general level of financial intelligence and investigation resources, and permit more allocation of these against environmental crimes of particular kinds, and thereafter reduce environmental harms. Haenlein and Keatinge (2017) advocate such a strategic and focused approach to conserve wildlife in East Africa, though it is not clear what order of magnitude of changes in resourcing and mindset may be needed to achieve major results. The sort of political will and evidence-based investigative skill they suggest may have an impact on that sector. However, anyone seeing these follow-the-money approaches as a ready solution to the entire range of environmental degradation might be well advised to think again. The stepping up of control efforts might lead to the use of more intermediaries to place more distance between the corporations and harms, and though banks might be pressurised by increased legal risks to exercise more supply chain control over firms with which they do business – as they have done in bribery and modern slavery legislation – it may be difficult to tell how much aggregate impact this has upon eco-crime or upon environmental harms without good 'before and after' measures and investigative input measures linked to outcomes, all of which are currently inadequate.

References

Ant-Lkbn Antara. 2005. 'Integrated [anti-]illegal logging operation in Papua should be just and fair, Minister says', *Indonesian government press release*, 14 March.

APG. 2005. 'Working to outlaw money laundering and terrorism financing in Asia Pacific', *Australian Transaction Reports and Analysis Centre*, 14 July.

APG. 2008. *The Asia/Pacific Group on Money Laundering (APG) Typologies Report: Illegal Logging and Money Laundering Issues.* Available at: apgml.org (accessed 19 August 2017).

APG. 2017. *APG Yearly Typologies Report 2017.* Sydney.

Artingstall, D., Dove, N., Howell, J., and Levi, M. 2016. *Drivers & Impacts of Derisking*, London: Financial Conduct Authority.

ASEAN, Indonesia and the EU. 2016. 'EU and Southeast Asian nations share progress in addressing illegal logging and timber trade', *Joint press release*, 6 December.

Bricknell, S. 2010. *Environmental Crime in Australia.* Canberra: Australian Institute of Criminology, Research and public policy series no. 109.

Brisman, A. and South, N. (2017). 'Green criminology', in *Oxford Handbook of Criminology*, edited by A. Liebling, L. McAra and S. Maruna. Oxford: Oxford University Press, 6th edition, 329–349.

Carrington, K., Hogg, R.G. and Sozzo, M. 2016. 'Southern Criminology', *The British Journal of Criminology* 56 (1), 1–20.

CGD. 2015. *Unintended Consequences of Anti–Money Laundering Policies for Poor Countries.* Washington DC: Center for Global Development.

Chatham House. 2017. 'EU and Vietnam complete negotiations on a deal to combat illegal logging and promote trade in legal timber', *Press release*, 11 May.

Council of the European Union. 2016. *Draft Council Conclusions on Countering Environmental Crime – Adoption.* 15184/16, Brussels 6 December.

Defensor, M. and Fathoni, T. 2005. 'Joint statement by Philippines and Indonesia regarding strengthening of the Forest Law Enforcement and Governance process', Governments of Indonesia and the Philippines, 21 March.

Dorn, N. and Levi, M. 2008. 'East meets west in anti-money laundering and anti-terrorist finance: policy dialogue and differentiation on security, the timber trade and 'alternative' banking', *Asian Journal of Criminology* 3(1), 91–110.

ESAAMLG. 2016. *A Special Typologies Project Report on Poaching, Illegal Trade in Wildlife and Wildlife Products and Associated Money Laundering in the ESAAMLG Region.* Nairobi: Eastern and Southern Africa Anti-Money Laundering Group.

Edwards, A. 2016. 'Actors, scripts, scenes and scenarios: Key trends in policy and research on the organisation of serious crimes', *Oñati Socio-Legal Series* 6(4), 975–995.

Edwards, A. and Levi, M. 2008. 'Researching the organisation of serious crimes', *Criminology and Criminal Justice* 8(4), 363–388.

Environment Agency. 2017. 'Payback for illegal waste crimes', *Press release*, 24 February.

Environmental Investigation Agency. 2003. 'Environmental investigators expose laundering of illegal Indonesian timber by Malaysia and Singapore', *Press release*, 15 May.

Environmental Investigation Agency. 2017. *Repeat Offender: Vietnam's Persistent Trade in Illegal Timber.* London and Washington: Environmental Investigation Agency.

Eurojust. 2014. *Strategic Project on Environmental Crime.* The Hague: Eurojust.

Eurojust. 2016. *Annual Report.* The Hague: Eurojust.

European Commission. 2003. *Communication from the Commission to the Council and the European Parliament, Forest Law Enforcement, Governance and Trade (FLEGT), Proposal for an EU Action Plan.* Brussels, COM (2003) 251 final.

European Commission. 2005. 'Seventh ASEM foreign ministers' meeting, Kyoto, 6–7 May 2005', *Press release*, 10 May.

European Commission. 2016a. *EU Action Plan Against Wildlife Trafficking*. Brussels, COM (2016) 87 final.

European Commission. 2016b. *Proposal for a Directive of the European Parliament and of the Council on Countering Money Laundering by Criminal Law*. Brussels, COM (2016) 862 final.

European Commission. 2017. *EU Action Plan Against Wildlife Trafficking: One Year After – Overview of Actions and Initiatives Taken by the EU Member States and the European Commission*. Available at: http://ec.europa.eu/environment/cites/pdf/Achievements_WAP_overview.pdf (accessed 19 August 2017).

Europol. 2013. *Threat Assessment 2013 Environmental Crime in the EU*. The Hague: Europol.

Europol. 2017. *Serious and Organised Crime Threat Assessment 2017*. The Hague: Europol.

FATF. 2012. *International Standards On Combating Money Laundering and the Financing of Terrorism & Proliferation: The FATF Recommendations*. Paris: FATF/OECD.

FATF. 2017. *Methodology Assessing Technical Compliance with the FATF Recommendations and the Effectiveness of AML/CFT Systems*. Paris: Financial Action Task Force.

Felson, M. 2006. *The Ecosystem for Organized Crime*. Helsinki: Heuni, Paper 26.

Gregory, M. 2015. *Stashing the Cash: Banks, Money Laundering and the Battle Against Illegal Logging. Reflections from Fern*. Moreton-in-Marsh and Brussels: Fern.

Haenlein, C. 2017. *Below the Surface: How Illegal, Unreported and Unregulated Fishing Threatens our Security*. London: RUSI.

Haenlein, C. and Keatinge, T. 2017. *Follow the Money: Using Financial Investigation to Combat Wildlife Crime*. London: RUSI.

Halliday, T., Levi, M. and Reuter, P. 2014. *Global Surveillance of Dirty Money: Assessing Assessments of Regimes to Control Money-Laundering and Combat the Financing of Terrorism*. Chicago: American Bar Foundation.

Haseman, J. and Lachica, E. 2005. *Toward a Stronger U.S.-Indonesia Security Relationship*. Washington & Jakarta: United States–Indonesia Society.

Hillyard, P. and Tombs, S. 2017. 'Social Harm and Zemiology', in *Oxford Handbook of Criminology*, edited by A. Liebling, L. McAra and S. Maruna. Oxford: Oxford University Press, 6th edition, 284–305.

Kluin, M. 2016. 'Accidents with dangerous substances in the Dutch chemical industry'. in *Hazardous Waste and Pollution*, edited by T. Wyatt. Switzerland: Springer International Publishing, 125–146.

Kluin, M., and Jagtman, E. 2016. 'A decade of violations in the Dutch chemical industry', in *Environmental Crime and Its Victims: Perspectives Within Green Criminology*, edited by Toine Spapens, Rob White and Wim Huisman. Farnham: Ashgate, 149–169.

Levi, M. 2010. 'Combating the financing of terrorism: A history and assessment of the control of 'threat finance',' *British Journal of Criminology* 50(4), 650–669.

Levi, M. 2012. 'States, frauds, and the threat of transnational organized crime', *Journal of International Affairs*, 66(1) , 37–48.

Levi, M. 2018. 'Punishing banks, their clients and their clients' clients', in *The Handbook of Criminal and Terrorism Financing Law*, edited by C. King, C. Walker and J. Gurule. London: Palgrave Macmillan.

Levi, M., Dakolias, M. and Greenberg. T. 2007. 'Money laundering and corruption', in *The Many Faces of Corruption: Tracking Vulnerabilities at the Sector Level*, edited by J. Edgardo Campos and S. Pradhan. Washington, DC: the World Bank, 389–426.

Levi, M. and Osofsky, L. 1995. *Investigating, Seizing, and Confiscating the Proceeds of Crime*. London: Home Office, Crime Detection and Prevention Series Paper 61.

Levi, M., Reuter, P. and Halliday, T. (2017) 'Can the AML/CTF system be evaluated without better data?', *Crime, Law and Social Change 69*(2), 307–328.

Maguire, T. and Haenlein, C. 2015. *An Illusion of Complicity: Terrorism and the Illegal Ivory Trade in East Africa*. London: Royal United Services Institute for Defence and Security Studies.

Nellemann, C., and INTERPOL Environmental Crime Programme (eds). 2012. *Green Carbon, Black Trade: Illegal Logging, Tax Fraud and Laundering in the Worlds Tropical Forests. A Rapid Response Assessment*. Arendal: UNEP and GRID-Arendal.

Newman, J. 2015. 'Targeting wildlife crime bosses – it's all about the money', *Environmental Investigation Agency*, 27 November.

SEPA. 2016. 'Waste recycling firm given highest confiscation order for environmental offences in Scotland', *Press release*, 15 February.

Setiono, B. and Barr, C. 2003. *Using Anti-Money Laundering Laws to Fight Forestry Crime in Indonesia*. Bogor: Center for International Forestry Research (CIFOR).

Setiono, B. and Husein, Y. 2005. *Fighting Forest Crime and Promoting Prudent Banking for Sustainable Forest Management*. Bogor: Center for International Forestry Research (CIFOR).

Sinaga, A., Gnych, S. and Phelps, J. 2015. *Forests, Financial Services and Customer Due Diligence: Efforts to Target Illegality, Money Laundering and Corruption in Indonesian Forests*. Bogor: Center for International Forestry Research (CIFOR).

Speechly, H. 2004. *Money Laundering and Illegal Logging – Application of UK Legislation, Summary of Points Made at Two Seminars Held at the Royal Institute for International Affairs*. London: Royal Institute of International Affairs.

Tacconi, L., Boscolo, M. and Brack, D. 2003. *National and International Policies to Control Illegal Forest Activities*. Bogor: Center for International Forestry Research (CIFOR).

Tacconi, L., Obidzinski, K. and Agung, F. 2004. *Learning Lessons to Promote Forest Certification and Control Illegal Logging in Indonesia*. Bogor: Center for International Forestry Research (CIFOR).

UNODC. (2016. *World Wildlife Crime Report 2016*. Vienna: United Nations.

Walters, R. (2017), Global Kitchens and Super Highways: *Social Harm and the Political Economy of Food*, Bristol: Policy Press.

White, R. 2014. *Environmental Harm: An Eco-Justice Perspective*, Bristol: Policy Press.

White, R. 2018. 'The global context of transnational environmental crime in Asia', in *The Palgrave Handbook of Criminology and the Global South*, edited by K. Carrington, R. Hogg, J. Scott and M. Sozzo. Basingstoke: Palgrave MacMillan, 281–300.

10 Wildlife and laundering

Interaction between the under and upper world

Daan van Uhm

Introduction

'[L]aundering is one of those terms that evokes images of sophisticated multinational financial operations that transform proceeds of drug trafficking into clean money' (Levi 2002, p. 182). However, laundering can also have another meaning in the context of wildlife trafficking: hiding its illegal origin to enable wildlife to be legitimately traded. This chapter analyses the involvement of legitimate companies in wildlife laundering; how actors transform financial profits obtained from trading in illegal wildlife and related offences into legitimate assets; and sheds light on the interaction between the criminal underworld and the upper world in the context of wildlife trafficking.

Ancient practices and new interpretations

Wildlife trafficking and money laundering are both activities related to the earliest civilisations. In ancient Egypt, for example, Hatshepsut and Cleopatra displayed imported wildlife in their royal menageries to represent imperial power over far-flung lands, while Roman rulers such as Caesar and Pompey systematically collected wildlife for entertainment, slaughter and display in the arenas and amphitheatres throughout the Roman Empire (van Uhm 2016a). Naylor (2004) argued that before the existence of the sovereign territorial state, there was also a need to hide financial transactions. 'It's a fair bet that the world's first genuine tax code, in Hammurabi's Babylonia, stimulated the imagination of those who sought to grant themselves a rebate' (p. 134). The high demand for exotic animals for the Roman games that was met by a private business on which an import tax of 2.5 per cent needed to be paid reflects how these two worlds may have historically converged.

While for a long time wildlife trafficking and money laundering have not been seen as serious crimes, in the past few decades both activities have become strongly linked to activities by underworld figures. Since the 1990s, reports by the United Nations (UN) increasingly underline the involvement of organised crime in both wildlife trafficking and money laundering (e.g. UN 2002, 2003,

2004).[1] Global thefts of rhino horns from museums by the Irish organised crime group the Rathkaele Rovers (Europol 2012), money laundering by the Italian members of the Cosa Nostra (Europol 2013a) or Chinese organised crime groups that supply traditional Chinese medicine containing derivatives of endangered species (Europol 2011) are examples thereof. More recently, the UN has emphasised that 'wildlife and forest crime has all the hallmarks of transnational organized crime and is frequently linked to other forms of serious crime such as fraud, corruption and money laundering' (UNODC 2017, p. 2).

Thus, gradually the wildlife trafficking and laundering nexus has become a popular topic in law enforcement in order to fight the multibillion-dollar wildlife industry. While many reports explicitly link illegal wildlife trafficking and laundering to organised crime activities (e.g. UNODC 2010; Europol 2013b; UNEP 2014), this chapter takes into account especially the role of another category of actors: legitimate traders in wildlife, in other words, 'green-collar' offenders.

The forgotten category of green-collar offenders

Criminology traditionally focuses on offenders from lower socio-economic classes committing street crimes such as theft and burglary. For a long time, powerful and large companies were not the object of study (Sutherland 1940, 1949; Coleman 1997; Friedrichs 1996). This changed when Edwin Sutherland introduced the concept of *white-collar crime*, referring to 'a crime committed by a person of respectability and high social status in the course of his occupation' (Sutherland 1949, p. 9). Corporate crimes are a subset of white-collar crimes committed by legitimate businesses and individuals within these companies (Sutherland 1949; Braithwaite 1984; Hoefnagels 1981). While mainstream criminology still focuses on crimes of the 'powerless' and continues to largely ignore crimes of the 'powerful', the concepts of white-collar crime and corporate crime have been gradually embraced by the discipline of criminology.

Corporate crimes committed to promote corporate interests vary from fraud, tax evasion and non-compliance with safety and other regulations, to even murder (Clinard and Quinney 1973; Friedrichs 2004; Passas and Goodwin 2004). Lynch and Stretesky (2003, 2014) and Ruggiero and South (2010, 2013) pointed out that powerful companies are also involved in environmental crimes. For this, Ruggiero and South (2010) introduced the term 'dirty-collar crime' in their study of fraud in the European waste and oil industries. Other authors (e.g. Barrett 1997; O'Hear 2004; Wolf 2011) used the term 'green-collar crime' to refer to and synthesise the concepts of white-collar crime and environmental justice related to green crimes.

---

1 The UN recently adopted a resolution on tackling illicit trafficking in wildlife that calls upon Member States to make illicit wildlife trafficking a 'serious crime' (Article 2b); and to include it in their Criminal Code as an offence punishable by a maximum deprivation of liberty of at least four years or a more serious penalty.

In the context of wildlife trafficking a number of investigations highlight the involvement of legitimate enterprises in the illegal trade in wildlife (e.g. Cook *et al.* 2002; Lyons and Natusch 2011). Even more so, a study of the professional background of wildlife crime offenders within the EU shows that a large proportion (> 30%) appear to work legally with wildlife (van Uhm 2016b).

Figure 10.1 shows different categories of wildlife crime offenders that were recorded in the European Union Trade in Wildlife Information eXchange database (EU-TWIX), the database of wildlife seizures in the EU (see also van Uhm 2016b).[2] For instance, these perpetrators include animal traders (14.2%), zoo or wildlife park owners (6.5%), antique dealers (4.3%), fashion trading companies (2.9%), wildlife breeders (1.4%), food traders (1.1%) and traditional Asian medicine suppliers (0.5%). It usually concerns the owners or employees of legitimate companies that conceal the illegal catching, trading or manufacturing of wildlife within legitimate activities involving wildlife (e.g. van Uhm and Moreto 2017). Illegal wildlife may end up with legitimate actors such as reptile meat and caviar in restaurants (2.5%), primates and bears in wildlife films (0.7%) and big cats in circuses (0.6%). The following sections illustrate that green-collar perpetrators are experts regarding the rules and regulations and know how to use loopholes to evade law enforcement.

Dealing with regulation

The most important and global legal instrument regulating the international trade in wildlife is the Convention on International Trade in Endangered Species (CITES). CITES regulates the trade in wild animals and plants through a system of licences (the CITES permits). Its aim is to ensure that the international trade in wild animals and plants does not threaten the survival of any species. CITES regulates the trade in more than 35,000 species, both animals and plants, through import and export permits. This multilateral treaty consists of three Appendices: CITES Appendix I refers to species seriously threatened with extinction.[3] Commercial trade in such species derived from the wild is therefore strictly forbidden.[4] In order to import CITES I species an import and export or re-export certificate is required. CITES Appendix II species are not directly threatened with extinction but consist of vulnerable populations.[5] It is assumed that if the trade is not regulated, these species may become threatened with extinction in the near future. CITES Appendix III includes species where the country of origin will offer protection.[6] For CITES II and III species no import permit is required; only an export permit is needed.

---

2 The data includes more than 20,000 shipments (N=22,204) of animals and animal products seized in the EU between 2001 and 2010.
3 Art. II.1, CITES.
4 Art. III.3.c, CITES.
5 Art. II.2.a, CITES.
6 Art. II.3, CITES.

Legally registered companies	%	Corrupt public actors	%	Outlets	%	Other professionals	%	Other	%
Animal trader	14.2	Public service administrative professionals	4.8	Restaurant owner	2.5	Businessman	11.4	Unemployed	6.9
Zoo/wildlife park owner	6.5	Armed Forces	4.4	Wildlife film producer	0.7	Liberal profession	7.2	Pensioner/Retired	5.9
Antique dealer	4.3	Diplomat	0.9	Circus, travelling exhibitions owner	0.6	Health professional	3.1	Student	4.5
Fashion (trading company)	2.9	Enforcement Agency (Police, Customs, etc.)	0.6	Falconer/Raptor displays/bird of prey centres	0.2	Taxidermist/Taxidermy seller	2.3	Truck driver	3.0
Breeder	1.4	Magistrate	0.2	Plant nursery/garden centre owner	0.1	Musician	0.4	Hobbyist	2.9
Food trader	1.1			Photographer	0.1	Hunter, angler	0.3	Sailor	2.5
Traditional Asian medicine supplier	0.5					Religious professional	0.1	Private collector	2.0
Luxury food supplies	0.1							Scientific expert	0.8
								Tourist	0.6
Total	31.0		10.9		4.2		24.8		29.1

Figure 10.1 Categories of perpetrators

Source: van Uhm 2016a

This regulation with three appendices seems to confuse law enforcement and provides opportunities for fraud. For example, CITES Appendix I species are regularly traded as Appendix II species. This may be difficult to detect, as Appendix I species may look like non-CITES species, as is the case with elephant ivory (Appendix I), which resembles walrus ivory (Appendix II) and mammoth ivory (unprotected). Another example would be the physical difference between a protected and unprotected turtle that may be just a dot on the cheek of the animal (van Uhm 2012). Moreover, due to the fact that no import permit is needed for Appendix II and III species (unless required by national law), the legality of the trade is not examined by the importing country that provides opportunities for illegal trade (e.g. providing CITES export permits through corrupt officials in the source country).

There is also another thriving issue: the aim of CITES is to ensure that the international trade in wildlife does not threaten 'wild' species. Therefore, CITES I species that were born and bred in captivity or were artificially propagated are considered as CITES II species and are allowed to be traded under Annex II conditions.[7] This provides a loophole for illegal trade, as the issuance of an import or export permit may be less strict (Lyons and Natusch 2011). On a regular basis, wildlife can be traded under permit if it is captive-bred, while in reality these animals consist of species from the wild; CITES trade data show large fluctuations between years in the amounts of captive-bred and wild-caught specimens traded (Nijman and Shepherd 2009; Lyons and Natusch 2011). Indeed, several surveys, site visits and interviews demonstrate unclear registration or simply that no capability of captive-bred farming in such commercial quantities is possible in countries of origin (Traffic 2012).

Wildlife laundering

Thus, the loopholes in regulation and the lack of control provide opportunities for fraud and *wildlife laundering*. Even though a broad concept of laundering in criminology may refer to the process of disguising the proceeds of crime and moving value through the use of trade transactions in an attempt to legitimise their illicit origins (Cassara 2015), narrow concepts of laundering refer to the process in which money obtained from illegal business is transformed into legitimate money (Levi and Reuter 2006). According to Reuter (2004, p. 1) 'money laundering is the conversion of criminal incomes into assets that cannot be traced back to the underlying crime'.[8] In laundering wildlife, the illegal origin

---

7 The classification with the highest demand is 'bred in captivity' (c) (Vinke and Vinke 2010).
8 For instance, the laundering of drug money by purchasing real estate with illegally obtained money whereby the property is sold to obtain legitimate money. In other words, the real estate is paid for in cash and with its sale the money will be back circulating in the economy as legitimate money.

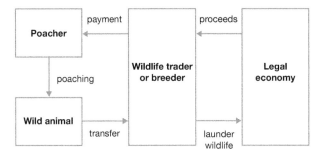

Figure 10.2 Wildlife laundering

Source: Author

of an animal or animal product is concealed. For instance, the wildlife is declared as being bred in captivity instead of poached in the wild (Wyatt 2013). Thus, a wildlife trader or breeder may order illegal wildlife from a poacher. The poacher provides the illegal wildlife and then the dealer declares that the wildlife is captive-bred or mixes it with legal wildlife trade. Subsequently, the wildlife is laundered and can enter the legal economy (Figure 10.2).

Globally, the size of this market in financial terms has yet to be estimated. However, increasing numbers of investigations indicate that for many species, this may very well be the case (e.g. Engler and Parry-Jones 2007; Nijman and Shepherd 2009; Vinke and Vinke 2010). For instance, Europol (2011) has pointed at criminal groups operating in north-west Europe that cooperate with breeders in other Member States to launder 'wild-caught' animals by using false documents and then to trade them as being captive-bred on the legitimate market.[9] Three examples of perpetrator categories from the EU-TWIX database will be discussed in order to understand the opportunities of wildlife laundering in the next sections.

Breeding centres

One of the main purposes of wildlife farming is to reduce pressure on wild populations (Revol 1995). In order to receive the classification of a commercial breeder, the breeding stock should be established in accordance with the requirements of CITES. For instance, mating must take place in a controlled environment (Vinke and Vinke 2010). However, Nijman and Shepherd (2009) and Lyons and Natusch (2011) noticed that commercial breeding seems to provide

9 For example, after the EU imposed a trade ban on wild-taken *Horsefield tortoises*, a sudden increase in captive-bred specimens was noticed. No less than 82,293 non-wild animals were imported into the EU between 2000 and 2006. Most of those captive-bred specimens (>90%) were imported from a country with no previous known history of captive-breeding this species (Ukraine). It is more likely that those animals were laundered on a large scale (Traffic 2012).

opportunities to launder illegally wild-caught animals. They described substantial discrepancies between the annually exported number of reptiles from Indonesia and the number of reptiles capable of being produced by Indonesian breeding farms. Nijman and Shepherd (2009) underline that young animals may have been captured in the wild and after growing up in captivity the reptiles are falsely declared as captive-bred. This type of wildlife laundering is extremely difficult to detect, because it is hard to differentiate between captive-bred and wild animals. Moreover, wild reptiles can be easily obtained in Indonesia and exporting wild reptiles (declared as captive-bred) is far less expensive than breeding the animals in captivity (Nijman and Shepherd 2009). For most reptile taxa within the study, the researchers found that recorded numbers were significantly lower than reported numbers. Comparably, Nijman, Shepherd and Stengel (2012) discovered large numbers of wild-caught birds, such as hornbills, parrots and birds-of-paradise, that were laundered into the global wildlife trade through the Solomon Islands by alleged breeders; again, they declared wild-caught animals as being captive-bred.

In relation to animal products similar issues have been found by Knapp *et al.* (2006), Sellar (2014) and van Uhm and Siegel (2016). Although aquaculture is mentioned as being the solution to the decline of the sturgeon population, several authors have argued that it could very well pose a risk to wild sturgeons. They highlight opportunities to launder illegally sourced caviar through aquaculture operations concerning sturgeons (Kecse-Nagy 2011; Jahrl 2013; van Uhm and Siegel 2016). For instance, wild-caught sturgeons for breeding purposes are being not released[10] or caviar from wild sturgeons will be sold as having been produced in fish farms. In 2009, the German authorities confiscated caviar labelled as farmed caviar where isotope analysis found that the caviar had originated from the Caspian Sea (NWCU 2013). Recent research in Bulgaria and Romania has also suggested the involvement of aquaculture operations in the Danube region in laundering wild caviar originating from the Caspian region (Kecse-Nagy 2011; Jahrl 2013). van Uhm and Siegel (2016) note that these companies may also launder illegally caught sturgeon under the pretence of scientific purposes. Statistical data covering several years after the ban on sturgeon fishing in the Caspian Sea demonstrates that 600 tons of caviar came from sturgeon caught for 'scientific purposes'.

Another example of breeding centres involved in the illegal wildlife trade concerns tiger farms in Asia. In China, while the population of wild tigers decreased from 4,000 in 1949 to 40–50 in 2012, the number of tigers kept in China's farms increased from 8–13 in 1986 to 6,000 in 2010 (EIA 2013). These farms were established before the 1993 ban on tiger bones for use in traditional Chinese medicine (TCM).[11] For instance, in the early 1990s Guilin Xiongsen

---

10 Generally fishing for sturgeons is forbidden, but there are exceptions. To increase wild populations, wild sturgeons may be caught for breeding purposes.
11 Article 11 Circular of the State Council on Banning the Trade of Rhinoceros Horn and Tiger Bone.

Tigers and Bears Mountain Village, keeping 400 captive-bred tigers at that time, regularly supplied bones to the TCM industry and a factory in Harbin manufactured half a million tiger bone plasters each day with a bone-crushing machine (Nowell 2000). While the sale of products derived from captive-bred tigers has not been allowed since 1993, breeders continue to openly sell tiger bone products to customers (van Uhm 2016a). While employees of these farms claim that they use tiger bones in tiger bone wine, on the ingredient list of the bottles the Latin name *Panthera leo* is mentioned. This would suggest that the bones are from lions instead of tigers. According to Nowell (2009) this may be a laundering method: the farms pretend that they are using lion bones (CITES II),[12] but in reality they use the forbidden tiger bones (CITES I).

Commercial traders

Commercial traders in all kinds of wildlife also have plenty of opportunities to launder protected wildlife. First, there seems to be an illegal market in CITES certificates (sometimes purchased from corrupt officials) and mark characteristics of captive-bred animals in the hands of wholesalers. For example, there is a thriving illegal trade in rings for captive-bred birds. The principle is that a correctly sized close ring can only be fitted to birds in the first days of life to demonstrate that the bird was captive-bred, and thus legal. However, many examples emphasise that birds are illegally caught and rings can be quite easily obtained and used to mark an illegal wild bird as legal for sale (van Kreveld 2007). Rings are also cut and reapplied and the inner diameter is enlarged, or has been made larger so that these rings are used to fit the leg of an adult bird caught illegally. This system enables illegal entrepreneurs to launder large numbers of protected wild birds into 'captive-bred' birds.[13]

Second, the same CITES certificates are reused multiple times for different animals. Theoretically, certificates should be sent back to the CITES authority when the animal dies but in practice this hardly happens. This allows commercial traders to transfer newly obtained illegal animals using those certificates. Another method is to re-use the same certificate for different shipments of animals and animal products. For example, a dealer orders a small batch of legal caviar, sends half of it back, and then uses his import licence to resell the illegal caviar (Knapp *et al.* 2006). Figure 10.3 illustrates how a caviar trader used an import permit for 500 kg of caviar to launder an additional amount of 250 kg of illegally obtained caviar.

A third method of laundering wildlife is claiming that it has come from stockpiles from before regulations came into effect (Wyatt 2013). A case of ivory

---

12 The use of lion bones in TCM is legal with certificates from the China State Forestry Administration (SFA) (EIA 2013).
13 There are even examples of chips that are implanted into other animals to launder them.

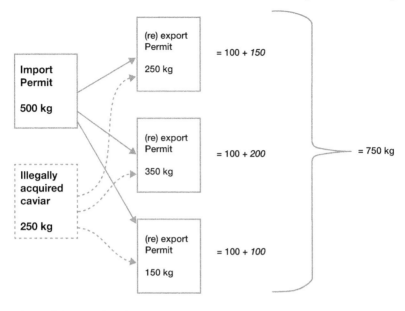

Figure 10.3 Caviar laundering
Source: van Uhm 2016a

laundering is an example. Hong Kong, for instance, has an extensive ivory business in which several shops openly sell ivory from stockpiles (Wong 2017). According to illegal traders, laundering ivory is easy as commercial traders use the stockpile of legal ivory as a cover while instead they sell illegally smuggled ivory (Lo and Edwards 2015). This would work in the same way for saiga antelope horns for use in traditional Chinese medicine (van Uhm 2016a). It is permitted for certain reputable sellers and producers to sell saiga horn from stockpiles. However, it has been calculated that stockpiles of saiga horn must have long been exhausted (Von Meibom et al. 2010).[14]

Zoos

The involvement of zoos and sanctuaries in the illegal wildlife trade is only incidentally mentioned. One of the most famous examples is the private zoo of the drug lord Pablo Escobar. From the late 1970s onwards he started to illegally

14 While in 1994 the total supply of saiga horn in China was estimated at 155,500 kg, in a second nationwide survey undertaken by the government (2005) the total volume was 55,000 kg (Von Meibom *et al.* 2010). This means that with a decrease of more than 100,000 kg in 10 years, the total amount of stockpiles would be minus 45,000 in 2015.

import endangered species from all over the world to Hacienda Napoles as he called his 530 hectares of jungle and grassland along the Magdalena River. He hired expert advice on which species could survive in this place and bribed customs officials to allow shipments of protected species to pass.[15] According to the police, camel and elephant droppings for his zoo were used in the wrapping of cocaine in order to confuse the law enforcers' drug-sniffing dogs (Toufexis 1993).

The fact that relatively high numbers of zoo and wildlife park owners appear in the EU confiscation data underlines the necessity of having a better look at these actors (van Uhm 2016b). Zoos are allowed to move endangered species with CITES documents for 'zoo purposes' such as breeding programmes. However, these may also be misused to explain the appearance of new animals. For instance, there are cases in which wildlife imported for zoo purposes is illegally traded.[16] Thus, fraudulent zoos may be used for import purposes, when the true intent of the import is commercial trade (UNODC 2016).

For instance, in 2002, four gorillas were exported from Nigeria to the Taiping Zoo in Malaysia. While the zoo claimed that the gorillas were captive-bred and part of an animal exchange programme, investigations revealed that the Nigerian zoo in question had no mating pair. In fact, a Nigerian wildlife dealer had illegally imported wild gorillas from Cameroon and reportedly received a combined price of USD 1.6 million for them. The gorillas were transported under valid CITES permits (Stiles *et al.* 2013). Recently, in another case, a criminal investigation uncovered how a criminal organisation used an illegal smuggling route involving zoos in Bulgaria and Dubai. While zoos are usually not allowed to commercially trade in protected species, the zoo imported the animals and illegally transferred them to a criminal organisation in the Netherlands (van Uhm 2016c).

Money and barter laundering

As was illustrated in the previous sections, legitimate companies involved in breeding and trading can be used to launder illegally obtained wildlife. They may, however, also sell illegal wildlife directly to 'trusted' customers. As these endangered

---

15 On 17 November 1983, Pablo was fined 450,000 pesos for the illegal importation of 85 animals, including camels, elephants, elk and a large Amazonian capybara.

16 Bird sanctuaries can also be involved in the illegal trade. A remarkable example is a bird sanctuary in the Netherlands, which, until recently, had a contract with the government and was paid to take care of birds that had been confiscated by the authorities. More than 50 per cent of the birds were not present at the sanctuary and very high mortality rates among the birds led to a police investigation that indicated involvement in the illegal trade in birds, including different kinds of parrots. The sanctuary sold the parrots under the table, registered the birds as deceased and replaced them with cheap other bird species, which were kept in the freezer and showed upon inspection, assuming that inspectors would be unable to tell the difference (van Uhm 2016c).

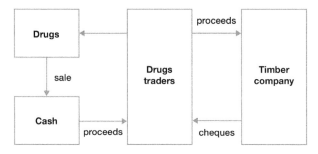

Figure 10.4 Money laundering from the sale of drugs

Source: Author

species can generate vast amounts of profits, this requires money laundering. Indeed, several reports associate wildlife trafficking with money laundering (e.g. UNODC 2010; Europol 2013b; UNEP 2014). For example, an abalone case illustrated that within nine months 335 cash deposits (each transaction was less than AUD 10,000 in order to avoid the cash transaction reporting threshold) were sent overseas via international funds transfer instructions by an employee of a company involved in illegal abalone fishing. More than AUD 3 million was transferred from Australia to Hong Kong and China and the employee received fees worth approximately AUD 30,000 from the abalone business owner (AUSTRAC 2010).

The wildlife trade may also be a cover to launder illegal money from other serious crimes, such as drug offences. For example, an agreement with an owner of a timber company provided a perfect cover to launder money from the sale of drugs.[17] The owner of the timber company received the proceeds of the drug sales and then provided the drug dealers with legitimate cheques, which were placed into personal accounts. The illegal money was mixed with legitimate funds from timber and the owner received 13 per cent of the laundered money (AUSTRAC 2010) (Figure 10.4).

There is also evidence that criminal groups exchange wildlife and other contraband on a cashless basis as part of the laundering of criminal proceeds. From this *broad* approach of laundering, the launderer may avoid the financial system entirely (van Duyne 2003). For larger transactions, even without money being exchanged, there may be tax implications for both actors; the bartered goods are supposed to be recorded at 'fair market value' (Cassara 2015, p. 125). For instance, planeloads of smuggled birds from Australia were being exchanged for heroin in Bangkok; the drugs were then transferred back to Australia (Cook *et al.* 2002). Another example includes criminal groups that exchanged wildlife with stolen contraband. For instance, criminal groups exchange stolen Mercedes cars for 500 g tins of caviar (van Uhm and Siegel 2016). From this barter system

17 Money laundering processes are mentioned regularly in the context of forest crimes (e.g. Nellemann 2012).

perspective, the wildlife trade can be used for such laundering schemes (CRI 1992; OECD 2012). The interface between wildlife trafficking and money laundering will be presented with the following three case studies.

The drug-wildlife kingpin

One of the first big wildlife crime cases in history, Operation Cobra, was a clear example of the interconnection between wildlife and drugs trafficking. The wildlife trader Tabraue was 'chairman of the board' of the Tabraue syndicate, a 79-million-dollar drug-smuggling operation and one of Florida's most violent organisations, according to Christy (2008). They 'owned' Miami police officers and politicians and were allegedly involved in a murder case.

The drug lord combined his cocaine trade from Colombia with an exotic animal business called Zoological Imports, one of the premier animal-importing companies in the United States (US). Critically endangered animals were illegally imported, such as a shipment of 35 endangered hyacinth macaws into the US inside PVC pipes. Subsequently, Tabraue sold the wildlife species in his store, borrowed some of the exotic animals to zoos and kept others as pets. The animal business turned out to be a perfect cover for his drug trafficking; they used codes such as 'I need three cockatoos', meaning three kilos of cocaine or 'three lesser-crested cockatoos', which meant three ounces (Scott 1992; Christy 2008). Moreover, the drug smuggling financed his collection of rare birds and animals (NOVA 1997). The syndicate would conceal the source, nature and amount of its illegal profits by the use of an offshore corporation, investments, cashiers' checks, false loans and mortgages, trusts and attorney trust accounts.[18]

After an investigation by the FBI the drug-wildlife kingpin was sentenced to 100 years imprisonment by a federal judge for racketeering, trafficking in cocaine, marijuana and murder (Christy 2008).[19] After 12 years he had already been released after testifying against other members of the Miami underworld. This case illustrates how Tabraue used his wildlife enterprise to hide the drug trade and to launder drug money through several investments, false loans and an offshore corporation.

The Lizard King

Another example is the case of Anson Wong, one of the most notorious wildlife smugglers, known as the Lizard King (the FBI identified Wong as 'King Rat') who headed a smuggling ring in wildlife products in Malaysia. He owned a private zoo in Penang as a legal business entity to hide the illegal trade in wildlife. Within a period of two years he successfully imported and sold more than 300

18 United States of America 'Operation Cobra indictment', 16 December 1987.
19 According to the court testimony Tabraue's associates discovered a government informant and murdered him (Christy 2008).

extremely rare and protected animals native to Asia and Africa, including critically endangered species such as the Komodo lizard from Indonesia (+/–30,000 USD per animal), Chinese alligators (+/–17,000 USD) and Ploughshare tortoises from Madagascar (+/–52,500 USD per animal) that are on the brink of extinction (Christy 2010; Mesko *et al.* 2011).

The Lizard King shipped the reptiles concealed in express delivery packages, airline baggage and large commercial shipments of legally declared animals. Allegedly, Wong was able to run his illegal business because he was protected by members of the Malaysian government (Spapens 2014). An undercover investigation led by the US, Operation Chameleon, led to successful infiltration into this wildlife trade. During this investigation, he offered to sell the agents 20 Timor pythons and several Spix Macaws, both of which were believed to be extinct (Morgan 2015).

The US conducted a sting operation to lure Wong out of Malaysia by starting to trade in reptiles with him (Schneider 2012). Consequently, he was arrested by Mexican officials based on charges from the US and pleaded guilty to 40 felony crimes, including conspiracy, smuggling and money laundering. He also agreed that the smuggled animals in the California case alone exceeded a market value of 500,000 USD. In this case, 51,183 USD was wire transferred from an account in Livermore in the name of an import-export company to an account in the name of Sungai Rusa Wildlife in Penang in violation of the laundering of monetary instruments.[20] He was sentenced to 71 months of incarceration and given a 60,000 USD fine for money laundering linked to wildlife trade in the US (Mesko *et al.* 2011). This case reflects how Wong's zoo provided opportunities to launder wildlife and how he was involved in laundering his money obtained through illegal wildlife trafficking.

The Groenewald syndicate

A recent case includes another serious indictment of laundering in Operation Crash. For over four years the Groenewald syndicate in South Africa, or the 'Musina group', is alleged to have kept rhinos for conservation purposes, while actually the real purpose was the dehorning and killing of rhinos to make profits from the sale of their horns (Rademeyer 2012; Ayling 2013). Among the people involved were wildlife veterinarians, professional hunters, a pilot and farm labourers. The case became one of the most serious cases regarding rhinos with 1,872 charges of racketeering, illegal hunting, dealing in rhino horns, and fraud and money laundering (Ayling 2013; Hübschle 2016).[21]

---

20 United States of America, Conviction case Operation Chameleon, No. 98–165, 5 July 2001.

21 Due to the involvement of professional hunters and game farmers predominantly made up of Afrikaners, these groups have been referred to as the 'Boere mafia' or 'khaki-collar criminals' (Milliken and Shaw 2012).

The criminal indictment includes money laundering and structuring deposits to avoid federal reporting requirements. Hunters allegedly paid between 3,500 and 15,000 USD for illegal rhino hunts.[22] The Groenewald gang told these hunters that because the dead rhinos were 'problem' animals, the horns were not allowed to be exported as trophies. According to the indictment the Groenewald syndicate sold the rhino horns obtained from these hunts to criminal networks. They therefore profited from the illegal hunts and subsequently from the illegal sale of rhino horns to criminal actors (Hübschle 2016).

The Groenewald group would have sold at least 384 rhino horns over a four-year period and made around USD 6.8 million from the illegal sale of rhino horn. They did not only dehorn rhinos on Groenewald's farm, Prachtig, but it is believed that they offered dehorning services to other rhino breeders in South Africa. Eight suspects are charged with money laundering (Jooste 2012). Allegedly the illegal money was transferred by wire transfer to and from banks located in the US and to and from banks outside the US and in South Africa and Botswana. The case has dragged on for years and is likely to resume soon. This indictment shows how a wildlife farm has allegedly been used to trade illegally in rhino horns and how the money obtained was laundered through banks abroad.

Discussion and conclusion

This chapter has demonstrated that the interconnection between the legal and illegal trade in wildlife appears to provide opportunities to launder valuable wildlife, and thus money. The actors involved in illegal wildlife trafficking and laundering consist of a variety of owners or employees of legitimate companies, such as animal traders, wildlife park owners, or wildlife breeders, who conceal their illegal practices. Findings show that these green-collar perpetrators are experts regarding the rules and regulations and know how to use loopholes to dodge law enforcement.

In the wildlife trade several methods are used to launder the illegal origin of protected species. A variety of modi operandi were described in the context of wildlife and money laundering and it turned out that wildlife is declared as not having been caught in the wild in order to obtain documents that prove its legality. For example, commercial wildlife traders are involved in fraud and forging mark characteristics to launder wild-caught animals into captive-bred animals. Whereas breeding farms for endangered wildlife may help to conserve biodiversity, they also provide a perfect opportunity for laundering illegally caught wildlife and to obtain proper documents. Zoos rightfully have a special position and are easily able to import wildlife for conservation purposes. However, the same role also allows criminals to launder wildlife and use breeding programmes to explain the appearance of new animals.

---

22 United States Department of Justice. 'Owners of Safari Company Indicted for Illegal Rhino Hunts', 23 October 2014.

In addition, several wildlife operations illustrate opportunities for money laundering involving proceeds from illegal activities. On the one hand, proceeds from illegal wildlife businesses were laundered and, on the other, proceeds from other serious forms of crime such as drugs were laundered through wildlife organisations. This happens directly through illegal money transfers or indirectly through other forms of trade and services (Stessens 2000). Although most types of wildlife trade related to money laundering eventually result in the 'injection' of money derived from criminal activities into the legal economy, some traders completely avoid the financial system by bartering wildlife for other illegal goods.

However, the concepts of laundering are influenced by Western perspectives. According to Cassara (2015, p. 4) 'we must put aside our linear Western thought process. Illicit money is not always represented by cash, checks, or electronic data in a wire transfer (. . .) The value represented by trade goods – and the accompanying documentation being both genuine and fictitious – can also represent the transfer of illicit funds and value'. The concept of wildlife laundering demonstrates how valuable protected wildlife can be transformed into legitimate wildlife by concealing its illegal origin, and barter laundering illustrates the broad sense of laundering. Thinking only in the classic money laundering techniques limits the field, and limits the understanding of laundering processes in the illegal wildlife trade.

References

AUSTRAC. 2010. *Typologies and Case Studies Report 2010.* AUSTRAC.

Ayling, J. 2013. 'What sustains wildlife crime? Rhino horn trading and the resilience of criminal networks', *Journal of International Wildlife Law and Policy* 16(1), 57–80.

Barrett, J.F. 1997. 'Green collar criminals: why should they receive special treatment', *Maryland Journal of Contemporary Legal Issues* 8, 107–117.

Braithwaite, J. 1984. *Corporate Crime in the Pharmaceutical Industry*. London: Routledge.

Cassara, J.A. 2015. 'Trade-based money laundering techniques: invoice fraud', in *Trade-Based Money Laundering: The Next Frontier in International Money Laundering Enforcement*, edited by J. Cassara. Hoboken NJ: John Wiley & Sons, 13–32.

Christy, B. 2008. *The Lizard King: The True Crimes and Passions of the World's Greatest Reptile Smugglers*. New York: Twelve.

Christy, B. 2010. 'The Kingpin', *National Geographic*, January 2010.

Clinard, M.B. and Quinney, R. 1973. *Criminal Behavior Systems: A Typology.* New York: Holt, Rinehart and Winston.

Coleman, J.W. 1997. *The Criminal Elite: Understanding White-Collar Crime.* New York: Macmillan.

Cook, D., Roberts, M., and Lowther, J. 2002. *The International Wildlife Trade and Organised Crime: A Review of the Evidence and the Role of the UK.* Wolverhampton: University of Wolverhampton.

CRI. 1992. *Milieuhandhaving en natuurbescherming; criminaliteitsbeeld van en om de handel in bedreigde plant en diersoorten.* The Hague: Centrale Recherche Informatiedienst.

Duyne, van P.C. 2003. 'Money laundering policy. Fears and facts'. in *Criminal Finances and Organising Crime in Europe*, edited by P.C. van Duyne, K. von Lampe and J.L. Newell. Nijmegen: Wolf Legal Publishers, 67–104.

EIA. 2013. *Hidden in Plain Sight: China's Clandestine Tiger Trade*. London: EIA.

Engler, M., and Parry-Jones, R. 2007. *Opportunity or Threat: The Role of the European Union in Global Wildlife Trade*. Brussels: Traffic Europe.

Europol. 2011. *Organised Crime Threat Assessment (OCTA)*. The Hague: Europol.

Europol. 2012. *OC-Scan Policy Brief. Involvement of an Irish Mobile OCG in the Illegal Trade in Rhino Horn*. The Hague: Europol.

Europol. 2013a. *Threat Assessment Italian Organised Crime*. The Hague: Europol.

Europol. 2013b. *EU Serious and Organised Crime Threat Assessment (SOCTA)*. The Hague: Europol.

Friedrichs, D. 1996. *Trusted Criminals: White Collar Crime in Contemporary Society*. Belmont: Wadsworth, Cengage Learning.

Friedrichs, D., 2004. 'Enron et al.: Paradigmatic white collar crime cases for the new century', *Critical Criminology* 12(2), 113–132.

Hoefnagels, G.P. 1981. *Witte boordencriminaliteit: opstellen over misdaad en macht*. Assen: Van Gorcum.

Hübschle, A.M. 2016. *A Game of Horns: Transnational Flows of Rhino Horn*. Universität zu Köln.

Jahrl, J. 2013. *Illegal Caviar Trade in Bulgaria and Romania – Results of a Market Survey on Trade in Caviar from Sturgeons (Acipenseridae)*. Vienna: WWF Austria and Traffic.

Jooste, J. 2012. *Supporting Affidavit*. Pretoria: Directorate for Priority Crime Investigations.

Kecse-Nagy, K. (2011). *Trade in Sturgeon Caviar in Bulgaria and Romania Overview of Reported Trade in Caviar, 1998–2008*. Budapest: Traffic.

Knapp. A., Kitschke, C. and Meibom, S. von (eds.) 2006. *Proceedings of the International Sturgeon Enforcement Workshop to Combat Illegal Trade in Caviar. Prepared by TRAFFIC Europe for the European Commission*. Brussels: Traffic.

Kreveld, van, A. 2007. *Gekweekt met de vangkooi. Verkenning naar illegale praktijken in de handel in wilde Europese vogels in Nederland*. Nijmegen: Stroming.

Levi, M. 2002. 'Money laundering and its regulation', *The Annals of the American Academy of Political and Social Science* 582(1), 181–194.

Levi, M. and Reuter, P., 2006. Money laundering, *Crime and Justice* 34(1), 289–375.

Lo, C. and Edwards, G. 2015. *The Hard Truth. How Hong Kong's Ivory Trade is Fuelling Africa's Elephant Poaching Crisis*. Hong Kong: WWF.

Lynch, J.M. and Stretesky, B.P. 2003. 'The meaning of green: Contrasting criminological perspectives', *Theoretical Criminology* 7(2), 217–238.

Lynch, M.J. and Stretesky, P.B. 2014. *Exploring Green Criminology: Toward a Green Criminological Revolution*. Farnham: Ashgate Publishing.

Lyons, J.A., and Natusch, D.J. 2011. 'Wildlife laundering through breeding farms: illegal harvest, population declines and a means of regulating the trade of green pythons (Morelia viridis) from Indonesia', *Biological Conservation* 144(12), 3073–3081.

Meibom, von, S., Vaisman, A., Neo Liang, S. H., Ng, J., and Xu, H. 2010. *Saiga Antelope Trade: Global Trends with a Focus on South-East Asia*. Brussels: Traffic Europe.

Mesko, G., Dimitrijević, D., and Fields, C.B. (eds.). 2011. *Understanding and Managing Threats to the Environment in South Eastern Europe*. Houten: Springer Science and Business Media.

Milliken, T. and Shaw, J., 2012. 'The South Africa–Vietnam rhino horn trade nexus', *Traffic*, 134–136.

Morgan, M.A. 2015. 'Exotic addiction', *Duke Law Journal Online* 65, 1–1.

National Wildlife Crime Unit (NWCU) 2013. *Strategic Assessment 2013*. London: NWCU.

Naylor, R.T. 2004. *Wages of Crime. Black Markets, Illegal Finance, and the Underworld Economy*. Ithaca NY: Cornell University Press.

Nellemann, C. 2012. *Green Carbon, Black Trade: Illegal Logging, Tax Fraud and Laundering in the Worlds Tropical Forests. A Rapid Response Assessment. United Nations Environment Programme*. Arendal: GRID- Arendal.

Nijman, V. and Shepherd, C.R. 2009. *Wildlife Trade from ASEAN to the EU: Issues with the Trade in Captive-Bred Reptiles from Indonesia*. Brussels: TRAFFIC Europe.

Nijman, V., Shepherd C.S. and Stengel C.J. 2012. *The Export and Re-Export of CITES-Listed Birds from the Solomon Islands*. Petaling Jaya, Selangor: TRAFFIC Southeast Asia, Malaysia.

NOVA. 1997. 'The Great Wildlife Heist', 11 March.

Nowell, K. 2000. *Far From a Cure: The Tiger Trade Revisited*. Cambridge: Traffic International.

Nowell, K. 2009. 'Tiger farms and pharmacies: the central importance of China's trade policy for tiger conservation', in *Tigers of the World: The Science, Politics, and Conservation of Panthera tigris*, edited by R. Tilson and P.J. Nyhus. Amsterdam: Elsevier, 463–475.

O'Hear, M.M. 2004. 'Sentencing the green-collar offender: Punishment, culpability, and environmental crime', *Journal of Criminal Law and Criminology* 95(1), 133–276.

OECD. 2012. *Illegal Trade in Environmentally Sensitive Goods*. OECD.

Passas, N. and Goodwin, N. 2004. *It's Legal But It Ain't Right: Harmful Social Consequences of Legal Industries*. Ann Arbor: University of Michigan Press.

Rademeyer, J. 2012. *Killing for Profit: Exposing the Illegal Rhino Horn Trade*. Cape Town: Random House Struik.

Reuter, P. 2004. *Chasing Dirty Money: The Fight Against Money Laundering*. Washington, DC: The Peterson Institute for International Economics.

Ruggiero, V. and South, N. 2010. 'Green criminology and dirty collar crime', *Critical Criminology* 18(4), 251–262.

Ruggiero, V., and South, N. 2013. 'Green criminology and crimes of the economy: Theory, research and praxis', *Critical Criminology* 21(3), 359–373.

Scott, P.D. 1992. *Cocaine Politics: Drugs, Armies, and the CIA in Central America*. Los Angeles: University of California.

Schneider, J. 2012. *Sold Into Extinction: The Global Trade in Endangered Species*. Santa Barbara: Praeger.

Sellar, J.M. 2014. *The UN'S Lone Ranger: Combating International Wildlife Crime*. Dunbeath: Whittles.

Spapens, T. 2014. 'Invisible victims: The problem of policing environmental crime', in *Environmental Crime and its Victims*, edited by T. Spapens, R. White and M. Kluin. Farnham: Ashgate, 221–236.

Stessens, G. 2000. *Money Laundering: A New International Law Enforcement Model*. Cambridge: Cambridge University Press.

Stiles, D., Redmond, I., Cress, D., Nellemann, C. and Formo, R.K. 2013. *Stolen Apes – The Illicit Trade in Chimpanzees, Gorillas, Bonobos, and Orangutans: A Rapid Response Assessment*. Arendal: United Nations Environment Programme/GRID-Arendal.

Sutherland, E. 1940. 'White-collar criminality', *American Sociological Review* 5(1), 1–12.

Sutherland, E. 1949. *White Collar Crime*. New York: Dryden Press.

Toufexis, A. 1993. 'The animal trade', *Time Magazine*, no. 29.

Traffic. 2012. *Captive Bred, or Wild Taken?* Cambridge: Traffic International.

Uhm, van, D.P. 2012. 'De illegale handel in beschermde diersoorten' *Justitiële verkenningen* 28(2): 91–100.

Uhm, van, D.P. 2016a. *The Illegal Wildlife Trade: Inside the World of Poachers, Smugglers and Traders*. New York: Springer.

Uhm, van, D.P. 2016b. 'Illegal trade in wildlife and harms to the world', in *Environmental Crime in Transnational Context*, edited by T. Spapens, R. White and W. Huisman. Farnham: Ashgate, 43–66.

Uhm, van, D.P. 2016c. 'De verwevenheid tussen de onder- en bovenwereld in de wildlife handel', *Cahiers Politiestudies* 38(1), 41–54.

Uhm, van, D.P. and Siegel, D. 2016. 'The illegal trade in black caviar', *Trends in Organized Crime* 19(1), 67–87.

Uhm, van, D.P. and Moreto, W.D. 2017. Corruption within the illegal wildlife trade: a symbiotic and antithetical enterprise, *The British Journal of Criminology* online first, doi.org/10.1093/bjc/azx032.

United Nations. 2002. Progress made in the implementation of Economic and Social Council resolution 2001/12 on illicit trafficking in protected species of wild flora and fauna.

United Nations. 2003. Illicit trafficking in protected species of wild flora and fauna and illicit access to genetic resources, report of the Secretary-General, 4 March 2003 (E/CN.15/2003/8).

United Nations. 2004. Strengthening international cooperation and technical assistance in combating money-laundering. ECOSOC Resolution 2004/29.

United Nations Environment Programme. 2014. *UNEP Year Book. Emerging Issues in our Global Environment.* Nairobi: UNEP.

United Nations Office on Drugs and Crime (UNODC). 2010. *The Globalization of Crime: A Transnational Organized Crime Threat Assessment*. Vienna: UNODC.

United Nations Office on Drugs and Crime (UNODC). 2016.*World Wildlife Crime Report: Trafficking in Protected Species*. New York: United Nations.

United Nations Office on Drugs and Crime (UNODC). 2017. *Financial Flows from Wildlife Crime*. Vienna: United Nations.

Vinke, T. and Vinke, S. 2010. 'Do breeding facilities for chelonians threaten their stability in the wild?', *Schildkröten im Fokus online* 1, 1–18.

Wolf, B. 2011. 'Green-collar crime': Environmental crime and justice in the sociological perspective', *Sociology Compass* 5(7), 499–511.

Wyatt, T. 2013. *Wildlife Trafficking: A Deconstruction of the Crime, the Victims, and the Offenders.* Basingstoke: Palgrave Macmillan.

11 The limits of ecological modernisation to effectively manage greenhouse gas emissions

A case study of carbon market crime

Ruth McKie

Introduction

Across the world a consensus has been reached that human-induced or anthropogenic climate change is one, if not, the greatest challenge facing human society (IPCC 2014; McKibben 1989, 2012; Rockström *et al.* 2009). Human polluting behaviour has caused significant disruption to the natural processes of Earth systems leading to unequivocal alterations to the entire eco-system (McKibben 2012). These harmful polluting activities have elevated Earth's temperature, causing ice caps to recede and releasing once trapped carbon dioxide (CO_2) and other greenhouse gases (GHGs). This has forced increases in temperatures leading to rising and warming sea levels (Hood *et al.* 2015). It has exacerbated drought seasons such as California in 2015 (Mann and Gleick 2015), while increased deforestation has depleted the number of carbon sinks that once stored the excess of GHGs (Canadell *et al.* 2007). Moreover, the cumulative impacts of humans polluting behaviour have yet to take full effect (Frank *et al.* 2015).

Global society is responding to existing and future problems of the well-documented increase in Earth's temperature (IPCC 2014). The adoption of the United Nations Framework Convention on Climate Change (UNFCCC) was the first substantive international effort to address climate change. It came into force in 1994 after the 1992 Rio Earth Summit. It devised an agenda to address climate change by incorporating a greater awareness of socio-natural relationships for sustainable development (Fiut 2012) while generating mitigation and adaptive technologies to limit GHGs (UN, www.un.org/geninfo/bp/enviro.html).[1]

---

1 The Rio Earth Summit reaffirmed the 27 proposals set out in the 1972 Declaration of the UN Conference on the Human Environment in response to the continued and newly emerging environmental challenges, including ACC. For further information, see Rio Declaration on Environment and Development.

Twenty years on, the outcome of the 2015 UNFCCC Conference of the Parties (COP21) saw 195 countries ratify a commitment to limit GHGs moving towards a zero carbon footprint by 2050 (UNFCCC 2015).

Aligned with the goals of the UNFCCC, one method to limit GHGs was first adopted under the Kyoto Protocol in 1997 (herein known as Kyoto). Kyoto entered into force in 2005 and was later reviewed in 2012. It established a set of binding emissions reduction goals using an international emissions trading system. At the end of its first commitment period in 2012 the Doha Amendment was adopted, establishing a second commitment period to Kyoto from 2013 to 2020. In an emissions trading system CO_2 (the GHG with the greatest impact on climate change) is commodified. These commodities, similar to that of fair trade produce (Lovell, Bulkeley and Liverman 2009), are used in financial transactions in a market place specifically designed to trade in CO_2 commodities. This emissions trading system is better known as carbon markets (Newell and Paterson 2009).

In this purposely provocative chapter, I contend that carbon markets cannot effectively manage GHGs because they are underpinned by a flawed political-economic ideology of ecological modernisation. Ecological modernisation is a school of thought among social scientists, which advocates economic development as a pathway to environmental reform (Spaargaren and Mol 2013). This incorporates an environmental regulatory strategy that makes a concerted effort to open up new economic markets to incentivise technological and social developments with the ecology in mind (Newell *et al.* 2006).

I use the contour of crime in carbon markets to illustrate the weakness of ecological modernised mechanisms to limit GHGs. First, I show that the structure of carbon markets hinders reductions in GHGs. Second, I echo comments made by other researchers on the wider flaws of ecological modernised economic mechanisms to limit GHGs as the antithesis to environmental reform (Carolan 2004; Foster 2000, 2012; O'Connor 1994; Pellow *et al.* 2000). That is, carbon markets were developed in line with neo-liberal governance strategies, which actually support fossil fuel based capitalism (Lohmann 2009, 2012). This is one of the root causes of ecological destruction (Cabello 2009; Foster 2000). Finally, I consider how a criminology that is critical of and advocates alternative mechanisms to these ecologically modern carbon markets may limit rising GHGs. In other words, using a criminological perspective that sees ecological modernised approaches to environmental reform as actually maintaining human polluting behaviour.

The flow of the chapter is designed to first describe the structure and evidence on carbon markets as they stand today. Following this, I outline the concept of ecological modernisation before showing how carbon markets are ecological modernisation in practice. Next, I consider the problems of carbon markets, ecological modernisation and what this means for limiting GHGs. This draws on critiques of ecological modernisation using social theories such as the treadmill of production. I then outline what steps have been taken to address crime in carbon markets and ecological modernisation. Finally, I draw conclusions and recommendations on potential ways forward to address carbon market crime and an alternative approach to ecological modernisation as a way to reduce GHGs.

Carbon markets

Under the guidance of the UNFCCC, carbon markets have been created to grapple with the effects of humans polluting behaviour. CO_2 and other GHGs from fossil fuel production is the largest contributor to climate change.[2] Trading in CO_2, where CO_2 is a commodity or trading unit allowing the right to emit (Button 2008), carbon markets have been introduced to help manage and reduce both unavoidable and excesses of emissions (Lehmann 2007). While some emissions are unavoidable, a reduction in fossil fuel use must be a priority (Lehmann 2007).

There are a number of different markets that have emerged across the world including the European Union Emissions Trading System (EU, ETS), New Zealand Emissions Trading System (NZ, ETS), California Emissions Trading System and the Swiss Emissions Trading System. In these markets CO_2 as a unit of trading is represented as a credit or offset (UNFCCC 1997). Carbon credits are allowances given to industries by governments or inter-governmental bodies that have set legal emissions limits. Industries that exceed emissions limits may purchase the equivalent units from those industries with a surplus of units (Perdan and Azapagic 2011). In other words, those industries that have used lower than their emissions limit can trade units of emissions for profit, although this is a far more complicated process than normal competitive financial markets (Smale *et al.* 2006). Thus, credits are there to incentivise market trading by reinforcing the additional costs to those industries that exceed their legal polluting limits, while emphasising the economic benefits of CO_2 reduction (Reyes and Gilbertson 2010). Individual countries are accountable for the amount of credits they distribute to different industries. The distribution of credits corresponds to the assigned international allowances prescribed under Kyoto and is otherwise known as Assigned Amount Units (AAU) (Aldrich and Koerner 2012).

Carbon offsets are an alternative way for firms or individuals to reduce the negative impacts of their polluting behaviour by allowing someone else to absorb or avoid releasing CO_2 and other GHGs (Kollmuss *et al.* 2008). Carbon offsets are emissions reduction projects and generally a source of 'funding for development and conservation in the Global South' (Bumpus and Liverman 2008, p. 128). These offset projects encourage sustainable, renewable and less polluting fuels for development. They are not associated with a polluting source such as credits, rather based on projects that reduce the amount of emissions released

---

2   There are six GHGs covered by the Kyoto protocol, CO2, methane (CH_4), nitro oxide (N_2O), sulphur hexafluoride (SF_6), hydrofluorocarbons (HFCs) and perfluoro-carbons (PFCs). These have been accumulated under a single carbon metric for trading purposes.

into the atmosphere by using alternative fuel sources, or by the introduction of carbon sinks such as forests to absorb excess CO_2 (Spash 2010).

Credits and offsets are traded in both involuntary (compliance) and voluntary carbon markets. The involuntary system operates at international, domestic and regional levels where firms in countries with emissions limits engage in a compulsory practice of buying and selling carbon allowances (Bayon *et al.* 2007). Involuntary markets such as the EU, ETS, Regional Greenhouse Gas Initiative (RGGI), are composed of one or more of three flexible mechanisms; (1) Cap and Trade, (2) Clean Development Mechanism and (3) Joint Implementation.

The Cap and Trade system works by allowing polluting industries in countries under Annex 1 of the Kyoto Agreement to purchase credits as allowances. Purchasing these allowances reduces the costs that would occur from emissions violations (Williams 2013). In other words, if an industry is likely to exceed their emissions allowance rather than incur penalties for pollution violations, they can purchase credits and stimulate this new financial mark. Annex 1 parties are 'composed of the industrialised countries that were members of the Organisation for Economic Co-operation and Development (OECD) in 1992, plus countries with economies in transition including the Russian Federation, the Baltic States, and several Central and Eastern European States' (UNFCCC 1998).[3] Industries that have been set emissions caps may purchase these from firms with a surplus of allowances, which will produce lower emissions under their cap. This process of buying and selling emissions is said to incentivise changes in behaviour, whereby it becomes profitable for an industry actor to reduce their emissions and sell a surplus of units in the carbon market place (Sorrell and Sijm 2003).

The voluntary system also operates at international, domestic and/or regional levels allowing firms and individuals the opportunity to offset their emissions by voluntarily purchasing a credit or offset (Bayon *et al.* 2007). This voluntary operation involves purchasing allowances in the form of Clean Development Mechanisms or Joint Implementations. Clean Development Mechanisms allow an industry to receive additional carbon credits if it financially supports carbon reduction offset projects. These offsets are often small-scale community projects built to improve local economies, enhance and protect biodiversity, and generate a path towards sustainable and low polluting futures in Non-Annex countries (Taiyab 2006). Non-Annex parties are 'certain groups of developing countries recognised by the Convention as being especially vulnerable to the adverse impacts of climate change, including countries with low-lying coastal areas and those prone to desertification and drought' (Atkins *et al.* 2000). The convention emphasises activities that promise to answer the special needs and concerns of these vulnerable countries through investment, insurance and technology transfer (UNFCCC 1998). For instance, since 2004, under the guidance of the African Development Bank (AfDB), a number of low carbon clean develop-

---

3   Economies in transition refer to economies that are expanding from a centralised economic system, largely controlled by the state, to a market-based economy (Jefferies 2013).

ment mechanism projects have been introduced to generate sources of electricity via alternative fuels over fossil fuels (AfDB 2011). Joint Implementations are similar to the Clean Development Mechanisms but operate on projects in industrialised countries (Bayon et al. 2007). In an early article reviewing joint implementation projects, Cullet and Mbote (1998) contend it has been implemented as a low-cost instrument under international agreements. It has allowed countries to fulfil their obligations under climate agreements by incorporating joint implementation projects into the market system at the lowest cost possible. (See also Kollmus et al. 2015). Some of these voluntary markets have introduced their own system of monitoring offsetting projects; for example, the Gold Standard. The Gold Standard is an organisation dedicated to the classification and monitoring of high quality offset projects designed to maximise economic and social development while incorporating climate friendly technological developments.[4]

Reasons for voluntary investment by corporate and industry actors in carbon markets are threefold. One, certain corporations such as those in heavy polluting industries do it as a tool to address the environmental concerns appearing as an eco-friendly, politically reputable investment (Wright and Nyberg 2015). This type of investment helps satisfy stakeholder and public concerns about rising GHGs and climate change (Lohmann 2012). Similarly, for individual investment in carbon markets, the notion of appearing environmentally friendly and satisfying their ecological concerns for their own polluting behaviour is a reason for investing (Paterson and Stripple 2010). Two, this investment also helps solidify a corporation's position as a green reputable organisation. These reasons have sometimes been criticised and labelled as a form of corporate greening. Corporate greening refers to the actions taken by corporations to positively frame environmentally harmful behaviour (Nyilasy *et al.* 2014). Now an integral part of organisational practice, investment in carbon markets may to a certain extent manipulate notions of environmental harm thereby redefining their actions as corporate environmentalism (Chrun et al. 2016). That is, heavily polluting industries in particular are able to justify high levels of emissions by appearing to support projects that reduce emissions elsewhere. Three, admitting to corporate violations, such as exceeding emissions limits, and/or promoting corporate environmentalism actively seeks to influence policy and environmental regulatory outcomes (Hillman *et al.* 2000) This means by advocating and participating in market mechanisms despite exceeding emissions limits undermines the ability to effectively punish and deter future violations if they believe they can pay their way out (Böhm 2009).

In sum, carbon markets have been developed to address rising GHGs emissions as the result of humans extensive historical and current polluting practices. Carbon credits or offsets are now 'tangible economic commodities that represent the avoidance or sequestration of GHG emissions' (Gillenwater *et al.* 2007,

---

4 See: www.goldstandard.org/our-story/what-we-believe.

p.85). These emissions reductions occur by asking other parts of the world – most often developing nations using the CDM system – to develop sustainable and low polluting technologies and minimise their impact on Earth's systems. This is instead of challenging the ways of life in those countries that have had arguably the greatest effect on Earth transformations (Cabello 2009). Why then, is this type of policy mechanism to limit GHGs supported over a tax on carbon emissions?

Ecological modernisation

The adoption of carbon markets as a mechanism to reduce GHGs is influenced by the global political-economic system (Heynen and Robbins 2005). That is, social forces driving consumptive and productive practices, those which have had detrimental effects on the environment, have created an opportunity to accumulate capital in the form of carbon markets (Lovins 2006). Capitalist ideology and, in particular, its manifestation in neo-liberalism refers to the belief in 'unfettered free markets with small governments . . . where governments have become capitalist referees . . . to ensure the fundamentals that enable capital accumulation' (Andrew *et al.* 2010, p.612). In other words, neo-liberalism is hegemonic (Cox 1987; Gramsci 1995; Robinson 1998) in so far as it is the dominant political-economic arrangement perceived as the only way of doing business. It is the belief that the market can achieve production and consumption reform required to limit GHGs (Humphreys 2009).

This political economic arrangement is reflected in global society's response to reducing GHGs and is labelled ecological modernised (e.g. Spaargaren and Mol 2013; Bailey *et al.* 2011; Boyd *et al.* 2011). As Mol and Spaargaren (2000) outline:

> Within principally the same modern institutional lay-out (a market economy, an industrial system, modern science and technology, a system of welfare states, etc.) we can thus look for – and design – radical environmental reforms.
>
> (p.36)

In other words, ecological modernisation argues that neo-liberal capitalism can incorporate an awareness of the risks associated with rising GHGs and adapt accordingly (Pellizzoni 2011). Largely independent of regulatory governance, market-based mechanisms are said to be the most effective way of fostering technological advancements eventually leading to a low carbon, political, economic and technological society that will mitigate and adapt to some of the existing and cumulative impacts of rising GHGs (Jänicke 1990). Nonetheless, neoliberal strategies to limit GHGs are not entirely self-governing and without regulation, yet remain competitive and private (Bäckstrand and Lövbrand 2006).

Those that adhere to this ecological modernisation perspective contend 'these transformations do not imply that one has to do away with those institutions of modern society that are involved in the modern organisation of production and consumption' (Mol and Spaargaren 2000, p. 19). Mol (1995) goes as far to argue that:

> environmental reform along the lines of ecological modernisation are the best (or even: the only feasible) way to conquer the ongoing burdening of modern society's sustenance base. If, and only if, modern society follows the path set out by ecological modernisation theory can the ecological crisis be controlled and eventually solved.
>
> (p.49)

That is, advocates of ecological modernisation such as Mol, contend rising GHGs can only be overcome by modernising neo-liberalism to incorporate environmental risks emerging from human's over-exploitation of nature into societies' response (Huber 2000; Kemp and Soete 1992). Rather than hinder environmental reform, they contend these same practices that have been complicit in rising GHG emissions can have the opposite effect.

Ecologically modernised influences on international environmental governance are intertwined with the construction of human attitudes and behaviours as they respond to environmental challenges (Spaargaren and van Vliet 2000). These responses are driven by a specific ecologically modernised discourse adopted by individuals across society (Hajer 1996). Assessing this discourse, Hajer (1996) concludes that ecological modernisation discourse is dominant in the political and public sphere by framing a set of scientific assessments and approaches to address the problem that are intrinsically linked with the preferred socio-political arrangement of neo-liberalism. Put another way, the construction of both scientific knowledge and policy environment is intrinsically linked with political-economic arrangements that prioritise economic growth over environmental reform (Bäckstrand and Lövbrand 2006). Analysis of this policy discourse has shed light on how society has come to acknowledge and generally see the best ways to manage rising GHGs emissions through a distinct market-oriented environmentalism (For a comparison see Keil and Desfor 2003).

Carbon markets as ecological modernisation in practice

While carbon markets continue to be a key component of negotiations to address rising GHGs, criticisms and questions about their effectiveness continue (Lo 2016; McAfee 2016; Millward-Hopkins 2016). This problem stems from the idea that carbon markets are an 'ideological fabrication' (Paterson 2010, p. 353). They are embedded within society's cultural norm that this economic system is the most appropriate way to limit GHGs. In other words,

> the fundamental rationale that paying for GHG reductions elsewhere is easier, cheaper, and faster than domestic reductions, providing greater benefits to the atmosphere as well as to sustainable development, especially when offsets involve projects in the developing world.
>
> (Bumpus and Liverman 2008, pp. 204–206)

However, the introduction of carbon trading systems that fund alternative development strategies in the developing world means there is very little or no change to the behaviour of industry and individuals in the most polluting countries by providing opportunities for others to reduce their impact on the environment (Bohm *et al.* 2012). Therefore, it has become the norm to associate environmental protection and sustainable development projects with ecological modernisation ideology paying other actors for any polluting activities that violate emissions caps. This does not necessarily mean reform of behaviour and change current consumption and production practices that curb emissions overall. That is, investing in credits and/or offsets to reduce the risk of emissions violations and appear environmentally friendly fails to achieve its GHG reduction goals and is in fact simply sustaining the unsustainable (Fournier 2008). As a result, the idea that economic development is one solution to stabilising and mitigating rising GHGs has become a force of environmentalism without fundamentally changing the social order (van der Heijden 1999).

Nevertheless, despite on-going criticisms that they have little to no impact on reducing GHGs (Lohmann 2008; Pearse and Böhm 2015) carbon markets have been introduced and continue to be a popular solution to reduce GHG emissions and mitigate climate change. For instance, under the COP21 agreement in Paris, a number of new policies incorporating carbon trading are scheduled to be introduced between 2016 and 2020 (Mansell 2016). This includes an emissions trading system in China, Ontario and certain states in the USA. However, future international action to limit GHGs needs to recognise the concerns on ecological modernised market mechanisms and asks the question, can such markets successfully minimise GHGs and other environmental harms? More specifically, can coupling economic growth and environmental welfare successfully mitigate rising GHGs, or does it in fact impose barriers to strategies that may provide success? I contend that the second is true. That carbon markets cannot necessarily reach the desired reductions in GHGs. One way in which to explore this is through an analysis of the growing literature on carbon market crime.

Carbon market crime

In 2013, Interpol released a report documenting the extent of criminal activity in carbon markets. They reported that a lack of understanding on this untraditional commodity – that is, not a traditional physical commodity – makes it particularly vulnerable to fraud and other illegal activities. They identified five types of illegal activity;

> (1) Fraudulent manipulation of measurements to claim more carbon credits from a project than were actually obtained; (2) Sale of carbon credits that either do not exist or belong to someone else; (3) False or misleading claims with respect to the environmental or financial benefits of carbon market investments; (4) Exploitation of weak regulations in the carbon market to

commit financial crimes, such as money laundering, securities fraud or tax fraud; and (5) Computer hacking/phishing to steal carbon credits and theft of personal information.

(Europol 2013, p. 11)

These findings indicated that carbon markets face the same risks as traditional financial markets. Examples include security fraud, embezzlement, money laundering and internet crimes. They add that the intangible nature of GHG emissions makes it easy for fraudulent measurements on the outcomes of offset projects. This leaves the market vulnerable to bribes and falsified records undermining the authority of the market to effectively reduce GHGs.

More recently, Transparency International's (2015) report found corruption risks in carbon markets continue. They reported the risks of over estimating the amount of emissions an industry will use. Thus, these industries overcompensate by applying for greater emissions limits. Offset projects may fraudulently claim greater emissions reductions than is the case. There are also great risks from cyber-crime because most carbon market transactions are conducted online. Therefore, greater internet security should be recommended to credit and offset investors, while also improved monitoring by specific government and carbon trading agencies. Furthermore, they note it is indeed difficult to find evidence of direct causal links between carbon markets and GHG reductions (see also Pearse and Böhm 2014).

Social scientists have also drawn attention to crime in carbon markets (Frunza *et al.* 2011; Gibbs *et al.* 2013; Walters and Martin 2012, 2013, 2012; McKie *et al.* 2015). In an early assessment of carbon market crime, Frunza *et al.* (2011) quantify missing trader fraud in the EU ETS. Missing trader fraud is the failure of traders to remit tax collected from sales to the government. In this case, the EU is unable to collect the tax owed via sales of carbon credits. Their findings revealed that prior to 2010 there was an estimated 1.3 billion Euros lost in the involuntary carbon market from missing trader fraud. Williams (2013) adds to this by formulating a typology of money laundering in the EU ETS identifying organised crime networks that have taken advantage of these deregulated markets to launder criminal proceeds. These points echo Bachram (2004) who argued criminal activity in carbon markets is the result of a laissez-faire environment lacking government monitoring and intervention. Laissez-faire refers to reduced state and (if any) government intervention in economic markets, encouraging a market led economic regime that generally emerged under the UK and US Thatcher and Reagan governments (Yeung 2000).

Gibbs *et al.* (2013) use routine activities theory to examine fraud in the EU ETS, pin pointing where the trading system is most vulnerable to criminal activity. Routine activities theory as a theory of crime facilitates the circumstances surrounding behaviour rather than individual offender characteristics (Cohen and Felson 1979). They contend that the social environment affects trends in intentional criminal or deviant behaviour. Gibbs, Cassidy and Rivers' application to carbon market crime is informative, illustrating how carbon markets tend to rely on online electronic registration, which is vulnerable to hackers who can obtain individual customer or firm information to then send scam emails. Also, the laissez-faire environment provides an environment for such criminal activity to emerge in carbon markets, suggesting this mechanism of trading is actually a bed for crime. Their research does not directly draw on the concept of ecological modernisation to explain criminal activity, however the problems they observe have in part emerged from these ecological modernised market mechanisms.

Walters and Martin (2012, 2013) identified how carbon market crime is symptomatic of this type of market. To do this they formulated a typology of carbon market crimes including computer crime, state crime, taxation crime, scams, corruption and bribery and structural fraud. More importantly, new markets, especially those trading in artificial commodities are weakly regulated and poorly monitored. This is an extension of neo-liberal governance, which has 'wider systematic properties' that are inherently corruptible (2012, p. 39). In other words, carbon markets conform to an economic system that is already problematic by creating a criminogenic environment. Not only is there the likelihood of market failures and collapse as the result of these weak regulatory strategies, there is also a platform for potential fraudulent activity. Although Walters and Martin do not draw directly upon ecological modernisation, their position easily aligns with the concept of ecological modernisation (i.e. the commodification of carbon to increase economic prosperity and reduce GHGs). From this position then, environmental reform that utilises neo-liberal market mechanisms is significantly compromised.

McKie *et al.* (2015) go further and directly expose a relationship between ecological modernisation and illegal activity in the voluntary carbon market. They examine what they identified as ecological modernised discourse used by illegal and legal operating credit and offset companies. Their findings indicated ecologically modern discourse was being used by illegal and legal traders making them indistinguishable. This is likely to increase the risk of defrauding investors. They argued that these results show how the market has facilitated 'motivated offenders and victims' (p. 483) who invest in offset markets in the pursuit of both monetary and personal profit to satisfy ecological concerns. That is, they have created a group of victims that have subscribed to ecological modernisation. It could be argued that ecological modernisation has not only created an environment – carbon markets – where crime takes place, it has also created victims and a group of actors willing to take advantage of misguided actions to reduce emissions.

There is also evidence concerning criminal activity under Reducing Emissions from Deforestation and Forest Degradation (REDD) projects. REDD projects are set up to protect natural mechanisms of carbon reductions. The gains made in reducing levels of carbon emissions have provided another avenue for the valuation of CO_2 (Skutsch and McCall 2010). While some of these REDD programmes have been incorporated into offsetting markets, they are also separate and supported by the EU and United Nations, but do not have a fully-fledged market system such as credits and offsetting (Skutsch and McCall 2010). In

2009, a guardian article reported that these projects like many others under CO_2 trading schemes were a recipe for destruction and may be hijacked by organised crime gangs (Videl 2009) (see also Böhm 2013).

In short, previous work clearly identifies different contours of carbon markets that are susceptible to criminal activity. Importantly, there is evidence to suggest that some of these problems stem from the root of markets built on ecological modernisation (see McKie *et al.* 2015). With this in mind, it is important to look closer at the weaknesses of ecological modernised mechanisms to limit GHGs.

The problem with ecological modernisation and carbon markets

It is clear that international governance strategies addressing rising GHGs are underpinned by ideas of ecological modernisation. Economic growth is coupled with environmental welfare, decreasing the role of the state in preference for market mechanisms and financial incentives. This has created a public and political consensus connecting environmental welfare with the importance of economic welfare and development. However, I contend that there are a number of problems associated with this approach.

First, society has subscribed to the idea that reductions in GHG can be achieved via flexible market mechanisms, yet these are poorly regulated and inherently corruptible (see also Böhm 2008; Lohmann 2009). As Walters and Martin (2013) note, reductions in regulation and state intervention in markets mean that market failures are possible and criminal activity is symptomatic. This is one reason why Michaelowa's (2010) labels the voluntary carbon trading system as the 'Wild West' of the market mechanisms in climate policy. 'They are evolving extremely rapidly without any centralized oversight and in a rather non-transparent fashion' (p. 239). In other words, the lack of adequate monitoring, regulation and policing of these markets leads to the inadequate management of GHGs, suggesting that the application of ecological modernisation has created an opportunity for crime to thrive (See also McKie *et al.* 2015; Lohmann 2009).

This point extends to the second criticism of ecological modernisation. In the case of crime in carbon markets, ecological modernised discourse has created opportunities for individuals believing they are satisfying their ecological responsibility to become the victims of criminal actors who also engage with this discourse. As McKie *et al.* (2015) point out it has created the opportunity for criminal actors to use this discourse and to take advantage of ecological concerns where there is a cultural pattern of investment of potential victims and offenders of carbon market crime in pursuit of psychological and economic profiteering.

Carrying out this criminal act is made easier as a result of the underpinning notions of ecologically modernised values. As noted above, ecological modernisation is hegemonic and emerging from this are ecological modernised discourses used to advocate practices that are the antithesis of ecological reform. Thus, whether at personal or firm level and in both the voluntary and involuntary markets, investment is simply to reduce a sense of guilt for the environmental harm caused by excessive pollution rather than challenging behaviour that would provide greater emissions reductions (Kotchen 2009). Criminal actors know this and by adopting the same discourse can create criminal opportunity using what could be argued are misguided notions that ecologically modernised practices can limit GHGs.

Again this does not challenge individual, industry and government behaviour, subsequently legitimising the system that is unlikely to curb GHGs and fails to dramatically alter behaviour that matches the ideological structures of a fossil fuel-based global capitalism. This leads to the third point, that is, policies to reduce GHGs, which rely on capitalist market traditions, are unlikely to effect change as capitalism, or the commitment to a neo-liberalism, is ecologically repressive (Foster 2000). That is, these market practices simply maintain the ecological destruction caused by GHGs (e.g. O'Conner 1998; Foster 1988; Schnaiberg 1980) because they fail to challenge the orthodoxy of current consumption and production practices.

Other social theorists have drawn similar conclusions about the problems of ecologically modern mechanisms to address environmental challenges. For instance, Schnaiberg (1980) argued that market-based policy developments do not stimulate environmental and social action, it simply 'greens' capitalism, ensuring that it is immune from an ecological critique (see also Curran 2009). Market solutions then do not address the entrenched role of fossil fuel, capitalist political economic infrastructure that undermines solutions to rising GHGs and subsequently ACC (Lohmann 2009).

Combatting the challenges of carbon market crime and ecological modernisation

Addressing the problems associated with carbon market crime and ecological modernisation can be split into two. First, a focus on the environment of carbon markets that facilitates crime. And second, addressing the overall commitment to ecological modernisation by presenting alternative economic mechanisms and policies to limit GHGs?

Regarding the first problem that focuses on the structural problem of carbon markets, a response requires greater regulation and monitoring of carbon markets. This should be the first step to address the weaknesses in the structural environment of market mechanisms. There are some monitoring mechanisms already in place. For instance, in the European trading system countries, or member states of the EU have to report their emissions according to monitoring plans accounting for the verification of offset projects and amount of GHGs emitted in accordance with permits (Verschuuren and Fleurke 2015). Not implementing these stronger and stricter regulatory strategies to market practices runs the danger of legitimising what continues to be an ineffective instrumental mechanism to manage GHGs (Christoff 1996).

Regarding the second point, that within the overall concept of ecological modernisation, the introduction of carbon taxes may be more effective in limiting

GHGs. Carbon taxes are a superior mechanism to reduce emissions than market mechanisms (Nordhaus 2007). The introduction of a carbon tax reduces the economic uncertainty of cap and trade mechanisms and a reliance on the pricing of CO2 commodities to stimulate reductions in GHGs (MacKenzie 2009). Similarly, advocating the ideas of de-growth also challenges the political-economic hegemony capitalism and ecological modernisation. De-growth in this sense is an oxymoron (Pansera and Owen 2016). It suggests action to limit GHGs goes against the technological progress made under ideas of green –growth and development. This may be the only satisfactory strategy to limit GHGs.

Thus, criminological investigation must assess the risks of ecological modernisation, in practice showing how it perpetuates environmental harm. Criminology must challenge this hegemonic ideology, the neo-liberal based practices that contribute to rising GHGs. It must be critical of the fundamental political-economic structure that underpins ecological modernisation ideology, which has created a carbon lock in (Lohmann 2009; Unruh 2000). Carbon lock in refers to a political-economic structure requiring constant capital accumulation that relies on fossil fuels (Unruh 2000). This has systematically created the opportunity to elevate GHG emissions and not challenge the unsustainable fundamental social structure that uses fossil fuels to fuel production and consumption.

Conclusions

Earlier in the chapter I posed the question, can coupling economic growth and environmental welfare successfully mitigate rising GHGs, or does it in fact impose barriers to strategies that may provide success? Turning to carbon markets, these can be described as the product of ecological modernised policy (e.g. Spaargaren and Mol 2013). That is, carbon markets are shaped by the notion that economic development leads to the most innovative ways to limit GHGs.

However, research examining carbon markets highlights clear structural weaknesses, which put in place barriers to fully achieve emissions reduction goals based on ecologically modernised mechanisms by creating opportunities for criminal activity. Moreover, the underlying ideological values driving this type of environmental reform deplete the ability of carbon markets to effectively reduce emissions. Ecologically, modern informed policy practices are failing to prevent current and future environmentally harmful behaviour by not challenging the root cause of rising GHGs.

This then supports the argument made in this chapter that ecological modernisation is likely to limit the reduction and management of GHGs rather than address it. To support this, I have explored carbon market crime that exists at international, domestic and regional levels revealing how ecological modernisation, combining the commodification of goods, economic development and incentives for environmental reform, has created the opportunity for crime and continually environmentally harmful behaviours. The reasons for the overall failing of ecological modernisation and carbon markets are threefold. One, evidence demonstrates the promotion of ecological modernisation has created offenders engaging with a discourse also adopted by 'green' victims. That is, the development of a flexible market practice for environmental reform is actually a driving force for criminal activity. This means also, that society's powerful commitment to ecological modernised policy ideas, which promote poor regulation and monitoring, is undermined if it is regularly the site for criminal activity. Advocates of ecological modernisation would argue this is an effective tool yet this does not seem to be the case. Three, the wider commitment to economic growth perpetuates a carbon lock in, where fossil fuel use underpins current production and consumption practices. This does not protect the environment injustices from fossil fuel intensive global capitalism.

In light of these findings, criminologists should continue their enquiry into carbon markets as recent research continues to indicate that carbon markets are still at risk from criminal activity. Criminologists may help identify these risks, as well as generate innovative solutions to these problems, which are likely to expand after the ratification of COP21 and potential expansion of carbon trading systems. Thus, caution should be aired if society implements strategies to reduce GHG and prevents further environmental harm under principles of ecological modernisation. Importantly, continuing a process of offsetting rather than mitigating human emissions runs the risk of inadequately addressing emissions levels and fails to prevent further climate changes.

References

Andrew, J., Kaidonis, M.A. and Andrew, B. 2010. 'Carbon tax: challenging neoliberal solutions to climate change', *Critical Perspectives on Accounting* 21(7), 611–618.

Aldrich, E.L. and Koerner, C.L. 2012. 'Unveiling Assigned Amount Unit (AAU) trades: current market impacts and prospects for the future', *Atmosphere* 3(1), 229–245.

Atkins, J.P., Mazzi, S. and Easter, C.D. 2000. *A Commonwealth Vulnerability Index for Developing Countries: The Position of Small States*. London: Commonwealth Secretariat.

Bachram, H. 2004. 'Climate fraud and carbon colonialism: the new trade in greenhouse gases', *Capitalism Nature Socialism* 15(4), 5–20.

Bäckstrand, K. and Lövbrand, E. 2006. 'Planting trees to mitigate climate change: contested discourses of ecological modernisation, green governmentality and civic environmentalism', *Global Environmental Politics* 6(1), 50–75.

Bailey, I., Gouldson, A., and Newell, P. 2011. 'Ecological modernisation and the governance of carbon: a critical analysis', *Antipode* 43(3), 682–703.

Bayon, R., Hawn, A., and Hamilton, K. 2007. *Voluntary Carbon Markets: An International Business Guide to What They Are and How They Work*. Abingdon, Oxon: Earthscan.

Böhm, S. 2009. *Upsetting the Offset: The Political Economy of Carbon Markets*. London: MayFlyBooks.

Böhm, S. 2013. 'Why are carbon markets failing', *The Guardian*, 10 April.

Böhm, S., Misoczky, M.C. and Moog, S. 2012. 'Greening capitalism? A Marxist critique of carbon markets', *Organization Studies* 33(11), 1617–1638.

Bumpus, A.G., and Liverman, D.M. 2008. 'Accumulation of decarbonisation and the governance of carbon offsets', *Economic Geography* 84(1), 127–155.

Button, J. 2008. 'Carbon: commodity or currency-the case for an international carbon market based on the currency model', *Harvard Environmental Law Review* 32, 571.

Cabello, J. 2009. 'The politics of the Clean Development Mechanism: hiding capitalism under the green rug', in *Upsetting the Offset: The Political Economy of Carbon Markets*, edited by S. Böhm, and S. Dabhi, 192–202.

Canadell, J.G., Le Quéré, C., Raupach, M.R., Field, C.B., Buitenhuis, E.T., Ciais, P., Conway, T.J., Gillett, N.P., Houghton, R.A. and Marland, G. 2007. 'Contributions to accelerating atmospheric CO2 growth from economic activity, carbon intensity, and efficiency of natural sinks', *Proceedings of the National Academy of Sciences* 104(47), 18866–18870.

Carolan, M.S. 2004. 'Ecological modernisation theory: what about consumption?', *Society and Natural Resources* 17(3), 247–260.

Christoff, P. 1996. 'Ecological modernisation, ecological modernities', *Environmental Politics* 5(3), 476–500.

Chrun, E., Dolšak, N. and Prakash, A. 2016. 'Corporate environmentalism: motivations and mechanisms', *Annual Review of Environment and Resources* 41(1), 341–362.

Cohen, L.E. and Felson, M. 1979. 'Social change and crime rate trends: a routine activity approach', *American Sociological Review* 44(4), 588–608.

Cox, R.W. 1987. *Production, Power, and World Order: Social Forces in the Making of History (Vol. 1)*. New York: Columbia University Press.

Cullet, P. and Kameri-Mbote, A.P. 1998. 'Joint implementation and forestry projects: conceptual and operational fallacies', *International Affairs* 74(2), 393–408.

Curran, G. 2009. 'Ecological modernisation and climate change in Australia', *Environmental Politics* 18(2), 201–217.

Fiut, I.S. 2012. 'Sustainable development: the upcoming civilizational revolution?', *Problemy Ekorozwoju–Problems of Sustainable Development* 7(2), 43–50.

Foster, J.B. 2000. 'Capitalism's environmental crisis – is technology the answer?', *Monthly Review – New York* 52(7), 1.

Foster, J.M. 2012. *The Sustainability Mirage*. London: Earthscan Routledge Publishing.

Fournier, V. 2008. 'Escaping from the economy: the politics of degrowth', *International Journal of Sociology and Social Policy* 28(11/12), 528–545.

Frank, D., Reichstein, M., Bahn, M., Thonicke, K., Frank, D., Mahecha, M.D., Smith, P., Velde, M., Vicca, S., Babst, F. and Beer, C. 2015 'Effects of climate extremes on the terrestrial carbon cycle: concepts, processes and potential future impacts', *Global Change Biology* 21(8), 2861–2880.

Frunza, M.C., Guegan, D., and Lassoudiere, A. 2011. 'Missing trader fraud on the emissions market', *Journal of Financial Crime* 18(2), 183–194.

Gibbs, C., Cassidy, M.B., and Rivers, L. 2013. 'A routine activities analysis of white-collar crime in carbon markets', *Law & Policy* 35(4), 341–374.

Gillenwater, M., Broekhoff, D., Trexler, M., Hyman, J., and Fowler, R. 2007. 'Policing the voluntary carbon market', *Nature Reports Climate Change*. Published Online October 2007. Available at: doi:10.1038/climate.2007.58 (accessed 25 May 2016).

Gramsci, A. 1995. *Further Selections From the Prison Notebooks*. Minneapolis: University of Minnesota Press.

Hajer, M. 1996. 'Ecological modernisation as cultural politics', in *Risk, Environment and Modernity: Towards a New Ecology*, edited by S. Lash, B. Szerszynski and B. Wynne. London: Sage Publications, 253–278.

Heijden, van der H-A. 1999 'Environmental movements, ecological modernisation and political opportunity structures', *Environmental Politics* 8(1), 199–221.

Heynen, N. and Robbins, P. 2005. 'The neoliberalization of nature: governance, privatization, enclosure and valuation', *Capitalism Nature Socialism* 16(1), 5–8.

Hillman, A.J., Cannella, A.A. and Paetzold, R.L. 2000. 'The resource dependence role of corporate directors: Strategic adaptation of board composition in response to environmental change', *Journal of Management Studies* 37(2), 235–256.

Hood, E., Battin, T.J., Fellman, J., O'Neel, S. and Spencer, R.G. 2015. 'Storage and release of organic carbon from glaciers and ice sheets', *Nature Geoscience* 8(2), 91–96.

Huber, J. 2000. 'Towards industrial ecology: sustainable development as a concept of ecological modernisation', *Journal of Environmental Policy and Planning* 2(4), 269–285.

Humphreys, D. 2009. 'Discourse as ideology: neoliberalism and the limits of international forest policy', *Forest Policy and Economics* 11(5), 319–325.

IPCC. 2014. *Climate Change 2014: Impacts, Adaptation, and Vulnerability. Part A: Global and Sectoral Aspects. Contribution of Working Group II to the Fifth Assessment Report of the Intergovernmental Panel on Climate Change.* Cambridge, United Kingdom and New York, NY, USA: Cambridge University Press.

Jänicke, M. 1990. *State Failure, the Impotence of Politics in Industrial Society.* University Park, PA: Pennsylvania State University Press.

Jefferies, I. 2013. *Economies in Transition.* London/New York: Routledge.

Keil, R. and Desfor, G. 2003. 'Ecological modernisation in Los Angeles and Toronto', *Local Environment* 8(1), 27–44.

Kemp, R. and Soete, L. 1992. 'The greening of technological progress: an evolutionary perspective', *Futures* 24(5), 437–457.

Kollmus, A., Schneider, L. and Zhezherin, V. 2015. *Has Joint Implementation Reduced GHG Emissions? Lessons learned for the design of carbon market mechanisms.* Stockholm Environmental Institute, Working Paper 2015–07.

Kollmus, A., Zink, H. and Polycarp. C. 2008. *Making Sense of the Voluntary Carbon Market. A Comparison of Carbon Offset Standards.* World Wildlife Fund, Germany.

Kotchen, M.J. 2009. 'Offsetting green guilt', *Stanford Social Innovation Review* 7(2), 26–31.

Lehmann, J. 2007. 'A handful of carbon', *Nature* 447 (7141), 143–144.

Lo, A.Y. 2016. 'Challenges to the development of carbon markets in China', *Climate Policy* 16(1), 109–124.

Lohmann, L. 2008. 'Carbon trading: a critical conversation on climate change, privatization and power', *Development Dialogue* 48 (September), 460–462.

Lohmann, L. 2009. 'Neoliberalism and the calculable world: the rise of carbon trading', in *Upsetting the Offset: The Political Economy of Carbon Markets*, edited by S. Böhm and S. Dabhi. London: Mayflybooks, 25–37.

Lohmann, L. 2012. 'Financialisation, commodification and carbon: the contradictions of neoliberal climate policy', *Socialist Register* 48, 85–107.

Lovell, H., Bulkeley, H. and Liverman, D. 2009. 'Carbon offsetting: sustaining consumption?', *Environment and Planning A* 41(10), 2357–2379.

Lovins, L.H. 2006. 'Natural capitalism: path to sustainability?', in *The International Handbook on Environmental Technology Management*, edited by D. Marinova, D. Annandale and J. Phillimore. Cheltenham: Edward Elgar Publishing, 93–103.

MacKenzie, D. 2009. 'Making things the same: gases, emissions rights and the politics of carbon markets', *Accounting, Organisations and Society* 34(3), 440–455.

Mann, M.E. and Gleick, P.H. 2015. 'Climate change and California drought in the 21st century', *Proceedings of the National Academy of Sciences* 112(13), 3858–3859.

Mansell, A. 2016. 'What's ahead for carbon markets after COP21?', *Biores*, 19 February.

McAfee, K. 2016. 'Green economy and carbon markets for conservation and development: a critical view', *International Environmental Agreements: Politics, Law and Economics* 16(333), 1–21.

McKibben, B. 1989. *The End of Nature*. New York: Random House.

Mckibben, B. 2012. *The Global Warming Reader: A Century of Writing about Climate Change*. Penguin.

Mckie, R.E., Stretesky, P.B., and Long, M. 2015. 'Crime in the voluntary carbon market: an exploration of modernisation themes among a sample of criminal and non-criminal organisations', *Critical Criminology* 23(4), 122–129.

Michaelowa, A. 2010. 'Voluntary carbon markets', *Climate Policy* 10(2), 239–240.

Millward-Hopkins, J.T. 2016. 'Natural capital, unnatural markets?', *Wiley Interdisciplinary Reviews: Climate Change* 7(1), 13–22.

Mol, A.P. 1995. *The Refinement of Production. Ecological Modernisation Theory and the Chemical Industry*. Utrecht: Van Arkel.

Mol, A.P. and Spaargaren, G. 2000. 'Ecological modernisation theory in debate: A review', *Environmental Politics* 9(1), 17–49.

Newell, P. and Paterson, M. 2009. 'The politics of the carbon economy', in *The Politics of Climate Change: A Survey*, edited by M. Boykoff. Oxford: Blackwell Publishing Ltd, 80–99.

Newell, R.G., Jaffe, A.B. and Stavins, R.N. 2006. 'The effects of economic and policy incentives on carbon mitigation technologies', *Energy Economics* 28(5), 563–578.

Nordhaus, W.D. 2007. 'To tax or not to tax: alternative approaches to slowing global warming', *Review of Environmental Economics and Policy* 1(1), 26–44.

Nyilasy, G., Gangadharbatla, H. and Paladino, A. 2014. 'Perceived greenwashing: the interactive effects of green advertising and corporate environmental performance on consumer reactions', *Journal of Business Ethics* 125(4), 693–707.

O'Connor, M. (ed.) 1994. *Is Capitalism Sustainable?: Political Economy and the Politics of Ecology*. New York: Guilford Press.

Pansera, M. and Owen, R. 2016. 'Innovation for de-growth: A case study of counter-hegemonic practices from Kerala, India', *Journal of Cleaner Production*. Published online July 2016.

Paterson, M. 2010. 'Legitimation and accumulation in climate change governance', *New Political Economy* 15(3), 345–368.

Paterson, M. and Stripple, J. 2010. 'My space: governing individuals' carbon emissions', *Environment and Planning, Society and Space* 28(2), 341–362.

Pearse, R. and Böhm, S. 2015. 'Ten reasons why carbon markets will not bring about radical emissions reduction', *Carbon Management* 5(4), 325–337.

Pellizzoni, L. 2011. 'Governing through disorder: neoliberal environmental governance and social theory', *Global Environmental Change* 21(3), 795–803.

Pellow, D.N., Schnaiberg, A. and Weinberg, A.S. 2000. 'Advanced industrial countries: putting the ecological modernisation thesis to the test: the promises and performances of urban recycling', *Environmental Politics* 9(1), 109–137.

Perdan, S. and Azapagic, A. 2011. 'Carbon trading: current schemes and future developments', *Energy Policy* 39(10), 6040–6054.

Reyes, O. and Gilbertson, T. 2010. 'Carbon trading: how it works and why it fails', *Soundings* 45(12), 89–100.

Rockström, J., Steffen, W., Noone, K., Persson, Å., Chapin, F.S., Lambin, E.F., and Foley, J.A. 2009. 'A safe operating space for humanity', *Nature* 461(7263), 472–475.

Schnaiberg, A. 1980. *Environment: From Surplus to Scarcity*. Oxford: Oxford University Press.

Skutsch, M.M. and McCall, M.K. 2010. 'Reassessing REDD: governance, markets and the hype cycle', *Climatic Change* 100(3), 395–402.

Smale, R., Hartley, M., Hepburn, C., Ward, J. and Grubb, M. 2006. 'The impact of CO_2 emissions trading on firm profits and market prices', *Climate Policy* 6(1), 31–48.

Sorrell, S. and Sijm, J. 2003. 'Carbon trading in the policy mix', *Oxford Review of Economic Policy* 19(3), 420–437.

Spaargaren G. and Mol, A.P. 2013. 'Carbon flows, carbon markets and low carbon lifestyles: reflecting on the role of markets in climate governance', *Environmental Politics* 22(1), 174–193.

Spaargaren, G. and Vliet, van, B. 2000. 'Lifestyles, consumption and the environment: the ecological modernisation of domestic consumption', *Environmental Politics* 9(1), 50–76.

Spash, C.L. 2010. 'The brave new world of carbon trading', *New Political Economy* 15(2), 169–195.

Taiyab, N. 2006. *Exploring the Market for Voluntary Carbon Offsets*. London: International Institute for Environment and Development.

Transparency International. 2015. 'Carbon market corruption risks and mitigation strategies', 24 September.

Unruh, G.C. 2000. 'Understanding carbon lock-in', *Energy Policy* 28(12), 817–830.

Verschuuren, J. and Fleurke, F.M. 2015. 'Enforcement of the EU ETS in the Member States', *Environmental Law Network International Review* (1+2), 17–23.

Videl, J. 2009. 'Copenhagen agenda: emissions, carbon markets and a UN grilling on CDM', *Guardian*, 8 December.

Walters, R. and Martin, P. 2012. *Risks of Carbon Fraud. Centre for Crime & Justice Website*. Brisbane: Queensland University of Technology.

Walters, R. and Martin, P. 2013. 'Crime and the commodification of carbon', in *Emerging Issues in Green Criminology: Exploring Power, Justice and Harm*, edited by R. Walters, D. Westerhuis and T. Wyatt. Basingstoke: Macmillan, 93–104.

Williams, C.C. 2013. 'A burning desire: the need for anti-money laundering regulations in carbon emissions trading schemes to combat emerging criminal typologies', *Journal of Money Laundering Control* 16(4), 298–320.

Wright, C. and Nyberg, D. 2015. *Climate Change, Capitalism, and Corporations: Processes of Creative Self-destruction*. Cambridge: Cambridge University Press.

Yeung, H.W.C. 2000. 'Neoliberalism, laissez-faire capitalism and economic crisis: the political economy of deindustrialisation in Hong Kong', *Competition & Change* 4(2), 121–169.

12 Financial investigation in environmental crime cases in the Netherlands

Rudie Neve and Nanina van Zanden

Introduction

An important goal of Dutch crime policy in recent decades is that criminals should be stripped of their illicit assets.[1] The approach was first aimed at serious and organised crimes such as drug trafficking and production, human trafficking and large-scale fraud. An example of the latter is a case of price fixing in the construction industry (the *Bouwfraude* case), which even led to a Parliamentary enquiry (van der Boon and van der Marel 2009). However, it took a long time before financial concerns affected environmental crime investigations. In environmental crime, as in other types of crime, the perpetrators' main aim is financial gain, and they often achieve this by operating a legitimate business and by circumventing environmental regulations that apply to that particular business activity. Financial investigation often requires advanced financial and administrative expertise, because the illegal activities are usually (but not always) intertwined with the legitimate activities of the company. However, types of environmental crime such as the trade in protected species and illegal fireworks greatly resemble markets for 'traditional' illicit or regulated goods such as controlled drugs and firearms.[2] For about the last five years, an attempt has been made to make up arrears when it comes to financial investigation of environmental crimes. In this chapter, we explore the state of affairs and the bottlenecks that occur.

Since the beginning of the 1990s, criminal investigation in the Netherlands has increasingly focused on confiscation of perpetrators' illegally obtained income and assets. In 1993, confiscation legislation – the Deprivation of Criminal Assets Act[3] – was first introduced, initially under the slogan 'strip them bare' (*pluk ze*

1 The authors would like to thank Central Unit's Translation and Interpreting Services Team, especially Dr Maria Sherwood-Smith, for their help with translating the article.
2 Unlike in many other countries, trafficking illegal fireworks is considered part of environmental crime in the Netherlands.
3 Dutch Bulletin of Acts and Decrees 1993, no. 11. In Dutch: *Ontneming van wederrechtelijk verkregen voordeel*. The legislation is informally called the 'strip them bare' Act ('*pluk ze*' *wet*).

in Dutch), and a start was made on developing financial expertise within law enforcement. Since then, the government has prioritised financial investigation and confiscation under criminal law pertaining to criminally obtained assets. When investigating crime and prosecuting suspects, the Netherlands Police, the special investigative services of the various ministries (*Bijzondere opsporingsdiensten*, BODs),[4] and the Public Prosecution Service (*Openbaar Ministerie*, OM) increasingly focus on financial aspects (see also Chapter 9). To implement this policy, the Ministry of Justice and the police have initiated several programmes and projects, including the initial Programme on Financial Investigation (Faber and van Nunen 2002) and the Financial and Economic Crime Programme that was launched in 2007 (IVJ 2012). At the strategic level, the aforementioned law enforcement agencies draw up annual performance agreements on the scope of illegally obtained assets to be confiscated and the number of prejudgement attachments to be levied on assets. In 2014, for example, the confiscation target for the Public Prosecution Service was €70.1 million (OM 2015). In the end, they actually confiscated €136 million, mainly due to a transaction in the SBM Offshore NV case.[5]

In order to also promote financial investigation in environmental crime cases the National Public Prosecutor's Office for Financial, Economic and Environmental Offences (the department of the National Public Prosecutor's Office specialising in environmental crime), set up a special unit to support the investigative services in financial investigations, which includes public prosecutors as well as accountants specialising in financial investigation. This unit was merged in with the specialised prosecution office for fraud and environmental crime in 2013. That year, the Netherlands Police Academy organised a conference with the title 'Environmental Crime: how does it work and how much does it pay?', which aimed at increasing practitioners' awareness of the subject of financial investigation in environmental crime cases (van Heel *et al.* 2013). During the conference, van Heel *et al.* (2013) presented the results of a study commissioned by the Dutch Police on the question of whether money laundering occurred in environmental crime cases. They found a number of case examples in which money was given a seemingly legal origin, for instance via foreign legal entities or by 'shelling out' a private limited company.[6] In cases that concerned larger

---

4 The four special investigative services are: the Human Environment and Transport Inspectorate – Intelligence and Investigation Department (ILT-IOD), the Netherlands Food and Consumer Product Safety Authority (NVWA-IOD), the Fiscal Intelligence and Investigation Service (FIOD) and the Social Affairs and Employment Inspectorate's Investigation Directorate. These services are part of the relevant ministries.

5 This company builds floating oil platforms; in 2014, it paid a sum of 240 million USD, consisting of a fine of $40 million and confiscated proceeds of crime adding up to 200 million, most of which (139 million) was paid in Brazil. The company had bribed officials and others.

6 This laundering method entails that money is drawn from a legal entity, e.g. through charging management fees, etc.

sums of illegally obtained money, perpetrators usually falsified documents, including invoices and bills of carriage to conceal the origin of the crime money. However, money-laundering charges were often only based on the fact that perpetrators held assets they could not account for with their legitimate income. Under Dutch law, such inexplicable possession of assets is considered as money laundering. From this study, it was concluded that it is essential to attach specially trained financial investigators to environmental investigation teams in order to improve the results of financial investigations (van der Leest and van der Zon 2012). This was also expressed in a recent policy re-evaluation document (Herijkingsnota), which states that financial knowledge and expertise will be enhanced on the one hand by hiring external expertise, and by training existing staff on the other (Ministry of Security and Justice 2015a). In a way, these intentions already anticipate the findings of the study discussed in this chapter.

In the next section, we address the state of affairs with regard to confiscation in cases of environmental crime at the beginning of 2015, as well as success and failure factors that could lead to recommendations for improvement.

Success and failure factors

Emphasis put on financial investigation resulted in a paradigm shift in the approach to environmental crime cases. In recent years, the financial part of investigation plans has become an important topic of discussion during case selection meetings. Because of the high priority given to confiscation of illegal assets following the motto that 'crime should not pay', the Netherlands Police wanted to assess whether at present financial investigation in environmental crime cases is successful in terms of implementation and outcomes. In 2015, we reported our findings to the Portfolio Holder for Environmental Crime with the Netherlands Police.[7] The present chapter is based on that report.

To answer the research questions, the files of 23 criminal investigations carried out by the special investigative services[8] and the police were analysed.[9] Case selection focused on important environmental issues such as illegal export

---

7 The report is not publicly available.
8 These were police cases mostly. Three cases each came from ILT-IOD and NVWA-IOD.
9 The registration system contains cases starting from 2012, of which 87 concerned environmental crime in which financial investigation was reported. Then, 15 others that were not (yet) registered were added in consultation with the services. Finally, from this database cases were selected in cooperation with the prosecutors, who advised on the cases they considered most informative in view of the research plan. These were the larger and more complicated cases within the total of 92 cases, in which more different aspects of financial investigation were expected to be present. This is in line with case study methodology literature (e.g. Stake 2006).

of waste, trade in protected species, crime involving polluted soil, and non-compliance with safety regulations in high-risk companies. The investigations were selected from the Public Prosecution Service's registration system, in consultation with prosecutors and police experts. For these 23 cases, we retrieved the case files, of which the financial reports contained most information relevant to the research questions. In addition to studying the files, we conducted semi-structured interviews with the people involved in the investigations, such as the financial investigators or experts connected with the case, and team leaders. All interviewees were employed by the police, a specialised investigation service or the prosecutor's office, except one who was a private consultant hired by an investigation team. An interview topic list was used, including questions on how the goal of the criminal investigation was formulated, the expertise of the detectives involved, the methods and equipment used as well as behaviours of the suspects with regard to concealment of their illegal activities and money laundering. Success and failure factors were assessed through the use of open interview questions and were not specified beforehand. These concerned aspects of the organisations and employees involved, as well as their training, cooperation and facilities relevant to the investigation. For the purpose of our study interviews were the primary data source, because the files contained little information answering the research questions. For instance, the files give information about choices that a team made, but say little about the considerations with respect to these choices.

In addition to interviews with investigators and team leaders, seven interviews were conducted with employees of the public prosecutor's office. Most of them were involved in one or more cases, but were also asked questions about their more general expertise and views. The background of these respondents varied from public prosecutors to financial experts involved in the confiscation of illegally obtained assets. This ensured that the entire range of staff involved in the financial side of the investigations was covered.

Confiscation of proceeds of crime under criminal law

The options for confiscating criminally obtained assets under criminal law

Under Dutch law, criminally obtained assets can be confiscated under criminal law, but also under administrative and civil law.[10] This study was limited to confiscation under criminal law. The criminal-law measures and penalties addressed in this study may be aimed at confiscating illegally obtained assets, but also at confiscation of indirect asset components, such as stopping business activities, or at the full or partial deprivation of certain rights. The legal grounds

---

10 This section is based on the work of George van der Zon, who at the time worked as a specialist in environmental law at the National Police.

for these punitive sanctions are laid down in the Dutch Code of Criminal Procedure, the Criminal Code and the Economic Offences Act. The primary option for taking away proceeds of crime under criminal law is imposing a fine. The main supplementary measure imposed by the court is the confiscation of illegally obtained assets. Furthermore, the National Public Prosecutor's Office for Financial, Economic and Environmental Offences can impose various incidental punishments and measures, such as halting a company's operations or ordering it to pay damages to third parties. Thus, the Office has at its disposal various methods to put the measures into effect. The criminal case and the confiscation case may be dealt with separately in court. It is possible to bring a case with a focus on demanding the confiscation of illegal assets against a person who has already been convicted. Out-of-court settlement, which will be discussed later, is possible in the criminal case as well as in the confiscation case.

Recently, systematic methods have been developed for the calculation of the proceeds of environmental crime.[11] For confiscation to be successful it is vital that the suspect's assets are actually identified. The National Public Prosecutor's Office for Financial, Economic and Environmental Offences employs specialised asset identification officers for this purpose. To prevent suspects from diverting their assets out of reach of the police and the judiciary, a prejudgement attachment can be levied.

Economic Offences Act

Whereas crimes such as document fraud are a criminal offence under the Criminal Code, offences against regulatory law, including environmental legislation, are punishable under the Economic Offences Act. This Act offers the possibility to impose measures that have indirect consequences for someone's assets, such as halting a company's business operations or making public a judicial decision. The Economic Offences Act not only supplements the instruments for confiscation under criminal law, but also offers specific investigative powers, such as the independent requisition and confiscation of information and documents from suspects; powers not provided by the equivalent sections of the Code of Criminal Procedure. In the Code of Criminal Procedure, the *nemo tenetur* principle applies: a suspect can withhold information that would facilitate his conviction. However, under the Economic Offences Act, a suspect is required to comply with a specified request to hand over documents and other information.

---

11 After attending a number of case selection meetings, accountants of the prosecution service provided the investigation services with a classified document in which proper calculation in several types of cases is discussed. The main distinction is calculation over a period of time on the basis of the estimated proceeds of specified illegal activities on the one hand, and calculation based on the comparison of patterns of spending with legal earnings on the other.

Results

In this section, we describe the results from our study, in accordance with the three stages of an investigation process: the preparation phase, the actual investigation and finally the prosecution phase in which the Public Prosecution Service has to choose between going to court or aiming for an out-of-court settlement. The option to charge the criminal offence of money laundering is discussed separately.

Preparation of the financial investigation

Although financial aspects have played a more prominent role in environmental investigations over the past few years, working methods are still in development. Depending on the choices made at the start of an investigation, attention given to the financial aspects of the case may vary. If an investigation starts ad hoc, such as after an incident, it often takes some time before the option of a financial investigation is discussed. However, if an investigation is planned and launched on the basis of a well-thought-out project plan, a financial section is often already included in the proposal, considering the options for financial investigation and ensuring that the personnel required for the investigation are available.[12] Most interviewees consider determining the financial objectives and designating the required expertise at an early stage as contributing to the success of a criminal investigation. Financial experts can play a role in the process, as can various instruments and tools that have been developed by the Investigation Services over the past years, including a computer programme that guides investigators through the options for financial investigation.[13] Determining the objectives of a criminal investigation emphasises its direction and helps control its duration and the deployment of personnel. This is considered to increase the chances of the financial investigation being successful.

When determining the deployment of personnel, one should consider both financial investigators who are directly involved in the investigation, and experts such as accountants who are not part of the investigation team but can advise or participate in more complex cases. The actual availability of the financial investigators and experts plays a role when planning an investigation project and putting together a team of detectives. The Netherlands Police and the special investigative services employ a range of financial experts with very different backgrounds and qualities, depending on their education and experience. Some hold university degrees and have developed their skills working in other

---

12 In the Netherlands, criminal investigation proposals are decided upon in case selection or 'weighting' committees, led by the prosecution service, where cases are discussed in view of the set priorities and policy.

13 The *Afpak*-app (from *afpakken*, 'to take away') is a computer program that guides the team through the options in a criminal investigation offered by Dutch law, depending on properties of the case, in the form of a decision tree.

professions, whereas others learned their trade on the job and may be more knowledgeable about environmental investigations. Ideally, team leaders have a choice as to the deployment of financial experts with the proper background, depending on the aims and expectations of a financial investigation.

However, in practice they have to make do with the available personnel because of the scarcity of financial experts within the Netherlands Police and the various special investigative services. Our interviews showed that in many cases no financial experts were available at the start of the investigation, causing financial investigation to take place too late in the process or not at all. At present, a trend can be noticed within the Dutch police organisation to concentrate specialised personnel in central departments.[14] Team leaders then have to submit a well-founded request for the deployment of these experts. Some team leaders are worried that those responsible for assigning these experts will prioritise more 'traditional' organised crime cases, such as drug cases. Many environmental investigators feel that higher police management is not all that committed to tackling environmental crime (Spapens 2012). However, it appears possible to also interpret the current guidelines in favour of the option of allocating financial experts to environmental crime teams. This is possible when a combination of expertise of financial as well as environmental legislation is required. However, financial expertise remains scarce and is frequently lacking. Recently, the Ministry of Security and Justice addressed the necessity of investing in financial expertise (Ministry of Security and Justice 2015a).

In addition to financial expertise, investigation of digital data is essential for the confiscation of proceeds of crime. Recovering and analysing data from applications such as bookkeeping software plays an important role when the records of a suspected company are seized or when money flows need tracing. Here, linking digital investigators to environmental teams has proven to be a success factor. If financial data can be read out and stored adequately, digital and financial investigators can analyse the data correctly and produce an accurate calculation of the illegally obtained assets. Bottlenecks encountered when drawing up a financial report include malfunctioning of the software used by the various services or, more frequently, its incompatibility; that is, data produced by one programme cannot be read by the software of another service.

According to the experts, new opportunities have recently opened up for the digital part of financial investigation because the police have adopted methods such as EDP-auditing (audit using Electronic Data Processing). This method was initially developed for improving information processes in companies, but can also simplify examination of a company's books. All data, including those stored on networks or in the Cloud, can be retrieved in a general format and analysed with software available to the investigation team.

14 Concentration of experts in central departments is a police policy that does not occur in the special investigation services.

Interviewees have stressed the importance of determining the objective of a criminal investigation, and thus the direction it should take. More general policy goals apply as well, such as decreasing environmental crime and its impact on society. Performance agreements that have been concluded between police, special investigation services and the public prosecution service formulate quantifiable output, such as the number of confiscations and the amount of money confiscated or put under prejudgement attachment. However, such a performance agreement may result in twisted incentives leading to performing action only for the sake of raising numbers in management reports, putting the goals of intervention, such as decreasing environmental crime, in the background. According to van Duyne, Kristen and de Zanger (2015), performance agreements on prejudgement attachment are unrealistic and show that authorities are too 'greedy' when confiscating proceeds of crime. This could result in the levying of large sums of prejudgement attachments that are not in proportion to the final confiscation to be expected and do not contribute to meeting the general objectives of the policy, i.e. reducing environmental crime. The employees of the National Public Prosecutor's Office for Financial, Economic and Environmental Offences interviewed in the study were aware of the risks of such 'strategic' behaviour, but they also emphasised that performance agreements can be used as an instrument to guide the organisation in a specific direction. A change of course is called for if 'ticking boxes' appears to be becoming an objective in itself. They agree that performance agreements create awareness among managers and investigators of the possibilities that financial confiscation offers and the results that can be achieved.

The financial investigation as part of the criminal investigation

A number of points must be considered when an investigation into environmental crime is launched. As was shown in the previous section, setting a clear objective for the investigation and monitoring its direction are important aspects. Furthermore, the prosecutor and the team need to decide at an early stage who are considered suspects in the criminal investigation and what charges will be brought against them.

In determining the charges, the leader of the investigation can choose from various articles in the Dutch Criminal Code and the Economic Offences Act.[15] According to various experts it is difficult to prove environmental crime on the basis of the Economic Offences Act and convict the perpetrators. A complicating factor is that the Economic Offences Act, and even more so the environmental legislation and regulations that it penalises, is subject to frequent amendments, sometimes even while an investigation is in progress, which complicates criminal

---

15 The Economic Offences Act is a framework law that documents the penalisation of the violation of various other laws and regulations, such as the Environmental Management Act, the Fertilizers Act and the Fisheries Act.

investigation. For this reason, the leader of the investigation may sometimes choose to charge a suspect with an offence under general criminal law, such as document fraud. However, charging a suspect on the basis of the Economic Offences Act also has advantages, because it allows the requisitioning of data and documents and requires suspects to cooperate whereas under the Criminal Code the *nemo tenetur* principle applies. There are, of course, a number of requirements that have to be met. A demand must be sufficiently underpinned, no data can be requisitioned that the suspect has yet to create, and all semblance of a 'fishing expedition' (to find grounds for suspicion) must be avoided. In some investigations, this has resulted in the decision not to carry out a search of the premises, but rather to requisition the financial records. Although this saves on personnel, there is a risk that suspects will withhold some of the incriminating information because they themselves are responsible for providing the information requisitioned. An alternative to requisitioning information is to carry out a premises search on the basis of the Code of Criminal Procedure. Investigators feel that a search must be thoroughly prepared in consultation with the financial advisor to produce important leads for the investigation. Digital and financial expertise is also needed during a search to ensure that the relevant information is gathered.

The fact that the various laws and measures cannot be applied simultaneously must be taken into account when investigative measures are selected from the Code of Criminal Procedure. It is impossible to switch to investigative measures provided by the Economic Offences Act if initially the choice was made to use the Code of Criminal Procedure. Therefore, it is vital to consider the best legislative option for the investigation at hand.

In addition to formulating the exact charges, it is important to determine whether a natural person or a legal entity is charged as the suspect. Many punishable environmental acts are part of company activities. As a result, a case can be made for either option: a natural person, such as a manager for instance, or a legal entity.[16] In this situation, interviewees felt the most important thing was to consider who benefited from the criminal offences and for this to be reflected in the charges. If more than one natural person emerges as a suspect in a case, it may be possible to charge them with membership of a criminal organisation, on the basis of Art. 140 of the Criminal Code. In such cases, the extent of the profit gained must be proven for each individual suspect[17] before the proceeds of crime can be confiscated.

---

16 Prosecution of legal persons and natural persons in a single case is legally possible but not very common. A non-financial example is the Odfjell gas leakage case where prosecution of individuals as well as the company were seriously considered by the Prosection Office ('t Sas 2013).

17 A legal entity can formally be charged with membership of a criminal organisation based on art. 51 of the penal code but this seems to occur in very few cases. More commonly, criminal organisations own, use or abuse a legal entity (Kruisbergen *et al.* 2012).

To calculate the illegally obtained gain, an investigation team can ask an examining magistrate for permission to start a criminal financial investigation (*Strafrechtelijk Financieel Onderzoek*, SFO). The objective of the SFO is to identify and trace illegally obtained gain and assets. The investigation team and the public prosecutor are given certain powers to achieve this. They can, for instance, requisition relevant documents. An SFO is also a covert procedure; the fact that an investigation is ongoing does not have to be revealed to a suspect until the day he or she is interviewed for the first time. Thus, it may have an adverse effect if a suspect finds out while the criminal investigation is ongoing that a financial investigation is also in progress. The suspect might take measures to hide his assets. This is why timing is crucial when launching an SFO. Once a confiscation order has been issued, the SFO has to be terminated. In 2011, at the request of the Public Prosecution Service, the legislator determined that after the confiscation order has been issued, an additional SFO can be started if the investigation team sees possibilities to trace more assets.

If an SFO is to be applied successfully, then there are some important considerations to be taken into account. First, if in a given investigation a lot of information needs to be gathered, an SFO may save the police much time because not all actions require the consent of a public prosecutor. Second, an SFO offers the chance of longer and more intensive investigation, which can be an advantage in more complex cases, for instance if several legal entities are involved. Third, environmental crime is often transnational; an SFO simplifies cooperation with foreign partners, as they have a tendency to prioritise investigations authorised by an examining magistrate. Given that an SFO has both advantages and disadvantages, it is advisable to consider what role an SFO could play right at the start, when determining the aim of the investigation. In addition, it is important to note that, according to the Ministry of Security and Justice's *Contourennota*,[18] the SFO as such will not be included in the upcoming revised Code of Criminal Procedure (Ministry of Security and Justice 2015b). The Public Prosecution Service expects, however, that the powers attached to the current SFO will be included in the new legislation under the same conditions and with the same scope.

Within an SFO, a public prosecutor can independently, without the intervention of an examining magistrate, levy a prejudgement attachment on a suspect's assets. Assets can also be confiscated on the basis of Article 103 of the Code of Criminal Procedure. As in the case of an SFO, it is advisable to discuss the range of confiscation options when determining the aims of the investigation, to make clear when, what, how and from whom assets will be confiscated. The timing of the confiscation may be relevant; for instance, once a suspect realises that a financial investigation is in progress, they may try to siphon off assets.

---

18 Ministry of Security and Justice (2015) *Contourennota*, a memorandum outlining future amendments of the Dutch Code of Criminal Procedure, which is still in process as this chapter is being written.

A good moment to confiscate the assets is as soon as a suspect becomes aware of the financial investigation (for instance as a result of an interview or a search). If a company's assets are confiscated, the suspect may sometimes prefer to submit a bank guarantee. This secures the assets just as well as a confiscation, and it is not possible to file a complaint about it, since it is requested by the suspect. Whether the investigation team opts for classical confiscation, prejudgement attachment, or no confiscation at all may have major consequences for a suspect, such as negative publicity, reduced turnover, or even bankruptcy. For this reason, most experts advise taking the principle of proportionality into account in applying this measure. According to several respondents, the part of the company not involved in the crime should be able to continue to function without being hampered by the confiscation.

Respondents differed in their opinions about whether the natural persons behind a suspect company should also be subject to attachment or confiscation. Everybody agrees that this should be done in the case of an individual who has received large personal gains from the crime committed. However, the criteria and degree of priority may vary from one public prosecutor to another. One argument in favour is that it serves as a warning; perpetrators should not believe they can hide behind their company and remain unassailable. On the other hand, some suggest, on the basis of the principle of proportionality that confiscation from natural persons should be applied as little as possible, and that if this measure is indeed opted for, only items of considerable value should be confiscated, such as exorbitantly expensive boats or cars. However, in some cases, personal belongings with emotional value to a suspect have been confiscated, a practice that is criticised by some as being a mere bullying. As long as confiscation takes into account when, what, how and from whom assets are to be confiscated, and the value of the confiscation is in proportion to what can be expected to be requisitioned, this constitutes a successful confiscation model.

Cooperation with other partners is an important element in reducing environmental crime, since different parties play a role in inspection, investigation and prosecution in relation to these types of crimes. The situation is no different when it comes to confiscating criminal assets. The people interviewed in this study indicated that close cooperation between the Netherlands Police, the special investigative services, not only those already mentioned but also the Fiscal Intelligence and Investigation Service (FIOD), is essential to arrive at the right confiscation option. For financial investigators, the most important element turns out to be close cooperation with the financial experts of the Confiscation Department of the National Public Prosecutor's Office for Financial, Economic and Environmental Offences, where investigation teams can consult specialists in the field of calculating illegally obtained gain and the legal options for confiscation. Cooperation with private-sector partners or with the business association in question may also be advisable. For instance, in this way it could be possible to reduce the opportunities for facilitators, by making known the risk. Also, it could be possible to include the suspect's financial network when applying confiscation measures, for example when a suspect hides assets with friends or relatives. Within the police or a given special investigation service, too, it is important to stimulate close cooperation between tactical, digital and financial investigators. Interviewees agree with each other that an important success factor when it comes to confiscation under criminal law is the extent to which *all* members of the investigation team are aware of the financial aspects of the case. Mutual inspiration and cooperation between tactical and financial experts leads to the best results in generating evidence in the criminal proceedings, as well as in the asset-confiscation proceedings.

Money laundering

The study by van der Leest and van der Zon (2012), mentioned above, focused on money-laundering constructions. The authors presented members of various environmental crime teams with a list of descriptions of money-laundering constructions. It emerged that most of these money-laundering constructions had not been explored in detail in the course of criminal investigations. This led the authors to call for more attention (human and financial resources) for investigating money-laundering charges in environmental crime cases (van der Leest and van der Zon 2012). However, our study shows that money laundering is rarely mentioned in the summons for environmental crime cases. In those few cases where it is mentioned, it is mainly restricted to constructions involving legal persons abroad, including one instance in which a facilitator had set up a construction of this kind.[19] For instance, in one case it could be proven that a consultant had set up a legal entity for a suspect in order to launder money. This consultant was charged with money laundering, whereas the main suspect (a company) faced environmental crime charges.

In most cases the suspect is not charged with money laundering, but with an environmental crime, sometimes in combination with forgery of documents or another offence under communal law. And in most cases an attempt is then made to confiscate illegally obtained gains. However, unlike van der Leest and van der Zon (2012), the present study does not conclude that perpetrators should be charged for money laundering more often. The reason is that in many cases the perpetrator derives advantage above all from not doing things that, according to the law, they ought to have done ('crimes of omission'). Their crime lies therefore in *not* spending money that they *should have* spent so it is not necessary for them to manufacture apparent legal origins for the money 'after the event'. However, this does not alter the fact that proceeds of crime can, in principle, be calculated and confiscated. Charging money laundering would be possible, legally speaking, since holding assets that cannot be traced to a legal origin amounts to

19 Incidentally, constructions involving several legal entities, abroad or within the country, are often legitimate and may be employed in business for various purposes, such as spreading risk and liability.

money laundering, even if no special construction of any kind is used to give it an apparently legal origin.

Thus, although in many cases a charge of money laundering would be an option, it is seldom actually chosen. The investigative team and the public prosecutor take into consideration what the added benefit is of charging the suspect with money laundering. If in the public prosecutor's assessment it will not make any difference either for the penalty to be imposed or for the confiscation proceedings, they choose to leave it out. This line of reasoning for instance appears in cases in which money laundering was initially included in the project plan, but was subsequently dropped.

Nevertheless, some of those interviewed actually advocated bringing charges of money laundering more often. On the one hand, they argued that it is an efficient way to prosecute suspects without having to prove an environmental crime, which is as described above often perceived as a complex process. On the other, interviewees recognise that the specific expertise on money laundering is often lacking among the environmental teams of the Netherlands Police and, to a lesser extent, the special investigative services. Moreover, the Dutch Supreme Court's case law has indicated that the basic offence must remain the central charge in criminal cases. This seems to contradict the idea of circumventing a complicated proof-furnishing process by choosing a money-laundering charge (Rozemeijer 2015).

Prosecution phase of the financial investigation

An investigating team concludes its financial investigation at the point when the case file is handed over to the Public Prosecution Service. The public prosecutor then decides what the next steps will be and thus how the file will be dealt with in court. Obviously, the investigating team expect the case to be dealt with by the court in a reasonable space of time and that they will receive feedback on the progress of the case. Detectives of the police and the special investigative services interviewed indicated that they were not always very satisfied in this regard. The Public Prosecution Service is well aware that it sometimes takes a very long time before a case is dealt with in court. There are several reasons for this. For example, the defence council may have certain requests, such as the hearing of witnesses, which at this stage must be carried out by an examining judge. Another factor is that in the case of environmental crime it is rare for natural persons to be held in detention, which means that the associated brief time limits for bringing the case to court do not apply. Unfortunately, the long processing times may lead the judge to use their powers of mitigation, which often results in reduced sentences in both the criminal case and the confiscation case. This is perceived by many as a bottleneck: the financial report submitted is not in proportion with the outcome of the court case, which is believed to result in a limited impact on those involved in environmental crime.

Also, in many cases feedback from the public prosecutor to the investigators is limited, even when they specifically ask for information. Interviewees from the

Public Prosecution Service admit that there is often insufficient communication with the investigation team on the progress of the case and the choices made. They attribute this mostly to time pressure due to the large number of cases they have to deal with, but some also admitted that communicating with investigation teams was not always given proper priority.

In addition to taking a case to court, a public prosecutor can choose to seek an out-of-court settlement. Given that bringing environmental crime to court is often a lengthy process, various examples of such settlements occurred in the study.[20] The choice for an out-of-court settlement depends on the Public Prosecution Service's aim. One reason might be to punish the perpetrator as swiftly as possible, to give a clear signal to society that certain crimes are undesirable. For this reason, prosecutors demand high sums to be paid as well as publicity on the outcome. In a case that might lead to new case law or which is intended to draw the attention of the legislative authority, an out-of-court settlement is not preferred. An alternative is to take the criminal case to court, creating exposure for the firm in question, and to aim for a settlement in the confiscation case. Both may be combined in a transaction that includes the confiscation, which makes it a kind of 'package deal'. The choice for out-of-court settlement does not depend solely on the Public Prosecution Service's aim, however, but also on the personal view of the competent public prosecutor. In the opinion of some of those interviewed out-of-court settlements are only justified if there are special reasons not to take the case to court. Their priority is the criminal case and punishing the natural persons who profited from the crimes committed. However, others state that out-of-court settlements inherently comprise an element of punishment, so that this constitutes a proper handling of the case. They point out that specific measures may be included in the settlement terms, such as publicising the outcome of the case. The investigating teams are somewhat hesitant about out-of-court settlements, as they often feel that such deals do not do justice to their hard work and do not help enough to change the suspects' behaviour. In contrast, other financial investigators state that out-of-court settlements could well lead to confiscation of even higher amounts, since the parties involved in the deliberations may be more inclined to put their cards on the table. This is supported by recent research that shows that for perpetrators, when compared to cases dealt with in court, out-of-court settlement in confiscation cases is in financial terms far more costly (de Voogd 2013). However, it should be noted that the study only looked at the percentage of the estimated illegal gain and did not consider whether actual policy goals, such as a reduction of environmental crime, were realised.

Publicity is considered a success factor in the fight against environmental crime. An investigation into compliance with environmental rules and regulations

20 As most of the cases analysed were still ongoing, it is not possible to report numbers or a percentage of cases in which settlements were proposed. Nevertheless, it appeared to be an issue generating much debate.

showed that the media may play a role in enforcing more compliance. Negative publicity and damage to one's reputation may be more of a threat to big companies than a fine (van Wingerde 2015). The Public Prosecution Service has the option, through the Economic Offences Act, of demanding that the outcome of the case is to be publicised and what form this publicity should take. The costs involved, for instance those of putting an advertisement in the papers, are then borne by the sentenced party. According to those interviewed, publicity is indeed a deterrent for both perpetrators and industry. However, using naming and shaming as a form of punishment is still in the preliminary stages; time will tell whether such measures will lead to the desired increase in compliance with environmental regulations.

Conclusion and discussion

The aim of this chapter was to provide insight into current developments in the Netherlands with regard to the confiscation of assets in environmental crime cases. Although this study emphasised options for confiscation of criminal assets under criminal law, it is important to keep in mind that other options are available as well. An administrative measure such as revoking a permit is seen by most respondents as an effective form of taking away criminal assets, as it is assumed also to impact on the turnover of the perpetrator's company.

On several occasions it was reported that financial investigations were unsuccessful because no financial investigator was available or because financial investigators had to divide their attention among too many different cases. The most important recommendation derived from our study is therefore that the police need to acquire more financial expertise, both in qualitative and quantitative terms, if they are to meet the authorities' ambitious targets with regard to confiscation. In the allocation of resources, it is important to ensure that the environmental teams receive sufficient support from specialised financial investigators. The need to allocate expertise and resources if the ambitious policy goals and performance agreements are to be realised is also expressed in Dutch policy studies on confiscation of criminal assets. In an evaluation study on the programme Financial Investigation of Crime, which ran from 1997 to 2002, it was concluded that the ambitions of the police and the public prosecution office were not reflected in the resources made available for the programme, let alone for the implementation of its findings in daily practice (Faber and van Nunen 2002). Later, the Netherlands Court of Audit (2008), in a study on fighting money laundering and finance of terrorism, found that results were poor, notwithstanding the priorities and ambitions set by five successive governments. The most recent evaluation of the Programme Financial and Economic Crimes (Finec) by the Ministry of Justice also found that the goals of the programme were not met. The organisation and resources were insufficient, as was the cooperation between the police and its partners (IVJ 2012). Although more financial investigators have been hired since then, this has not solved scarcity problems in the field of environmental crime.

Nevertheless, we conclude that progress has been made in confiscation of proceeds of environmental crime, although less so than probably would have been the case if recommendations of earlier studies had been followed. And as we saw, in environmental crime cases confiscation of proceeds of crime was already lagging behind when compared to other types of crime. This was in fact the reason the study was performed: the police leadership realised that there is ground to be made up when it comes to a financial approach of environmental crimes. In many of the environmental crime investigations an attempt has been made at least to estimate and confiscate the illegally obtained gain. Public prosecutors are more aware of the possibilities than before. The special investigative services of the Living Environment and Transport Inspectorate of the Dutch Food and Consumer Product Safety Authority seem to be ahead of the police in terms of financial capacity and its deployment from the start of investigations. However, since most of the cases that were analysed for this study are still in progress, it remains to be seen how the results in terms of amounts confiscated – relative to estimated assets – actually turn out in the end, when the cases have been treated in (appeal) court.

A number of bottlenecks need to be removed in order to achieve further improvements. Hiring or training more financial investigators is necessary but will also have strong budgetary consequences. However, cheaper measures, such as raising awareness of the financial aspects of an investigation among the environmental teams are also possible. It might prompt police officers to seize essential financial documents during the first search of a premise. A small team of experts working with the teams could make all the difference.

In the course of our study it became evident that perspectives varied with regard to a number of aspects. These differences can only partly be traced back to differences in knowledge and experience. There are striking divergences in the ideas about the use of criminal financial investigations, laying prejudgement attachments on natural and legal persons, and out-of-court settlements. It seems a good idea to allow police officers and team leaders to run their investigations their own way, on the condition that they make explicit the considerations with respect to the choice for certain steps, which makes it possible to evaluate the results. The study makes no claim to have the answer to the question of what approach works best. Such an assessment would also depend on which criterion one wants to apply: is it about the height of the fine or the amount of money confiscated, or is the ultimate goal to reduce environmental crime? Obviously the latter effects would be far more difficult to measure.

References

Boon, van der, V. and Marel, van der, G. 2009. *De vastgoedfraude: Miljoenenzwendel aan de top van het Nederlandse bedrijfsleven*. Amsterdam: Nieuw Amsterdam.

Court of Audit. 2008. *Bestrijden witwassen en terrorismefinanciering*. Den Haag: Algemene Rekenkamer.

Duyne, van, P.C., Kristen, F.H.G and Zanger, de, S. 2015. 'Belust op misdaadgeld: de werkelijkheid van de voordeelsontneming', *Justitiële Verkenningen* 41(1), 100–116.

Faber, W. and van Nunen, A. 2002. *Het ei van Columbo? Evaluatie van het project Financieel Rechercheren*. Oss: Faber organisatievernieuwing BV.

Heel, van, A., Nieuwdorp, A. and Vanlandschoot, A. 2013. *Milieucriminaliteit, hoe en wat schuift het, Congres 31 mei 2013*. Apeldoorn: Politieacademie.

IVJ. 2012. *Follow the money! Onderzoek naar financieel opsporen door de politie in het licht van het landelijk programma FinEC Politie*. The Hague: Inspectie Veiligheid en Justitie.

Kruisbergen, E.W., Bunt, van de, H.G and Kleemans, E.R. 2012. *Georganiseerde criminaliteit in Nederland. Vierde rapportage op basis van de Monitor Georganiseerde Criminaliteit*. Den Haag: Boom Lemma uitgevers.

Leest, van der, W. and Zon, van der, G.A. 2012. 'Witwasmethoden bij grensoverschrijdende milieucriminaliteit', *Justitiële Verkenningen* 382, 76–90.

Ministry of Security and Justice. 2015a. *Herijkingsnota. Herijking realisatie van de nationale politie*. Den Haag: Ministerie van Veiligheid en Justitie.

Ministry of Security and Justice. 2015b. *Contourennota aanpassing Wetboek van Strafvordering*. Den Haag: Ministerie van Veiligheid en Justitie.

OM. 2015. *Jaarbericht 2014*. Den Haag: Openbaar Ministerie.

Rozemeijer, J.P. 2015. 'Witwasonderzoeken zonder aantoonbaar gronddelict. Het rechtelijk toetsingskader en efficiënt opsporen in zes stappen', *Justitiële Verkenningen* 41(1), 24–36.

Sas, 't, S. 2013. 'OM: 'Opnieuw strafrechtelijk onderzoek Odfjell', *EenVandaag* 14 November.

Spapens, T. 2012. *De complexiteit van milieucriminaliteit: De aard van het misdrijf, de opsporing en de samenwerkingsrelaties*. Den Haag: Boom Lemma uitgevers.

Stake, R.E. 2006. *Multiple Case Study Analysis*. New York: The Guildford Press.

Voogd, de, H. 2013. *Koopman of dominee. Verkennend kwalitatief onderzoek rondom de opbrengsten en inzet van de schikking ex artikel 511c Wetboek van Strafvordering*. Apeldoorn: Politieacademie bachelor thesis.

Wingerde, van, K. 2015. 'The limits of environmental regulation in a globalized economy. Lessons from the Probo Koala', in *The Routledge Handbook of White-Collar and Corporate Crime in Europe*, edited by J. van Erp, W. Huisman, and G. VandeWalle. London and New York: Routledge, 260–275.

13 Sentencing environmental offenders

It is not just about the money

Rob White

Introduction

The impetus for this chapter is the frequent claim made in criminological, legal and socio-legal research that courts (in a generic sense, but generally referring to lower-level courts) deal with environmental issues in a trivialising and/or uninformed way, and that the penalties imposed by courts tend to be lenient and thereby inconsequential in terms of deterrence or reprobation (de Prez 2000ab; Fogel and Lipovsek 2013; Chin *et al.* 2014; Cochran *et al.* 2016; Lynch *et al.* 2016). These issues have been acknowledged in a number of jurisdictions including Sweden, Canada, the United States and the United Kingdom, and Europe more generally (Bell and McGillivray 2008; O'Hear 2004; Environment Audit Committee 2004). They have also been noted in Australia, although they have never been empirically tested (Bates 2013).

Related recent Australian research on sentencing by the New South Wales Land and Environment Court (NSWLEC) has also examined the questions of consistency and proportionality; that is, how consistent the Court has been in applying additional maximum penalties in cases where they appear to be warranted (Burke 2016). While not focused on the issue of leniency *per se*, consistent with prior research the study has demonstrated that a substantial number of cases involved sentences that are well below the expected penalty threshold.

The empirical foundation for evaluating the accuracy of this widespread belief about leniency is nonetheless scant, insofar as the number of studies on this topic is still relatively small. Therefore, opinion about this should be seen as open-ended and indicative rather than conclusive. Accordingly and in light of this, the purpose of this chapter is to consider the ways in which the New South Wales Land and Environment Court sentences those found guilty of environmental offences. This is done through examination of a select number of cases involving harm to non-human environmental entities such as animals and trees and other plant species. Specifically, the concern is with how the NSWLEC apportions penalties as part of its role in future deterrence and thereby responds to the damage to, death of, or destruction or degradation of the non-human environmental entity (such as trees, animals and other vegetation). While legislation sets the definitions and limits of both harm and the available penalties relevant to that harm, it is up to the Court to determine the specific nature of the harm and translate this into an appropriate sentence.

The New South Wales Land and Environment Court

Australia's court system is extensive and incorporates several tiers within both federal and state jurisdiction (White and Perrone 2015). State courts deal with the vast majority of offences and disputes arising in Australia. Federal courts customarily deal with matters falling beyond the jurisdiction of state laws, including Constitutional matters. At the state and territory level, there are three tiers. Inferior courts – variously referred to as the Magistrates' Court, Court of Petty Sessions, Local Court and Court of Summary Jurisdiction – are the lowest tier and have jurisdiction enabling them to deal with both criminal and civil matters of a relatively minor nature. The courts are presided over by magistrates and enjoy a limited range of sentencing options, and generally, therefore, the penalties imposed at this level are relatively lenient. Over time, specialist courts (for example, Coroner's and Children's) and problem-solving courts (indigenous, drug, mental health and family violence) have been created as divisions of the traditional courts existing at this level, to deal with specific types of offences and/or offenders regarded as requiring special attention. These courts are the busiest in terms of number of cases determined. Nonetheless, courts at this level do not carry the same prestige, legal weight, remuneration or resources of the higher courts. They also do not 'shape' the laws by creating precedent, and they involve a preponderance of guilty pleas.

Intermediate courts deal with cases of a more serious criminal and civil nature than the inferior courts and are presided over by judges, who have extensive legal experience. Courts at this level are referred to as District or County Courts depending on the state. The vast majority of all indictable criminal offences, such as assault, robbery, rape and culpable driving, are determined in these courts with the assistance of a jury, and proceedings tend to be formal. Intermediate courts are also able to hear appeals relating to conviction and/or sentence, as forwarded to them from inferior courts, if suitable ground for such an appeal exists.

Superior courts – known as Supreme Courts – are also officiated by an experienced judge and involving a jury in contested matters, and deal with the most serious criminal cases, including homicide and related offences (that is, all are indictable cases). In some instances, these courts are also able to take on federal jurisdiction to deal with offences committed under Commonwealth (or federal) law, such as drug importation and fraud offences. They also act as key courts of criminal appeal from lower courts. At the federal level, the High Court of Australia sits at the summit of the Australian court hierarchy and is the custodian of the Australian Constitution. This court is also the highest Court of Appeal for criminal matters, thereby setting the authoritative precedents that are binding on all lower courts throughout the land.

The New South Wales Land and Environment Court (NSWLEC) was chosen as the focus for the present case study for several reasons. It is the oldest specialist court of its kind in Australia (one of only three in Australia dealing specially with environmental matters). It has criminal jurisdiction and thus deals directly with environmental crimes (in contrast, for example, with the Queensland environment court that does not deal with criminal matters). It has superior status to magistrate courts and therefore can provide an indication of how courts operate when environmental harm is deemed serious enough to warrant higher court attention. Whereas much of the extant literature on environmental crime and courts is critical of lower court activity in this domain, little has been written on either specialist environmental courts, or on courts that have higher court status. From this vantage point, it may well be that the issues of leniency, ignorance and inappropriateness either melt away or manifest in quite different ways (Burke 2016).

The NSWLEC was created by the *Land and Environment Court Act* in 1979. The Court was established in the light of two key objectives: rationalisation (whereby diverse environmental, planning and land matters could be dealt with in the single court) and specialisation (through appointment of appropriate personnel and the Court's wide jurisdiction in relation to the matters before it) (Pearlman 2010; Preston 2014). The NSWLEC is part of the New South Wales court system, and is equivalent to the Supreme Court in the hierarchy of courts in New South Wales. The judges of the Court have the same rank, title and status as judges of the Supreme Court of New South Wales.

The NSWLEC has a wide jurisdiction to hear and determine many different types of case. These are grouped by the relevant class of the Court's jurisdiction, and include Class 5 cases, namely, criminal proceedings for offences against planning or environmental laws. The Court needs to be cognisant of the elements constitutive of 'ecologically sustainable development' as outlined in the *Protection of the Environment Administration Act 1991 (NSW)*. The PEA Act provides that ecologically sustainable development can be achieved through the implementation of particular principles and programs (such as the precautionary principle, inter-generational equity, conservation of biological diversity and ecological integrity). This is relevant to the concerns of the present chapter insofar as these principles also implicitly include consideration of the health and wellbeing of non-human entities, including specific ecosystems, flora and fauna.

The findings presented in this chapter are based upon detailed textual analysis of 14 cases relating to the sentencing of offenders for criminal breaches of the *Native Vegetation Act 2003 (NSW)* [NVA] and 18 cases pertaining to sentencing for breaches of the *National Parks and Wildlife Act 1974 (NSW)* [NPWA]. These cases included all cases in the NSWLEC involving harms against non-human environmental entities, including flora (e.g., illegal cutting down of trees) and fauna (e.g., destruction of habitat of koalas), between 2003–2013. While the findings of the study are context-specific, they nonetheless provide generalisations that may be of relevance to jurisdictions and case law outside the remit of the present study.

Sentencing and environmental offences

Sentencing is a core function of those courts invested with responsibility for adjudicating criminal cases. In deciding sentence, the court typically weighs up a range of matters, including sentencing aims, sentencing principles, offender-specific factors, offence-specific factors, legislative intent and the specific facts of the case. The sentencing of adult offenders in New South Wales is governed by the *Crimes (Sentencing Procedure) Act 1999* (NSW) that sets out the purposes of sentencing in Section 3A. These aims include punishment, deterrence, rehabilitation, denunciation and community protection. Although not explicitly included in sentencing purposes, increasingly the aim of restorative justice is being incorporated into sentencing provisions, including in the specific area of environmental offences. However, within the context of the criminal law and particular mandate of the NSWLEC, there is no specific or explicit reference to 'restorative justice' *per se* as a method or remedy (White 2017). In the history of the NSWLEC there has in fact been only one instance in which restorative justice, involving processes of mediation and community conferencing, has been used, although a number of opportunities to do so have occurred over time (Hamilton 2014).

The various sentencing options that are available in sentencing for environmental offences reflect purposes of sentencing such as general deterrence, restoration and reparation (Preston 2007ab). Additional orders in the *Protection of the Environment Operations Act 1997 (NSW)*, for example, include orders for restoration and prevention; orders for payment of costs, expenses and compensation; orders to pay investigation costs; monetary benefit orders; publication orders; environmental service orders; environmental audit orders; payment into an environmental trust; order to attend a training course; order to establish a training course and order to provide financial assistance. No Australian jurisdiction has specified a ranking of sentencing purposes or a primary rationale, and each is weighed up in importance on a case-by-case basis (Mackenzie *et al.* 2010; Bagaric and Edney 2014).

The sentencing practices of the Court are shaped by legislation that sets out the hierarchy of sanctions available within this jurisdiction (such as, for example, the *Crimes (Sentencing Procedure) Act 1999* (NSW). A significant legislative development in this regard was the introduction of new sentencing measures in the *National Parks and Wildlife Amendment Act 2010 No 38 (NSW)*. For the criminal offences covered by *NPWA*, this meant the possibility of creative and innovative ways for dealing with offenders. This, too, was of great interest to the present research because, as noted previously, courts have been criticised for both leniency in sentencing environmental offenders, and general ineffectiveness in either remedying or preventing harm (Chin *et al.* 2014). Less severe sentences are described in terms of leniency, which is a common criticism of sentencing in relation to environmental criminal offences (de Prez 2000ab; Fogel and Lipovsek 2013; Cochran *et al.* 2016; Lynch 2017). The question for the present chapter is how best to gauge the severity of the sentence given.

Seriousness of offence is indicated in the application of the principle of proportionality, which refers to the idea that the severity of punishment should be commensurate with the seriousness of the criminal conduct. *Ordinal proportionality* concerns the relative seriousness of offences compared to other offences (for example, murder versus burglary). *Cardinal proportionality* relates to the notion that the penalty (within a scale of punishments) should not be out of proportion to the gravity of the crime involved (Preston 2007b). An overarching question, therefore, is whether, both legislatively and judicially, the level of seriousness of environmental harm is sufficiently acknowledged.

A rough survey of various countries seems to point to the trend that most offences involving the environment are prosecuted in lower courts (or dealt with by civil and administrative penalties), and that most penalties are on the lower rather than higher end of the scale. For example, over 90 per cent of all environmental crimes in the United Kingdom are dealt with in the Magistrate's Court and the most common sanction is fines, and these are low level (Bell and McGillivray 2008). A comparison of European states in regard to environmental prosecution and sentencing found that the fine is the criminal penalty most commonly used in legal practice, and that the amounts imposed are apparently relatively low on average (Faure and Heine 2000). In the United States, there is the anomaly that at the same time when appellate courts were interpreting environmental guidelines so as to provide for increasingly severe sentences, the district courts were actually imposing increasingly lenient sentences (O'Hear 2004).

Prison time has remained the exception not the norm (Lynch *et al.* 2016). In jurisdictions such as Flanders, Belgium even when prison sentences are imposed they are not always executed, but are often used as a suspended or probationary sentence (Billiet and Rousseau 2014). In the United States, where incarceration for federal environmental offences occurs, the mean sentence lengths are small and occur when the defendant is an individual rather than a corporation (Lynch 2017). Imprisonment tends to be given to offenders who have violated non-environmental laws as part of their offence (such as conspiracy, tax fraud, drug or firearm offences) (Lynch 2017). Moreover, it seems that low-culpability defendants may receive harsher sanctions than high-culpability defendants given how appellate courts have ignored culpability considerations when interpreting ambiguous provisions under environmental sentencing law guidelines (O'Hear 2004).

In Canada, recent analysis has once again confirmed the ambiguities in law and leniency in punishment when it comes to environmental offences (Fogel and Lipovsek 2013). Internationally, concern has been expressed that many emerging definitions of environmental crime have actually constrained the term by limiting it to crimes associated with breaches of environmental and/or endangered species legislation only. Typically, therefore, environmental crime is seen only as an infraction or misdemeanour – that is, less serious – than felony or indictable offences (Nelleman *et al.* 2016, p. 25).

Even where there are severe penalties available, they may not be applied by the judiciary, especially if they are not familiar with environmental crime and its consequences (Hayman and Brack 2002). This then relates to cardinal proportionality. The experience in the United Kingdom has been that the trivialisation of environmental offences in the courtroom serves to impede enforcement as a whole and to diminish the threats posed by prosecution (Environmental Audit Committee 2004). Specifically, the level of sentence given in courts, principally magistrate's courts, for environmental crimes has been seen to be too low for them to be effective either as punishment or a deterrent. This is not necessarily due to the legislative regime within which they work, but includes factors such as perceptions by magistrates regarding the seriousness of environmental crime and their relative inexperience in dealing with such crimes.

Range of penalties imposed

Nonetheless, a range of penalty types, approaches and mechanisms have emerged in Australia in recent years in regards to environmental sentencing, and these indicate a shift upwards in ordinal rankings of seriousness (that is, these sorts of crimes compared to other crime types) and attempts to fashion responses that better match the nature and dynamics of environmental harm (White 2010). Altogether such measures appear to denote a change in the seriousness with which the community regards environmental offences, as reflected in legislative changes to offence classifications and sentence regimes (Preston 2007b). How this burgeoning range of sentencing options translates into sentencing outcomes warrants ongoing and close scrutiny, and is of particular interest to this chapter. This is important because prosecutorial and judicial interventions around environmental harm provide concrete evidence of the specific valuing of environmental harm in and by the criminal justice system at any point in time.

Sentencing options available to the NSWLEC for enforcement and compliance purposes are provided under the *Protection of the Environment Operations Act 1997 (NSW)*. Options include terms of imprisonment, fines, clean-up or preventative action orders, and orders for compensation to those who suffered damage to property as a result of the offence or who incurred costs in taking steps to clean up the harm caused by the offence.

The *National Parks and Wildlife Act 1974 (NSW)* was amended in 2010 to expand the range of measures a court may impose. These include additional orders that provide the court may do any one or more of the following:

(a) Order the offender to take specified action to publicise the offence (including the circumstances of the offence) and its environmental and other consequences and any other orders made against the person,

(b) Order the offender to take specified action to notify specified persons or classes of persons of the offence (including the circumstances of the offence) and its consequences and of any orders made against the person (including, for example, the publication in an annual report or any other notice to shareholders or a company or the notification of persons aggrieved or affected by the offender's conduct),

(c) Order the offender to carry out a specified project for the restoration or enhancement of the environment in a public place or for the public benefit,

(d) Order the offender to pay a specified amount to the Environmental Trust established under the Environmental Trust Act 1998, or a specified organisation, for the purposes of a specified project for the restoration or enhancement of the environment or for general environmental purposes,

(e) Order the offender to attend, or to cause an employee or employees or a contractor or contractors of the offender to attend, a training or other course specified by the court,

(f) Order the offender to establish, for employees or contractors of the offender, a training course of a kind specified by the court.

(s205(1) National Parks and Wildlife
Amendment Act 2010 (NSW)

The *National Parks and Wildlife Amendment Act 2010* also includes general provisions pertaining to matters to be considered in imposing penalty. S 194 states:

1   In imposing a penalty for an offence under this Act or the regulations, the court is to take into consideration the following (so far as they are relevant):

(a) The extent of the harm caused or likely to be caused by the commission of the offence,

(b) The significance of the reserved land, Aboriginal object or place, threatened species or endangered species, population or ecological community (if any) that was harmed, or likely to be harmed, by the commission of the offence,

(c) The practical measures that may be taken to prevent, control, abate or mitigate that harm,

(d) The extent to which the person who committed the offence could reasonably have foreseen the harm caused or likely to be caused by the commission of the offence,

(e) The extent to which the person who committed the offence had control over the causes that gave rise to the offence,

(f) In relation to an offence concerning an Aboriginal object or place or an Aboriginal area – the views of Aboriginal persons who have an association with the object, place or area concerned,

(g) Whether, in committing the offence, the person was complying with an order or direction from an employer or supervising employee,

(h) Whether the offence was committed for commercial gain.

Section 194 (2) extends the purview of the Court beyond the specific factors laid out in s 194(1) by permitting the Court to 'take into consideration other matters that it considers relevant'. This gives the NSWLEC wide discretion in determining what factors to take into account in sentencing offenders. Analysis of the penalties imposed by the NSWLEC provide insight into how legislatively provided sentencing options are being translated into penalties at the concrete level, and how the Court is utilising these wide discretionary powers.

As noted previously, a fine is the most common penalty for environmental offences in places such as the USA, the UK, Belgium and Australia (Bates 2013; Billiet and Rousseau 2014; Stretesky *et al.* 2013). In Australia, it has also been observed that while overall most jurisdictions are strengthening penalties for environmental offences, the fines nonetheless remain low, especially relative to the maximum statutory penalty limits (Pepper 2012). These findings imply that both ordinal proportionality (the seriousness of environmental offences compared to other criminal offences) and cardinal proportionality (the penalty levels within the overall scale of punishments) do not fully reflect the seriousness of the offence as construed by those arguing that offenders who transgress against ecosystems, animals and plants should be more fully held to account.

Yet, the existing data in regards to the use of fines, particularly around questions of leniency and harshness in sentencing, require further analysis and elaboration. For example, concerns that warrant further attention include the difference in sentencing outcomes between the NSWLEC and the Local Court, comparisons between criminal proceedings for offences against environmental laws and other roughly equivalent offences involving criminal proceedings, systematic empirical evidence regarding trends in fine levels over time, and comparisons of NSWLEC sentencing outcomes with fines imposed in other countries. Moreover, the nature of the 'intuitive synthesis' – which encapsulates consideration of objective harm and subjective circumstance – means that factors such as capacity to pay have a bearing on sentencing determinations as well as indicia pertaining to environmental harm. The Court weighs up a wide range of factors and does so in accordance with sentencing principles such as consistency and proportionality. A serious offence, therefore, does not always result in a high range penalty outcome, depending upon circumstances.

If the purpose of the NSWLEC is seen to reside primarily in terms of reparation of harm and deterrence of future offending, then what counts is how sentencing can best contribute to these purposes (White 2017). Fines, in this instance, are not simply a 'cost of business' (Bricknell 2010; see also Stretesky *et al.* 2013). They are intended to be large enough to have a deterrent effect but, just as importantly, they are translated into meaningful projects and programmes that attempt to concretely remediate the damage and repair the harm. The linking of fines to specific environmental purposes thereby marks it off from more generic fine schemes in which the money is channelled into consolidated revenue.

The tailoring of sanctions and remedies by the court, over time, particularly in the direction of reparation is significant. When specific remedies are examined, they seem to indicate evidence of specialist knowledge and expertise by the judiciary about the nature of environmental harm and sustained efforts to ensure that the sentence fits the crime. This requires sensitivity to the importance of ecological principles, including regeneration and reparation, as well as knowledge of what might be most suitable in given circumstances. The content of extended environmental service orders also indicates reliance upon and/or awareness of scientific knowledge and methodological *nous*, as well as reflecting experience of likely offender behaviour post-hearing. With respect to this, the fact that the New South Wales Land and Environment Court is a specialist court also seems to be particularly important.

The principles of ecologically sustainable development as set out in the *Protection of the Environment Administration Act 1991 (NSW)* form part of the blueprint for decisions made in the NSWLEC. However, putting principles into practice in an effective manner requires a combination of informed decision-making, the ability to exercise judicial discretion and suitable legislatively provided sentencing regimes to be in place.

When it comes to sentencing outcomes, it is the imposition of orders, particularly in respect to the *NPWA* that is of special note. This is because, rather than use of just the one punitive option (for example, a fine), the NSWLEC has, since 2010, exhibited even greater flexibility and discretion in tailoring sentences to fit the specific circumstances of the offender and the offence. Not only does this ensure a better fit between problem and response, it also represents punishment that in many instances is of greater burden to the offender than imposition of a fine only.

It has been suggested that the effectiveness of combining different types of orders is that they put a spotlight on the fact that a crime has been committed, while simultaneously producing an environmental good (Bricknell 2010). If this is indeed the case, then such sentencing processes appear to address matters of the seriousness of environmental crime better than former approaches. They also reflect a regard for the appropriateness of penalty in relation to matters of ecological integrity. For instance, not only does the NSWLEC determine the nature of the harm to non-human environmental entities such as trees and animals by reference to ecological criteria, it imposes penalties that include measures designed to ensure the maintenance, restoration or preservation of the harmed plant and animal species, ecological community and ecosystem.

Innovative sentencing

A penalty regime need not be solely about application of criminal penalties, since the overarching issue is how best to address matters pertaining to environmental harm as circumstances dictate. For example, in some instances administrative sanctions can be more severe than criminal sanctions (such as when they involve revocation of licences) and similar to criminal penalties they may be oriented to prevention and punishment (Chin *et al.* 2014). Nonetheless the imposition of criminal penalties provides a clear indication of the severity of the offence.

International experience demonstrates that environmental crime tends not to attract harsh penalties and/or that its seriousness entirely depends upon the jurisdiction within which the crime is committed (European Union Action to Fight Environmental Crime 2016; Lebovitz *et al.* 2013). Even where other jurisdictions ostensibly are in favour of taking environmental crime seriously (or more seriously than previously), there are obstacles that have made this difficult to achieve in practice. For example, the *Directive 2008/99/EC of the European Parliament and of the Council of 19 November on the protection of the environment through criminal law* is intended to bolster efforts to deal with nine specific environmental offences, which include reference to discharges and emissions, hazardous materials, deterioration of habitat, and protected flora and fauna. The Directive underlines that penalties have to be substantial and that Member States take the necessary measures to ensure that the offences are punishable by 'effective, proportionate and dissuasive criminal penalties' (Article 5 Penalties).

The phrase 'effective, proportionate and dissuasive' is subject to different interpretations, and the institutional and legislative contexts within which criminal penalties for environmental offences are to be executed vary greatly within the European Union context (European Union Action to Fight Environmental Crime 2016). For present purposes, these three notions are taken to indicate certain basic requirements: 'effectiveness' deals with matters of specific and general deterrence, restoration of harm, and prevention of future harm; 'dissuasiveness' deals with deterrence, as well as harm to society, potential benefits to perpetrators and the probability of detection; and 'proportionality' makes reference to what or who is harmed, and acknowledges that concrete harm is more serious than endangering an interest (Faure 2011).

The NSWLEC appears to have addressed most of the concerns expressed in regards to effectiveness, dissuasiveness and proportionality. The NSWLEC operates in statutory context that provides for substantial penalties for environmental offences, and that provides a broad spectrum of sanctions that can be drawn upon in sentencing offenders. The cost to offenders therefore can be substantial and involve financial, reputational and resource implications. Many of the penalties imposed by the NSWLEC also include requirements that the defendant *do* something. That is, they are not simply passive recipients of penalties such as fines (or, indeed, of imprisonment). Rather, punishment is something that must also be accomplished *by* the offender. This has been described as an instance when a 'problem-solving model makes executives 'useful' at their own expense instead of simply levying them a fine or mandating time in prison' (Boyd 2008). This is time, energy and resource consuming, especially if it involves relatively substantial remediation or rehabilitation works. Combining financial sanctions such as fines with activity-based sanctions such as remediation means that compared to many other jurisdictions, the NSWLEC imposes sentences of greater burden to the offender than otherwise has been the case.

The Court is also futures-oriented, not only in regards to the deterrent effect of combined penalties, but also in regards to repairing the harm. This entails making available resources for non-human environmental entities (through for example funding being directed to suitable conservation organisations, and via direct remedial action). This can be termed 'reparative justice' to distinguish it from the more familiar term 'restorative justice' (White 2017).

Once the nature, extent and seriousness of environmental harm has been determined, the next question is how best to respond to it. Typically, in many jurisdictions the main response has been use of a fine. The imposition of fines, as such, is limited. Nevertheless, there has been suggestion that better use of fines may provide better outcomes. The use of cumulative penalties, as in the case of points systems in motoring offences, so that a penalty infringement notice (PIN) does not become 'routine' or permit wealthy operators the 'right' to pollute, has for example been suggested (Bell and McGillivray 2008). The more often you cause harm, the greater the penalty each time. Likewise, the United Nations Environment Programme's 'Global Judges Programme' includes reference to the imposition of deterrent fines based upon 'economic benefit of noncompliance' (EBN). This takes account of the value to the violator of deferred compliance, that is, the money that should have been spent on environmental improvements that was presumably invested elsewhere, earning a rate of return on an annual basis (United Nations Environment Programme 2007).

It is not only fines that are seen to provide limited value as a punishment. While prison sentences are used on occasion as a sanction for environmental crime, their specific use depends upon the context of their imposition. For example, in Flanders, Belgium prison sentences are usually combined with other sanctions such as fines or community service orders. However, the Belgian practice is one of suspending the execution of prison sentences and there has also evolved a policy of non-execution of 'short' effective sentences, thereby reducing the credibility of the threat of harsher penalties for non-compliance (Billiet and Rousseau 2014).

The NSWLEC utilises sanctions in ways that appear to overcome some of the pitfalls identified above, while also building upon some of the suggested courses of action as well. The present range of orders has been characterised as falling into two broad groups (NSW Environment and Heritage 2013).

Orders aimed at restoration/preventing a recurrence of the offence

- Clean up orders
- Compensation orders
- Investigation costs orders (order the offender to pay costs and expenses incurred during the investigation of an offence)
- Monetary benefits penalty orders (order the offender to pay a sum up to the amount of the monetary benefit derived from the offence)
- Environmental audit orders (order the offender to carry out a specified environmental audit of activities carried on by the offender)

Orders aimed at punishing or deterring offenders

- Fines/custodial sentence
- Environmental service orders (order the offender to carry out a specified project for the restoration or enhancement of the environment in a public place or for the public benefit)
- Publication orders (order the offender to publish details of the offence and the orders made by the court in, for example, a newspaper and/or in a company's Annual Report).

The basis for the use of penalties is initially guided by two considerations. The first is the legislatively provided range and type of sentencing options available. The wider the range and number of options, the greater the degree of judicial discretion in what penalties to use and how best to use them in given circumstances.

Second, in criminal cases the determination of sentence is based upon 'intuitive synthesis' involving judicial decision-making as informed by consideration of objective harms and subjective factors. Yet, this method is simultaneously shaped by precedent (given judicial concerns with consistency) and the possibilities of innovation (depending upon the variety and type of remedies available to the Court). It is thus both backward looking and forward looking.

The NSWLEC is drawing upon a wide range of sentencing options in response to specific offences and offenders. It is not only this range that is significant however. What also appears to make a difference is the *combination of sanctions*. It is the combining of different sanctions to match circumstances (and specific offenders and offending) that allows the Court to provide tailor-made solutions to the problem of environmental harm before it.

Table 13.1 describes the types of penalties (including non-penalty costs to the offender, such as payment of prosecutor's costs) actually utilised by the NSWLEC across all cases examined in the research undertaken. Essentially, the New South Wales Land and Environment Court is able to draw upon the selected measures that best suit each particular situation, and that combine punitive as well as reparative elements. This also provides for more supportive and nuanced responses to the harms against non-human environmental entities than application of fines as a punitive measure in its own right. There is a demonstrated concern on the part of the NSWLEC with remediation and reparation – both in ascertaining the scope and nature of environmental harm, and in responding with appropriate penalties where harm has occurred (White, 2017).

From the point of view of sentencing purposes, this broad approach enables the NSWLEC to impose punishments that are both punitive and reparative at the same time. Sentencing is informed by the notion of problem solving. For the NSWLEC, the legislatively established sentencing options provides opportunity for remedies that are intended to deter future offending, while also contributing to remediation and rehabilitation of the environmental damage (White 2017).

Table 13.1 Types of penalties imposed by the NSWLEC 2002–2013

Type of penalty imposed	Specific Order
Fines	General consolidated revenue
	Directed to Environmental Fund
	Directed to Specific Environmental Project
Costs	Prosecutor costs
	Investigation costs
Community Service Order	General community benefit
Reprobation *(in relation to defendant)*	Publication Order
	Public Notice (in regards to specific site)
	Publicity related to Fine Order (so as not to benefit from financial contribution ordered as part of an offence resolution)
Rehabilitation *(in relation to environment)*	Environmental Service Order
	Monitoring
	Rehabilitation/remediation

The flexibility of the penalties thus provides for greater scope to address the harms directly, rather than simply punish the offender.

Conclusion

This chapter has examined the way in which the New South Wales Land and Environment Court (NSWLEC) approaches the task of determining criminal sentences for offenders who breach environmental laws involving nonhuman environmental entities such as flora and fauna. It has shown that the NSWLEC has applied penalties that convey the message that environmental crimes are taken seriously by the Court. As such, these findings suggest an opportunity to develop further best practice guidelines for courts dealing with offences against environmental laws, and provide a platform for improving judicial practice and legislative options in other jurisdictions. Legislative systems vary greatly in the types of remedies and penalties available in regards to combatting environmental crime, but knowledge of different and novel sentencing options, and the innovative application of these at a practical level, may provide the basis for relevant law reform pertaining to criminal provisions.

There are many variables that determine the outcome when criminal cases involving environmental harm to non-human entities are prosecuted. These include, for example, which courts the cases are heard in (e.g., magistrates or a superior court), what kind of court (e.g., generalist or specialist), what types of penalties can be assigned to offenders (e.g., fines or action orders), and what remedies might be invoked for the harm caused (e.g., remediation).

Perennial problems in this area in many jurisdictions compared to that of the NSWLEC have included the perception that environmental crime is not a real crime. It would be expected that such problems would be compounded when the 'victim' is in fact a non-human environmental entity such as a river, plant, bird or animal, given the complications arising from assessing harm in relation to the non-human environmental entity (such as reliance upon specialist expertise).

The practical experience of the NSWLEC can serve as an exemplar of good practice in dealing with environmental crime. The types of penalties imposed by the Court illustrate an on-going concern to address the health and wellbeing of particular species and ecosystems via remediation and reparation. The Court has exhibited a consciousness of and sensitivity to ecological integrity, biodiversity and the importance of environmental protection. This has been buttressed by the availability of a wide range of orders so that tailored penalties can be provided; and the combining of sanctions in ways that are oriented toward repairing the harm while simultaneously creating appropriate burdens for the offender. Compared to other courts and what is occurring in many other jurisdictions, then, the experience of the NSWLEC demonstrates that offences involving harm to non-human environmental entities are best dealt with when there are clear guidelines and multiple options at the statute level, and specialist expertise informing discretionary interpretations at the court level.

References

Bagaric, M. and Edney, R. 2014. *Sentencing in Australia*. Sydney: Lawbook Company.

Bates, G. 2013. *Environmental Law in Australia* (8th edition). Sydney: LexisNexis Butterworths.

Bell, S., and McGillivray, D. 2008. *Environmental Law* (7th edition). London: Oxford University Press.

Billiet, C. and Rousseau, S. 2014. 'How real is the threat of imprisonment for environmental crime?', *European Journal of Law Economics* 37, 183–198.

Boyd, C. 2008 'Expanding the arsenal for sentencing environmental crimes: would therapeutic jurisprudence and restorative justice work?', *William & Mary Environmental Law and Policy Review* 32(2), 483–512.

Bricknell, S. 2010. *Environmental Crime in Australia*. AIC Reports Research and Public Policy Series 109, Canberra: Australian Institute of Criminology.

Burke, A. 2016. 'Threatened species, endangered justice: how additional maximum penalties for harming threatened species have failed in practice', *Environmental Planning and Law Journal* 33, 451–466.

Chin, S., Veening, W. and Gerstetter, C. 2014. *Policy Brief 1: Limitations and Challenges of the Criminal Justice System in Addressing Environmental Crime*. European Union Action to Fight Environmental Crime [EFFACE].

Cochran, J., Lynch, M., Toman, E. and Shields, R. 2016. 'Court sentencing patterns for environmental crimes: is there a 'green gap' in punishment?', *Journal of Quantitative Criminology* DOI 10.1007/s10940-016-9322-9.

Environmental Audit Committee, House of Commons of the United Kingdom. 2004. *Environmental Crime and the Courts*. London: House of Commons.

European Union Action to Fight Environmental Crime [EFFACE]. 2016. *Environmental Crime and the EU: Synthesis of the Research Project*. Berlin: Ecologic Institute.

Faure, M. 2011. *The Implementation of the Environmental Crime Directives in Europe*. Paper presented at the 9th INECE Conference, Whistler, 18–24 June.

Faure, M. and Heine, G. 2000. *Criminal Enforcement of Environmental Law in the European Union*. Copenhagen: Danish Environmental Protection Agency.

Fogel, C. and Lipovsek, J. 2013. 'Green crime in the Canadian courts', *Journal of Politics and Law* 6(2), 48–52.

Hamilton, M. 2014. 'Restorative justice intervention in an aboriginal cultural heritage protection context: conspicuous absences?', *Environmental Planning and Law Journal* 31, 352–367.

Hayman, G. and Brack, D. 2002. *International Environmental Crime: The Nature and Control of Environmental Black Markets*. London: Sustainable Development Programme, Royal Institute of International Affairs.

Lebovitz, M., Newbigging, H. and Puritz, A. (eds.) 2013. *Empty Threat: Does the Law Combat Illegal Wildlife Trade? An Eleven-Country Review of Legislative and Judicial Approaches*. London: DLA Piper.

Lynch, M. 2017. 'The sentencing/punishment of federal environmental/green criminal offenders 2000–2013', *Deviant Behavior* 38(9), 991–1008.

Lynch, M., Barrett, K., Stretesky, P. and Long, M. 2016. 'The weak probability of punishment for environmental offences and deterrence of environmental offenders: a discussion based on USEPA criminal cases, 1983–2013', *Deviant Behavior* 37(10), 1095–1109.

MacKenzie, G., Stobbs, N. and O'Leary, J. 2010. *Principles of Sentencing*. Sydney: Federation Press.

New South Wales Department of Environment and Heritage. 2013. *Guidelines for Seeking Environmental Court Orders*. Sydney: Environment & Heritage.

O'Hear, M. 2004. 'Sentencing the green-collar offender: punishment, culpability, and environmental crime', *Journal of Criminal Law & Criminology* 95(1), 133–276.

Pearlman, M. 2010. '20 years of the land and environment court of NSW', *Australian Planner* 38(1), 45–49.

Pepper, R. 2012. *Recent Developments in Sentencing for Environmental Offences*. Paper presented at the Australasian Conference of Planning and Environment Courts and Tribunals, Perth, 28 August–2 September.

Preston, B. 2007a. 'Principled sentencing for environmental offences – Part 1: purposes of sentencing', *Criminal Law Journal* 31(2), 91–100.

Preston, B. 2007b. 'Principled sentencing for environmental offences – Part 2: sentencing considerations and options', *Criminal Law Journal* 31(3), 142–164.

Preston, B. 2014. 'Characteristics of successful environmental courts and tribunals', *Journal of Environmental Law* 26(3), 365–393.

Prez, de, P. 2000a. 'Excuses, excuses the ritual trivialisation of environmental prosecutions', *Journal of Environmental Law* 12(1), 65–78.

Prez, de P. 2000b. 'Beyond judicial sanctions: the negative impact of conviction for environmental offences', *Environmental Law Review* 2, pp. 11–22.

Stretesky, P., Long, M. and Lynch, M. 2013. 'Does environmental enforcement slow the treadmill of production? The relationship between large monetary penalties, ecological disorganization and toxic releases within offending corporations', *Journal of Crime and Justice* 36(2), 233–247.

United Nations Environment Programme. 2007. *Judicial Training Modules on Environmental Law: Application of Environmental Law by National Courts and Tribunals.* UNEP.

White, R. 2010. 'Prosecution and sentencing in relation to environmental crime: recent socio-legal developments', *Crime, Law and Social Change* 53(4), 365–381.

White, R. 2017. 'Reparative justice, environmental crime and penalties for the powerful', *Crime, Law and Social Change* 67(2), 117–132.

White, R. and Perrone, S. 2015. *Crime, Criminality and Criminal Justice.* Melbourne: Oxford University Press.

Index

Locators in *italics* refer to figures and those in **bold** to tables.

3M Corporation 117

Afghanistan: conflict with United States 20–21; economic motives 33
African Development Bank (AfDB) 218
aggregate profitability effects 118
air pollution 94; *see also* carbon markets; Volkswagen dieselgate scandal
Allee effect: Anthropogenic Allee Effect 4, 74, 83–84; definition 73–74; wildlife trade 83–84
AML/CFT context 180–181, 185–186
animal trade *see* illegal wildlife trade
Anthropogenic Allee Effect 4, 74, 83–84
anthropogenic climate change *see* climate change
anti money laundering *see* AML/CFT context
Asia: illegal logging 183–184, 191–192; tourism 193; wildlife trade 74–75, 203–204, 208–209
Australia: environmental offences 253–255; innovative sentencing 258–261, **262**; New South Wales Land and Environment Court 251–252; range of penalties imposed 255–258; response to wildlife trade 77–83; sentencing overview 250–252
automobile industry *see* Volkswagen dieselgate scandal

Balzac, de Honoré 15–16
barter laundering 206–210; *see also* money laundering

birds trade 204
brand reputation 116
breeders, wildlife trade 76–77, 202–203
business *see* corporations

California Air Resources Board (CARB) 96–97
Canada, sentencing 254
Cap and Trade 218
capital, environmental performance 114, 121–123
capitalism: carbon markets 220–221, 226; corporate crime 93; treadmill of production 2
captive breeding 76–77
carbon markets: criminal activity 222–225; ecological modernisation 221–222; operation of 217–220
carbon offsetting 217–218, 224–225
carbon taxes 226–227
cardinal proportionality 254
car industry *see* Volkswagen dieselgate scandal
caviar trade 204, *205*
certification, wildlife trade 204
chemicals industry: corporate crime 133–143; hazardous waste 148
China: natural resource possession 21; wildlife trade 74–75, 203–204
Clean Development Mechanisms 218–219
climate change: carbon markets 217–220, 221–222, 225–228; ecological modernisation 220–222, 225–228; natural resource decline 25; natural

resource possession 22–23; responses to
215–217; Trump administration 2
Code of Criminal Procedure 237, 241,
242–243
Colombia, economic motives 33
commercial traders, wildlife 204–205
Committed Compliers (compliance style)
138, 140–141
Company.info 134–135
compliance *see* environmental compliance;
health and safety compliance
conflict: conservation 34–35;
environmental harm 4, 19–20, 26–27,
35–36; financial behaviours 32–35;
typology of environment-conflict
relationships 19–32
conservation, and conflict 34–35
consumerism: customer loyalty 116;
environmental performance of firms
113–114, 115–116; and fraud 192;
philosophy of desire 14–16
Convention on International Trade in
Endangered Species (CITES) 72–73,
199–201, 206
corporate crime 129–131, 143–145;
capitalism 93; case study approach and
data 133–143; criminological
approaches 198; economic licence
131–133; firm size 130, 132–133;
money laundering 180–181; organised
crime distinction 152–153; profitability
131–133; State-corporate crime
perspective 93, 105–108; waste market
157–162
corporate crime theory 157–158
corporate ethics 92
corporate sustainability, public relations
130–131; *see also* environmental
performance
corporations: corporate crime 162;
environmental compliance 138–143,
144; environmental performance 126;
firm size 130, 132–133; Volkswagen
company characteristics 102–105;
Volkswagen dieselgate scandal 92–100;
Volkswagen top management 92–94,
100–105; *see also* environmental
compliance; environmental
performance; management

corruption: conservation 35; and
consumerism 192; illegal logging
186–189; Italy 42–43; tourism 193
cost efficiency 116–117
cost of capital 121–123
cost of debt 123, 125
cost of equity 121–122, 125
cost of green crime 2–3, 129
countering the financing of terrorism
see AML/CFT context
courts 5–6; Australia's response to wildlife
trade 77–83; the Netherlands
confiscation of proceeds of crime
233–234, 236–237; the Netherlands
financial investigations 233–236,
238–248; sentencing in Australia
250–252
credit: carbon markets 219; environmental
performance 123, 125; illegal logging
186–187, 191
crime *see* green crime
crime prevention: complex crime
168–169; corporate crime 162; green
criminological theory 166–167;
organised crime 156–157; *see also*
enforcement; sentencing
Crimes (Sentencing Procedure) Act 1999
253
criminal justice responses 3; confiscation
of proceeds of crime 233–234, 236–
237; financial investigations 233–236,
238–248; waste industry 162, 166–167;
wildlife trade 77–83
criminal organisations *see* organised crime
customer loyalty 116; *see also* consumerism

debt *see* credit
degradation: conflict that destroys
environments 26–30; natural resource
decline 23–25
Democratic Republic of Congo (DRC):
economic motives 33; natural resource
possession 21–22
desire, philosophy of 3–4, 14–17
destruction: conflict 26–30; economics
9–17
development: legal regulation 13–14;
poverty 12–13
diesel engines 94–95

'dieselgate' *see* Volkswagen dieselgate scandal
drought *see* water resources
drug-wildlife trafficking 208

Eastern and Southern African Anti-Money Laundering Group 182–183
eco-labelling 115–116; *see also* environmental performance
ecological modernisation: climate change 220–222, 225–228; EU emissions trading system 5
eco-mafia 42–43, 54–55
econometric methodology 57–58
economic licence, corporate crime 131–133
economic motives 1–3; confiscation of proceeds of crime 233–234, 236–237; environmental harm 32–35; and environmental performance 113–121, 125–126; financial investigations 233–236, 238–248; green crime 2–3, 129; Italy's waste trafficking 55–56; Volkswagen dieselgate scandal 105–108, 109; *see also* money laundering
Economic Offences Act 237
economics: habit and domination 11–12; legal regulation 13–14; poverty 12–13; and science 9–11; *see also headings under* costs
efficiency, cost 116–117
electric cars 109
emissions *see* carbon markets; pollution; Volkswagen dieselgate scandal
emissions trading system, EU 5, 223–224
endangered species 72, 74–75, 76, 82–83; *see also* illegal wildlife trade
end-of-life vessels 160–161
end-of-waste criteria 44
enforcement 5; AML/CFT context 182; environmental compliance 142–143; illegal logging 187–188; the Netherlands environmental crime cases 238–248; sentencing severity 254–255; Volkswagen dieselgate scandal 107–108; *see also* courts; crime prevention; sentencing
Environmental Code (EC) 51

environmental compliance: corporate crime prevention 162; corporations 4; economic licence 131–133; management 138–143, 144; Volkswagen dieselgate scandal 104–105; waste 50–51; *see also* sentencing
Environmental Courts or Tribunals (ECTs) 84
environmental harm 1–3; conflict 4, 19–20, 26–27, 35–36; destruction 9–17; green criminological theory 163–167; illegal and questionable financial behaviours 32–35; typology of environment-conflict relationships 19–32
environmental justice 164
Environmental Laggards (compliance style) 138, 139–140
environmental performance: corporate sustainability 130–131; corporations 4; cost of capital 114, 121–123; and firm value 113–121, 125–126; profitability 4, 113–121, **119**, 125–126, 132; valuation 124
Environmental Protection Agency (EPA) 94
Environmental Strategists (compliance style) 138, 141–142
Eurojust 180
European Union: diesel engines 96; emissions trading system 5, 223–224; illegal logging 184–185, 187–188; money laundering 180; sentencing 259; Volkswagen dieselgate scandal 98–100, 105–108; wildlife trade 199
externalities 10–11
extraction conflicts 30–32

falconry trade 76
Financial Action Task Force 179, 181–182
financial gain *see* economic motives
financial instruments 3, 5; *see also* sentencing
Financial Intelligence Units (FIUs) 182, 183, 187, 189, 193
financial investigations, the Netherlands 233–236, 238–248
fines 3; *see also* sentencing

firms *see* corporations
firm size, corporate crime 130, 132–133
fishing, natural resource extraction 30–31
follow-the-money approaches 183, 192, 193
food markets: environmental performance 113–121; illegal wildlife trade 75, 81–82
Forest Law Enforcement, Governance and Trade agreement (FLEGT) 188
fossil fuels conflict 28; *see also* climate change

General Motors (GM), López affair 101
Germany: car industry 96, 99–101, 103, 105–109; organised crime definition 153
global context: environmental crime 35–36; environmental performance 121; illegal logging 188–189, 191–192; money laundering 182–183; sentencing 259; waste crime 167, 168; wildlife trade 74–75, 83–84
Global North: AML/CFT context 182–183, 185–186, 193; money laundering 190–191
Global South: AML/CFT context 182–183, 193; carbon offsetting 217; environmental justice 164
Global Sustainable Investment Review 121–122
Gold Standard, carbon markets 219
governments: Australia's response to wildlife trade 78–83; State-corporate crime perspective 105–108
green-collar crime, wildlife trade 198–199
green crime 1–3; carbon markets 222–225; environmental harm 32–35; waste market 149–152, 167–169; *see also* corporate crime; corruption; crime prevention; illegal logging; illegal wildlife trade
green criminological theory, waste 163–167
greenhouse gases 215; *see also* carbon markets; climate change
Greenpeace 168–169
Groenewald syndicate 209–210
growth, and regulation 13–14

Hahn, Carl 103
hazardous waste 148; corporate crime 158, 159–161; organised crime 153–155; radioactive waste 150–151; *see also* chemicals industry
health and safety compliance 139–143
Henri Robert Morgan v R 80–81
historical context, wildlife trade 197

illegal environmental action *see* green crime
illegal logging: conflict 22; money laundering 183–184, 186–189; policy context 183–185
illegal wildlife trade 4, 5; Australia's response to 77–83; contexts, causes and constructs 74–77; financial turnover 72; global industry 74–75, 83–84; green-collar offenders 198–199; green criminology 73–74; historical and contemporary context 197–198; and laundering 197, 206–211; legal regulation 72–73, 83–84, 199–201; money laundering 182–183; operation of 201–206, *202*
implied cost of capital (ICC) 122–123
income from green crime 2–3
indigenous peoples: land ownership 36; pipelines protests 32
indirect costs 3
innovative sentencing 258–261, **262**
interdependence, poverty 12
international context *see* global context
Interpol: carbon markets 222–223; corporate crime 129
intuitive synthesis 261
inverse density dependence 73–74
Italy: hazardous waste 154; legal regulation 43–51; organised crime definition 153; waste market 4, 42–43, 51–55
ivory trade 33–34, 75, 201, 204–205

Joint Implementations 218–219

KLD (environmental performance) 120–121, 122
Korean War 27

labour leader scandal 101

land ownership conflict 20–23, 36

laundering *see* illegal wildlife trade; money laundering

legality 11

legal regulation 3, 5; Australia's response to wildlife trade 77–83; Australia's sentencing 250–258; confiscation of proceeds of crime 233–234, 236–237; economics 13–14; green criminological theory 163–167; illegal logging 183–185, 187–189; money laundering 179–180, 182–183, 190–191; Volkswagen dieselgate scandal 98–100, 105–108; waste market 43–51; wildlife trade 72–73, 83–84, 199–201; *see also* courts; enforcement; environmental compliance

legitimacy 12

Lizard King case 208

logging *see* illegal logging

López affair 101

Lotz, Kurt 102–103

Love Canal case 159

management: corporate crime 162; environmental compliance 138–143, 144; environmental performance 126; Volkswagen dieselgate scandal 92–94, 100–105

meat markets, illegal wildlife trade 75, 81–82

meum-tuum distinction 10

militarism 28–30

Mock, Peter 96

money laundering 3, 5, 179–183, 191–193; AML/CFT context 180–181, 185–186; Global North 190–191; illegal logging 183–185, 186–189; the Netherlands cases 234–235, 244–245; wildlife trade 206–210, *207*

municipal solid waste 44, 50–51

Myanmar, natural resource extraction 30–31

National Parks and Wildlife Act 1974 252, 253, 255–257

nation state *see* governments

Native Americans, pipelines 32

Native Vegetation Act 2003 252

natural resource decline 23–25

natural resource extraction 30–32

natural resource possession 20–23, 36

nemo tenetur principle 237, 241

neoliberal economics 3–4, 9–11

neo-liberalism, carbon markets 220–221

the Netherlands: complex crime 168–169; confiscation of proceeds of crime 233–234, 236–237; financial investigations 233–236, 238–248; waste industry corporate crime 133–143, 144–145, 158, 159–160; waste industry organised crime 153, 155

New South Wales Land and Environment Court 250, 251–252

NGOs: complex crime 168–169; follow-the-money approaches 193; green criminological theory 167; illegal logging 184–185; waste crime 158, 160–161, 166–167

Niger Delta case study 165–166

nitrogen oxide 91, 96; *see also* Volkswagen dieselgate scandal

offence types, sentencing 253–255

offenders: Australia's response to wildlife trade 78–83; corporate crime 149; Global North 190, 193; green-collar crime 198–199; green crime 1–2; green criminological perspective 166; Volkswagen dieselgate scandal 96–98; waste market in Italy 53, *54*, 57; wildlife trade 75–76, 78–84, 198–199, **200**

oil, natural resource extraction 30–31

Operation Cobra 208

ordinal proportionality 254

organisations *see* corporations

organised crime: corporate crime distinction 152–153; Italy 42–43, 55–69; Italy's waste trafficking 51–55; waste market 5, 148–150, 152–157

organised crime theory 152–153

ownership conflict 20–23, 36

paper mills industry 132–133

Paris Agreement 222

penalties *see* sentencing

Peru, natural resource possession 22
pet markets 75
Phillips v State of SA 81–82
philosophy of desire 3–4, 14–17
Piëch, Ferdinand 94, 95, 100–102,
    103–105
pipelines conflict 32
poaching 34–35; *see also* illegal wildlife
    trade
policy *see* legal regulation
pollution: environmental responsibility of
    firms 124; green criminological theory
    165; *see also* carbon markets
population, wildlife 73–74
poverty, as trigger of development
    12–13
prevention *see* crime prevention
Probo Koala case 159–160
profitability: corporate crime 131–133;
    environmental performance 4, 113–
    121, **119**, 125–126, 132; of green
    crime 2–3, 129; illegal wildlife trade
    72; waste industry 136–137; *see also*
    economic motives
proportionality 254
Protection of the Environment
    Administration Act 1991 252, 253,
    258
Protection of the Environment Operations
    Act 255
Public Prosecution Service, the
    Netherlands 234, 236, 242, 245–246,
    247
public relations: corporate sustainability
    130–131; the Netherlands
    environmental crime cases 246–247
pulp and paper mills industry 132–133

radioactive waste 150–151
rarity: Allee effect 74; wildlife trade
    83–84
Reducing Emissions from Deforestation
    and Forest Degradation (REDD)
    224–225
regulation *see* legal regulation
Reluctant Compliers (compliance style)
    138, 140
reparative justice 260
reptiles trade 208–209

resources *see under* natural resources
restorative justice 260
return on assets (ROA) 115, 118–120,
    119, 121
revenue, corporate crime 134–135
revenue effects 115–116
rhino horn trade 209–210
Rio Earth Summit 215–216
Ronchi Decree 46
routine activities theory 223–224
R v Degelder 82–83
R v Petersen 79–80

scarcity, natural resource decline
    23–25
Schneiderman, Eric 105
science, and neoliberal economics 9–11
Scottish Environmental Protection Agency
    (SEPA) 190
Selective Catalytic Reduction (SCR)
    94–95
self-regulation 162; *see also* environmental
    compliance
sentencing 250–251, 262–263; in
    Australia 255–258; environmental
    offences 253–255; innovative
    sentencing 258–261, **262**; New South
    Wales Land and Environment Court
    250, 251–252; range of penalties
    imposed 255–258
Sharia law 186–187
Shell pollution case 165–166
shipping, waste crime 160–161
social licence 133
socioeconomic context, Italy's waste
    trafficking 57–58
South Africa, Groenewald syndicate
    209–210
special waste 44, 47–50
state *see* governments
State-corporate crime perspective 93,
    105–108
supply and demand, wildlife trade 74–77,
    83–84
supply chains, environmental performance
    of firms 117–118
sustainability: sentencing guidelines 258;
    technology 125–126
Syria, natural resource decline 23–25

taxation, carbon 226–227
technology: carbon markets 218–219; environmental performance of firms 117–118; sustainability 125–126
territorial heterogeneity, Italy 62–63
terrorism, and poaching 34–35
tiger trade 203–204
timber trafficking *see* illegal logging
Tobin's q 124
top management *see* management
tourism, and corruption 193
trafficking *see* illegal wildlife trade; waste trafficking
transnational crime *see* global context
Transparency International 223
transportation, wildlife trade 76–77
treadmill of production 2; green criminological theory 163; wildlife trade 4, 74, 83–84
trucking industry 133
True Believers (compliance style) 138, 141–142
Trump administration, climate change 2
Turbocharged Direct Injection (TDI) engines 94–95

United Kingdom: AML/CFT context 182; environmental crime 190–191; illegal logging 186–187; sentencing 254; waste crime 167–168
United Nations: Global Judges Programme 260; wildlife trade 197–198
United Nations Environment Programme (UNEP) 129
United Nations Framework Convention on Climate Change (UNFCCC) 215–216, 217
United States: conflict that destroys environments 27–30; conflict with Afghanistan 20–21; corporate crime 161; organised crime 154; Volkswagen dieselgate scandal 98
utilitarianism 10–11

valuation, environmental performance 124; *see also* economic motives
Volkswagen dieselgate scandal 4, 91–92, 108–109; case overview 94–100; company characteristics 102–105; role of top management 92–94, 100–105; State-corporate crime perspective 105–108; theoretical framework 92–94
voluntary systems: carbon markets 218–219, 225; self-regulation 162

war *see* conflict
War on Drugs 26
waste market 148; complex crime 167–169; corporate crime 130, 133–143, 157–162; and crime 149–152, 169; criminal organisations 5, 152–157; data description and empirical strategy 57–69; green criminological perspective 163–167; Italy 4, 42–43, 51–55; legal regulation 43–51; theoretical background and hypotheses 55–56
waste production crimes 158
waste trafficking 51–55
waste treatment crimes 158, 160
water resources decline 24–25
Weber, Max 11–12, 13–14
white-collar crime 198–199
wildlife populations 73–74
wildlife trade *see* illegal wildlife trade
willingness-to-pay 115–116
Winterkorn, Martin 95–96, 97, 100–101, 103–105

zoos, wildlife trade 205–206, 208–209

Taylor & Francis eBooks

www.taylorfrancis.com

A single destination for eBooks from Taylor & Francis
with increased functionality and an improved user
experience to meet the needs of our customers.

90,000+ eBooks of award-winning academic content in
Humanities, Social Science, Science, Technology, Engineering,
and Medical written by a global network of editors and authors.

TAYLOR & FRANCIS EBOOKS OFFERS:

A streamlined
experience for
our library
customers

A single point
of discovery
for all of our
eBook content

Improved
search and
discovery of
content at both
book and
chapter level

REQUEST A FREE TRIAL
support@taylorfrancis.com

For Product Safety Concerns and Information please contact our EU
representative GPSR@taylorandfrancis.com
Taylor & Francis Verlag GmbH, Kaufingerstraße 24, 80331 München, Germany

www.ingramcontent.com/pod-product-compliance
Ingram Content Group UK Ltd.
Pitfield, Milton Keynes, MK11 3LW, UK
UKHW021012180425
457613UK00020B/907